Cecil B. DeMille and American Culture

Cecil B. DeMille and American Culture

The Silent Era

Sumiko Higashi

UNIVERSITY OF CALIFORNIA PRESS
Berkeley   Los Angeles   London

University of California Press
Berkeley and Los Angeles, California
University of California Press
London, England
Copyright © 1994 by The Regents of the University of California

Library of Congress Cataloging-in-Publication Data

Higashi, Sumiko.
    Cecil B. DeMille and American culture : the silent era / Sumiko
Higashi.
        p. cm.
    Includes bibliographical references and index.
    ISBN 0-520-08556-6. — ISBN 0-520-08557-4 (pbk. : alk. paper)
    1. DeMille, Cecil B. (Cecil Blount), 1881–1959—Criticism and
interpretation. I. Title.
PN1998.3.D39H54 1994
791.43′0232′092—dc20   94-6580
                                                                              CIP

Printed in the United States of America
1 2 3 4 5 6 7 8 9
The paper used in this publication meets the minimum requirements
of American National Standard for Information Sciences—Perma-
nence of Paper for Printed Library Materials, ANSI Z39.48-1984 ♾

To my parents

whose voices were silenced

in an American concentration camp

and

to Bob

for sharing the burden of my historical legacy

CONTENTS

ILLUSTRATIONS

ACKNOWLEDGMENTS

As a graduate student years ago, I traveled to George Eastman House and met James Card, the distinguished former curator who established one of the world's great film archives by depositing most of his private collection in the museum. A memorable first screening of DeMille's *Old Wives for New*, accompanied by a witty commentary, has since been repeated with different films in different venues, as Card has generously arranged screenings for me over the years. I shall always be indebted to him and to his dedicated colleague, the late George Pratt, for encouraging my interest in silent cinema.

Since this book has been in production for many years, I have incurred several other debts as well. James V. D'Arc, who spent over a decade establishing the massive DeMille Archives at Brigham Young University, has been knowledgeable, gracious, and supportive. Ned Comstock at the University of Southern California sent many thoughtful communications that extended beyond the usual service accorded library patrons on research trips. At George Eastman House, Paolo Cherchi Usai (now at Cinémathèque Royale de Belgique), Jan-Christopher Horak, and Edward E. Stratmann in the film department, and Becky Simmons in the library graciously provided access to research materials. Howard H. Prouty at the Academy of Motion Picture Arts and Sciences, David Parker at the Library of Congress, and Holly Hankinson, my former student, at the UCLA Film and Television Archive, also provided valuable assistance. Closer to home, I am thankful to Robert Gilliam at interlibrary loan, not only for his bibliographical expertise but also for his intellectual range. And James Dusen in photo services rescued me from misadventures with several cameras and developed innumerable prints.

As important as individuals who assisted me with my research were readers who helped me with my writing. Francis G. Couvares not only provided the book's title but also thoughtful suggestions and forceful injunctions to minimize language borrowed from critical theorists. For invaluable comments on drafts of various chapters in varying stages of completion, I wish to thank David Desser, Clayton R. Koppes, Janaki Bakhle, Robert Rosenstone, Arthur Nolletti, Jr., Ronald Gottesman, Nick Browne, Robert Lang, and Eugene C. McCreary. Also helpful were intelligent critiques written by a University of California Press reader and an editorial board member. Edward Dimendberg, my editor, deserves credit for being venturesome and taking on an interdisciplinary project to which he lent his intellect and support.

As for institutional assistance, I profited from a sabbatical leave granted by the State University of New York College at Brockport. Additionally, a summer stipend and two travel grants from the National Endowment for the Humanities funded some of my research.

I should acknowledge debts of a personal nature as well. A daughter of Japanese-American immigrants whose dreams turned into an arid landscape with barbed wire and armed sentries, I was not a likely candidate to write this book. I am grateful to my sister, Kimiko Higashi, a brilliant psychotherapist, for helping me clarify the relationship between family dynamics and a historical legacy that has dictated either invisibility or incarceration.

Lastly, I am thankful to my husband and colleague, Robert J. Smith, who spared the time while writing his own book to help me in countless ways, from repairing hard drive crashes to editing drafts. Apart from his generosity of spirit, I have been sustained by his empathy and wit.

Parts of this book have been presented as papers, and earlier drafts of chapters have been published as essays. A condensed version of chapter 1 was read at the Society for Cinema Studies conference at the University of Iowa in 1989 and published as "Cecil B. DeMille and the Lasky Company: Legitimating Feature Film as Art," *Film History* 4 (1990). Chapter 2 appeared as "Melodrama as a Middle-Class Sermon: *What's His Name,*" in Paolo Cherchi Usai and Lorenzo Codelli, eds., *The DeMille Legacy* (Pordenone: Edizioni Biblioteca dell'Immagine, 1991), the catalogue for the DeMille retrospective at Le Giornate del Cinema Muto. A section of chapter 3 was delivered as a slide presentation at the Organization of American Historians in Anaheim in 1993 and at The Movies Begin: History/Film/Culture at Yale University in 1993. An abbreviated version of chapter 4 appeared as "Class, Ethnicity, and Gender in Film: DeMille's *The Cheat,*" in Lester Friedman, ed., *Unspeakable Images: Ethnicity and the American Cinema* (Urbana: University of Illinois Press, 1991).

Introduction

*If we are looking for the relations between literature and society, we cannot either
separate out this one practice from a formed body of other practices, nor when we
have identified a particular practice can we give it a uniform, static and
ahistorical relation to some abstract social formation.*
—RAYMOND WILLIAMS

In December 1913 Cecil B. DeMille abandoned a stage career that was his
family legacy and boarded a train for California to assume a post as director-
general of a recently organized film studio, the Jesse L. Lasky Feature Play
Company. A year later, his indomitable mother, Beatrice, who continued to
manage his debt-ridden finances and to make useful contacts in New York,
wrote: "Who should walk into the office this morning but Mary Rinehart.
She has a fine idea about a combination of Movie and play . . . if you want
it pipe up quick. She is pretty valuable these days the only writer [*sic*] except
London and Tarkington who can and does get $6000 for the serial rights
alone of a short story."[1] A business opportunity for a noted theatrical agent
who was also a devoted mother, this episode illustrates the strategy developed by the Lasky Company, subsequently Famous Players-Lasky, to resituate cinema for "better" audiences with adaptations of literary works. At the
time the studio was founded, the motion picture industry was just beginning
to showcase feature-length films in lavish downtown movie palaces to acquire cultural legitimacy. Indeed, an argument repeated in trade journals
representative of industry discourse called for upgrading production and
exhibition practices to attract "high-class" as opposed to "low-class" patrons to film theaters.

DeMille, who represented cultural capital as a member of a distinguished
Broadway family, quickly won acclaim by producing feature film adaptations
of stage melodramas, novels, and short stories as intertexts familiar to
middle-class readers. The director, in other words, inserted the photoplay
into genteel culture by exploiting parallel discourses deemed highbrow in
an era characterized by conspicuous racial, ethnic, and class distinctions. An
adaptation of *Carmen* (1915), starring Metropolitan Opera diva Geraldine
Farrar, for example, attracted a blue blood audience to its Boston premiere.

1

Although emphasis on the intertextuality of feature film, legitimate theater, and grand opera at first precluded recognition of DeMille's own claim to authorship, by the time the Lasky Company merged with Famous Players in 1916, he had established credentials in his own right. Critical discourse on film authorship in fact constituted a sign of the increasing recognition of motion pictures, at first compared to theatrical productions and paintings by famous artists, as a separate art form.

Why was DeMille—today mostly remembered, if not dismissed, as the director of overblown biblical epics—an exemplar of genteel culture in the early twentieth century? What confluence of economic, social, and cultural forces enabled him to construct feature film as spectacle articulating middle-class ideology? Why was the legacy of Victorian pictorialism that character-ized his signature as a filmmaker so influential in classic Hollywood cinema, and how is it still evident in today's postmodern electronic age? And why did the director, having legitimated film with reference to intertexts in high-brow culture during the Progressive Era, become a fashion trendsetter who influenced consumer behavior in the 1920s? Answers to such questions require an interdisciplinary perspective based on close readings of film as texts—a practice eschewed in traditional historical works—in relation to studies of the genteel middle class by American cultural and social histo-rians. Acknowledging the failure of the historical profession to develop a vocabulary to analyze visual media, Neil Harris nevertheless asks a pertinent question: "What use is the demonstration of changes in visual coding unless some larger implications can be developed?"[2] I focus therefore on the relationship between texts as cultural commodities and the social world in which they circulated as a sign of gentility. A scrutiny of middle-class culture, moreover, provides evidence of how the dynamics of social change influ-enced the construction of feature film, addressed first to cultivated readers and then across class and ethnic lines to a mass audience consisting in-creasingly of women.

Perhaps most significant in the evolution of the middle class, increasingly differentiated between "old" property owners and "new" salaried profes-sionals, was the privileging of sight in a cultural formation dominated by spectacle. An enthusiastic clergyman reacting to a DeMille epic stated rather succinctly that sight constituted "the most royal of all the faculties." Genteel response to a pluralistic urban milieu populated by threatening strangers thus stressed visual codes such as self-theatricalization in social rituals as a sign of good breeding, as Karen Halttunen argues.[3] Yet social entertainment as well as the staging of private theatricals were hardly confined to the well-appointed interiors of the domestic or private sphere. Indeed, the spectacle of elaborate parlor games became interchangeable with displays mounted by department stores, museums, world's fairs, and civic pageantry, as well as sets designed for stage and film melodrama. Antithetical to such an emphasis upon appearances, the mechanism of production in genteel culture was tucked behind living room drapery in fashionable homes and hidden from view in spectacular venues in the public sphere. The moral legacy of sentimentalism and evangelical Protestantism, so essential to the formation of an "old" middle class characterized by probity and self-restraint, was thus diluted as home and marketplace became indistinguishable. Although the cinema was associated with storefront nickelodeons for the lower orders, the moving image became a crucial text in a consumer culture that was at first an expression of the social ambition of the respectable middle class. A filmmaker who capitalized on the congruence of cultural forms in genteel society, DeMille not only replicated the familiar sights of both the private and public spheres in his pictorial mise-en-scène but was so innovative that he left his own stamp on "the society of the spectacle."

DeMille quickly achieved product differentiation for Lasky Company films through dramatic low-key lighting effects marketed as "Lasky lighting" or "Rembrandt lighting." Although he borrowed the Victorian trope of darkness and light from a rich tradition of pictorial realism, the director achieved international renown with inventive lighting in combination with color tinting in *The Cheat* (1915), an early feature starring stage actors Fannie Ward and Sessue Hayakawa. Critics acclaimed his feature films as artistically superior productions that equalled or surpassed legitimate stagecraft. Yet, to the extent that film language was articulated with respect to established forms of genteel culture, stylistic or technical advances became part of status quo discourse. The evolution of feature film in relation to existing cultural practice thus meant the articulation of middle-class ideology in an era that stressed Americanization as a response to cultural diversity. An essential aspect of representations that commodified the urban "Other" as spectacle for voyeuristic consumers, for example, were Orientalist fantasies. A Western discourse that projected a taste for sybaritic luxury and depraved sexuality onto new immigrants perceived as threats to the existing body politic, Orientalism pervaded DeMille's texts.[4] Such was especially the case in the Jazz Age films that rationalized consumption in the sacrosanct terms of cultural refinement, on the one hand, and bizarre Orientalist behavior, on the other. Contrary to the earlier films of the Progressive Era, however, DeMille challenged middle-class mores by setting consumer trends in fashion and home furnishing during the 1920s. As a matter of fact, his spectacles provided the advertising industry with valuable intertexts to promote consumption, albeit in mise-en-scène increasingly noted for outré set and costume design rather than innovative lighting.

At the center of the director's famous sex comedies and melodramas was the transformation of the sentimental heroine into a sexual playmate in a childless marriage. A symbol of the consumer culture, the "new woman" was no longer a thrift-conscious and resourceful housewife but a fashion plate who embodied market forces invading the privatized domestic sphere. Abstraction or reification of social relations that earlier characterized performance rituals as a coded sign of gentility in well-appointed parlors now permeated the boudoir or back region of respectable homes. DeMille's Jazz Age films thus represented matrimony as a game of musical chairs with spouses as interchangeable parts, a scenario that exemplified the dominance of exchange value in commodity production. According to Georg Lukács, who articulated the notion of reification as a dominant force in bourgeois existence, "the essence of commodity-structure has often been pointed out. Its basis is that *a relation between people takes on the character of a thing* [my italics]." Furthermore, the production of oversized spectacle itself constituted a form of consumption uniting filmmaker and spectator alike in commodity fetishism, that is, the displacement of desire from human relations onto material objects. Assessing "the society of the spectacle," Guy Debord argues that "the tangible world is replaced by a selection of images which exist above it, and which simultaneously impose themselves as the tangible."[5] As DeMille demonstrated in the Biblical Prologue of *The Ten Commandments* (1923), even religious or spiritual uplift was subject to commodification. At the end of his tenure as director-general of Famous Players-Lasky in 1925, his texts had become a primer not only on the reification of social relations in a consumer culture but on the religious spirit itself as a consumable image inspiring awestruck audiences.

Any study of DeMille's silent film career must take into account an embarrassment of riches with respect to source materials accruing from singular efforts to create an industry persona. Convinced, but scarcely assured, of his stature in motion picture history, the director built a vault on his hilltop estate to house the nitrate prints that constituted his filmography. With respect to the silent era, a total of twenty-four out of seventy films were produced in the brief period of time before the Lasky Company merged with Famous Players in 1916. When DeMille left Famous Players-Lasky in 1925 after protracted disagreement over his escalating production budgets, he had made all but four of the fifty-two films that comprised his silent productions. Aside from prints of most of his films, the director amassed a vast collection of documents, including correspondence, contracts, financial statements, interview transcripts, scrapbooks, scripts, production and still photos, preproduction artwork, memorabilia, movie trailers, and radio broadcast recordings. An invaluable resource, much of this material has been bequeathed to research institutions, notably Brigham Young University, although correspondence dating back to the earliest years was lost for decades and has only recently been recovered.[6] Unfortunately, the director's personal possessions and collections of objets d'art, which comprised valuable sources for material culture studies, were auctioned by Christie's in 1988.[7]

In sum, DeMille left enormous traces of his authorship long before François Truffaut and Andrew Sarris made the term *auteur* fashionable in cinema studies. Precisely because I am interested in the relationship between early feature film and genteel middle-class culture, I chose not to employ auteurist reformulations such as recent Foucauldian concepts of an *author-function*, in which the director is displaced by textual processes as these construct an implied narrator. The filmmaker has been disembodied, as David Bordwell argues, as components of a signature style, and thus reappears in many studies as the text's mise-en-scène or editing. As a cultural historian who acknowledges the value of critical theory, I nevertheless subscribe to a belief in human agency, however restricted, and do not construe the relationship between a film director and a specific historical context as a theoretical abstraction; thus I write about DeMille not only as a figure who was shaped and influenced by the forces of his era but as a filmmaker who left his own signature on the culture industry.[8]

Since DeMille was such a prolific filmmaker in the silent period, the selection of specific texts for close readings proved to be a challenging task. I concentrate more on the lesser known but acclaimed features of the Progressive Era because these are more informative about the ways in which cinema was legitimated as art, more varied in terms of genre formulations, more daring in the development of film technique such as lighting effects and color processes, and more revealing as representations of a middle-class culture in transition. Discussion of the better-known sex comedies and melodramas of the Jazz Age has been restricted to a single, lengthy chapter. Absent are analyses of films like *The Girl of the Golden West* (1915), which circulated in the exemplary *Before Hollywood* archival film series, and *Male and Female* (1919), famous for its bathroom sequence, as well as lesser-known efforts such as *Till I Come Back to You* (1918) and *Triumph* (1924), justifiably excluded at the DeMille retrospective at Le Giornate del Cinema Muto.[9]

Although it would surely be useful to expand the intertextual approach of this study by comparing DeMille's texts with those of other directors, notably D. W. Griffith, or analyzing *Carmen* in relation to movements such as Film d'Art, or scrutinizing Lasky Company and Famous Players-Lasky features with those of other producers, I have chosen instead to ask different questions. "The concept of *inter-textuality*," as Tony Bennett and Janet Woollacott argue, need not refer to "the system of references to other texts which can be discerned within the composition of a specific individual text [but may refer] to the social organisation of the relations between texts within specific conditions of reading."[10] I concentrate therefore on the relationship between DeMille's feature films and traditional forms of genteel culture during a significant moment of transition not only in the film industry but also in American history.[11] Assessing a lack that characterizes the three volumes in the prizewinning *History of the American Cinema*—and in my view, film history in general—Dana Polan states in an otherwise laudable review that texts are unrelated to context as American society recedes into the background.[12] Unlike film historians who analyze the evolution of film langauge and/or production, distribution, and exhibition practices, I focus on DeMille's texts as these relate to class, ethnic, and gender hierarchies signifying the exercise of power in the "real" world. A film history that takes into account the dynamics of social change outside the studio gate, this study explores the issue of intertextuality from a perspective that emphasizes the congruence of feature film with established cultural forms as a sign of gentility. Such an approach best clarifies the director's significance both as an auteur who legitimated cinema and as an architect of modern consumption. Straddling the late Victorian era and a consumer culture that shifted into high gear in the 1920s, DeMille personified a transformation in genteel middle-class culture whose trajectory he first mapped and then influenced as a major filmmaker.

ONE

The Lasky Company
and Highbrow Culture:
Authorship versus Intertextuality

THE CONSUMPTION OF CULTURE:
HIGHBROW VERSUS LOWBROW

When Cecil B. DeMille decided to abandon an unspectacular stage career for filmmaking in 1913, he was undeterred by the low repute of one-reelers associated with workers and immigrants in storefront nickelodeons. Such a rash move, however, prompted his older brother, William, a celebrated playwright, to react: "You do come of a cultivated family. . . . I cannot understand how you are willing to identify yourself with a cheap form of amusement . . . which no one will ever allude to as art. Surely you know the contempt with which the movie is regarded by every writer, actor and producer on Broadway." William's condescending attitude toward motion pictures was not unrehearsed. Previously, he had corresponded in a similar vein with Broadway producer David Belasco when Mary Pickford, who had appeared in one of his father's well-known plays, abandoned the stage. The playwright was so contemptuous of films that not even curiosity could induce him to enter a nickelodeon to see one-reel adaptations of his own works.[1] Cecil had the last word, however. A year after the formation of the Jesse L. Lasky Feature Play Company, William himself succumbed to the lure of motion pictures as a new democratic mode of expression. What led to this dramatic reversal of convictions regarding the nature of cinema? What role did Cecil play in persuading not only his playwright brother but respectable middle-class consumers that film was indeed an art form? To put it another way, what intertextual relationship existed during the Progressive Era between the legitimate stage and early feature film as a photoplay?

Adolph Zukor, president of the Famous Players Film Company, commented on successful stage productions as a standard for filmmakers when

7

he affirmed in a trade journal: "The moving picture man must try to do as artistic, as high-class, and as notable things in his line of entertainment as such men as . . . Charles and Daniel Frohman were doing in high-class Broadway theatres."[2] A chapter in film history that has yet to be thoroughly investigated, the legitimate theater rather than vaudeville served as a model for the production of feature film exhibited in movie palaces. A mode of representation intended to legitimate cinema for "better" audiences, multi-reel film adaptations of stage plays constituted a significant industry development that requires a study of the intertextuality of cultural forms in the genteel tradition. Although motion pictures were most likely patronized by the lower- as opposed to the upper-half of an expanding middle class before World War I, filmmakers like DeMille developed representational strategies for sophisticated audiences conversant with highbrow culture.[3] Pivotal to the success of the Lasky Company was exploitation of the well-known DeMille family name, for it had been associated with the celebrated stage productions of impresario David Belasco. Indeed, DeMille's contract stipulated that he would obtain the motion picture rights to the "plays and scenarios . . . controlled by the . . . DeMille Agency [his mother's company] and the . . . DeMille Estate."[4] Consequently, the director's arrival on the West Coast was part of a wholesale importation of Broadway producers, actors, playwrights, art directors, and music composers to legitimate cinema as art. The production of feature film adaptations was thus based on the name recognition of established writers and stage artists as signifiers of cultural legitimacy. Such an emphasis upon intertextual modes of address, however, rendered the question of early film authorship problematic, a dilemma that was resolved once cinema achieved recognition as an art form in its own right.

Understanding DeMille's contribution to the legitimation of cinema and of film authorship first requires a consideration of American cultural practice in relation to class dynamics during the late nineteenth and early twentieth centuries. Concepts of cultural hierarchy that pervade our thinking today, as Lawrence W. Levine argues, did not always exist. For the first half of the nineteenth century, a fairly homogeneous American audience enjoyed such art forms as Shakespearean theater and Italian opera as "*simultaneously* popular and elite." Shakespeare was thus not infrequently "presented as part of the same milieu inhabited by magicians, dancers, singers, acrobats, minstrels, and comics."[5] Similarly, museums displayed "Indian arrows, mammal bones, [and] two-headed pigs alongside casts of Greek sculpture and paintings by Gilbert Stuart and Thomas Sully."[6] Such cultural juxtapositions, seemingly incongruous today but for the intervention of postmodernism, were emblematic of a social formation that had receded into the past before the Victorian era drew to a close. During the latter part of the nineteenth century, American culture was subject to a process of sacralization accelerated by an increasingly professionalized culture industry and by the impulse of the genteel classes to distance themselves from urban workers and immigrants. Although the differentiation of cultural consumption according to class was an urban phenomenon that also occurred in Europe, the legacy of evangelical Protestantism and a more secularized Unitarianism predisposed the American patrician elite to recast culture in moral and didactic terms. Furthermore, the influence of Matthew Arnold, who emphasized a perpetual striving for self-improvement in pursuit of human perfection, was not only considerable but had strong religious overtones. Arnold's concept of culture as a force that could transcend individual and group differences was severely tested, however, as the urban scene became increasingly pluralistic. American intellectuals, already concerned about the debasement of cultural forms by the middle class, were undoubtedly alarmed by the practices of the lower orders. As the consump-, tion of culture became an expression of class and ethnic hierarchies, the genteel classes not only attempted to reform the recreation of the lower classes but also mapped out a *cordon sanitaire* for their own forms of conspicuous leisure. Consequently, performances of Shakespeare, opera, and symphonic music for the edification of the elite were elevated above popular entertainment. A sign of the increasing fragmentation of cultural production, the term "legitimate" denoted stage plays enshrined in the pantheon of art as opposed to cheaper amusement such as vaudeville, burlesque, and the circus. Pursuit of recreation and leisure became part of social practices that reinforced class and ethnic lines as the mid-nineteenth-century model of a harmonious civic culture receded into the past.[7]

The differentiation of American culture into highbrow and lowbrow—originally phrenological terms based on cranial shapes to equate racial types with intelligence—occurred at a time of demographic change associated with rapid industrial and urban growth. Unprecedented immigration from southern and eastern Europe, which crested in 1907, resulted in a more heterogeneous population in bustling American cities. The arrival of large numbers of seemingly unassimilable immigrants, especially Italians and Jews, and labor unrest culminating in the Haymarket riot and the Homestead and Pullman strikes were interrelated developments that sparked a revival of nativism. Characteristically, the response of the Anglo-Saxon elite to the centrifugal forces of a market society resulting in fragmentation was to impose cultural and moral order. As arbiters of good taste, they established the canon of legitimate theater, music, and art; validated modes of representation; and dictated audience reception that was respectful. Cultural refinement thus became part of a distinctive style of living in which ritualistic attendance at theaters, concert halls, and museums represented a sign of gentility vis-à-vis urban workers and immigrants.[8]

Since the genteel middle class defined its social identity in terms of its cultural practice, film entrepreneurs intent on escaping the lower-class stigma of storefront nickelodeons were determined to upgrade both production and exhibition. Significantly, their effort to uplift motion pictures coincided with that of the custodians of culture who were motivated by a sense of Progressive reform and moral rectitude. Although historians disagree about the nature of the relationship between these two factions, the attraction of cinema as entertainment for workers and immigrants influenced reformers to establish mechanisms of censorship and to regulate exhibition practices restricting the industry.[9] Ultimately, film magnates, pursuing respectability as well as profit, and Progressive reformers, intent on mediating film spectatorship to educate the urban masses, were at cross-purposes. Whereas the self-appointed elite struggled against the erosion of their authority through a process of sacralization to reinforce the status quo, profit-driven film entrepreneurs developed economic practices, such as vertical integration of the industry, that resulted in an increasing homogenization of cultural production if not reception. As filmmakers like DeMille exploited the genteel tradition to legitimate cinema, cultural forms became more interdependent and less amenable to concepts validating hierarchies of aesthetic modes. Within this context, the accelerating growth of the leisure industry meant that class and ethnic divisions reinforced by cultural consumption became less distinctive with each succeeding decade. What emerged, therefore, was a significantly different basis for a homogeneous population than had existed in mid-nineteenth-century civic culture. As opposed to a sense of community based upon shared commitment and moral values, twentieth-century popular culture represented the homogeneity of democratized access to commercialized amusement—especially as a form of visual appropriation—if not to actual consumer goods like tableware and furniture signifying upward social mobility.[10]

TEXTS AND INTERTEXTS: A QUESTION OF AUTHORSHIP

The Jesse L. Lasky Feature Play Company, cofounded by former vaudeville producer Lasky, his brother-in-law and glove salesman Samuel Goldfish (later Goldwyn), attorney Arthur S. Friend, and DeMille, was quick to announce its strategy to upgrade cinema for respectable middle-class audiences. As *Motion Picture News* reported in December 1913, the production company would film adaptations of "familiar novels and plays for presentation on the screen."[11] Although the company was named after Lasky because he was the best-known of the four cofounders, DeMille's theatrical legacy represented cultural capital that could immediately be exploited. Adolph Zukor, who merged his Famous Players Film Company with the Lasky Company in 1916, recalled that the DeMilles were "so closely associated with the stage that he was surprised Cecil . . . was becoming associated with the screen."[12] A *Photoplay* writer anticipated Zukor's reaction in 1915: "For more than a generation the name of DeMille has been closely linked with that of Belasco, both synonymous with high altitudes of dramatic art. Consequently when the first DeMille turned to the screen there was marked the beginning of a new epoch in film annals."[13] A beneficiary of the cultural legacy established by his father and brother as well-known playwrights, DeMille quickly attempted to validate his authorship in a related new medium. Problems that he encountered resulted from the questionable status of motion pictures compared then to more traditional forms of genteel culture. Although the director was able to establish the validity of his signature within a relatively short period of time, narrative and marketing strategies that exploited stage and literary works proved at first to be a mixed blessing.[14]

Consider, for example, DeMille's first three releases, *The Squaw Man* (1914), *The Virginian* (1914), and *The Call of the North* (1914). All were adaptations of stage Westerns that, in the last two instances, were in turn adapted from novels written by Owen Wister and Stewart Edward White, respectively. A fourth feature, *What's His Name* (1914), was a domestic melodrama based on a minor work by George Barr McCutcheon, a best-selling author whose earlier fiction had been successfully adapted as stage plays and feature films. Significantly, the credits of all four features attribute authorship to well-known writers, whereas DeMille is only acknowledged as having "picturized" the screen version. Not until his fifth feature, *The Man from Home* (1914), an adaptation of a Booth Tarkington and Harry L. Wilson play about American innocents abroad, did DeMille begin to identify himself in the credits as a producer equivalent to the Belascos of the stage. But his claim to authorship remained tenuous until the industry ceased to foreground writers, signifying cultural legitimacy, and represented cinema as the artistic expression of the director.

Credit sequences of early Lasky Company features illustrate the extent to which novelists and stage actors rather than directors were privileged as film authors. An intertitle in *The Call of the North*, for example, reads "Mr. DeMille Presents the Cast to Stewart Edward White," author of *The Conjuror's House*, a novel previously adapted for the stage by George Broadhurst. DeMille is seated on the extreme left, at times practically out of the frame, whereas White, seated prominently in the center, meets the costumed actors who represent the characters he invented in his novel. Robert Edeson, the Broadway actor starring in the dual role of Canadian frontiersmen, *père et fils*, is introduced last, turns to his left, and shakes the hand of his creator. In *What's His Name*, trumpeted as an adaptation of "The Celebrated Novel by George Barr McCutcheon," Lolita Robertson and Max Figman emerge on screen as poster board characters who come to life. Figman, interestingly, bows to the audience as if he were acknowledging applause on stage. Dustin Farnum, hero of the stage version of *The Virginian*, claimed that he was criticized for prostituting himself in the film adaptation of *The Squaw Man*,

1. Broadway actor Max Figman bows to the audience as if he were taking a curtain call in the credits of *What's His Name*, an adaptation of the novel by George Barr McCutcheon (1914). *(Photo courtesy George Eastman House)*

but a succession of theatrical stars, including Ina Claire, Marie Doro, Fannie Ward, Charlotte Walker, Theodore Roberts, Thomas Meighan, and Elliott Dexter appeared in DeMille's early features and became part of the Lasky studio's equivalent of a stock company. Since the appearance of Broadway actors on screen was considered a noteworthy event, trade journals regularly publicized the recruitment of theatrical stars who signed contracts with film studios. In March 1914 *Photoplay* claimed that more actors were abandoning the stage to appear in motion pictures on a permanent basis, a sign of the growing financial profitability as well as increasing cultural legitimacy of the cinema.[15]

The authorship of early film adaptations constructed as intertextual modes of address is an issue complicated by the role of talent behind the camera as well as publicity accorded writers and stage stars. When DeMille boarded a train to film *The Squaw Man* on the West Coast, he had never before directed a motion picture and was thus accompanied by filmmaker Oscar Apfel. Calling attention to this event, the *New York Dramatic Mirror* headlined, "Oscar Apfel to Direct Company Leaving for Pacific Coast

Soon," and described the director in a follow-up article as "well-known in film circles." Previously, Apfel had enjoyed a successful theatrical career as stage manager and director of several stock companies and worked with Belasco's assistant director, Will Dean. After leaving the theater, Apfel had also written and directed scores of motion pictures for the Edison Manufacturing Company, the Mutual Film Company, and Pathé Frères Film Company. According to Robert Grau's characterization of the struggle of independent film producers against the Motion Picture Patents Company, which was declared in restraint of trade in 1917, Apfel's Reliance productions for Mutual "contributed more to the 'Independent' cause than any single factor one may name."[16] The Lasky Company had thus recruited a considerable talent for its first filmmaking venture, but DeMille fortunately proved to be a quick study.

A consideration of *The Squaw Man* illustrates some of the basic filmmaking techniques that DeMille learned from Apfel, credited as codirector. Adapted from Edwin Milton Royle's stage play (1905) and starring Dustin Farnum, the film was a melodrama in the tradition of dime novels about the Wild West and foregrounded issues regarding class, ethnicity, and gender. Apfel and DeMille adroitly used parallel editing[17] to narrate the adventures of Captain James Wynnegate (Farnum), British aristocrat turned cowpuncher, who settles on the frontier after assuming blame for a crime committed by the husband of the woman he secretly loves. As evident in *The Squaw Man,* Apfel's filmmaking style was technically advanced and distinguished by composition for depth, a high ratio of medium shots, camera movement for reframing, parallel editing, eye-level shots with occasional use of high angle and even reverse angle shots, superimpositions and split-screen effects to show a protagonist recalling past events, and intertitles as exposition and dialogue, all characteristic of DeMille's early features. Significantly, the use of low-key lighting effects in night scenes with a fireplace or a match as naturalistic light sources are not as dramatic as in later DeMille films that would benefit from the expertise of Belasco's former set designer, Wilfred Buckland. Yet such lighting is used in two scenes to convey intimacy in Jim's tabooed relationship with an Indian chief's daughter, Nat-u-ritch (Red Wing), and thus prefigures the way in which DeMille typically constructed mise-en-scène to express moral dilemmas. Indeed, the director's striking use of "contrasty" lighting in a succession of feature films not only achieved product differentiation for the Lasky Company but also contributed to recognition of his own claim to authorship.

The reaction of enthusiastic film critics, who recognized Apfel's work when *The Squaw Man* was premiered in New York, must have been instructive for DeMille as he sought to establish himself as an author in his own right. Aside from this first acclaimed Lasky Company film, the director's collaborations with Apfel were never listed as titles in his filmography. Apfel continued to direct features as one of the studio's stable of filmmakers but was soon eclipsed in reputation by his apprentice. Probably, DeMille, who was extremely competitive with his brother William, was not predisposed to advance the career of yet another rival. At the beginning of its history, however, the Lasky Company profited from Apfel's mastery to establish a reputation for quality film with its very first release. A *Moving Picture World* critic who admired *The Squaw Man* claimed, "I have not seen Oscar Apfel's name made prominent in connection with this winner, but I recognize his handiwork without difficulty." The *New York Dramatic Mirror* tactfully stated, "As director-general, we presume the first credit for a skillfully directed drama belongs to Cecil B. DeMille, but this need not detract from the honor due Oscar C. Apfel, who, we understand, bore the brunt of the actual work." Indeed, a photograph taken on December 29, 1913, the day shooting commenced on the film, shows Apfel in command as director while DeMille is standing unobtrusively with cast and crew. One account of the production attributes camera angles and editing to Apfel and acting direction to DeMille.[18] Such a division of labor is feasible given noticeable contrasts between *The Squaw Man,* a collaborative work, and *The Virginian,* DeMille's third release, second feature, and first solo effort. An adaptation of Owen Wister's acclaimed best-seller about a Westerner (Dustin Farnum) who delays his marriage to an Eastern school teacher (Winifred Kingston) for a shootout, *The Virginian* is the most technically flawed of the director's early features. DeMille violates screen direction in editing several scenes, represents contiguous space in separate shots that are awkward with respect to scale and direction, makes erratic use of fades, and has a lower ratio of medium shots for intimate scenes such as one in which the Virginian bids farewell to a friend about to be hanged for cattle rustling. DeMille's later features, especially *Carmen* (1915), were reedited as reissues, but such was apparently not the case for this Western. Yet *The Virginian* does feature dramatic low-key lighting effects, as in nighttime campfire scenes repeated in *The Warrens of Virginia* (1915)—a Civil War saga based on William deMille's play—which are absent in *The Squaw Man* and most likely attributable to the genius of Belasco's set designer, Wilfred Buckland.

Although DeMille boasted, "I brought the whole Belasco crew out here . . . the men who had made the Belasco productions great," he attributed Buckland's recruitment as art director to the persuasive powers of his mother, Beatrice DeMille.[19] She was able to capitalize on professional ties dating back several decades because Buckland had acted in her husband's play, *The Main Line* (1886), and taught makeup at the American Academy of Dramatic Arts, where he counted Cecil and William among his pupils and had himself studied under Belasco.[20] Acclaiming him as a "decorative artist and an electrical expert in stage lighting," *Moving Picture World* announced his move to Los Angeles in May 1914 in a piece titled "Getting

Belasco Atmosphere."[21] Because Buckland's arrival at the West Coast studio coincided with the use of low-key lighting in campfire scenes in *The Virginian,* DeMille's attempt to establish his authorship was still problematic. But "Lasky lighting," also labeled "Rembrandt lighting," became the most distinctive if not dramatic aspect of the director's visual style before the First World War. Although Buckland served as art director until 1920 when set and costume design became decidedly more outré, DeMille in all likelihood proved himself to be once again a quick study. Scripts of the early feature films include details about the use of lighting effects, occasionally in the director's own handwriting. As he later recalled, cameramen were rated at the time according to "how clearly you could see under the table . . . how clearly you could see the back corner of the room—both corners . . ." Undeniably, the filmmaker's rapid progression from flat, uniform lighting that flooded the entire set, to modeled lighting with highlight and shadows that could be attributed to naturalistic sources, to dramatic low-key lighting that was combined with color tinting were technical advances reinforcing his claim to authorship.[22] DeMille never ceased to acknowledge Buckland's contribution, however. Studio correspondence attests that he was personally involved in the art director's salary negotiations in the midst of the Famous Players-Lasky merger.[23] At the end of his decades-long career, he still observed: "Buckland is a man who has not been given credit that he deserves. . . . Belasco's productions were something nobody in the world could equal, and that was because of Buckland."[24]

At the time that Buckland abandoned the legitimate theater, the Lasky Company was still exploiting audience perception of stage and screen as intertexts by negotiating for the rights to Belasco's plays. *Moving Picture World* touted an industry coup by announcing "the greatest tour de force of the season": "Lasky Gets Belasco Plays." According to Goldwyn, DeMille's family connections with Belasco were useful in outbidding Adolph Zukor's Famous Players in negotiations with the Broadway producer.[25] Given Belasco's stature, the significance of the Lasky Company acquiring the rights to his plays cannot be minimized. Belasco pontificated on the occasion: "The main feature of my agreement with Mr. Lasky and his company is their promise to put my plays on film in a manner befitting their success and reputation." Apparently reversing an earlier opinion regarding the cultural legitimacy of cinema, the producer shrewdly realized that motion picture rights would provide lucrative income after a stage play had completed its engagement and exhausted its stock company value. The transaction was worth one hundred thousand dollars.[26] For its part, the Lasky Company proved adept in exploiting the coup to attract middle-class patrons of the legitimate theater to its films. Ads in trade journals emphasized the intertextuality of stage and film productions in order to influence exhibiting practices and thereby audience reception. For example, an ad for

2. Broadway producer David Belasco wearing his everyday attire, a clerical collar.
(Photo courtesy Brigham Young University)

DeMille's first Belasco adaptation, *Rose of the Rancho* (1914), set in California after the Mexican War, trumpeted "Jesse L. Lasky in association with David Belasco presents . . ."

Such billing was not lost on DeMille, attempting to assert his own authorship, as he learned to model his persona after Belasco's. Although the director succeeded in dictating details about the display of his name when he achieved status as an author two years later, the marquee value of

Broadway personalities was then unquestioned. Ads for *The Warrens of Virginia* thus featured Belasco as producer of the stage hit and William deMille as playwright. Underneath and in smaller letters, Cecil was identified as film director. But events in early film history, including the legitimation of cinema in relation to the stage and as a separate art form, developed very quickly. By 1916 the announcement of Lasky's acquisition of the rights to additional Belasco plays was buried at the bottom of a page in *Moving Picture World*. By 1918 *Photoplay* was contemptuous of Belasco's judgment that stage drama was superior to the screen and described "this greatest of American producers" as "speaking in ponderous generalizations of things concerning which he has, obviously, almost no knowledge."[27]

As filmmakers who relied upon intertexts to address educated middle-class audiences, DeMille and Lasky initially considered scriptwriting to be the key to success. During his first year in Los Angeles, DeMille wrote to Goldwyn, who dealt with distribution and exhibition in the company's New York office: "I had always thought . . . that if the same technical and dramatic knowledge were applied to the scenario as to the play, the result would go far toward raising the standard of the photoplay." Similarly, he stated in an interview two years later, "If the scenario were written with the same care that is given to the writing of a drama, and were produced with . . . care and thought . . . , it would create an absolutely new clientele for motion pictures." When the West Coast studio was reorganized in 1915, Lasky announced, "We paid particular attention to the scenario department . . . [it] wholly controls the whole situation for the producer."[28] At the very least, DeMille must have been aware that his own assertion of authorship depended on his control of the scriptwriting process. A significant development occurred, therefore, when his brother William agreed late in the previous year to become the first head of the newly organized scenario department. The *New York Dramatic Mirror* reported his defection from the legitimate stage in September 1914: "Some surprise was caused [because] deMille . . . was one of the great playwrights of the decade and at the hey-day of his success on the stage." Shortly after he arrived at the studio and was cast as an extra in *Rose of the Rancho*, William wrote to his wife about his new craft: "There is very much to be learnt about the structure of a scenario. . . . It is very tricky work and requires absolute concentration."[29] Assisted by former New Yorkers who had also abandoned the stage, namely Margaret Turnbull, a novelist and playwright with whom he had collaborated, and her brother Hector Turnbull, a former drama critic of the *New York Tribune*, William quickly wrote several scripts. As part of a public relations effort to promote screenwriting, he even exploited his affiliation with his alma mater, Columbia University. The Lasky Company supported the institution's decision to establish a special course of lectures on filmmaking by announcing a scholarship for the student who wrote the most original scenario. With

3. DeMille, on the right, and his brother, William, dressed as adventurers in their early days at the Lasky studio in Hollywood. *(Photo courtesy Brigham Young University)*

respect to film authorship, however, William quickly surmised, as did Lasky, that the role of the director was pivotal despite movie ads trumpeting Broadway names. Several months prior to the Lasky Company's merger with Famous Players, he stated, "really good directors in this game are worth almost any amount," and renounced writing in favor of directing. Although Lasky wrote to Goldwyn, "I have been concentrating on . . . directors and scenario writers," he also concluded, "the fate of a picture is so much in the hands of the director, even though the scenario department turns out first-rate scenarios."[30]

A bold move to consolidate feature film production for middle-class audiences, the merger—contemplated in 1915 but negotiated a year later—strained an understaffed scenario department but demonstrated the astuteness of focusing on screenplays to upgrade films. When DeMille wired that his scriptwriting methods were being undone in the midst of reorganization, Lasky, now headquartered in New York, countered that he was overwhelmed because Famous Players lacked not only a scenario department and a backlog of scripts but positive reviews of recent releases. By contrast, the Lasky Company had been in a strong position to negotiate favorable terms for the merger. According to Lasky, "I always claimed we made better, if fewer, pictures than Famous Players in the early days." Indeed, DeMille had boastfully written to Goldwyn during his first year on the West Coast, "I can make Zukor productions for you in three weeks; in fact I will guarantee to turn you out a half a dozen 'Eagle's Mates' [a Famous Players film] weekly."[31] Under pressure to consolidate and streamline the newly formed corporation, Lasky, who assumed the role of vice-president under Zukor, named Hector Turnbull as head of a scenario department relocated in New York. Although the executive remained committed to producing high-quality films, he was impressed with Famous Players' cost-cutting practices, if not its organization, and quipped to DeMille, "my slogan is 'Dividends first and art second.' Or rather a blend of the two."[32]

As the Lasky Company and Famous Players demonstrated even before their well-publicized merger, the cultural legitimacy of feature films meant increased profit. And as the cinema became increasingly recognized as an art form in its own right, DeMille began to assert his claim to film authorship. On this subject, Lasky sided with his director-general and explained to Goldwyn a year prior to the merger:

> Cecil showed me a copy of a letter he had written to you on publicity for himself. It seems that this has been in his mind for some months. . . . Cecil has proved his value to the firm in many ways and . . . there can be no question of his loyalty to us. That being the case, I think it a very good business move for us to build up his name as we are trying to build up Blanche Sweet's name. You know the public go to see a Griffith production, not because it may have a star in the cast, but because Griffith's name on it stands for so much. It seems to me that the time has come for us to do the same with Cecil's name. If we

4. Casually dressed as director-general of the studio, DeMille confers with executive Adolph Zukor and scriptwriter Jeanie Macpherson. *(Photo courtesy Brigham Young University)*

> can accomplish this, we could let Cecil stage the plays that have no stars and his name in large type on the paper, advertising, etc., would undoubtedly in time take the place of a star's. In a word, he is the biggest asset we have, so let's use it for all it is worth.[33]

But before DeMille's reputation as an auteur eclipsed the stars in his productions, the arrival of Metropolitan Opera soprano Geraldine Farrar resulted in extraordinary fanfare for the debut of a spectacular leading lady.

GERALDINE FARRAR: A DIVA COMES TO HOLLYWOOD

A year before merging with Famous Players, the Lasky Company advanced its strategy to exploit the congruence of cultural forms in the genteel tradition by focusing on the intertextuality of feature film and grand opera. A standard exhibiting practice for releases distributed through Paramount at first-run theaters was a balanced program that included the engagement of an orchestra and vocalists to perform operatic music before and after screenings. At the Strand Theatre in New York, for example, audiences who attended screenings of DeMille's comedy *Chimmie Fadden* (1915) heard the overture from *Cavalleria Rusticana,* a duet from *La Forza del Destino,* and the sextet from *Lucia di Lamermoor.*[34] Considerable publicity was thus generated

5. DeMille poses with Jesse L. Lasky, Adolph Zukor, Samuel (Goldfish) Goldwyn, and Albert Kaufman after the Famous Players-Lasky merger. *(Photo courtesy Brigham Young University)*

when Geraldine Farrar, an internationally acclaimed soprano who had refused offers to sing in big-time vaudeville, signed a contract to star in DeMille's feature films. She became an asset to the Lasky Company equivalent to Famous Players' biggest marquee attraction, Mary Pickford.[35] Grand opera, especially in an age when culture was sacrosanct, was the citadel of highbrow culture. Farrar, an American-born singer and Hohenzollern protégée, had made her debut in Berlin and was an accomplished diva who could sing in German, Italian, and French. She brought to film the aura of high culture patronized by European royalty. *Moving Picture World* pronounced: "Next to the entry of Belasco . . . , the distinguished apostle of American art to the . . . screen, the resolution of this marvelously gifted young woman to employ her talents in . . . films is the greatest step in advancing the dignity of the motion picture, in freeing it from the bane of prejudice, in winning for it the good opinion of the public." A sign of the correspondence between theater and opera as intertexts appropriated by film entrepreneurs, Farrar's contract was negotiated on her behalf by Morris Gest, a close personal friend who was also Belasco's son-in-law.[36] An admirer of the Metropolitan Opera diva, Belasco had consulted her about the premiere of Puccini's opera, *La Fanciulla del West*, which was based on his stage play about a California romance, *The Girl of the Golden West*. She had previously appeared with Enrico Caruso in Puccini's *Madama Butterfly*, also based on a Belasco play, in a performance that had been attended by the composer himself.[37] Years later when Farrar left the Lasky Company after a dispute over the career of her husband, Lou Tellegen, best known as Sarah Bernhardt's leading man, she again worked with Belasco to stage the operatic version of his play, *Zaza*, a role that became part of her repertoire.[38]

Farrar's screen debut in *Carmen* in October 1915 was the occasion for immense publicity that is very revealing about marketing strategies to elevate the status of motion pictures in relation to highbrow culture.[39] By coincidence, Fox Film Company also released an adaptation of the opera starring Theda Bara, but Farrar's prestige guaranteed that the Lasky Company version would be the focus of unusual attention. Prior to the release date, trade papers announced that Farrar's film would be exhibited only on the Paramount program and that exhibitors could expect to "add . . . clientele that have never before been approached by the motion picture." Similarly, *The Opera Magazine* predicted that lines of automobiles, a sign of well-heeled patrons, would be drawn up in front of movie theaters. Ads for the film were printed in script to simulate formal invitations to upper crust social and cultural events.[40] Arranging a premiere attended by a glittering audience composed of the Brahmin elite, certainly more blue-blooded than the social register in New York, Jesse L. Lasky engaged Boston's Symphony Hall and a full orchestra. Significantly, William's name as scriptwriter was billed over Cecil's in a strategy to dignify Farrar's first film release with emblems of respectable middle-class culture. Publicity accorded the soprano's screen debut in a silent version of a well-known opera was a bonus for the Lasky Company but, for the moment, obscured DeMille's effort to establish himself as an author in his own right.

Because the Lasky Company could not obtain the rights to Georges Bizet's opera, William deMille based his screenplay on the Prosper Mérimée novel that had inspired librettists Henri Meilhac and Ludovic Halévy. Dispensing with minor characters and subplots, William focused instead on the characterization of the fiery gypsy heroine, a move that paid off because Farrar proved to be as riveting on screen as she was on stage. An equivalent to the ominous chords of the operatic overture foreboding violent death, the art titles in the credits show Carmen and Don José in dramatic low-key lighting that establishes the mood of their doomed relationship. As opposed to introducing all the main characters before the first sequence of the narrative, DeMille presents them as the plot unfolds so that Farrar's appearance is delayed until she sights gypsy smugglers on a mountainside. Surrounded by foliage in dappled sunlight, she is playful and confident as she appears in a medium long shot that identifies her with nature. When she overhears that Don José (Wallace Reid) cannot be bribed, she boasts to her compatriots, "I will give you this incorruptible officer bound hand and foot—by love."

Apart from the clamor that resulted from Farrar's screen debut, *Carmen* deserved critical acclaim for its visual style albeit the only print extant is a reedited version reissued in 1918.[41] DeMille used art titles with drawings that prefigure the shot beginning the next sequence; low-key lighting in conjunction with color tinting in shades of red, pink, amber, and blue to produce shimmering textures; a high ratio of medium shots and medium close-ups, especially of the diva; a spectacular high angle shot of the bull-fighter with Carmen, seated in the foreground of the ring, as she throws him a favor; and several deep focus shots of the gypsy campsite and tavern. A closer analysis of the amber-tinted sequence in which Carmen dances for her admirers reveals how artfully DeMille staged Farrar's screen debut. Escamillo, the toreador (Pedro de Cordoba), arrives at the tavern and queries its owner Pastia (Horace B. Carpenter) about the gypsy's whereabouts. DeMille cuts to a darkened screen. Suddenly a door swings open to reveal Carmen, an ornament in her hair and flowers pinned to her neckline, standing in the light emanating from the room behind her. Advancing to the stairway railing in a close medium shot, she is maddeningly provocative and flirts with several admirers while sighting Don José in the distance. A close-up of Escamillo in a profile shot in low-key lighting, as he gazes to his right, complements a close-up of Don José staring to his left while the light plays on his helmet and epaulettes. Pinned between the gaze of these two possessive suitors, Carmen has fewer options than her free spirit warrants.

Farrar, who had proven herself a drawing card for operagoers on two continents, won kudos for her screen debut despite Pennsylvania censors objecting to her impassioned portrayal. According to the *New York Times*, which did not yet review films on a regular basis, "among movie actresses she is one of the best," but "her playing is . . . bold, bald, and in dubious taste." Undoubtedly, Farrar's portrayal of Carmen as a sensual woman unbound by the conventions of romance violated Victorian definitions of womanhood. The soprano retained her realistic film acting style, however, and slapped Caruso during a controversial performance of the opera at the Metropolitan. Jerry, as she was called, became a magnet for throngs of filmgoers who crowded the so-called "high-class" theaters. *Motion Picture News* commented on the significance of this development by repeating that "nickelodeons are bound to be very largely superceded by the better class of motion picture entertainment." Advertising suggests, however, that while the Lasky Company was courting "better" audiences, an opportunity to

6. Metropolitan Opera soprano Geraldine Farrar appears in her screen debut as *Carmen* (1915), a film with dramatic low-key lighting, billed in the industry as "Lasky lighting." *(Photo courtesy George Eastman House)*

7. As the audacious and seductive gypsy, Farrar flirts with several admirers, including Wallace Reid, on the left, in the role of Don José. *(Photo courtesy George Eastman House)*

attract segments of the lower-middle and upper working classes, drawn to highbrow culture as a status symbol, was also being exploited. At the Chicago Strand, refurbished for an engagement of *Carmen,* the program stated, "To see Miss Farrar in 'Carmen' at the Metropolitan Opera House would cost five dollars a seat. The work of Paramount Pictures Corporation has enabled you to see her in a film at regular motion picture admission prices," ranging from fifteen cents for the balcony to one dollar for loge seats.[42] Fittingly, in the 1918 reissue, *Carmen* was preceded by shots of Farrar costumed in her various operatic roles including Butterfly, Tosca, and Manon.

Critical response to *Carmen* in the trade papers was self-congratulatory. *Motion Picture News* headlined, "Critics of the Dailies, Who Had Shown Inclination to Hold Aloof from Photo Plays, Are Compelled to Acknowledge by the Lasky Presentation the Importance of Film Drama." The *New York Dramatic Mirror* crowed, "What is to become of opera if singers learn to act? About the first innovation would be a new set of Metropolitan critics who . . . recognize the relationship between operatic and pantomimic art, as practiced in the despised 'movies.'" As a matter of fact, opera critics objected to the "violent wrenching of Mérimée's text" as adapted by William deMille and the reorchestration of Bizet's music as accompaniment. Controversy about the artistic merit of feature film compared to opera did not, however, prevent seasoned reviewers from observing that the use of dramatic low-key lighting and location shooting resulted in a technically superior production.[43] Assessing the film decades later, Kirk Bond praised the composition, lighting, and acting of the film and concluded, "DeMille tells the old story with such brio, such power indeed, that it becomes new."[44] *Carmen* represents a milestone because DeMille's artistry, though overshadowed by Farrar's acting debut, equalled her international renown and charismatic screen presence. As the director continued to earn critical acclaim in 1915, he would become less indebted to established forms of genteel culture in order to legitimate cinema and to establish his own credentials.

CRITICAL DISCOURSES

As Jesse L. Lasky recalled, perhaps with more nostalgia than accuracy, "feature pictures were established in 1914, [but] they didn't become respectable until late in 1915."[45] Discourse in trade journals supports his argument that cinema was not then widely recognized as an art form. Geraldine Farrar's sensational debut and attendant press reaction could have occurred only during the early years when the industry had yet to achieve cultural legitimacy. Such events demonstrated that producers like the Lasky Company and Famous Players deployed the right strategy to establish multi-reel features as the industry standard to attract middle-class audiences. According to discourse in trade journals and fan magazines, however, as late as 1914 there was by no means unanimity on the subject of features, a term coined by *Motion Picture News* in the previous year. Captain Leslie T. Peacocke, who was affiliated with Universal Film Manufacturing Company and wrote *Photoplay*'s column on scriptwriting, cautioned that "all the companies are vieing [*sic*] to secure . . . leading attractions without taking into consideration whether the five and ten cent audience—who constitute the big patrons of the film drama and will always do so—will enthuse themselves over a play . . . or a book . . . of which they have never heard."[46] Asserting an opposite point of view in *Moving Picture World*, Jesse L. Lasky and Adolph Zukor disputed William Selig and Carl Laemmle on the desirability of features as against one- and two-reelers. Lasky argued:

> Features . . . have accomplished what the "one reel" subjects failed to attain in fifteen years . . . to interest the classes. . . . Fronts were changed, interiors rearranged, music improved, prices elevated, and advertising in the press resorted to. Features compelled recognition in the daily press. Regular reviewers . . . began reviewing feature photoplays from the same angle that the legitimate dramas are criticized. . . . The production of features have attracted [*sic*] a large number of men to the ranks of motion picture purveyors who could do naught else than dignify the industry.[47]

As Lasky recognized, feature films prompted critics to write reviews comparable to those of stage plays in newspapers and periodicals that influenced middle-class reception. The *New York Times*, for example, did not yet review films on a regular basis, as did trade papers and fan magazines, but it devoted space to adaptations starring celebrated artists like Farrar. Discourse in trade journals was more consistent, but critics still valorized screen adaptations in terms of intertextual references to traditional art forms. Consequently, they too legitimated film according to the standards of genteel culture but in so doing diminished the authorial claim of filmmakers like DeMille. Critics, in other words, were still expressing uncertainty regarding the nature of film aesthetic during an important transitional period in the evolution of cinema. DeMille's first release, *The Squaw Man*, for example, was hailed as "one of the best visualizations of a stage play ever shown on screen." Yet the critic also asserted that the director should "realize the art of producing moving pictures is to be measured by its own canons alone." Another critic reacted to *Rose of the Rancho* with this comparison: "If the best stage plays can be picturized with such success then the picture even excels the play." Belasco's favorable response to the film, "This is better than the play," was widely publicized to validate the screen version. Significantly, the production of spectacles that surpassed those orchestrated on stage called attention to increased realism as a desirable characteristic distinguishing the new medium. Critics were thus impressed with "a real soda fountain" in *What's His Name*, "the ambushing and destruction of the supply train" in *The Warrens of Virginia*, and "picturesque settings" in *The Captive* (1915). Anticipating such reviews, DeMille had written to Goldwyn in 1914, "The scope of the photoplay is so much wider than that of the legitimate drama. In the first place we DO things instead of acting them. When a big effect is necessary, such as the burning of a ship, the blowing up of a mine, the wrecking of a train, we do not have to trick the effect with lights and scenery, we DO it."[48] As critical response became focused on the formal properties of a new mode of representation, film acquired greater currency as an art form. Within this context, the publication of Vachel Lindsay's *The Art of the Moving Picture* (1915), one of the first serious and extended essays on film aesthetic, is telling: the work asserted an independent status for cinema while discussing it with reference to traditional art forms like architecture and sculpture.[49]

DeMille's attempt to establish his credentials as an author when film had yet to achieve cultural legitimacy was initially compromised by his reputation for lighting effects. Given the fact that low-key lighting and color tinting on nitrate prints resulted in a pictorial mise-en-scène, critics referred to famous paintings as intertexts. Artwork such as chromolithographs had long since been commercialized for middle-class consumption, but paintings exhibited in museums still retained the aura of unique art objects. Critics thus simultaneously conferred and withheld authorship by focusing on DeMille's mise-en-scène. W. Stephen Bush, for example, claimed in *Moving Picture World* that the director's representation of a tenement district in *Kindling* (1914) was "as graphic as anything that ever came from the hands of Hogarth or Rembrandt." After viewing the *The Golden Chance* (1915), a Cinderella story based on an original screenplay, Bush exclaimed: "If the paintings in a Rembrandt gallery or a set of Titians or Tintorettos were to come to life . . . and transferred to the moving picture screen the effect could not have been more startling." Similarly, the *New York Dramatic News* praised "the masterly handling and lighting of Cecil deMille [*sic*]" in *Carmen* and noted that "the use of direct and only mildly suffused light in almost every picture emphasizes the figures and the play of facial muscles, and creates a quality akin to the tone of oil painting." DeMille himself maintained in a much-repeated anecdote that when Goldwyn objected to the shadowy effects of low-key lighting—most likely in scenes in *The Man from Home* or *The Warrens of Virginia*—he replied, "To Hell with it—tell them it's Rembrandt lighting." Since DeMille's claim to authorship had not yet been substantiated, credits of his early features signified his role as filmmaker with the phrase "picturized by" as opposed to "produced by" or "directed by." Aptly, an article in the *New York Dramatic Mirror* was titled, "The Director as a Painter and the Players His Colors," a comparison that would cease to be accentuated when film became an independent art form.[50]

Although the intertextuality of cultural forms in genteel society served to dim as well as illuminate his achievement, DeMille exploited convictions regarding the sanctity of culture to assert his status as an author. Consistent with Protestant beliefs as well as Arnoldian concepts stressing human perfectibility, artists were then prompted to produce realistic representations that could be read as spiritual messages.[51] Belasco, not coincidentally, wore a clergyman's collar as part of his everyday dress and was dubbed an "apostle of art." As his heirs apparent in the cinema, the DeMille brothers reinterpreted the tradition of Victorian pictorialism so that it became an essential aspect of their mission as filmmakers. While still a playwright, William had claimed that "the primary essential of a play is that it shall teach a lesson." Cecil asserted that "to preach is to invite disaster, but . . . to be afraid to develop a message in the story is to miss a great possibility." Although the brothers shared a belief in the didactic function of art, they had serious ideological differences that would later become more apparent. William, a liberal, had married the daughter of single-tax reform advocate, Henry George, and sympathized with the people against the "highbrows" and "uplifters"; he had even championed stage drama as "the art of the people as a whole" rather than "for a cultivated few."[52] Cecil was conservative and retained toward the public a stance of cultural stewardship that he shared with the elite classes of the Progressive Era.

Within the context of Progressive reform based on moral imperative, film critics too were proponents of the sanctity of culture and responded to DeMille's features in language saturated with didacticism. Such expressions accorded with the objectives of genteel reformers intent on assimilating immigrants and workers by emphasizing the value of education. Motion pictures were thus not just entertainment; they were "a titanic engine for popular education . . . [and] for the cultivation of the public mind." Accordingly, one critic waxed rhapsodic about film in relation to "the refining and intensifying of the emotions, the logic of civilization, and the development of the soul." Critics also used the rhetoric of uplift to describe the improving quality of feature film. A reviewer of *The Call of the North* proclaimed in *Moving Picture World* that the feature had reaffirmed his "faith in the approaching kingdom of quality." Similarly, *Photoplay* announced with awe and anticipation, "We stand at the threshold of the full-length screen play, as the living body of a higher and finer programme."[53] In sum, critics demonstrated that the sacrosanct language associated with highbrow culture could be employed to legitimate the emergence of a popular mass medium. Although this practice was useful in securing for DeMille the status of a cultural custodian in his endeavor to establish authorship, ultimately the interpenetration of cultural forms contributed to a process of desacralization. The intertextuality of grand opera, stage melodrama, and feature film, in other words, signified that the elite would find the preservation of a cultural hierarchy unmanageable in a technological age.

FILM: THE NEW DEMOCRATIC ART

Although film entrepreneurs initially exploited the intertextual relationship between feature film and traditional art forms, they were not shortsighted about the future of the industry. At the time he abandoned vaudeville for motion pictures, Jesse L. Lasky predicted, "Eventually we will have stories by authors of recognized standing and written expressly for the screen." The mode of production of early feature film was so fast-paced in response to market demand that filmmakers could not indefinitely rely on theatrical and literary sources for adaptations. DeMille therefore resorted to formulaic screenplays that not only gave him more stature as an author in his own right, but proved cheaper than negotiating for costly rights and was more tailored to the abilities of actors under contract. Studio emphasis on original scenarios also streamlined production because expensive delays attributed to scriptwriting problems, as Lasky complained to Goldwyn, meant that directors and stars had to be paid while awaiting rehearsals. Working at breakneck pace, DeMille doubled the number of his releases from seven in 1914 to thirteen in 1915, including three features, *The Captive*, *The Cheat*, and *The Golden Chance*, that were based on original screenplays. As director-general, moreover, he supervised the production of twenty-one features, including his own films, in 1914 and thirty-six in 1915.[54] Toward the end of 1915 and prior to the Famous Players-Lasky merger in June 1916, he began to include in his output original screenplays written by Jeanie Macpherson and Hector Turnbull. Macpherson, interestingly, had previously been employed under Oscar Apfel at the Edison Manufacturing Company and had written scenarios and directed films for Universal Film Manufacturing Company and Criterion Features.[55] After the merger, DeMille relied almost exclusively on Macpherson's formulaic scenarios, even though a general manager assumed his supervisory duties as director-general so that he could produce special features at a slower pace.

Undoubtedly, the extraordinary success of *The Cheat* and *The Golden Chance*, films based on original screenplays that DeMille simultaneously directed during a hectic production schedule, influenced his move away from adaptations. Critics responded with hyperbole even though they still compared film with the legitimate stage. The *Motion Picture News* critic, for example, referred to the theater when he claimed that "in staging 'The Cheat,' [DeMille's] genius reached a climax," but he also noted that the film "should mark a new era in lighting as applied to screen productions." Acknowledging film authorship, the *New York Dramatic Mirror* critic detected "the master hand of Cecil DeMille . . . throughout 'The Golden Chance'" and claimed the production could "be favorably compared to anything that either the stage or the screen has brought forth." As both Goldwyn and William deMille later recalled, critical acclaim for *The Cheat*, a sensational melodrama focused on an interracial relationship, elevated DeMille to the pantheon of early film directors.[56] After a series of successful features during a year when the names of Belasco, Farrar, and his brother William had been emblazoned above his own, Cecil was finally in a position to dictate that his name be "prominently displayed upon all motion pictures." When he signed a contract with Famous Players-Lasky shortly after the merger, he achieved recognition in the industry equivalent to that accorded luminaries of the legitimate stage and opera.[57] Fittingly, DeMille, hailed as "Creator of Artistic Productions Embodying High Box-Office Value," was the only director besides D. W. Griffith to be inducted into the *Motion Picture News* Hall of Fame in 1922.[58]

What was the significance of filmmakers like DeMille who came of age during the sacralization of culture and exploited a theatrical legacy to legitimate cinema and film authorship? Since motion pictures were a popular attraction for workers and immigrants in storefront nickelodeons before entrepreneurs sought legitimacy, middle-class film reception signified an important shift in patterns of cultural consumption. A number of social and cultural historians as well as film historians have debated whether early film attendance exemplifies a trickle-down or bottom-up model with respect to class and ethnic interaction in an urban environment. Were middle-class audiences patronizing nickelodeons at a much earlier date than has been assumed, as Russell Merritt and Robert C. Allen argue? Or was filmgoing, as Roy Rosenzweig asserts, a working-class diversion as late as 1914 and thus evidence of a radical change in middle-class cultural practice? Significantly, Merritt and Allen do not distinguish between the upper and lower middle classes in their empirical studies, although Tom Gunning points out that by 1910, 25 percent of filmgoers were lower-middle-class salaried workers. Were lower-class immigrant women indeed setting trends for middle-class women by patronizing commercialized amusement, as Kathy Peiss claims? Or were they, as Elizabeth Ewen contends, subject to the assimilative process of Americanization as represented on the screen? Were sociable immigrants translating Habermas's concept of the public sphere into neighborhood nickelodeons only to be textually constructed as spectators, as Miriam Hansen maintains? Or was the filmgoing experience of the working class, as Lizabeth Cohen asserts, significantly mediated by subcultures well into the 1920s? With respect to representational strategies and reading practices, were producers creating a mass audience by persuading the lower classes to join their "betters" in nickelodeons, as Janet Staiger argues, or were they in league with elite constituents, as William Uricchio and Roberta E. Pearson contend, to make films that could be read by the middle as well as working classes?[59]

The formation of producers like Famous Players and the Lasky Company, as well as distributors like Paramount, in my view, meant that entrepreneurs purposely developed a strategy to resituate cinema for "better" audiences during the years 1912–1915. Given the importance of cultural rituals and commodities to signify genteel status, industry leaders chose to upgrade production and exhibition practices to legitimate cinema and to enhance profit. Although filmgoing was most likely entertainment for the lower as opposed to upper middle class before World War I, the practice of showcasing features in downtown movie palaces overlapped and to some extent displaced a preexisting plebeian film culture. A reading of specific DeMille texts will show, moreover, that the representational strategy of feature films based on traditional cultural forms articulated genteel middle-class ideology to appeal to cultivated audiences. What appears ironic in retrospect is that filmmakers unwittingly contributed to the homogenization of culture that threatened the social identity of the very classes whom they were courting. Writers in trade journals did employ terms like "high-class" and "low-class" to differentiate clientele, but the eventual legitimation of film rendered such distinctions less meaningful. According to Douglas Gomery, by the mid-1920s approximately 50 percent of audiences in large urban centers were patronizing first- and second-run theaters.[60] The reception of cinema as entertainment that began to transcend established patterns of cultural consumption based on class and ethnicity thus proved to be a meaningful development.

The Lasky Company strategy to upgrade film in terms of intertextual readings indeed heightened contradictions that attenuated the sacrosanct status of genteel culture in an age of commercialized amusement. Distinctions between *highbrow* and *lowbrow*, for example, were difficult to sustain even in the legitimate theater whose aura filmmakers sought for the cinema. Critical discourse on the Henry C. DeMille-David Belasco domestic melodramas staged in fashionable theaters in the 1880s and 1890s was not always appreciative, as will be discussed later. As theatergoing became pervasive among genteel middle-class audiences demanding Broadway productions, critics expressed concern about such issues as style over substance. When William deMille's Civil War melodrama, *The Warrens of Virginia*, went on tour in 1908 after a successful run at the Belasco Theatre in New York, the *Cincinnati Inquirer* observed that it "proved more interesting as a production than as a drama." A few years later, *The Bookman* reacted to William's popular melodrama *The Woman* as "the best directed play Mr. Belasco ever yet produced" but "distinctly a well made play [that] expands no theme . . . of permanent importance to humanity."[61] As the new stagecraft displaced Victorian melodrama in the 1920s, Belasco was dismissed for stage plays that were more notable for pictorial realism than for literary merit.[62] Subject to the leveling impact of market conditions, the cultural consumption of the genteel classes, as shown by their taste in theatergoing, did not always adhere to Arnoldian standards of excellence.

Within this fluctuating context, the marketing of feature film adaptations further undermined cultural distinctions that were based on notions of excellence and buttressed by class and ethnic hierarchies. Fan magazines such as *Photoplay*, for example, published novelizations of motion pictures illustrated with stills that not only served as advertising but rendered film narrative as well as its intertexts more accessible. The May 1914 cover of the magazine read, "In This Issue: The Squaw Man. A Complete Novelette From the Feature Film." Adapted for the screen by DeMille, Edwin Milton Royle's stage play was subsequently novelized for fan magazine readers. At times, this circuitous practice led to novelizations of already existing novels. DeMille's *The Virginian* was "Novelized from the Film . . . Based on the Original Novel by Owen Wister [and the stage version by Kirk LaShelle]." Staff writers did not feel compelled to refrain from invention, as was the case when Bruce Westfall concluded his version of DeMille's *Rose of the Rancho*— adapted from the Belasco and Richard Walton Tully play—on a more conciliatory and less realistic note.[63] Aside from generating publicity, novelizations were probably useful to less educated audiences who were unfamiliar with the novel or stage version of convoluted plots such as DeMille's *The Call of the North*, a Western set in Canada that spanned two generations.[64] Yet narrative forms were undeniably diluted in the recycling process that screen adaptations set in motion. As more space in fan magazines was allocated to articles about movie stars, a sign of growing preoccupation with celebrities rather than narrative, a smaller percentage of pages was devoted to novelizations. Possibly, these recycled stories became redundant when film narration advanced to the point where an audience could follow complicated plot developments. As early fan magazine staples, however, novelizations illustrate the impact of filmmakers who, while claiming the aura of art for feature film, unwittingly collapsed distinctions between highbrow and lowbrow and paved the way for categories like middlebrow. The term *middlebrow*, which signified a decline of Arnoldian standards of excellence, was not coined until 1925, but the leveling impact of the market on cultural commodities had been in evidence for many decades. DeMille could not have exploited the genteel tradition so artfully if middle-class consumers had not already been seduced by stage plays and best-sellers whose titles would scarcely merit recognition today. As a description of class and ethnic distinctions in patterns of cultural consumption, the term *highbrow* has its uses as a label, but it was not necessarily synonymous with high art and could thus be reconfigured as middlebrow by the culture industry.[65]

Although the success of feature film ultimately contributed to the increasing homogenization of culture as an index of social status, could it then be argued that the cinema succeeded mid-nineteenth-century theater as a new democratic art form?[66] To be sure, film reception continued to be mediated by a number of variables including gender, class, ethnicity, religion, age group, and geographical region.[67] The significance of film as a revolutionary and powerful new medium with widespread appeal, however, was not lost upon the filmmakers themselves. William deMille was quite prescient when he observed in 1915 that "for the first time in history a new art is being born that is more democratic than the drama." Indeed, his abandonment of a prestigious stage career can in some measure be attributed to his liberal politics and to his vision regarding the future of the cinema. Asserting a similar viewpoint, *Photoplay* observed, "films . . . are a basic amusement, recreation and instruction for the entire world—for the highbrow and for the fellow whose cowlick grows into his eyebrows."[68] Given the context of turbulent class and ethnic relations in the early twentieth century, this industry development was not inconsiderable. Despite the conclusion of a trade journal survey that the building of picture palaces had not diminished the importance of small houses as the "bread and butter" of the business, the existence of first-run theaters in major cities signified not only the increasing cultural legitimacy of film but its broad appeal.[69] Certainly, the newly built or renovated movie palaces had seating arrangements, as in nineteenth-century theaters partitioned into boxes, gallery, and balcony, that reinforced social distinctions. Specific showtimes meant less accessibility than continuous screenings at nickelodeons. Notwithstanding the preference of workers and immigrants for neighborhood venues, "high-class" theaters proved more accessible for them than other forms of middle-class culture. Granted, programs offered a selection of orchestral and vocal music that appealed to more educated listeners, but feature film, newsreels, educational footage, and comedies were hardly inaccessible to a younger generation of working-class and ethnic groups. As Richard Koszarski has pointed out, the diverse components of a balanced program at first-run theaters had more in common with vaudeville, initially a working-class and ethnic diversion, than with the legitimate theater.[70] Whether exhibited in movie palaces or neighborhood houses, feature film ultimately represented a form of expression that merged art and entertainment to exert an appeal transcending social barriers. What resulted was a shared cultural experience based to a significant extent on representations of genteel values that would become pervasive even as the cultural distinctiveness of the middle class, especially its lower rungs, became tenuous in an age of mass culture. A contextualized reading of DeMille's early feature film adaptations therefore demonstrates how middle-class cultural practice became the basis for a redefinition of cinema as a democratic art form.

TWO

Self-Theatricalization in Victorian Pictorial Dramaturgy: *What's His Name*

MELODRAMA AS A MIDDLE-CLASS SERMON

On July 13, 1914, seven months into his first year as director-general of the Lasky Company, DeMille began to film an adaptation of *What's His Name*, a minor novel that had not previously won acclaim on the legitimate stage.[1] Since his first three features, *The Squaw Man, The Call of the North,* and *The Virginian,* were screen versions of well-known plays that could boast the location shooting, action scenes, and frontiersmen typical of Westerns, *What's His Name* was a significant departure. A domestic melodrama based on an unconventional sex-role reversal, it represented DeMille's first effort to rewrite a genre that his father, Henry C. DeMille, had formulated in collaboration with David Belasco in the 1880s and 1890s. To put it another way, melodrama translated from stage to screen as an intertext was in some measure a DeMille family enterprise. According to the tradition of well-made plays crafted by his father and by his brother, William, DeMille resolved the personal and family dilemmas signifying the ethical crises of modern urban life by constructing his mise-en-scène as an instructive tableau. That he was unable to do so with the moral clarity so compelling in late-nineteenth-century stage melodrama reveals a great deal not only about the evolution of the genre but about the transformation of middle-class culture in the early twentieth century.

A discourse on gender, *What's His Name* registers ambiguity about social change during an era when a broadly defined middle class, differentiated between "old" independent farmers and small businessmen and "new" salaried white-collar workers, was undergoing a transition in its composition, ethos, and life-style. Caught between visible extremes of urban wealth and poverty, middle-class families, with annual incomes ranging from $1,200 to

$5,000, sought to define their social identity in terms of a distinctive style of living.[2] The old ingrained habits of self-denial, restraint, and frugality were giving way to an investment in comfort and refinement as signifiers of genteel status. As *What's His Name* demonstrates, however, such a practice was fraught with danger because it remapped private versus public spheres based on traditional definitions of gender and vitiated the differentiation between home and marketplace.[3]

What's His Name takes place in Blakeville, a small town whose inhabitants engage in simple pleasures such as enjoying refreshments at a soda fountain, but not so small that it is unexposed to touring companies that travel by rail and provide the lure of big city attractions. At the beginning of the narrative, Harvey, unidentified by a surname and destined to become "What's His Name," marries his sweetheart Nellie against the objections of Uncle Peter, a crusty bachelor who resists the tyranny of domestication. DeMille moves his camera in for a medium shot at the wedding as Harvey plunges out of a crowd of guests to search frantically for the ring, a nervous gesture that betrays his uneasiness. An intertitle, "Three Years Later," marks the passage of time. Nellie has become disenchanted with housewifery and mothering a young daughter named Phoebe. Attracted by a musical comedy troupe performing in town, she responds eagerly to an opportunity to join the chorus at a salary of twenty dollars a week. A sign of his diminished status in the role of maternal substitute and lackey, Harvey is carrying Phoebe as well as luggage at the train station when the family departs for New York.

After an auspicious debut, Nellie becomes the "Toast of Broadway" and attracts the attention of a millionaire named Fairfax, who typifies the silk-hatted, paunchy villain signifying greed in Progressive Era cartoons.[4] A scenario representing the moral dilemma of a consumer culture, *What's His Name* shows a small-town comedienne neglecting her family and succumbing to the lure of upper-class finery. But the morality of self-denial personified by Uncle Peter and characteristic of the propertied "old" middle class ultimately prevails. When her child becomes seriously ill, Nellie relinquishes the excitement of theatrical life and resumes her duties as a wife and mother. As discourse on women and the family, the film thus reconstructs traditional gender roles but not without the ambiguity rendered by lighting effects in the final tableau. A close analysis of this melodrama is intriguing, but it first requires contextualization with respect to the role of women in the formation and social reproduction of the middle-class family; their control over social and theatergoing rituals as these defined the self in relation to others in genteel society is especially relevant for an informed reading.

As historians and sociologists point out, the access of the middle class to education meant that particularly the upper level of this socioeconomic group, albeit subject to the homogenizing forces of the leisure industry, would nevertheless exercise cultural power disproportionate to political

8 and 9. Cecil B. DeMille's parents: playwright Henry Churchill DeMille, and (*opposite*) theatrical agent Matilda Beatrice Samuel DeMille. (*Photos courtesy Brigham Young University*)

power. The genteel middle class in fact wielded enormous influence through its redefinition of womanhood and the family. As established by the practice of native-born, Protestant households, the privatized family became a refuge from the marketplace, especially in suburban communities built away from downtown business districts after the Civil War. Particularly essential in middle-class formation, as Mary P. Ryan argues, was the role of women who supplemented family income by taking in boarders, shopped with great economy, and saved enough money to educate sons. Given a

pattern of financial investment in the education of sons, matrilineal ties persisted in the lives of young men.[5] A case in point is DeMille's own family. When his mother became a widow with three children in 1893, she resolutely provided for the future. A resourceful woman, Beatrice DeMille founded the Henry C. DeMille School for Girls at the Pompton, New Jersey, estate that her husband had purchased two years before his untimely death. She also capitalized on the rights to the celebrated DeMille-Belasco plays to establish herself as a theatrical agent for playwrights. Although she never learned to manage finances and heavily mortgaged the family estate, she made certain William was educated at Columbia University and Cecil at the Pennsylvania Military College. When her younger son decided to gamble on filmmaking in 1913, she sold her theatrical agency for twenty-five thousand dollars to provide him with the requisite capital.[6] Years later, he confided to an interviewer, "we have to bring out the tremendous personality that she was and how much I am 'operating' from her, because it's an awful lot."[7]

Women demonstrated resourcefulness in transforming the middle-class family under their own supervision because men were no longer heads of "corporate and patriarchal households" characteristic of an agrarian era.[8] A feminization of American culture thus occurred under the leadership of women allied with clergymen because both, lacking traditional access to power, elevated passivity to a virtue in sentimental discourse. The pervasiveness of sentimentalism in genteel circles understandably provoked a surge of the martial ideal in definitions of masculine selfhood and in pursuit of American foreign policy at the turn of the century. According to T. J. Jackson Lears, middle- and upper-class men who felt suffocated by over-civilization, luxury, and effeminacy endorsed the strenuous life exemplified by Theodore Roosevelt in his frontier, hunting, and military exploits. Distinctions between manual and nonmanual labor as an index of class and ethnicity, in other words, meant that privileged men would ritualize the pursuit of athleticism. After the Census Bureau declared the frontier closed in 1890, for example, the Westerner became a compelling figure in such best-sellers as *The Virginian* (1902), dedicated to Theodore Roosevelt by a Harvard classmate.[9] DeMille's first three adaptations, including *The Virginian,* also exemplify the revitalization of men as frontier heroes in Westerns. A domestic melodrama, *What's His Name* affirms to the contrary that male bravado expressed barely submerged fears of castration. Such a contrast in discursive modes reveals fault lines based on gender within the privileged social strata. To put it another way, sentimentalism with its polite evasiveness about urban conflict, on the one hand, and masculine quest for potency with its emphasis on self-realization, on the other, were expressions of sexual conflict in an age when class hegemony remained intact. As manifestations of Victorian homosocial or sex-segregated culture, however, both sentimentalism and embattled masculinity served to accommodate the growth of consumer capitalism because the rhetoric of spiritual uplift was co-opted to rationalize self-fulfillment.[10]

The influence of genteel women in establishing middle-class culture as a matrix that governed the formation of the self in relation to a consumer

Offices of

Mrs. H. C. De Mille
220 West 42nd Street
New York

Phone {330}{331} Bryant

Cable, "Iliacal"
New York-London

June 11th 1914.

Dear Boy:-

I forgot the other night to enclose your life policy. I had a most satisfactory talk yesterday afternoon with Mr. Friend about your affairs, particularly the Casey ones. It will all be adjusted to-day, with poor Billy as usual the victim ! He is the one who has to wait until you can pay him his share of the advance, which Classmates and Stroheart mostly used up !

I had to borrow the money and pay Mrs. Flebbe what would have been he advance pro rata, had the $2250. been evenly divided between the thirteen plays contracted for. I could not afford to lose Mrs. Beulah Dix Flebbe's friendship which has stood by me so many years. Things look good for you.

Have just returned from seeing The Lost Paradise, it is a splendid picture It makes my soul sick not to have any rights in the moving picture. Some of Roeder's treachery many years ago. We see The Only Son this afternoon.

Much love—

Mother ————— over

10. Correspondence addressed to DeMille by his mother, Beatrice, who continued to manage his finances after he became director-general of the Lasky Company. *(Photo courtesy Brigham Young University)*

society cannot be underestimated. Particularly relevant were theatrical modes of self-representation in polite forms of social intercourse and in elaborate parlor games that anticipated the reemergence of the elite in fashionable theaters. The publication of numerous etiquette manuals implied that an entrée into society was possible, but rituals such as the "ordeal by fork" at dinner parties required elegant comportment and dress, thus winnowing the field. As families with disposable income began to spend increasingly on comfort and refinement, social practices like ceremonial callings in genteel parlors became preludes to concourse in ostentatious public settings such as theaters, department stores, and museums.[11] A sign of private and public spheres intersecting in the art of self-theatricalization, middle-class women learned how to gesture and pose according to the Delsarte system of acting. A notable foreign import, this French schematic expression of human behavior was introduced in the 1870s by Broadway producer Steele MacKaye at the Lyceum Academy, subsequently renamed the American Academy of Dramatic Arts by Henry C. DeMille.[12]

Anticipating the revival of theater attendance among the upper middle class, dramaturgical modes of self-representation and social interaction flourished in the form of mid-nineteenth-century parlor games and theatricals. As Karen Halttunen has documented, upper-middle-class society engaged in performances of charades, proverbs, burlesques, farces, tableaux vivants, and shadow pantomimes that were quite elaborate in the use of costumes, sets, lighting, sound, and special effects. What accounts for this fascination with artifice in an industrial and urban setting? Why was play-acting so integral to middle-class culture, especially in an era of increased consumption? According to Halttunen, the urban environment represented a "world of strangers" that endangered social relations and thus required adherence to a semiotics of performance rituals ensuring gentility. Social intercourse in this guise resembled a charade, however, in which actors engaging in self-theatricalization signified the decline of character based on moral virtue and the rise of personality associated with consumption. Consequently, the private theatrical represented a play-within-a-play because the parlor had become a stage for observances in which proper attire and decorum were but aspects of a performance. Yet these communicative acts, as Erving Goffman argues, were nevertheless morally implicated because they raised questions about the nature of "claims" and "promises" being transmitted.[13] The social transactions of a consumer culture thus resulted in ethical dilemmas such as those involved in performance rituals that the genteel classes by no means succeeded in resolving.

Undeniably, upper-middle-class society was being transformed in drawing room pursuits that placed a premium on self-commodification, a problematic basis for a personal sense of identity as well as for social interaction. Genteel women thus presided over rituals that eroded a legacy of evangelical

Protestantism expressed as moral empowerment in sentimental discourse. But if cultivated women stepped off their pedestals, they succeeded in dictating the terms of access to respectable society and thereby extended their influence into the public sphere. All the world became a stage as the middle class began to engage in ritualistic theatergoing after having earlier abandoned the scene to the boisterous lower orders in the gallery. While congregating in lavish foyers or enjoying a performance on stage, formally attired audiences engaged in a form of playacting scripted according to social conventions. Across the country, a building craze responded to middle-class demand for grandiose theaters as a setting for self-display and social intercourse. The Providence Opera House, for example, was built in record time with a budget exceeding expenditure on all the city's previous theaters combined. Unveiled in 1871, the magnificent new structure showcased a melodrama titled *Fashion, or Life in New York* because "it gave the ladies an opportunity to show some handsome dresses." Similarly, Pittsburgh's aspiring middle class demanded a "New York" theater without galleries that seated the lower classes to accommodate syndicated shows in the 1890s.[14]

The construction of ornate theaters of "Moorish and rococo designs" not only represented a shift in patterns of genteel middle-class consumption but signified a decline in the Victorian practice of separate spheres for the sexes. As a social agency, the theater became the site of transition between the privatized home and the marketplace as these two institutions began to converge. An important aspect of this transformation in theatergoing, previously dismissed as the object of religious and social opprobrium, was the successful rewriting of melodrama for genteel audiences. Understandably, the reformulating of a genre that was derived from popular forms of entertainment for the urban working class was essential in an age when culture was differentiated between lowbrow and highbrow forms of consumption. Within this context, the success of the society drama associated with the names of Henry C. DeMille and David Belasco proved to be a significant development. A brief but successful collaboration on four domestic melodramas resulted in a legacy that Cecil B. DeMille would later transmit to the screen as an intertext designed for theatergoers accustomed to social ritual as performance.

A GENTEEL AUDIENCE: REWRITING DOMESTIC MELODRAMA

Although the relationship between the legitimate stage and early feature film is a subject that needs to be further explored, a brief investigation shows that movie moguls were indebted to the theater not only for intertextual modes of address but also for entrepreneurial practices.[15] Adolph Zukor's vertical integration of the film industry, for example, was similar to organizational patterns established in the theatrical business. Subject to the same standardized and cost-efficient practices essential to the success of late-nineteenth-century industrial firms, American theater, in contrast to European tradition, depended on box-office revenues rather than state subsidies.[16] When middle-class audiences began to patronize the stage in growing numbers, they represented an increased demand that, together with technological advances, enabled entrepreneurs to establish a monopoly. Upon completion of transcontinental railroad construction, the success of the single-play combination, or road company, featuring Broadway stars in established hits signified the end of local resident companies. Also stimulating the growth of theater as big business was the production of realistic and sensational plays associated with big-name directors and requiring large capital investment for complex machinery, set design, and lighting equipment.[17]

In 1896 Charles Frohman capitalized on these developments by organizing the Syndicate: it monopolized booking agencies serving as middlemen between producers and local playhouses, acquired theater chains in large cities on major railroad stops, and financed productions for the legitimate stage. Programs of theatrical performances show that Frohman anticipated film exhibition practices. Attempting to create a solemn atmosphere in lavish theaters built for cultivated audiences, he provided orchestral performances of works by Rossini, Verdi, and Johann Strauss rather than popular tunes and patriotic airs.[18] So that only the fashionable crowd could attend, ticket prices ranged from $1.50 in the orchestra to 50 cents in the dress circle for reserved seats that had to be secured in advance.[19] At the height of its power in the first decade of the twentieth century, the Syndicate invested in long runs of single plays with type casting and popular stars rather than repertories.[20] When demand shifted from legitimate stage plays to feature film during the 1910s, Frohman joined Adolph Zukor's Famous Players in an attempt to repeat his pattern of marketing mass entertainment.

Since middle-class preoccupation with performance rituals represented a demand that led to the building of fashionable playhouses, melodrama, a popular art staged in "East Side rialtos" as well as in more felicitous venues, was rewritten for genteel consumption.[21] Although the well-made play that came into vogue was still characterized by Dickensian incidents and reversals of fortune, "after 1895 the kidnapped orphans, the ghosts, the papers, the foreclosed mortgages, the providential accidents, the disguises, the rescuing comics, the missing heirs, and even the *reconnaissance* went into discard; the rhetoric was brought under control; and the sentimentality was tempered." A theatrical form that had largely been abandoned by serious British writers, melodrama was now the province of American playwrights.[22] Consequently, the success of Henry C. DeMille and David Belasco in formulating society dramas that appealed to the genteel sensibility proved to be a noteworthy achievement. American melodrama arrived on the New York stage in the

1889–1890 season, as Frank Rahill argues, with the success of five native plays, including a DeMille-Belasco collaboration titled *The Charity Ball*. Unlike three of the productions that were rural in theme and played to less prosperous downtown audiences, *The Charity Ball* focused on drawing room society.[23] As such, it appealed to the fashionable middle class at the Lyceum, an uptown theater that was also the initial site of the American Academy of Dramatic Arts. Part of a series of four domestic melodramas that DeMille successfully devised with Belasco, the play was based on upper-class characters, drawing room situations, and literate dialogue. In short, it exemplified a more sophisticated melodramatic form crafted for middle-class theatergoers accustomed to social rituals as performance.

Apart from the enactment of social observances related to everyday life, what accounts for the immense appeal of the DeMille-Belasco society dramas? Why were these productions especially relevant to middle-class experience in the late nineteenth century? And what changes were formulated to suit the genre to the sensibility of fashionable theatergoers? As entertainment for the lower orders, melodrama was a mode of expression that dramatized sensational issues such as class conflict in a capitalistic economy. According to Robert Heilman, the "melodramatic form seizes upon the topics that spring up with the turns of history and consciousness—slavery, 'big business,' slums, totalitarianism, mechanization of life, war, the varieties of segregationism. . . . In a more general sense, melodrama is the realm of social action, public action, action within the world."[24] DeMille and Belasco successfully reversed this formula by foregrounding the domestic sphere of courtship, marriage, and the family as a crucible for performance against a related public sphere of societal, financial, or political intrigue. A consequence of the more intimate scale, the consciousness and actions of individual characters acquired more weight in contrast to catastrophic events controlling their fate. Accordingly, the ideological concerns of genteel middle-class audiences who were invested in the privatized family—an institution increasingly threatened by patterns of consumption that nevertheless signified genteel status—were translated into the moral quandaries of the society drama.

Unquestionably, the effectiveness of the society dramas was in large measure the result of Belasco's careful staging and innovative lighting. A producer whose reputation would later enable him to challenge Frohman's Syndicate, Belasco became known for directing ensembles in a naturalistic style that was the result of numerous rehearsals and mise-en-scène integrating actors and sets. As a means of focusing attention on the action of individual characters, he used baby spots and orchestrated subtle changes in mood or atmosphere through "color, intensity, and diffusion of light." Since the box setting, which came into use in the late nineteenth century, consisted of three walls and a ceiling to simulate an actual room, middle-class audiences could identify with social rituals as performances taking place behind the "fourth wall."[25] For his part, Henry C. DeMille, acknowledged as a talented dialogue writer, employed the rhetoric of Victorian sentimentalism and religiosity to characterize upper-middle-class relationships.[26] Consider, for example, the exchange of a married couple in *The Wife* during a moment when their future is in doubt, a scene rendered even more poignant by Belasco's lighting effects:

HELEN: [Low and tearfully] My husband!

RUTHERFORD: Yes, for by that word, we have the sacred right to know each other's hearts, as they are known by Him, that, knowing, we may help each other. Let us not mistake, as the world so often does, the bond that unites man and wife. [Ring music]

HELEN: Oh! Is it not broken?

RUTHERFORD: "Wilt though love her, comfort her, honor and keep her, in sickness and in health, forsaking all others, keep thee only unto her, so long as ye both shall live?" [By this time the moonlight has faded into darkness and the fire has almost died away. He tenderly takes her face between his two hands, reverently kisses her on the forehead, and speaks in a low voice husky with emotion] God—bless—you and give—you—rest. [. . . She slowly turns away from him with bowed head and . . . stops before the door. He goes to the fireplace. She pauses for a moment with the door open, the dim light from the hall falling upon her. . . . Rutherford sinks abstractedly into armchair and gazes into fireplace, where the last flickering spark at that moment disappears][27]

Although theatergoing became part of respectable middle-class culture, the transition from family-centered leisure shaped by maternal guidance to entertainment outside the home, that is, the diminution of separate spheres based on gender, was not accomplished without qualms. A critic who praised *The Charity Ball* expressed concerns regarding the lower-class morality associated with commercialized amusement:

To demonstrate gently but efficaciously that the human heart still beats responsive to the chivalrous, the gentle, and the wholesomely sentimental, is something that every man and woman who believes in the potency of faith and refinement, and has a spiritual anchorage in a mother and a home will hasten to rejoice discreetly over, for it must be admitted with something like reproach that the theatre of our day oftener reflects the surface discontent and the cheap despair of the saloon and the cafe, than the abiding trust and creative confidence of the home.[28]

Abandoning the pulpit for the stage as a vocation, Henry C. DeMille successfully crafted plays for cultivated audiences by translating Protestant belief in economics as an index of character into the personal terms of domestic melodrama. As a playwright, he facilitated the secularization of evangelical Protestantism, once so essential to middle-class formation, by employing religious rhetoric to characterize the quotidian. As Peter Brooks argues, "Melodrama represents both the urge toward resacralization and the impossibility of conceiving sacralization other than in personal terms" in a "frightening new world in which the traditional patterns of moral order no longer provide the necessary social glue."[29] Although this generalization was made with respect to revolutionary France, it is also applicable to the urban scene in late-nineteenth-century America. Among the genteel classes, cultural refinement provided the social cement in coded transactions conducted in an increasingly industrialized and secularized milieu. Precisely because social relations in a strange city were fraught with danger and entrapment, as dramatized by the DeMille-Belasco melodramas, the middle class became preoccupied with the semiotics of performance.[30] A critic aware of societal trends noted at the time that DeMille "was the first to conventionalize to the needs of scenic representation certain phrases and characteristics of American society whose theatric effectiveness . . . had escaped previous writers."[31]

As a sermon, domestic melodrama conveyed the message that middle-class apprehension about the eclipse of the privatized home, itself subject to contradictions, was not unfounded in an age of commercialized leisure. Indeed, the very success of the DeMille-Belasco society dramas attested to the interpenetration of home and marketplace. DeMille had begun his theatrical career, not coincidentally, as a playreader at the Madison Square Theatre. An establishment situated at the intersection of private and public theatricals, the Madison was associated with famed producer Steele MacKaye, who introduced the Delsarte style of acting, and represented the investment of shrewd businessmen who marketed religious periodicals. Assessing a situation in which a vast middle class found their amusements restricted to "Sabbath-school picnics, strawberry festivals, sociables, and possibly an organ recital," these Broadway investors exploited Victorian sentimentalism to attract a new theater audience. A successful venture meant that "not only did there spring into flourishing existence a new school of dramas, but a new body of theatre patrons."[32] The DeMille-Belasco society dramas thus demonstrated that the feminization of American culture in effect subjected the privatized home to the intrusions of the marketplace. A private theatrical staged in the opening act of the first DeMille-Belasco melodrama, *The Wife*, provides an apt illustration. Clearly, the nature of commodity exchange or marketplace transactions was not unrelated to modes of self-theatricalization as dramatized in a parlor game wedding:

> MRS. A: . . . These private theatricals will be the death of me. I don't remember when I've been so excited. If Nelly had been obliged to act the bride without the wreath, the entire performance would have been ruined. [Enter Silas, L.E.]
>
> SILAS: If ever I permit myself to be cajoled into quitting business again for a holiday, and wheat, choice red, going from 82½ to 83¾ and back again!

[Crossing, L.C.] It's bad enough to be roused out of sleep by the boat's arrival at three in the morning, and thrust into the pleasures of Newport half awake—[33]

Although the four DeMille-Belasco productions, *The Wife* (1887), *Lord Chumley* (1888), *The Charity Ball* (1889), and *Men and Women* (1890), enjoyed lucrative runs on Broadway before going on nationwide tour, critical discourse attests that the success of society dramas, albeit crafted for the educated middle class, raised issues about cultural excellence. As part of the "notable" gathering of the elite described in theater reviews, middle-class audiences participated in a process that simultaneously sacralized and desacralized culture in Arnoldian terms. Cultural refinement, in other words, involved questions of taste that encompassed the intellect as well as appearances maintained by attention to proper deportment, dress, and decor. Yet genteel sensibility became restrained and even tepid as a result of being subjected to rigorous forms of self-representation and social rituals dictated by women. A chorus of male critics thus bemoaned the DeMille-Belasco plays as reasonably entertaining stage fare but trite, vapid, and prosaic. As the *New York Sun* observed about Daniel Frohman, Charles's brother and manager of the Lyceum Theatre, where three of the four society dramas were staged:

> He has induced the more fashionably intelligent people of New York to form fine audiences for his house, and he is aware that they require considerable substance and no offence in their theatrical entertainment. . . . Therefore his pieces must be polite without inanity, humorous without crudity, and strong without coarseness. . . . This is . . . done . . . by having the plays manufactured in his establishment. They are written by Henry C. deMille, and constructed by David Belasco under Mr. Frohman's own direction. In that way "The Wife" was produced, and last night another result . . . met with a deservedly heartier acceptance. . . . its scenes were laid in the midst of American riches and elegance, and its personages were such men and women as may be found in Fifth avenue homes of opulent refinement.[34]

Similarly, *The Illustrated American* summed up in an acerbic tone:

> For several seasons [DeMille and Belasco] spread upon the boards of theatres of the first fashion and patronage, the mush and milk of mawkish sentiment, sickly humor, and colorless emotion. Silliness, insipidity, and bathos were never before put to such prosperous account. And yet these men addressed themselves to audiences of presumable taste and intelligence. They did not write "for the gallery." . . . Perhaps it is to be regretted. . . . It would have been interesting to note how the quick and pitiless wits of the topmost tier regarded the puerilities and vacuities that delighted the discriminations of box and parquet.[35]

William Winter, the respected *New York Daily Tribune* critic who later wrote a two-volume biography of Belasco, labeled *The Wife* "sentimental confectionary and antic farce" and compared it unfavorably with the canonical works of the legitimate stage. Significantly, he referred to photography, construed and dismissed as a mechanistic representation of reality, to criticize the play:

> Its scene is laid at Newport, New York and Washington, in the present day; and its dialogue is written mostly in a strain of the commonplace colloquy which is assumed to be characteristic of fashionable society in its superficial mood and general habit. The artistic standard of the authors of "The Wife"—which is the artistic standard of many dramatists—may be inferred from this latter peculiarity. To reflect persons of everyday life and to make them converse in an everyday manner seems generally to be thought sufficient to fill the ambition of the playwright and to satisfy the taste of the public. This was not the limitation of Congreve and Sheridan. . . . That old method of writing comedy . . . appears to have given place to the far inferior and much easier method of literary and theatrical photography.[36]

A year later, the *Spirit of the Times* expressed a similar viewpoint while invoking Shakespeare in a review of *Lord Chumley:* "The critics say what ought to be left out. The public say what they like kept in. The manager works at it, alters, cuts, amends, adds, and at last we have such a success as The Wife. . . . This is not playwriting; but, like Mercutio's wound, 'twill serve."[37] Also attuned to the commercial appeal of *The Wife* was a *Tid Bits* reviewer who observed:

> It will be liked and enjoyed, if not greatly admired, by the run of theatergoers. For say what we will—and no one is more conscious of it than Mr. [William Dean] Howells, for instance, who protests . . . against sentiment and romance—the people, the great big, dear masses, who pay for seats at the theater, and buy the novels, are in their secret hearts hopelessly enamored of sentiment.[38]

Yet the *New York Times* and the *Herald* asserted that *The Wife* was an important American play and a significant contribution to dramatic literature.[39]

Although critics cited Shakespeare, Congreve, and Sheridan as models of excellence to whom DeMille and Belasco could not be compared, realist discourse demonstrates that middle-class sensibility, even as it palled within sentimental confines, required artifice. As theater historians point out with respect to forms of realism dominant in the late nineteenth and early twentieth centuries, two variations existed on stage: "romantic realism, in which dramas with idealized subjects are mounted in extremely detailed and historically accurate settings and costume; and true realism, in which plays based on nonidealized contemporary subjects are presented in settings designed to show significant interaction of environment with character and action." The DeMille-Belasco society dramas exemplified the first as opposed to the second category (which also included naturalism) like most stage fare at the time. Assessing the development of such conventions in theatrical productions, A. Nicholas Vardac points out, "The more romantic the subject matter, the more realistic must be its presentation upon the boards."[40] The legitimate theater, in other words, constituted a forum in which romantic and realist modes coexisted in melodrama that was authentically staged yet appealed to the Victorian sensibility. After concluding that *Lord Chumley* did not measure up to Shakespeare, for example, the *Spirit of the Times* added insult to injury by observing, "The play is located in England; but the furniture and fittings and stove in the second act are American." Belasco's sets did elicit rave reviews, however, when an impressive scene in *The Charity Ball* was staged in a reproduction of a corridor of the Metropolitan Opera House.[41]

Despite the fact that some critics found the DeMille-Belasco society dramas lacking, either in intellectual stimulus or in authentic set design, they would by no means have embraced Ibsen's form of realism. The *Graphic* stated quite summarily, "If we want unconventional realism, the Lord knows we can go to the novels these days and be satisfied." Charles Frohman's Syndicate, to be sure, displayed little interest in experimentation and exploited works with broad audience appeal. Dissenting actors like Minnie Maddern Fiske, who was married to Broadway producer and *New York Dramatic Mirror* publisher, Harrison Grey Fiske, championed Ibsen but did not attract large audiences.[42] A *New York World* reviewer of *The Charity Ball* voiced critical as well as popular opinion by asserting:

> Messrs. Belasco and DeMille have in a measure accomplished in a sentimental way what it is claimed Ibsen is trying to do in a didactic way. . . . "The Charity Ball" retains enough of the essentials of the better part of our serene and wholesome life of the present to preserve it against all the protests of the morbid, the outworn, the pharisaical.[43]

In sum, the DeMille-Belasco society dramas, patronized by the "best people," posed a dilemma in that these works did not exemplify Arnoldian standards as the "best that has been thought and known in the world." As such, middle-class theatergoing, an extension of social rituals performed in elegant parlors, signified the commodification of culture in an age of commercialized amusement. With respect to considerations of gender (as well as class and ethnicity), however, Arnoldian concepts prove inadequate for conceptualizing about culture. At issue, as Jane Tompkins argues, is sentimentalism as the distinguishing characteristic of Victorian female sensibility. An expression of gender conflict, male discourse on society dramas was part of a larger reaction to culture reorganized to suit the social agenda of women committed to the moral legacy of evangelical Protestantism. As works that were "halfway between sermon and social theory," the DeMille-Belasco domestic melodramas expressed a woman's point of view.[44] According to a reviewer of *The Charity Ball* in the *New York Mirror*, theatergoing was in effect a social ritual that appealed to female rather than male audiences: "There is . . . just enough pathos to evoke feminine tears, and just enough humor to keep the masculine portion of the audience from falling asleep."[45] Since critics often devalued sentimental discourse as an exercise in female emotions, more to the point was an astute observation in *Once a Week:*

> "The Charity Ball" is . . . the most daring attempt that has ever been made to introduce religion on the stage. The greater portion of the play occurs in a rectory immediately adjoining a church and the text is full of scriptural quotations, while the dialogue is occasionally interrupted by the pealing of the organ and the chanting of hymns.[46]

Several decades would elapse before film exhibitors courted the patronage of respectable middle-class women as a sign of cultural legitimacy. Cecil B. DeMille's legacy of Victorian pictorial dramaturgy as an intertext related to pious and sentimental literature would then stand him in good stead. As demonstrated in *What's His Name,* the director successfully rewrote domestic melodrama so that it continued to address the ethical concerns of both the "old" and "new" middle class in an era of transition.

CHARACTER VERSUS PERSONALITY: *WHAT'S HIS NAME*

As a means of exploring the ethical dilemma of the "old" middle class in an increasingly secularized and consumer-oriented society, Cecil B. DeMille purposely focuses on small-town or village life rather than drawing room society in *What's His Name*. Since his credentials as an author had yet to be established, the credits announce that the film is an adaptation based on the novel by George Barr McCutcheon, a lesser light among Indiana Hoosiers such as Booth Tarkington and Theodore Dreiser. An author who sold over five million copies of such novels as *Graustark* (1901) and *Brewster's Millions* (1903), adapted on Broadway and in feature film, McCutcheon represented the Victorian sentimental tradition pervasive in genteel culture. *What's His Name,* published by both Dodd, Mead and Grosset and Dunlap in 1911, was a minor effort with strong autobiographical elements because it was written during an identity crisis in part attributed to failed theatrical ambitions. DeMille successfully translated the novel about a small-town soda jerk and a Broadway comedienne, inspired by Minnie Maddern Fiske, into a Progressive Era discourse on gender, marriage, and the family.[47]

A rewriting of domestic melodrama, *What's His Name* foregrounds intertextual references to moral dilemmas in society dramas and in social rituals as performance. Pervading the film adaptation is the quality of a play-within-a-play that characterized parlor games such as the private theatrical

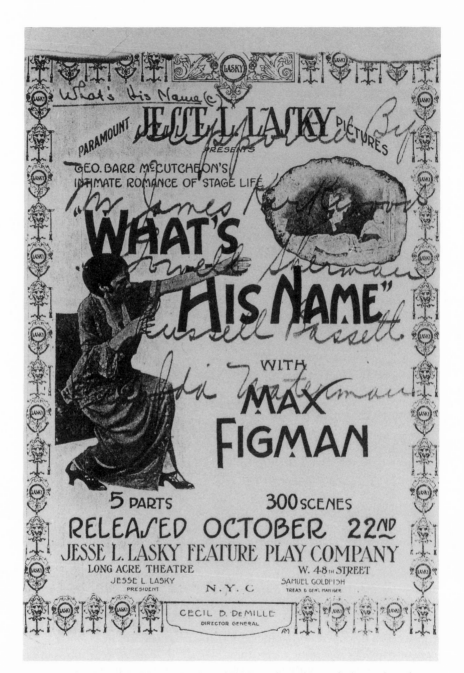

11. Advertisement for *What's His Name* (1914), a domestic melodrama based on a minor novel by a best-selling author.

staged in *The Charity Ball*. DeMille thus constructs the mise-en-scène of an opening night, filmed at a Los Angeles theater, so that a high angle shot shows a conductor in the orchestra pit roped off from the audience in middleground and background. The composition of the shot, with the conductor's head peering out of the pit in extreme foreground, is unbalanced until the camera tilts up to reveal an usher leading a formally attired couple down an aisle and to their seats. Another well-dressed couple subsequently arrives and is also seated. DeMille shows the performance that follows by cutting between the proscenium stage photographed in extreme long shots and audience reaction shown in reverse angle shots. Clearly, the filmgoing audience, identified with theatergoers, was being positioned to engage in a series of moral judgments concerning the nature of performance in a scenario about the sanctity of the family.

Drawing attention to the elusive nature of performance, whether in the public or private sphere, Broadway stars Max Figman and Lolita Robertson come to life during the credits as figures in a billboard poster and astonish the puzzled billsticker. Figman had in fact appeared on stage with Robertson before their marriage and acted in productions associated with such noted theatrical producers as Augustin Daly, Charles Frohman, and Harrison Grey Fiske. Since the husband-and-wife team engaged in performance not only as characters wedded in the film but as Broadway stars married in real life, they added another dimension to the film's narrative structure as a play-within-a-play. Audience reception was undoubtedly influenced by fan magazine and news articles publicizing the fact that Figman managed his wife's career and that the couple made a point of traveling together with their children.[48] Such awareness introduced a note of false suspense into a domestic melodrama in which gender roles are dramatically reversed and then reconstituted during an ambiguous conclusion. Partly the result of his stage persona and of his publicity, Figman's portrayal of Harvey as a good-natured but ineffectual soda jerk is much more resonant than McCutcheon's extremely lackluster protagonist.

As an adaptation, *What's His Name* foregrounds authorial and intertextual issues to reveal the inscription not only of the director but of the novelist and leading actors. Although the contributions of McCutcheon, Figman, and Robertson should be taken into account in attributing authorship, *Moving Picture World* rightly noted that "the production must have been difficult on account of the condensation, but it is filled with signs of good direction."[49] DeMille's signature is unmistakable in the use of lighting effects, mise-en-scène, and editing to rewrite domestic melodrama as a film genre. A clever construction of the mise-en-scène, for example, conveys the sex-role reversal essential to the film's representation of a lower-middle-class family. Harvey, Nellie, and their daughter Phoebe eat their meals in a cramped apartment furnished with cheap goods. A plain dining table occupies much of the foreground in a medium long shot that shows a crude hutch beyond the door in the rear wall. After leaving some money to pay for a bill, Harvey exits through the door to his left, while Nellie, clearing the table, looks out the window to see a poster advertising a musical comedy. DeMille apparently simplified, improvised, and eliminated shots while learning his craft because this scene is more revealing as detailed in the script: "Combination of Dining and Living Room: Nellie leaves the window—starts to carry the dishes out. Door bell rings, Nellie goes out, returns with butcher's boy, starts to pay the bill, glances through window, gives him $2.00, explains that she will pay other later. Butcher boy goes out."[50] Nellie, according to the script, is already engaging in selfish and extravagant behavior detrimental to her family's welfare. An inversion of the breakfast table mise-en-scène in the couple's New York apartment, where they have moved so that Nellie may pursue a stage career, is very telling. Although a door in the rear still leads to an adjoining room and a table is still prominently in middleground, the entry is now to the right and the time of day is evening rather than morning. Nellie returns home after a strenuous and discouraging day of rehearsal, while Harvey has busily been preparing dinner. Hanging on the rear wall is a sign, "GOD BLESS OUR HOME," an aphorism that for many Victorians meant material goods rather than spiritual blessings.[51]

DeMille's mise-en-scène in sequences filmed at the theater reveals that although Nellie has escaped the confines of housewifery in an uneventful small town, she is now in the clutches of venal and unethical men. On opening night, she commits a hilarious blunder that singles her out as a crowd pleaser but compromises her personal integrity. The semiotics of female performance was indeed complex and required an interpretation of a spectrum of behavior. Although Victorian women engaged in self-theatricalization in social engagements, such rituals were highly codified as opposed to self-display violating norms of modesty and decency. Acquiring notoriety, as Nellie did, by committing a comic faux pas that drew attention to herself was distinctly unladylike. A comedienne would in fact have found it more difficult than a dramatic actress to claim the mantle of art for her profession. What then does Nellie's performance signify? Clearly, she has embarked on a treacherous course of self-commodification that exceeds proper bounds and may thus be equated with prostitution. Progressive reformers, it should be noted, waged vigorous campaigns against sexual misconduct as a sign of urban change by advocating social purity and social hygiene.[52]

DeMille's inventive mise-en-scène unmistakably represents the precarious situation in which Nellie has become entrapped. A long shot behind the parted curtains of an aisle shows Fairfax (Fred Montague) and the company manager in the foreground as they frame the stage to negotiate a deal. A repetition of this mise-en-scène backstage underscores Nellie's predicament. Costumed as a clown, she is squeezed in the background between the figures of the two men in dark formal attire as they dominate the foreground. A dialogue title conveys the manager's blunt proposal as he confronts the inexperienced chorus girl: "You'll get more salary and meet Mr. Fairfax, a millionaire, besides." As a matter of fact, the theme of self-display as prostitution was established earlier in the film when Ruby, a chorus girl, reluctantly introduces the manager, intent on engaging an attractive new recruit, to Nellie, by warning him: "If you're on the level, all right, if not, nothin' doin'." Since Fairfax is coded as a paunchy villain who represents plutocratic corporate greed, Nellie has become the object of class as well as sexual exploitation. She must choose, in other words, between domestic confinement that precludes personal and sexual gratification, and public exposure that transforms her into a commodity. Yet genteel reformers would consider Nellie and Fairfax to be equivalent in a setting of commercialized vice as an underworld analogue of corporate greed.[53] The chorus girl, like the millionaire, craves the power, prestige, and luxury that money buys. Attentive to her manager's rule, "No husbands wanted," she ensconces Harvey and Phoebe in suburban Tarrytown, assumes the stage name Miss Duluth, and flirts openly with Fairfax. Actresses were then commonly billed as "Miss" to enhance their attraction for male spectators, surely an aspect of commodification that implied prostitution.[54]

DeMille, who calculated that he spent 20 percent of his time in the cutting room, uses parallel editing to show the deterioration of family life as Nellie becomes a temperamental star and neglects her domestic duties.[55] On Christmas Day, Harvey's plight becomes painfully clear when gifts arrive for Phoebe and the servants while he is ignored. Sensitive to her father's dilemma, Phoebe attempts to console him with a present in a gesture that suggests she is a stand-in for her mother. A cut to Nellie's boudoir reveals the actress, absent from the family hearth even on Christmas, as she compares a modest pin from Harvey with a jewel-encrusted butterfly symbolizing her metamorphosis. Successive close-ups of each pin from her point of view emphasize the lure of temptation to which she succumbs. A cut back to the Tarrytown living room shows Fairfax arriving a short time later in formal dress with cane and bowler. Arrogant and pugnacious, he aggressively dominates the frame, demands agreement to a divorce, and provokes a scuffle. As the two men exchange blows, the Christmas tree is toppled and lies on the floor. Harvey is so distraught that he retires to his room, turns a portrait of Nellie face down on the table, and attempts to commit suicide by switching on the gas lamp. Fortunately, the serviceman arrives to disconnect the utilities so that the unhappy husband awakens, as if in a dream, in a shot with an earlier and happier Blakeville scene superimposed over the bedroom.

Undeterred, Fairfax returns with Nellie who demands custody of Phoebe, but, forced to choose between parents, the child turns to her father. Movers subsequently arrive to place the furniture in storage and cart away the Christmas tree as well as the "GOD BLESS OUR HOME" sign. An insert informs the audience that Harvey has notified his cantankerous Uncle Peter (Sydney Deane), who functions as his alter ego, that he and Phoebe are homeward bound. Parallel editing shows father and daughter traveling in extremely straitened circumstances, while Nellie entertains actresses of dubious character and travels to Reno to obtain a divorce. Symbolically, Harvey and Phoebe are abruptly awakened and ejected from a railroad car but find a ride home on a horse-driven wagon during the last phase of their trip. The journey from New York to Blakeville thus represents a move away from the sinful temptations of city life and a reaffirmation of traditional small-town and rural values.

DeMille's use of lighting effects is as significant as mise-en-scène and parallel editing to convey a didactic message that would appeal to sentimental middle-class audiences. Unlike his later adaptations, such as *Rose of the Rancho* (1914), *The Girl of the Golden West* (1915), *The Warrens of Virginia* (1915), *Kindling* (1915), and *Carmen* (1915), in which lighting effects are used throughout to advance the narrative, DeMille singles out specific shots representing the family for what he labeled *contrasty* lighting. Clearly, he had already used Buckland's talent to his advantage in *The Virginian,* their first collaboration and his first directorial effort, in campfire scenes absent in *The Squaw Man,* an otherwise superior film.[56] DeMille recalled years later that his lighting setups were not standard practice and that he had to issue specific instructions to cameraman Alvin Wyckoff:

> I was trying to get composition and light and shadow, and I would say to him, "You musn't make this part so light, under the table musn't be light—it should be dark and back corner of the room shouldn't be light—it should be dark." So they all said, "He likes it '*contrasty*'"—contrasty!—that was the phrase. I was known as the man who—there were some terrific battles because of that, because that meant expose it for contrast. It didn't mean shadow it, it just meant make the whites whiter and the black blacker.[57]

In *What's His Name,* DeMille began to codify the use of contrasty lighting to represent moral dilemmas such as those engulfing the family in a society increasingly preoccupied with consumer values.[58]

The director first uses dramatic lighting effects in an intimate scene following a surprise backstage visit that reveals Nellie dining with Fairfax. At bedtime, Harvey and Phoebe are both lit in the foreground against a darkened background as they recite prayers and exchange an affectionate good-night kiss. Lying on the corner of the bed is a very large doll that serves as a substitute for the child. As both father and daughter assume maternal functions in Nellie's absence, their relationship is endangered by incestuous feeling, a scenario rendered all the more intriguing by the fact that DeMille cast his only child, Cecilia, as Phoebe.[59] A variation of this mise-en-scène occurs later in a boxcar strewn with straw, signifying religious representations of the Holy Family in Bethlehem, as Harvey and Phoebe take shelter during their long journey back to Blakeville. DeMille moves his camera in closer for a medium shot, in contrast to a preponderance of medium long shots, as once again the father joins his daughter in prayer, tucks her under a jacket, and kisses her good night. Phoebe's gigantic doll occupies the space between them as Harvey falls asleep in the space to her right. All three are dramatically lit against the darkness of the boxcar but not from any naturalistic light source. Lastly, DeMille uses contrasty lighting to recuperate Nellie as a maternal figure after she spurns Fairfax in Reno, a sign of sexual restraint suitable for domestic rather than theatrical life, and responds to a telegram regarding Phoebe's illness. The description of the final tableau in the script is rather pedestrian and shows how much DeMille improvised to achieve his results on film:

> Photographer's Studio: Harvey and Uncle Peter nursing Phoebe—Nellie on— Picture—Uncle Peter starts to become violent—Harvey stops him, indicates Phoebe. Nellie comes to other side of couch, kneels over Phoebe. Harvey opposite her—Phoebe tosses—Both start to put covers over her—and eyes meet—Nellie's head goes down on bed—Harvey watching her—Uncle Peter standing at head of bed, shows disgust, turns his back and walks away.[60]

As photographed, all four members of the family are lit in a medium long shot against the darkened backdrop of Uncle Peter's studio. Phoebe sleeps in the foreground as Nellie sits by her bedside to the left. Forming an arc, Harvey leans toward his repentant wife in a conciliatory gesture, while Uncle Peter stands rigidly apart in disapproval as a strong vertical in the center of the screen. Ashamed, Nellie lowers her head so that a broad-brimmed hat obliterates her from the family picture during a moment of restoration, reconciliation, and moral resolution.

DeMille's translation of domestic melodrama as an intertext from stage to screen represents the ethical dilemma of middle-class families caught between the values of self-denial signifying moral character, on the one hand, and personality defined by commodities and performance, on the other. A consumer culture, in other words, meant a rearticulation of gender roles or a remapping of private and public spheres that imperiled sentimental ideals about womanhood. Since *What's His Name* was based on a novel that, according to one critic, was condensed in the adaptation, a comparison of these parallel discourses shows how each author dealt with the issues of gender, marriage, and the family. McCutcheon's version avoids pronouncements about motherhood that could be interpreted as saccharine and focuses instead on the inability of the title character to assert his manhood. A small-town soda jerk unable to comprehend the exchange value of commodity production in urban life, Harvey exemplifies sentimental traits such as selflessness, charity, and forgiveness. Nellie, on the contrary, gratifies her whims by obtaining a divorce and marrying Fairfax, as well as assuming custody of Phoebe. She is punished, however, by a fatal illness that provides the occasion for a reconciliation with her magnanimous former husband.

By contrast, DeMille shifts the focus of the narrative to sex-role reversals as these affect the welfare of the child. Although the lighting in the final shot of *What's His Name* renders ambiguous Nellie's recuperation as a maternal figure, the film nevertheless emphasizes "the potent effect," to quote a reviewer, "of the mother['s] love for her child." Granted, Nellie's rush to Phoebe's bedside may be interpreted as a narrative rupture, but she finally adheres to the dictum that the well-being of children is the purpose of middle-class family life.[61] As Beatrice DeMille stressed in a pamphlet advertising the Henry C. DeMille School for Girls, "only through home life may a rounded development be attained."[62] Significantly, DeMille's first three adaptations, albeit Westerns, have lengthy and meaningful sequences that emphasize adult commitment to the welfare of children, as do his prewar Lasky Company features such as *The Captive* (1915), *Kindling* (1915), and *The Heart of Nora Flynn* (1916). But his better-known Jazz Age sex comedies and melodramas, including *Don't Change Your Husband* (1919), *Why Change Your Wife?* (1920), and *The Affairs of Anatol* (1921), focus on companionate marriage or childless couples involved in marital and extramarital misadventures. The absence of children from these later features in effect underscores threats posed to family commitment in a secularized consumer culture.

Although focused on the disintegration of the family under the impact of a sex-role reversal, DeMille's adaptation addresses the crucial problem of masculine identity in an era when revolt against feminization ranged from silly posturing to fascist glorification of warriors. What was the fate of a young man molded according to sentimental principles espoused by genteel women and clergymen in charge of child rearing practices? What were the costs of genteel culture, in other words, for men who did not have the option of escaping into fantasies such as Orientalism or pursuing energetic adventures at home and abroad? Pathetically, Harvey represents the product of a lower-middle-class upbringing, that is, a lackluster white-collar worker with limited aspirations and mobility in a competitive marketplace. Critical response to this Milquetoast figure varied. According to the *New York Dramatic Mirror*, "the character presented by Max Figman retains a fund of good, manly qualities notwithstanding the burden of indignities." Certainly, Figman is not nearly as passive, inept, and inconsequential as McCutcheon's unheroic hero. A *Hartford Current* reviewer, however, describes Harvey as a "weak husband," a judgment affirmed by the film's superego, Uncle Peter, in his disavowal of marriage as a threat to masculine independence.[63]

Since Uncle Peter is a photographer with privileged access to the nature of reality, his censorious behavior in the last scene, which takes place in his studio, renders the resolution as ambiguous as does the lighting. Although he occupies the center of the screen, he also stands apart from the family reunited in the foreground. Perhaps the curmudgeonly bachelor is too uncompromising in his dedication to the small-town values of self-denial, restraint, and thrift. Yet Harvey discovers that assuming a persona means playing oneself false in the only scene in which he enjoys celebrity status as the result of a performance. Dressed like Fairfax and sporting a cane and bowler, he returns to the drugstore to find that news stories about his divorce have portrayed him as a neglectful husband and a ladies' man, a reputation eliciting bravos from curious and admiring townsfolk. Basking in the lime-light is cut short, however, by news of Phoebe's illness as a reminder of family obligations. For all his weaknesses, Harvey still personifies sincerity, a trait compromised in sophisticated parlor games and therefore associated with simple village life.

As opposed to Harvey, Nellie represents personality defined by perfor-mance and consumption and thus signifies the danger of the marketplace invading the privatized home. She is an actress who not only performs on stage but also portrays the penitent role of the absent mother in the final tableau. Self-theatricalization thereby compromises sincerity even in the back region of the house or in the inner circle of family relations. Yet the ethical conflict of *What's His Name* is not between the polarities of wealth and sexuality as symbolized by Fairfax, on the one hand, and selflessness as personified by Harvey, on the other. Rather, DeMille rewrites the moral contest as one between character based on the Protestant values of the "old" middle class versus personality representative of a "new" middle class in-vested in consumption.[64] Consequently, the film yields no easy solutions in terms of closure. According to the conventions of melodrama as a nostalgic reaffirmation of a golden age, the director resolves the moral dilemma in favor of small-town values. *What's His Name* reaffirms character as defined by "old" middle-class traits such as "benevolence, self-reliance, humility, sincerity, perseverance, orderliness, frugality, reverence, patience, honesty, purity, punctuality, charity," and so forth.[65] But in the final tableau, DeMille aptly sacrifices the moral clarity of a resolution in favor of an ambiguity more consistent with the uncertain values of a middle class in transition.

Given the context of social change in the Progressive Era, DeMille re-formulates domestic melodrama in *What's His Name* to address the concerns of an evolving middle class. A discourse on the erosion of the Victorian practice of separate spheres, the film foregrounds moral issues regarding the role of women in the family. Since an accelerated shift from a producer to a consumer economy occurred during a period of sustained inflation, debate grew about the wisdom of increased family spending to achieve a more refined standard of living. Essential to the survival of the middle class was the resourceful and prudent housewife who had negotiated transactions in the marketplace long before the advent of a modern consumer culture. She had been enjoined for decades to avoid extravagance and fashion, a sign of social ambition foreign to the "old" propertied middle class.[66] But women were being seduced by an increasing array of enticing consumer goods. Divorce cases, alarmingly on the rise among native-born Protestants, attested to the unreasonable demands and household neglect of wives who wished to increase expenditures. For middle-class audiences accustomed to discourse on the virtues of self-denial as opposed to comfort and refinement, the character of Nellie in *What's His Name* must have struck a resonant chord. As she is literally effaced by the low-key lighting in the final scene, a tableau that imparts a moral lesson, the actress represents the dangers confronted by the middle-class family in a secular age of increased consumption and leisure.

DeMille's early filmmaking style aptly conveyed such a message, even though a number of interesting details regarding characterization and plot are unintelligible due to a lack of medium shots and medium close-ups. Ruby is characterized as a questionable chorus girl, for example, because she is shopping for cosmetics and wearing a watch on her ankle, details in the script that escape the audience. What registers on account of the high ratio of medium long shots, however, is the intertextuality of feature film, stage plays, and parlor theatricals in Victorian sentimental culture. The director's visual style, specifically mise-en-scène, low-key lighting, and parallel editing, was thus appropriate for the reformulation of melodrama as a sermon for filmgoers accustomed to patronizing the legitimate theater. An unconventional narrative of a sex-role reversal certain to provoke censure, not to mention hilarity, the adaptation served to underscore the continuing need for social convention in middle-class life. As *Moving Picture World* concluded, "The story . . . has a philosophy that the average spectator will like."[67] DeMille's rewriting of domestic melodrama as a form of Victorian pictorialism thus succeeded as a cinematic articulation of the ideological concerns of both the "old" and "new" middle class at a historical crossroads.

THREE

The Lower East Side as Spectacle: Class and Ethnicity in the Urban Landscape

A few weeks before his premature and untimely death as a result of typhoid, Henry C. DeMille was reading political tracts such as Hamlin Garland's "A New Declaration of Rights" (1892). Swayed by the moral fervor of populist reform, Garland claimed, "at last, under the leadership of Henry George, the single-tax men of America have made that immortal old parchment blaze with light!" and prophesied "the abolition of all slavery, white slavery, the slavery of women, the slavery of the farmer."[1] DeMille could not then know that his liberal elder son, William, would become a playwright and marry Henry George's daughter, or that his conservative younger son, Cecil, would articulate middle-class ideology in early feature film. As signified by the elder DeMille's choice of literature, discourse on social change represented by urban workers and immigrants was an ideologically charged exercise for the genteel classes.

Although his family entertained populist Henry George, Cecil B. DeMille's adaptations of works about the urban landscape were based to a significant extent on realist representation that existed in tension with Victorian sentimentalism.[2] A sign of social upheaval, the destitute were not always welcome in genteel drawing rooms, not even in discursive modes like realism that essentially legitimated existing social hierarchies. As an unsympathetic novelist claimed, "we are hobnobbing with persons with whom we could not in real life bear a moment's interview."[3] The ambiguity of middle-class response to realist aesthetic was symptomatic not only of class and ethnic differences but, equally significant, of conflicting concepts of culture organized on the basis of gender. A masculine mode of social observation based on clinical detachment, realism countered the sentimental worldview of genteel women. Yet the tendency to stress spiritual and emotional uplift mitigated empirical investigations into the nature of reality. Pictorialism, for example, became increasingly realist as a result of technological advances such as halftones, but as stage melodrama it translated social forces into personal dilemmas to impart the lessons of sentimental culture.[4] A more detailed discussion of this issue in relation to cinematic discourse on urbanism first requires a consideration of the nineteenth-century view of the city.

According to the language of cinematography, representations of the urban milieu in the late nineteenth century could be divided into panoramic or high angle shots and medium shots or medium close-ups. A spectacular illustration of the first category, according to Peter B. Hales, is the grand-style photography that prevailed after the Civil War. Panoramic vistas dignified shots of building facades with Beaux Arts ornamentation, broad avenues intersecting the city in geometric patterns, landscaped parks with scenic promenades, and technological marvels like harbors, railroad yards, and steel bridges. Grand-style photography, like early documentary film, emphasized the monumentality of the urban landscape and thus imposed unity upon diverse peoples reduced in scale or rendered invisible in high angle or extreme long shots.[5] A representational strategy appealing to the genteel classes, this photographic style was ideologically informed by the Protestant image of America as a "city on a hill" and rooted in small-town experience. An attempt to foster that experience in a modern urban setting, the City Beautiful movement sought to promote civic growth in accordance with the principles of harmony, balance, and order.[6] Visions of the American city as an arcadian landscape were thus grounded in an aesthetic that articulated the political ideology and social experience of the elite.

From the closer perspective of medium shots, however, a more troubling view emerged to contrast with the grandiose designs inspired by the fabled "White City" of the World Columbian Exhibition in Chicago (1893).[7] Indeed, a disturbing picture of degenerate city life had prevailed since the mid-nineteenth century in fiction, periodical literature, sensationalized news stories, muckraking journalism, and vice commission reports.[8] As the sense of community that had been founded on middle-class participation in local civic activities disintegrated under the impact of urbanization, cultural differences based on class and ethnic hierarchies became more visible and disquieting.[9] Particularly noteworthy in influencing middle-class response to urban life was George Foster's "New York in Slices" in the *New York Tribune*. Anticipating the social photography and magic lantern slide lectures of Jacob Riis, as well as realist literature, Foster employed direct address in conducting a tour of the Lower East Side: "Go on with us, and see . . . the actual condition of the wicked and wretched classes.''[10] As dwellers of a dark, mysterious, and evil metropolis, immigrant and working-class peoples constituted a spectacle as the urban "Other" for the edification of the middle class. The term "ghetto," interestingly, was not then in common use so that slum areas were referred to as "colonies," a label obviously applied to subjugated alien peoples under an imperialistic flag.[11] An integral aspect of explorations of the urban scene thus involved a sense of tourism and voyeurism that reinforced social hierarchies. Absent in an era in which exotic travel could refer not only to Orientalist visions of the Middle or Far East but also to the Lower East Side was the postmodernist concept of "the indignity of speaking for others."[12] In fact, Henry George, who preached economic reform entailing a redistribution of wealth, complained that the poor were treated as a "different species from the rich, . . . to be inspected and regulated and instructed and kindly helped by their betters."[13] Precisely this condescension, if not Foucauldian panoptic surveillance, characterized attitudes toward immigrants and workers in discourse on urban social problems.[14]

Aestheticized visions of a "city on a hill" and realistic engravings and photographs of the tenements provided early filmmakers like DeMille with a rich legacy of intertexts to represent social change. Although realism became a dominant mode of expression in late-nineteenth-century urban life, it was informed by sentimental values. Underlying this tension in representational strategies were signs of gender conflict in discourse that otherwise preserved the status quo. An investigative mode associated with research that privileged the hard facts in delineating an urban environment, realism was in part a masculine response to sentimental culture. Alfred Habegger defines it as a male adversarial form of literature that occupied a middle ground between Victorian "scribbling females," to use Hawthorne's pejorative phrase, and twentieth-century modernism.[15] Yet the influence of genteel women in setting the cultural agenda of the middle class dictated that realist representation, itself subject to contradictions, be moderated by didactic values if not spiritual uplift.

Despite the increasing diversification of readership that resulted in the popularity of masculine genres in the late nineteenth century, genteel women still functioned as the guardians of culture; they were not likely to attend Ibsen plays or to purchase copies of *Sister Carrie* (1900). According to Henry F. May, a publishing "house might accept a late James novel, but it had to make up for it with an innocent costume novel or a tearful story of family trials and triumphs."[16] Such a dismissal of sentimental culture, however, ignores the strength of the moral commitment of middle-class women to family life and social experience.[17] Yet sentimentalism was circumscribed in the face of existing power relations even as it sought to redefine these in an industrialized environment. The limitations of the sentimental worldview became especially apparent as the bonds of community, including ethical precepts as the basis for social intercourse, began to dissolve in a pluralistic urban milieu. As the underpinning of reformist activity, moral certitude dictated philanthropy, social work, and political change, but in the form of noblesse oblige it also reinforced class and ethnic hierarchies.

Artists in revolt against Victorian sentimentalism, however, were themselves morally implicated by realist modes of discourse that objectified and commodified the urban "Other." Indeed, their representational strategies were not unrelated to an established pictorial tradition that employed didacticism to preserve social distance between the classes. A further consideration of realism, moreover, reveals that visual strategies involving objectification and reproduction expressed an impulse to impose order upon a chaotic, bewildering, and elusive landscape. According to Miles Orvell, the culture of imitation "thrived on a traffic in representations and replications" enclosed within a theatrical space or picture frame to provide spectators with an illusion of mastery. Orvell labels this form of middle-class sensibility, as expressed in the medium of photography, *artificial realism,* an oxymoronic label that is conceptually related to *romantic realism* in the theater.[18] An equivalent to genteel display of curios and bric-a-brac in parlors replicating aristocratic taste, the legitimate stage antedated photography and cinema as a representation stressing verisimilitude. David Belasco, for example, removed all the worn and soiled furnishings, fixtures, and wallpaper from a room in a disreputable boarding house for the sets in his production of *The Easiest Way* (1909).[19] Such celebrated stage reproductions constituted spectacle for the visual appropriation of the elite. Artificial or romantic realism, while encompassing the variety of experience in the city as a social matrix, thus did not qualify as an expression of cultural democracy.

As a filmmaker, DeMille was adept at drawing on both realist and sentimental modes of representation in continuing a narrative tradition that would dominate American cinema at least until the mid-twentieth century. Certainly, the vogue of artificial or romantic realism in genteel culture had implications for motion pictures as a medium for representing (and thus containing) social reality.[20] An intertextual reading of the director's adaptations of stage plays, for example, reveals that he diluted grim expressions of urban realism in favor of reconciliations dictated by sentimentalism. DeMille and the Lasky Company evidently intended to ensure the appeal of their productions to middle-class women in the audience. Although the director's early filmmaking style, such as brilliant use of lighting, set design, and split screen in *Kindling* (1915), was original, his technical innovations were unmatched on an ideological level by the progressive social thought that was his family's legacy. DeMille demonstrated, in other words, that to the extent narrative conventions were articulated with respect to established forms of genteel culture, stylistic advances in film language were integrated into status quo discourse. The evolution of feature film aesthetic in relation to existing cultural practice thus meant that cinema became a vehicle for the articulation of middle-class ideology. Granted, a variety of rich subcultures mediated working-class and ethnic reception of film in neighborhood venues despite a decline in such plebeian male pastimes as socializing in saloons. Yet the leisure industry exerted a powerful homogenizing influence during an era that stressed Americanization as a response to cultural diversity.

SOCIAL ILLS AND COMIC RELIEF:
THE *CHIMMIE FADDEN* SERIES

Although comedy appears at first to be unrelated to realist modes of representation linked to the urban experience, regional writers and local colorists had introduced to the reading public amusing characters who spoke in the vernacular. Chimmie (James) Fadden, a Bowery lad known to news and short story readers and to stage audiences before his appearance on screen, was such a character. Since DeMille was associated with the melodramatic playwriting tradition rather than comedy, the *Chimmie Fadden* series provides an interesting point of departure to investigate his articulation of urban relations. In fact, the *Chimmie Fadden* films are not pure comedies but also function as sentimental melodrama in that romance mitigates social tensions. Such a mixture of genres is revealing with respect to controversial issues involving not only ethnicity and class but also gender. Comedies exploiting cultural differences presumed social distance and thus violated the conventions of sentimental literature that stressed emotional identification with characters. Genteel women, moreover, considered laughter irreligious and a breach of tenets of self-control and performance required in the drawing room.[21] Yet a great deal of the humor in the *Chimmie Fadden* short stories and films is based on the hero's inability to comprehend or to conform to upper-class etiquette. By artfully merging comic and sentimental modes of expression in his adaptations, DeMille struck a compromise. Ultimately, he preferred melodrama to comedy, despite critical acclaim for the *Chimmie Fadden* series and the early Jazz Age films, because he indulged his penchant for orchestrating spectacle.

Unfortunately, there is no extant print of *Chimmie Fadden*, the first of at least two features in a series based on the well-known comic character. The reconstruction of any film that has not survived is problematical, but in this case there exists, in addition to the sequel, several reliable texts, including short stories and scripts of both the stage play and film adaptations. A character indebted to the correspondence of dominant cultural forms in an urban milieu, Chimmie progressed from print media to stage to screen in such a manner that sentiment increasingly displaced satire. As opposed to sustaining the hilarity provoked by extreme class differences in the short stories, DeMille registered a shift in genres, signified at times by lighting effects, to emphasize social reconciliation based on sentimental values. A closer reading of the *Chimmie Fadden* intertexts demonstrates that even before he was widely acknowledged as an author, DeMille left his own inscription on texts adapted from middle-class cultural practice.

Chimmie, an enterprising Irish tough who lives on the Lower East Side with his mother and brother, first appeared in the columns of the influential *New York Sun* in the 1890s. Although he was a fictional character invented by Edward W. Townsend, his credibility was enhanced by colorful dialect and scenes of slum life based on actual observations. So popular was this engaging rogue that Townsend, who later pursued a Congressional career, published several volumes of collected short stories. Adapted for the legitimate stage by Augustus Thomas, former art director of the Charles Frohman Company, and by Townsend himself, *Chimmie Fadden* played to audiences in New York and then toured the country.[22] A photograph of Broadway taken in the 1890s shows a huge sign painted on the side of the tallest building in the area to advertise the play.[23] Chimmie thereafter became a familiar character in theatrical entertainment. Victor Moore, recruited by Beatrice DeMille to star in the Lasky Company adaptations, was billed as "Broadway's most popular comedian" because he had previously played Chimmie as well as other Bowery types both on stage and in vaudeville.[24] Situated at a point of convergence for several media including newspapers, best-sellers, vaudeville, legitimate theater, and feature film, Chimmie mediated the experience of the urban poor for middle-class readers and spectators.

An intertext that provided the basis for several adaptations, Townsend's short stories in turn exploited middle-class familiarity with stage conventions. Chimmie, for example, continually affirms that he has no "langwudge" problem while addressing his readers, as would a vaudeville actor, in first person and in street dialect. At his best, he regales his audience with hilarious anecdotes about life as a footman for a Fifth Avenue household. Subject to ridicule are the idiosyncrasies of the rich, such as Miss Fannie's theatrics as lady bountiful in the slums. According to Chimmie, "Wese goes down dere in de street cars, cause dey strings ye down dere if ye goes in er carriage, an' Miss Fannie she puts on er dress wot she tinks looks like er factory girl's dress. . . . It looks like one er dem loidies wot plays on der stage when dey goes t' de war t' be nurses when dere fellys is sojers. See?" As Chimmie discerns, Fannie is deliberately engaging in a performance, a mode of behavior inaccessible to the untutored poor, to impress a suitor: "now dat 'e's back an' ev'ryting is up to de limit wid Miss Fannie, she ain't breakin' 'er neck no more 'bout no orphans, nor no kids in hospitals wid crooked legs, nor no old womin wot ain't got no good grub nor no Bibles in de slums. See?"[25] Assuming a satirical attitude toward the self-theatricalization of the well-to-do, Chimmie comments on the moral dilemma involved in genteel performance as a basis for social interaction. And for good measure, he expresses the resentment of tenement dwellers constantly subjected to the scrutiny of philanthropists, reformers, social workers, journalists, and social scientists.

Although laughter dissipated the reader's anxiety about unwelcome social problems in the pages of the *New York Sun,* Townsend focused on class antagonism in the stage version by introducing elements of melodrama. Larry, a young man who has just been released from prison, declares, "Well I ain't so much better out than in. A mug might as well be doing time at Sing Sing as being here with no graft to work, no job, square or crooked, to make the price of a meal with." Commenting on the plight of Miss Fannie's maid, he bitterly remarks, "you heard what Maggie said about her wages all going for rent, with nothing left to fill the cupboard or coal scuttle with."[26] DeMille, however, vitiates both the short stories as outrageous satire and stage melodrama as discourse on class conflict in the film adaptation. As a result, Larry is no longer an ex-convict who makes stinging observations about the plight of the poor but a delinquent brother in Chimmie's family. Chimmie himself loses some of his toughness and opportunism as a street character, if none of his charm, and is definitely a straight-arrow. According to the conventions of melodrama as romantic realism, the forces of social injustice are thus reduced to a question of individual ethics, a formula reworked in the social problem films that originated at the time.[27]

Drawing upon realistic illustrations of urban inequality in newspapers and magazines, DeMille begins the first Chimmie film with a contrast edit to juxtapose the circumstances of rich and poor. The script indicates: "Street scene in Bowery of Kelly sending Mrs. Murphy a pint of suds in pail, which Chimmie empties before it reaches the woman; then cut to [a scene DeMille has penciled in as] Van Cortlandts Summer Home on Long Island."[28] As sentimental heroines, Fanny, now spelled with a *y* and surnamed Van Cortlandt (Anita King), and her French maid, Duchess (Camille Astor), both lose their temperamental qualities in the role of ingénues. Fanny in fact ceases to be the butt of jokes as a lady bountiful and becomes an earnest social worker who pleads with her father, "Daddy—I need more money for the sick babies in the slums." Class difference, on the contrary, is satirized rather than sentimentalized in the stage version. When the Duchess accompanies Miss Fannie to the tenements, she exclaims in a reference to economic warfare in Paris, "Mon Dieu! is this what M'mselle calls slumming? It is worse than the commune!" As if to substantiate this observation, Larry steals Miss Fannie's purse and explains, "I wouldn't pinched nothing only Maggie told me dere wasn't money enough at home to pay the rent, and I wanted to save the old woman from being put out on the street."[29] DeMille, interestingly, rewrites this episode in the film so that Chimmie prevents an unidentified drunkard from seizing Fanny's pocketbook and is rewarded with employment as a footman, a sure sign of noblesse oblige.

DeMille's narrative strategy to defuse *Chimmie Fadden* as satire by sentimentalizing the characters did not, however, dilute the film's exploitation of vaudeville humor. According to the script of the first film, Victor Moore looks straight into the camera during the credits and addresses an audience already familiar with Chimmie's previous incarnations in newspaper columns, short stories, and stage plays. Similarly, the actor is introduced in an iris shot in the sequel, *Chimmie Fadden Out West,* as the camera tilts up the horizontal stripes of the back of his shirt. Yawning as he turns around to greet the audience in a close-up, he is quite likeable as he mutters, "Hello, Folks!" Unquestionably, his direct address recalls vaudeville that began as entertainment based on ethnic stereotypes for working-class audiences and became middle-class fare in big-time theaters built by the Keith-Albee circuit. According to *Variety,* the audience applauded Moore's entry and exit in the film as they would performers on a vaudeville stage.[30] Surely, they enjoyed outrageous antics and faux pas as a result of social interaction across class and ethnic barriers that remained firmly in place. An elegant dinner party provided just the right setting in the first film. Struggling into an ill-fitting uniform that elicits contempt from a haughty butler, Chimmie creates mayhem. As detailed in the film script, he rushes into the kitchen and "says, 'Give me the feed.' The cook hands him tray with cups of bouillon on it. Chimmie starts in a hurry through swinging door . . . looks at cups—decides it is tea, grabs sugar and cream from side board, puts bouillon down in front of guests and says, grandly, . . . 'Do yez take one lump or two?'"[31] Such comedy is obviously based on audience awareness of violations of social rituals conducted according to proper etiquette among the genteel classes.

Although Townsend's play was compared unfavorably with the work of Edward Harrigan, who invented Irish characters in the Bowery without "straining for the picturesque," DeMille's screen adaptation won favorable reviews.[32] While regretting that comedy "changed to sentiment," a shift in genres noticed by at least one critic, the *New York Dramatic Mirror* pointed out:

> One thing this picture would seem to prove . . . is that slapstick is nearing the termination of its present vogue. Victor Moore got more laughter in avoiding what the best of slapstick artists do than he could have in any other way obtained. . . . Rarely have we heard more enjoyment than the other night at a Strand performance. The audience literally howled itself hoarse, not only at Mr. Moore, but at the slangy inserts.[33]

Clearly, the middle-class audience enjoyed the humor of Chimmie's street vernacular, a sign that dialogue titles could provoke as many laughs as slapstick comedy constructed with sight gags. Assuming a different perspective, W. Stephen Bush emphasized the societal as opposed to the comic elements of the film in *Moving Picture World:*

> There is the fine dramatic story and the contrast between The Bowery and Fifth Avenue. The human bond which connects these extremes of society is most carefully constructed and most artistically. . . . The atmosphere is splendid, both of the Lower East Side with its struggling human bee hive and its picturesqueness, and of the Fifth Avenue section. . . . the settings and the photography . . . are up to the best Lasky standard.[34]

The critics' repeated use of the term *picturesque* as well as the audience's hilarious response to Chimmie's dialect implied that voyeuristic tours of urban slums had become commonplace. Unfortunately, DeMille's representation of tenements in the first Chimmie Fadden film, a product of his collaboration with Wilfred Buckland, has not been preserved in an extant print.

DeMille exhibited such a talented flair for comedy in *Chimmie Fadden* that the Lasky Company quickly announced plans to make a sequel. *Motion Picture News* informed the industry, "More 'Chimmie Fadden' Plays with Moore Coming. Popularity of the First One, Demonstrated by the First Few Showings and Letters Received by Exhibitors Prompts Lasky to Arrange for a Series Featuring the Comedian." E. W. Townsend, whose letter to Samuel Goldwyn was included as a testimonial in the article, applauded the adaptation of his stories: "Frankly, I was amazed as I was delighted with the vitality of the pictures. You have reproduced the group of people Chimmie fought, loved, teased, jollied, not only with quite astonishing fidelity to physical characteristics, but the very spirit of the character is shown."[35] Consistent with the Lasky Company's strategy to establish its reputation for quality film, ads for the sequel described Chimmie as "a character of American literature likely to live as long as Tom Sawyer or other familiar youths of fiction."[36] The exploitation of early film adaptations still relied heavily on the circulation of recognized intertexts in middle-class culture to achieve cultural legitimacy.

The sequel, *Chimmie Fadden Out West,* represented progress in DeMille's effort to establish himself as an author because he shared an original screenplay credit with Jeanie Macpherson, who later collaborated with him on the scripts of most of his silent features.[37] Characteristic of Macpherson's touch is the sentimental romance between the Irish rogue and the French maid. A tale of adventurous travel in the West, the initial story treatment shows the young hero discovering gold and beset by bandits. A dream sequence then presents Chimmie, dressed in gentlemen's clothes and riding in an automobile, as he apes the Van Cortlandts and dispenses charity on a tour of his former neighborhood.[38] But DeMille abandoned this story treatment of the Bowery boy makes good in favor of a script that contrasts Chimmie's sterling moral character with the greed of unscrupulous businessmen. Unlike his fate in the Townsend short stories, Chimmie does not prosper after marrying the Duchess, a spirited and savvy woman who arranges for him to serve as a valet. Indeed, his lack of employment in the film sequel constitutes a serious financial and romantic dilemma. Sadly, he tells the Duchess, "I wonder if I'll ever git enough coin so's we kin get spliced!" Contrary to the story treatment in which he discovers gold, Chimmie is drawn into a dishonest and speculative venture in the sequel by Van Cortlandt (Ernest Joy) and his business associate, Preston (Harry Hadfield). Acting in response to an urgent telegram from the company president, who insists on "*snappy* advertising" to stimulate business on the Southwest Railway, the two scoundrels persuade the Irish lad to fake a gold mine discovery in Death Valley. Chimmie, buoyed by the prospect of winning a fortune that will enable him to marry the Duchess, momentarily buries his scruples.

A script that appeals to middle-class sensibility, *Chimmie Fadden Out West* provokes laughter at the good-natured but inept poor and moralizing about the gluttonous rich. Again, a great deal of amusement results from class and ethnic differences expressed by Chimmie's costume, speech, and mannerisms. When he scrambles on board a train destined for Death Valley, for example, the Bowery lad knows nothing about sleeping car etiquette. DeMille uses tight framing, editing, and low-key lighting to dramatize a series of hilarious antics that occur in extremely crowded spaces on the train. Chimmie and an irate spinster, interestingly, serve as the butt of laughter rather than a black porter whose dialogue titles are grammatically correct. During a comic sequence filmed mostly in sleeping berths, Chimmie exclaims to authorities, who accuse him of designs on the old woman, "If I was goin' to get fixed up wid a dame, do you t'ink I'd grab dat!" Chimmie's antics in the Wild West are also hilarious. Dressed in a cowboy outfit that includes a kerchief, suspenders, shearling chaps, elbow-length gloves, knife, and gun—not to mention his trademark bowler—Chimmie finds uninhibited saloon behavior a bit tame. When drunken cowboys shoot up the floor, he comments, "Wid a little practice you guys might get by in New York."

Chimmie's comic adventures are overshadowed, however, in a melodramatic turn of events that foregrounds his moral dilemma. As he prepares for his wedding by donning formal dress, his brother Larry (Raymond Hatton) horrifies both their mother and the Duchess by exposing the fake gold mine as a crooked investment scheme. Ashamed, he confronts Preston and Van Cortlandt at the office and announces to reporters, "De Chimmie Fadden Mine is on de blink. Dese gents will hand back every cent!" Although he has redeemed his character, Chimmie returns dejected and empty handed to a darkened Bowery apartment. DeMille uses extreme low-key lighting in a medium shot in which Chimmie, seated at a table, stares at a

12. Broadway comedian Victor Moore, in the title role of *Chimmie Fadden Out West* (1915), buries his scruples and agrees to a dishonest investment scheme plotted by Eastern businessmen. *(Photo courtesy George Eastman House)*

13. As the Irish tough, Moore exchanges his bowler for a cowboy hat and elicits the admiration anad hopes of his proud mother (Mrs. Lewis McCord). *(Photo courtesy George Eastman House)*

wedding ring and is comforted by his mother. She removes his bowler, takes his hand, and kisses him on the cheek to signify both approval of his good deed and sympathy for his plight. A cut to a medium shot at the Van Cortlandt mansion, where the Duchess has resumed her duties as a maid, shows her listening to news about Chimmie's heroic action. DeMille moves his camera in for an even closer medium shot as he next cuts to the Duchess entering the dimly lit apartment to reconcile with her despondent lover. Addressing the audience he greeted during the credits, Chimmie exclaims, "Wot d'ye mean—I lost my gold mine!" and embraces the Duchess before a fade-out.

Among the first Lasky Company films to merit a review in the *New York Times, Chimmie Fadden Out West* drew a favorable notice for Victor Moore's acting and for humor that proved "a picture may be funny without even a single Chaplin kick." Also attesting to the success of the comedy, the *New York Dramatic Mirror* noted that it "called forth roar after roar of laughter."[39] Although the Chimmie Fadden series as nonslapstick comedy represented a departure for DeMille, melodrama subverted laughter so that a morality tale could be told. Class and ethnic antagonisms were thus resolved in a sentimental manner, ensuring that the audience experienced moral certitude as well as emotional uplift. At the conclusion of the first film in the series, Chimmie is accused of theft when he is caught returning goods stolen from the Van Cortlandt mansion by his brother Larry. Paranoia about the lower orders, it should be noted, characterized several films in which middle- and upper-class residents find their homes invaded by thieves. Class reconciliation is stressed, however, as the Van Cortlandts agree not to prosecute Chimmie's delinquent brother. In *Chimmie Fadden Out West*, thievery exists in a more sophisticated form as financial transactions in a capitalistic economy. A good-natured Bowery lad, Chimmie finds himself surrounded by corruption not only among Eastern businessmen but among frontier lawmen. Yet his honesty and decency prevail in the end.

DeMille's adaptation of the *Chimmie Fadden* stories defuses the issue of social injustice by focusing on the morality of sterling characters like Chimmie. Particularly noteworthy is the personification of Protestant or "old" middle-class values by slum inhabitants whose class and ethnic traits are otherwise a source of amusement. Such a narrative strategy has several implications worth considering. On the one hand, feature film adaptations based on romantic realism mediated the urban experience for middle-class audiences. A flood tide of immigration that peaked in 1907 intensified a resurgence of nativism and xenophobia as well as racism among native-born Americans, including the elite. Partly an impulse to impose order on a chaotic metropolitan landscape, realistic representations objectified the "Other" for genteel consumers touring slum areas as exotic sites. Film narratives such as the *Chimmie Fadden* series, moreover, focused on lower-class characters who were not only reassuringly comical but ethical as well.

On the other hand, features produced for the appropriation of sophisticated audiences in first-run theaters also became part of a preexisting plebeian film culture. A variety of working-class and ethnic subcultures undoubtedly mediated the reception of feature film adaptations at local exhibition sites. The issue of what constitutes humor for different cultural groups was particularly relevant for the *Chimmie Fadden* series because lower-class spectators may not have found the Irishman as amusing as patrons at downtown movie palaces. Indeed, the sequel's failure to attract as large a number of filmgoers as were flocking to Geraldine Farrar films led Lasky to conclude, "We think the name of Chimmie Fadden is keeping the people out of the Theatres."[40] Chimmie was most likely an unfamiliar character among uneducated audiences, but therein lay the limitations of marketing features based on highbrow intertexts consumed by the genteel classes. Yet as entrepreneurs succeeded in expanding film production based on middle-class aesthetic and ideology, a process of homogenization previously resisted by workers and immigrants began to occur, even as they were cinematically defined as the urban "Other." Contrary to their hostility to genteel reformers intent on shaping recreational activities, the lower classes became enthusiastic patrons of commercialized amusement.[41] Feature films, in other words, functioned as a primer on middle-class values for the lower orders being counseled to Americanize and assimilate.

A TOUR OF THE LOWER EAST SIDE: *KINDLING*

A few days after he completed the first Chimmie Fadden film on May 18, 1915, DeMille began work on *Kindling,* an adaptation of a stage melodrama that demonstrates the extent to which realist representation of the poor was based on intertexts in middle-class culture. A well-received theatrical work, *Kindling* had been adapted for the stage by newsman Charles Kenyon from a novel that he had written in collaboration with Arthur Hornblow, editor of *Theatre.*[42] Part of a series of adaptations, their fiction was in turn based on a magazine article about tenement life and a *New York Evening Sun* human interest story.[43] As literature that addressed the social concerns of urban middle-class readers, metropolitan news stories, often in sensationalized accounts, frequently provided playwrights like Kenyon with dramatic material.[44] After a trial run in Los Angeles, the stage version of *Kindling* opened to respectful reviews at the Daly Theatre in New York in December 1911. According to the *New York Telegraph,* "the so-called high-brow contingent and sincere students of the drama pronounced the play one of the best of recent years." Given the reaction of critics to the DeMille-Belasco society dramas as confection, the equation of the term *highbrow* with realism is notable. The *Chicago Record Herald* declared that *Kindling* was "the most vital, vigorous specimen of American drama yet given to the stage." Several

14. Advertisement for *Kindling* (1915). Ads in trade journals emphasized the marquee value of Broadway stars like Charlotte Walker, rather than filmmakers like DeMille who had yet to establish their authorship.

reviewers commented on the deleterious effects of urbanization, and one concluded that the play "ought to make people feel that they should do something to better these conditions, . . . to do something . . . for others." Although one of the critics emphasized class division by stating that "the poor have been made to feel like dime-museum curiosities as a result of the . . . visits of the uptown 'swells,'" another emphasized the melting-pot qualities of American life: "We are becoming one people, with a national pulse, infinite in its variations of beats, but one just the same."[45] In sum, realist representation as a response to urban pluralism provoked discourse on daunting social problems, but the reaction of the genteel middle class to these changes remained essentially conservative.

DeMille's adaptation of *Kindling* draws upon well-established visual conventions that circulated in middle-class culture to represent life on the Lower East Side. Indeed, an unprecedented revolution in visual media resulting from the use of halftones to reproduce illustrations and photographs had preceded and even anticipated the rise of cinema.[46] A pictorial artist himself, DeMille was surely familiar with the iconography of engravings, halftones, paintings, photography, stereographs, and magic lantern slides. Particularly in representations of the city there existed in the cultural practice of this era a rich cross-fertilization between high and popular (as distinct from highbrow and lowbrow) culture. Artists like Winslow Homer, for example, preceded Jacob Riis into police station lodging houses to capture the plight of the homeless sleeping on the floor for *Harper's Weekly* (1874).[47] Captioned engravings of slums that focused on laundry hung out to dry on clotheslines—a practice that contradicted views of tenement life as filthy and unsanitary—became a cliché recycled by photographers of urban scenes and by painters in the realist tradition.[48] John Sloan, who was trained as a magazine and newspaper illustrator like the rest of the Ashcan school, produced paintings such as *Backyards, Greenwich Village* (1914) that showed the family wash dominating the skyline of an alleyway.[49] An example of the cinematic appropriation of visual conventions, a shot in *Kindling* shows clothesline laundry in the foreground of a tenement building fire escape.

Committed to inventing a visual style appropriate for the urban landscape, Ashcan painters, or New York realists, including John Sloan, George Luks, William Glackens, and Everett Shinn, emphasized a dark palette and sharp contrasts. Under the leadership of Robert Henri, this innovative group earned the epithet, "the black school."[50] An exhibit of their work held in a Manhattan gallery in 1908 attracted considerable notice in the press and several thousand visitors. Stylistically opposed to the New York realists, Alfred Stieglitz also affirmed that contemporary street scenes and ordinary people were appropriate subjects for serious art. An international figure who influenced the reception of photography as art, he produced several photographs of Manhattan, including subjects popularized in magazines and newspapers by graphic artists.[51] An innovator like DeMille could therefore draw upon several established conventions to represent the urban scene, but so inventive was he that exact quotations were never a part of his vision. What the director did replicate, however, was the didactic tone of pictorial realism as a tradition mediating the urban experience for the middle class. The widely held belief that the purpose of art was to provide spiritual inspiration rather than sheer aesthetic pleasure still pervaded an era on the verge of modernism.[52]

Characteristic of discourse on urban poverty, then, was a didactic tone motivated by genuine social concern as well as condescension that was evident, for example, in the work of genteel reformers. When Charles Loring Brace, founder of the Children's Aid Society, published an illustrated account of his work among the indigent, he called it *The Dangerous Classes of New York and Twenty Years' Work among Them* (1872). Similarly, James D. McCabe, Jr., drew a moral lesson in an exposé aptly titled *Lights and*

Shadows of New York Life (1872). Undoubtedly most influential was Jacob Riis's *How the Other Half Lives: Studies among the Tenements of New York* (1890), a volume with forty-three illustrations, including halftone reproductions of photographs printed earlier as drawings in a *Scribner's* article (1889).[53] Darkness and light, in other words, represented moral values in realistic urban discourse that was pervaded by sentimentalism. As a result, "Rembrandt" or contrasty lighting, advertised by the Lasky Company to achieve product differentiation for DeMille's films, functioned not only as a sign of highbrow culture but also as a Victorian trope familiar to middle-class sensibility. The director's reputation as an author was established, not coincidentally, by means of dramatic low-key lighting effects in a series of acclaimed films.

Since DeMille experimented with selective and low-key lighting to represent the tenets of Victorian moralism, he begins *Kindling*, as he does *Chimmie Fadden*, with a pictorial contrast. Rather than juxtaposing rich and poor by means of editing, however, he contrasts good and evil through lighting effects. Deleting from the script the intertitle, "The Eyes of the City," which indeed suggests voyeurism and Foucauldian panoptic surveillance, he opens the film instead with a didactic title, "Where the Devil Wins." An exterior shot of a street in the slums at nightfall is detailed in the script with attention to lighting as follows:

> Typical summer night scene in New York slums. Light effect from all doors and windows. Light from street on corner. Standing light directly over "Private" entrance to saloon. One woman exchanges remarks from lighted doorway where she is standing to woman in lighted window above. Groups of men pass down street or lounge in doorways. One man and a couple of loudly dressed but very *young* girls come down street and enter "Private" door of saloon, laugh boisterously. As the shutters of the saloon on corner swing back and forth to let people out or in, men are seen from time to time drinking at bar. In the broad shaft of light from the saloon entrance, a "hurdy gurdy" and grinder have stopped. Into the light from somewhere come a couple of ragged little girls and start to dance delightedly. In the shadows near the "Private" to saloon, stands a rather languidly dressed woman who appears to be waiting for someone. Steve comes swaggering down street smoking. He exchanges a gesture with a man in lighted doorway as he approaches "Private" entrance.[54]

What does this tenement scene look like on film? It is dusk. A narrow street in extreme long shot is dimly lit although there are no visible awnings that cast dark shadows on the buildings. DeMille choreographs a great deal of movement so that the scene becomes animated with several characters, including a young boy seated on the curb before a littered street, two men stationed on or near beer barrels in front of the saloon, prostitutes soliciting men strolling by, a beggar picking through the trash, a belligerent man escorting a woman on his arm, and a cripple walking on crutches. Unlike the description in the script, these details add up to a more depressing street scene and accord with the use of atmospheric lighting that creates a somber mood. By contrast, DeMille's next title, "Where the Devil Loses," precedes a medium shot that foregrounds stevedore Heine Schultz (Thomas Meighan) as he sits in the center of his apartment and reads a newspaper. Slightly in the background and to the right, his wife Maggie (Charlotte Walker) busily prepares the evening meal. On the left is a shelf with bits of crockery and dishes. A solicitous spouse, Maggie pours Heine a cup of tea. As the couple engage in an affectionate exchange, they deliver the message that a proper home based on traditional gender roles provides a positive environment to counteract degenerate slum life.

DeMille was inventive in constructing a realist representation of tenement life that was nevertheless aestheticized and didactic; to put it another way, he illustrated the extent to which Victorian pictoralism could be converted into a commodity. A filmmaker who articulated middle-class ideology, he also demonstrated the limitations of genteel culture with respect to representing the urban experience of workers and immigrants. The Schultzes, for example, are insulated in their apartment to avoid contact with squalid surroundings, but privacy was neither possible nor practical in slum dwellings. Unlike comfortable middle-class families in privatized suburban homes, the poor depended for their survival on mutual exchange and sharing. Further, DeMille's degenerate street scene in front of a saloon calls forth instant moral condemnation when in fact street life provided a vibrant contrast to dehumanizing factory work. According to Kathy Peiss:

> Streets served as the center of social life in the working-class districts, where laboring people clustered on street corners, on stoops, and in doorways of tenements, relaxing and socializing after their day's work. Lower East Side streets teemed with sights of interest and penny pleasures: organ grinders and buskers played favorite airs, itinerant acrobats performed tricks, and baked-potato venders, hot-corn stands, and soda dispensers vied for customers.[55]

Despite the limitations of romantic realism as a form of sentimental discourse, DeMille struck the right chord when he began *Kindling* with an atmospheric street scene in contrast to the opening of the stage play, which begins inside a tenement building. Film critics who used the ideologically loaded term *picturesque* responded with rapt reviews. W. Stephen Bush, for example, commented that "to portray atmosphere and surroundings in one or two brief touches is art of the highest order. The scene . . . depicting a typical section of the tenement district of a big city, is as graphic as anything that ever came from the hands of Hogarth or Rembrandt."[56] As a matter of fact, DeMille most likely quoted Stieglitz rather than European artists in constructing this particular mise-en-scène. Founder of the Photo-Secessionists, whose gallery was a short walking distance from D. W.

Griffith's Biograph studio, Stieglitz had published and exhibited several photographs of New York street scenes.[57] Poetically titled *Winter—Fifth Avenue* or *Spring Showers,* these photos exemplified a "pictorial" as opposed to a "straight" or clearly focused style evocative of the camera as a mechanical instrument. Stieglitz, in short, favored impressionistic, atmospheric, and blurred images that subtly transformed quotidian subjects into art. Such decontextualization and appropriation of the lower classes, however, was an aesthetic equivalent of economic exploitation then condemned not only by reformers but by artists themselves.[58]

After an atmospheric shot of a street scene influenced by Photo-Secessionist style photography, DeMille quickly exhibits his brilliant eclecticism as he next quotes the work of Jacob Riis. Unlike the blurred outlines of Steiglitz's ragpickers and asphalters photographed in an ambient urban milieu, Riis's documentation of slum dwellers was a stark contrast in light and shadow. A journalist and reformer, he mediated the urban experience for middle-class consumers who comprised "the other half" ensconced in material comfort and bolstered by moral rectitude. The representational strategy of his photos, as contemporary critics argue, involved posed or even startled subjects who were objectified and commodified as spectacle.[59] Scrutinized by the camera lens, immigrants and workers were denied their subjectivity and appeared defenseless. Accordingly, DeMille constructs a similar mise-en-scène in *Kindling.* When Maggie goes to the dispensary to fetch Dr. Taylor, for example, she enters a waiting room that would have been an appropriate subject for Riis's camera. As described in the script, the patients who sit there passively include

> a number of distinctive slum types sitting in line on bench waiting for their turn. A woman with utterly discouraged face and small consumptive boy. Woman is frail and delicate. A very old man who has a cane, almost in tatters. A young tough poorly dressed and scratched in probable street fight. And a young Italian girl with tragic eyes and ear rings, whose fate is not hard to imagine. Each expression is characteristic but all have the patient look of the very poor except the young tough who fidgets nervously.[60]

Although this gallery of characters appears slightly altered in the film, it is unquestionably drawn from Riis's social photography and magic lantern slides. DeMille's condescending and stereotyped description of the destitute, including the equation of a young girl's "tragic eyes" with "ear rings," was not atypical of the period. Consistent with his objectification of the poor in the film was the casting of a Mexican child suffering from malnutrition as the Jones baby, another victim of slum conditions.[61] When the sick infant dies, Dr. Taylor blames its mother for inadequate sanitation, when in fact a high rate of infant death in the tenements resulted from the practice of commercial dairies bottling contaminated milk.[62] Poverty is represented,

15. In *Kindling* DeMille's vision of the Lower East Side was influenced by a rich tradition of pictorial realism, including the social photography of Jacob Riis. *(Photo courtesy George Eastman House)*

according to middle-class ideological belief, as a personal failing rather than the result of capitalistic exploitation.

Further examples of DeMille's familiarity with Riis's social photography and magic lantern slide lectures are visible in several sequences in *Kindling.* A shot of Jones's apartment shows the dejected mother seated to the right so that the rear wall, pockmarked with filthy and deteriorating plaster, is plainly visible. As critics point out, Riis's use of magnesium flash powder to illuminate dark tenement rooms exaggerated blemishes and surface irregularities.[63] Perhaps most evocative of Riis's lectures is the sequence initiated by Maggie's argument with Heine about rearing children. Secretive about her pregnant condition, the heroine has purchased a cradle at a fire sale and hidden it beneath the kitchen table. When she learns about the death of the Jones baby, she claims, "All the kids born down here don't die." But her husband retorts, "The health officer says that half of them die—and the rest grow up to be crooks," and points to their neighbors. Panning right to follow Maggie's movement to the rear window, the camera cuts to a point-of-view shot of a forlorn child alone on a fire escape with empty milk bottles and a clothesline. A scene that constitutes the beginning of a cinematic tour of the slums, this exchange is absent from the stage play and indebted to Riis's exercises in urban voyeurism.

Heine asks pointedly, "Would you like to have a kid of yours, cursin' you for the very life you gave it?" He then exits left into the littered hallway. Maggie, stealing a glance at the cradle hidden under the table, follows. The Schultzes emerge from the tenement building entrance, where a sullen young girl is caring for a child. A few moments later, a strategically placed medium close-up shows the couple as they glance left, a profile shot clearly intended to heighten spectator identification as they continue on their excursion. What they, as well as the audience, observe is a series of sordid incidents in slum life: a boy stealing a watch from a drunkard who is sleeping next to a trash can, a man emerging from a saloon with a pail of beer and offering a swig to a disheveled young girl, and two children fighting over refuse as they dig through garbage cans. Heine exclaims, "I'd rather kill a child of ours the day it was born than send it up against a game like that!" Maggie, looking crestfallen, agrees as they complete their tour. Such an exercise in voyeurism constitutes a narrative strategy that distances middle-class spectators who are concerned yet disdainful about "how the other half lives." The hierarchical relationship between the Schultzes and the degenerate slum dwellers whom they observe thus corresponds to existing social structures reenacted in the film theater as a form of film spectatorship.

As tour guides, Maggie and Heine enact the mediatory role of narrators and affirm for the middle class its perceptions about "the other half." The function of the magic lantern slide lecturer, in other words, has been incorporated into the text as characters whose point-of-view shots provoke a moral commentary reinforced by intertitles. Alternating with such views are composite shots in which motion picture stars are inserted into the sordid environment documented by social photography. Charlotte Walker as Maggie, for example, surreptitiously visits a neighborhood pawnshop (whose owner is stereotyped in the script as "an old nearsighted Jew"), photographed in low-key lighting that shows wire cages in the dim background. A mise-en-scène remarkably similar to Riis's photo, *What the Boys Learn on Their Street Playground,* focuses on the arrival of a chauffeured limousine in the slums. A scrutiny of both the photograph and the shot in the film shows a fire escape ladder dangling over a first story shop in the background.[64] Also notable is a long shot of Steve (Raymond Hatton), Maggie's disreputable neighbor, walking on a street in front of buildings papered over with large ads for barber shops and rooming houses, a familiar scene in magazine engravings and photographs. In sum, DeMille's representational strategy of alternating point-of-view shots with composite shots heightens spectator identification with stars as well as a sense of voyeurism that exploits class and ethnic differences.

16. Actress Margaret Illington realistically portrays a working-class woman who lives in a tenement building in the stage play *Kindling* (1911).

Aside from engaging in visual strategies that reinforce class distinctions, DeMille also cast the leads in such a manner that, as in the *Chimmie Fadden* series, he muted the social commentary of melodrama. Particularly significant are differences in the characterization of Maggie on stage as opposed to on screen. As portrayed in the theatrical version by actress Margaret Illington, reviewers found Maggie "a tenement house woman with red hands, scalped hair and ill-fitting clothes," a "dull, sodden creature of the tenements"—"slow-footed, coarse-featured, awkward, dull-witted, [but] good-natured"—a woman "bowed down with toil, crushed with the hopelessness of poverty and the dreary agony of living." Characterized as "ignorant and stupid," Maggie was redeemed by her longing for motherhood, a universal sentiment that, according to critics, transcended class barriers. Although Illington was not a conventionally beautiful woman, reviewers noted that as a slum dweller she "dimmed her beauty with ugly make-up and clothes" and submitted to a "courageous subordination of frocks and beauty."[65] The stage version of Maggie, in other words, was scarcely a character with whom middle-class audiences would identify on an excursion into the Lower East Side.

In contrast, Charlotte Walker, who plays Maggie in DeMille's adaptation, was an attractive actress noted for her portrayal of Southern belles on the legitimate stage. She had played the heroine of the Belasco production of William deMille's Civil War melodrama, *The Warrens of Virginia* (a role reprised by Blanche Sweet in DeMille's adaptation). As Maggie, she bore no resemblance to Illington's oppressed but spirited working-class character. She is, quite the contrary, an ingénue type. During the credits of the film, Walker is introduced in medium shot while scrubbing clothes. The lighting from an unidentified source to the right, presumably a window, defines her rounded form as soft and feminine. Pausing for a moment, she discovers a hole in Heine's sock, becomes quite amused, and expresses loving thoughts about her spouse. As opposed to the uneducated speech of the heroine in the play or the dialect spoken by the slum characters in the film, Maggie's dialogue titles are grammatically correct. Walker, in her screen debut, thus "plays" at being a slum woman in a performance that undermines realist representation but enhances spectator identification on the part of middle-class audiences. Critics, interestingly, agreed about the superior qualities of the narrative but differed about her effectiveness in the lead.[66] As a physical type, moreover, Walker is interchangeable with actress Florence Dagmar as Miss Alice, the socialite who does charitable work in her aunt's tenement buildings. When the two women encounter each other at the dispensary, they shake hands as if they were social equals. Maggie's neighbor Bates is rebuffed, however, when she extends her hand to Miss Alice's haughty aunt in the stage version. Clearly, the film adaptation of *Kindling* demonstrates that to the extent ethnic or working-class characteristics were being effaced on the screen, the star system promoted a process of Americanization based on Anglo-Saxon standards.[67]

A comparison of the portrayal of slum dwellers in the play with those on screen shows that in addition to casting glamorous stars in the lead, DeMille diluted social commentary by denying the characters their acerbic views. Among others, Bates, Heine, and Dr. Taylor are critical, if not caustic, about tenement conditions in the stage version. Further, Heine, dismissed by the rich as a tool of "demagogues" for going on strike, reads muckraking and socialist literature and resents the voyeurism of the well-to-do. When Maggie claims that "they're just people what likes comin' around doin' good," he sneers, "Same's their children likes feedin' monkeys in the park—The poverty and trouble o' me and my family ain't made for the pleasure of no man. They can go and do their . . . playin' somewheres else."[68] Such dialogue is excised in the film adaptation. DeMille himself changed Heine's sarcastic dialogue title, "The baby died from havin' too much *food* and *sunshine!*" to "The Jones baby downstairs is dead!"[69] The film adaptation thus mutes a chorus of voices raised against class privilege, on the one hand, and heightens a sense of voyeurism, on the other, to appeal to middle-class spectators.

Attention to the details of set design gives further evidence that class oppression articulated in the stage version of *Kindling* was vitiated in the film. DeMille's talented art director Wilfred Buckland did not replicate the stage sets representing utter squalor. According to a theater critic,

> The three acts pass within the four walls of a doleful, mouldy-green room. The paper is dropping from the walls, the plaster chipped. . . . a small window gives on a well. Another is let into the back wall to light the stairs and hallway. Out there stands the common sink, used by all the tenants on the floors above. For though the law requires it there is no plumbing higher up. Indeed the whole building is a mass of bad sanitation, disease-breeding dirt, and violations . . . of city ordinances.[70]

DeMille shows the stairway of the tenement building littered with trash and in need of repair, but the Schultzes' apartment, as emphasized in the script, has a "cheerful, peaceful home atmosphere."[71] Indeed, the "picturesque" opening shot of the slums, though somber in mood, remains highly aes-theticized on account of its atmospheric lighting effects. Significantly, the Lasky Company did not add Raoul Walsh to its roster of directors because his representation of slum life in *Regeneration* (1915), filmed on location in the Bowery rather than on a set, was an unsentimental indictment of class exploitation.[72]

Despite the fact that DeMille moderated the social commentary of the stage version of *Kindling,* film critics protested the realism of the Schultzes' tour of the slums. *Variety* claimed that the two children fighting over garbage "like groveling scavengers . . . in front of one of the Hell's Kitchen hovels . . . is so strong that it is enough to cause one to become ill."[73] Genteel audiences apparently enjoyed tours of urban scenes in order to appropriate realistic detail, but not so realistic as to disturb their insulation from the poor. As a matter of fact, both the stage and film versions of *Kindling* avoid coming to grips with compelling social problems in a conclusion that is evasive and unsatisfying. Class conflict, represented according to the con-ventions of realism on stage and romantic realism on screen, remains

17. A split screen in *Kindling* shows actress Charlotte Walker envisioning an agrarian landscape in the Far West as an ideal environment for rearing her child. *(Photo courtesy George Eastman House)*

insoluble. Consequently, the only recourse is a nostalgic return to the agrarian past. When Maggie confides news of her pregnancy to Bates (Mrs. Lewis McCord), she seizes upon the suggestion that her child should be reared in an idyllic farmlike setting. A former inhabitant of Wyoming, Bates informs Maggie that "the government has a plan what would set yer up wid a farm out west." Preceding this dialogue title is a medium shot of Maggie seated on the right side of the screen in front of her neighbor. A cut to a longer shot of this same scene, after the intertitle, shows a split screen in which two children on the left play in the fields before a large farmhouse; Maggie, with hands clasped to her bosom, turns to face left as if envisioning this pastoral scene. She is quickly deflated, however, when Heine returns home with news that he is on strike. Furthermore, Alice's aunt, Mrs. Burke-Smith (Lillian Langdon), pronounces during a tour of the building she owns that "children . . . are an economic error in the tenements."

Due to increasingly straitened circumstances, Maggie accepts Mrs. Burke-Smith's offer to become a seamstress at her Fifth Avenue mansion. She even becomes an accomplice in a burglary scheme that lends credence to the fears of the well-to-do of expropriation at the hands of deprived masses.

18. Florence Dagmar as a socialite and Charlotte Walker as a tenement woman are stars representing interchangeable feminine types in *Kindling.* Thomas Meighan stands between them. *(Photo courtesy George Eastman House)*

DeMille mitigates the fact of her collusion, however, by deleting from the film an insert of a map she has drawn of the mansion's floor plan.[74] Confronted by detectives at the film's conclusion, Maggie erupts, "I lied, I fought, I stole—to keep my baby from bein' born in this hell-hole of yours!" The wealthy matron, whose rent collector ruthlessly milks the poor, arrives on the scene, becomes instantly contrite, and refuses to prosecute. Miss Alice, who has just recovered her stolen brooch from the Jewish pawnshop, remains while the other characters leave to give Heine one hundred dollars for train fare to Wyoming. As the couple dream about their prospects, a dissolve from their apartment to an extreme long shot as they walk in an airy countryside signifies a happy ending. Audiences need not pause to reflect that their meager savings will not amount to the capital outlay required for a farming venture. Class conflict, temporarily defused, is left behind as part of urban blight absent in an Edenic paradise.[75]

A film about the social consequences of industrialization and urbanization, *Kindling* articulates American ambivalence regarding the machine age. Although the U.S. Census Bureau announced the closing of the frontier in 1890, Americans clung tenaciously to the myth of the West as a safety valve for urban congestion and poverty. The Homestead Bill, enacted by Congress in 1862, had become a bonanza for railroad and land speculators rather than an opportunity for small farmers, but the image of a bountiful landscape persisted.[76] DeMille's representation of the West in wholesome terms, however, was not uncontested even at the time. Women writers who published sentimental fiction made it clear that life in the country meant, at best, unremitting toil and, at worst, brutalizing poverty and viciousness. Indeed, serious discussion about rural life as isolated, narrow-minded, and even pernicious countered nostalgia for a bucolic landscape in the late nineteenth century.[77] Although *Kindling* remains an exercise in the condemnation of urbanism in favor of the nation's agrarian roots, DeMille paired his stars, Charlotte Walker and Thomas Meighan, in a later work, *The Trail of the Lonesome Pine* (1916), that waxed far less nostalgic. Based on a novel by John Fox, Jr., and plot contrivances in *The Warrens of Virginia,* the film portrays clannish moonshiners who are incestuous, irrational, and violent in their rejection of modernity. For the most part, however, the director retained a morally ambivalent attitude toward the benefits of urban life even as he himself was seduced by the consumer culture and became one of its most celebrated architects.

CINDERELLA OF THE SLUMS: *THE DREAM GIRL*

When DeMille returned to the theme of urban slum life in 1916, he was adapting fewer plays and relied instead on original scripts by Jeanie Macpherson. She concocted a Cinderella fantasy aptly titled *The Dream Girl.* Without the constraints of realistic representation in such intertexts as melodrama, news stories, and social photography, DeMille indulged Macpherson's embroidery of a plot with striking similarities to that of *The Golden Chance* (1915), an earlier screenplay about a woman trapped in the tenements. As signified by its title, *The Dream Girl* is essentially an exercise in escapist fantasy in which an Irish girl from the slums climbs up into the social register. Unfortunately, this film—starring former Ziegfeld star Mae Murray as Meg Dugan, daughter of an abusive Irish drunk—is unavailable in an extant print, but the script and stills provide data for the following observations. Although she is destitute, Meg is so captivated by the music of an Italian organ grinder that she scampers out of bed to give the man some money. According to an intertitle in the script, her father snarls, "Since when have ye been slippin' coin to dagoes?" Anxious to escape parental wrath, Meg hides in the ash heap of a refuse dump with a treasured copy of *King Arthur.* As detailed by the script, "in the doorway of saloon loafs a cigarette-smoking youth. Bartender in shirt sleeves comes out of saloon with a paste-board box (suit box) full of rubbish—such as old papers, 'Police Gazettes' cigars and cigarette stubs (half smoked) old corks and a couple of empty whiskey bottles (small)." The defenseless heroine buried under this trash, symbolic of degenerate slum life, is obviously in need of rescue. Enter Tom Merton, a young heir in the guise of Sir Galahad at an extravagant costume party that is a private theatrical.

Placed in an orphanage after her father's death in a scheme involving con artist English Hal, Meg meets Tom as she is exploring the grounds of an institution conveniently located next to an estate. Stricken by Meg's beauty as well as by an attack of noblesse oblige, Tom decides to adopt the young girl, who interests him romantically. When his snobbish sister, Alice, protests, "You don't mean you're going to bring that girl (pointing to Orphanage) into *this* house?" he registers, "Of course she is—she's so poor, it's our duty, etc." DeMille borrows a plot contrivance from *Lord Chumley* when English Hal reappears as Lord Henry Trevor, a frequent guest at the mansion and a suitor for Alice. Unlike other slum characters, English Hal gains an entrée into upper-class circles because he is adept in the conduct of social rituals. Since the Mertons accept his credentials as a British aristocrat, he exposes self-theatricalization as a charade rather than a sign of gentility ensured by the semiotics of performance. A product of the slums, Meg has not been educated according to the Delsarte school of acting, but her naive charm appeals to the bored and decadent rich. DeMille did not expose the contradictions of the social elite and the working class fantasizing about intermarriage until he later made a Jazz Age spectacle titled *Saturday Night* (1922).[78]

According to realist conventions, the director exploits the voyeurist attitude of the rich toward the poor in *The Dream Girl* when dinner party guests decide to amuse themselves on an excursion on the Lower East Side. A rather enthusiastic group, they exclaim, "Let's go slumming!" During the ensuing tour, Meg comes face-to-face with her drunken father, whom she thought dead, and decides to reject her suitor's marriage proposal. As she explains, "If I married you—Tom—Dad couldn't mix with the highbrows—and it ain't right to leave him!" The use of the term *highbrow* to refer to social status rather than to high art reveals the extent to which cultural consumption was perceived as a sign of class. All ends well, however, when the young woman's "lowbrow" father has an unaccustomed attack of parental conscience and disappears from her life to ensure her happiness.[79] Meg's elevation to upper-class status is prophetic regarding DeMille's penchant for staging extravagant spectacles in Jazz Age collaborations with Macpherson. During the 1920s, the director became preoccupied with fantasies about how the rich live to the exclusion of considerations about how "the other half" lives. *The Dream Girl* is therefore a significant transitional film in which the grim reality of tenement life in the Progressive Era provides a starting point for the realization of consumer fantasies.

To sum up, DeMille's representation of tenement life in screen adaptations drew on a pictorial tradition in which realism existed in tension with sentimentalism. Consequently, his early feature films enhanced voyeurism and muted social commentary in order to appeal to "better" audiences. What did this articulation of middle-class ideology signify insofar as profit-driven distribution practices transcended class and ethnic boundary lines? Granted, more cultivated filmgoers were attracted to downtown theaters showcasing features such as *Chimmie Fadden* and *Kindling*, but what meaning did these features project for lower-class audiences in neighborhood venues? As texts representing the urban "Other" to themselves, the significance of screen adaptations drawing on the iconography of the cultural elite cannot be minimized. At the very least, the success of feature films based on Victorian pictorialism competed with plebeian forms of expression in an age of increasing commercialized leisure. A significant effect of film distribution practices, in other words, was the articulation of middle-class values during the recreation of the lower classes, an objective that had largely eluded Progressive reformers. Although film reception was surely mediated by class and ethnicity in neighborhood theaters, the eventual decline of plebeian pastimes, albeit largely male-oriented, meant fewer modes of self-expression based on a localized sense of community. Since workers and immigrants had previously pursued recreation in saloons, firehouses, and clubs that contravened middle-class standards of propriety, the homogenizing influence of the culture industry paved the way toward increased assimilation in decades to come.[80] The emergence of feature film as an industry standard thus meant the dominance of modes of representation associated with highbrow consumption in cinema as a mass culture phenomenon.

FOUR

The Screen as Display Window: Constructing the "New Woman"

THE "NEW WOMAN" AS A CONSUMER

A sign of profound change regarding the Victorian practice of separate spheres for the sexes, the term *new woman* first appeared in the 1890s in publications like *North American Review* and *Outlook* that reported on public affairs. At the time, the "new woman" was alternately praised as a "more independent, better educated . . . companion to husband and children" and condemned for having failed "to prove that woman's mission is something higher than the bearing of children and bringing them up." Confusion regarding the energetic, spirited, and self-reliant "new woman" who pursued white-collar jobs and interests outside the home was not restricted, however, to late-nineteenth- and early-twentieth-century discourse. Contemporary women's historians have applied the label to two succeeding but contrasting generations: college-educated women who chose to forego marriage for social activism and careers before the First World War, and boyish flappers who symbolized the Jazz Age. Whereas the older women were emotionally invested in homosocial or sex-segregated relationships, the younger women became pals in companionate marriages.[1] Yet, despite differences in the character and priorities of these two generations, they both charted new paths leading out of the privatized household. Whether social activist or flapper, the "new woman" expected to function in both the public and private spheres despite controversy regarding the nature of her role.

DeMille acquired firsthand knowledge about the enterprising "new woman" who ventured into the public sphere because his mother, Beatrice, played such a role. Although he recalled that "she never did anything publicly while father lived," the *Philadelphia Record* featured a story about her

successful career as a theatrical agent in 1906. "Never before," the newspaper claimed, "have so many women been seeking support in the business
world. . . . A good illustration of what a woman can accomplish in the world's
work is suggested by Mrs. H. C. DeMille, the mother of the author of
'Strongheart' [a William deMille play]."[2] A laudable account of her professional achievement is balanced by references to her contributions to
family life. DeMille herself failed to differentiate between private and public
spheres, however, and spoke as if the theater were an extension of the living
room. She declared forthrightly in 1912:

> This is the woman's age. . . . Every relation between the sexes has changed,
> because woman has changed. Hereafter, no woman is going to be married
> without feeling that she is getting as much as she gives. . . . This theme—
> woman's equality—lies very close to my heart. . . . Because I am thoroughly
> aroused to the vast and . . . incalculable effects of this movement, I am anxious
> to make my contribution to it through the stage, because the stage gets the
> proposition to the masses. In the present condition of society, with its wide-
> spread habit of theatregoing, one can scarcely overrate the value of the
> playhouse as a means of propaganda.[3]

When her son Cecil abandoned the stage to become a filmmaker one year
later, she witnessed the growth of the cinema rather than the theater as a
medium for articulating a redefinition of womanhood.

What was the nature of early-twentieth-century discourse on changing sex
roles signified by the diminution of separate spheres based on gender? What
was the relationship, in other words, of the motion picture frame to the
proscenium stage, department store window, and museum and world's fair
exhibits as sites for constructing the "new woman"? A preface to a discussion of specific DeMille texts, such questions require an assessment of the
changing role of women in middle-class families, or the transformation of
privatized households based on sentimental values. Although unimaginable
today, men once assumed responsibility for marketing chores in business
districts configured as strictly masculine terrain.[4] The feminization of shopping, or the conversion of women into retail shoppers that began in the
mid-nineteenth century was thus a sign of the increasing interpenetration
of home and marketplace. Stocked with an increasing abundance and array
of commodities, merchants in downtown establishments began to court
female shoppers and effected a redesign in urban topography. Chicago
planners, for example, reconstructed not only the streets of the Loop but
the entire city, heretofore a male province, in order to provide women with
access to dry-goods stores operated by audacious entrepreneurs like Potter Palmer, Levi Leiter, and Marshall Field. When Field expanded his
department store in 1902, he built a lengthy facade of huge plate glass
windows that kept thirty to forty full-time trimmers busy year-round.[5] As

signified by the display window, the redefinition of middle-class women as consumers meant their decreased privatization at the cost of their increased commodification. The labor of thrift-conscious wives in the social repro-duction of middle-class families, in other words, was superceded by self-theatricalization in elegant living rooms, lavish theater foyers, and sump-tuous department stores. Precisely how this transformation was effected, especially at the site of opulent shopping emporiums, and what it implied in terms of psychic gains and losses for women will be explored here before a consideration of specific DeMille texts.

A replication of drawing room society, the Henry C. DeMille-David Belasco melodramas, as discussed in a previous chapter, were anticipated by upper-middle-class social rituals in which actors engaged in a performance. Such forms of entertainment required a distinction between the living room, or front region, where guests were admitted, and the private quarters, or back region, where hosts need not remain in character.[6] The mechanism of social reproduction was thus carefully disguised or hidden behind the drapery and walls of tastefully furnished houses. Genteel preoccupation with appearances and performance rituals in effect constituted a form of reifi-cation in which social relations became increasingly abstract. As Georg Lukács argues:

> Reification requires that a society should learn to satisfy all its needs in terms of commodity exchange. The separation of the producer from his means of production, the dissolution and destruction of all "natural" production units, etc., and all the social and economic conditions necessary for the emergence of modern capitalism tend to replace "natural" relations which exhibit hu-man relations more plainly by rationally reified relations.[7]

An emphasis on display that disguised the means of production and social reproduction characterized not only genteel homes, but department stores like A. T. Stewart's Marble and Cast Iron Palaces as sites of consumer capitalism.[8] Within these pleasurable shopping emporiums, all traces of the manufacturing of goods and the conduct of business were kept out of sight so that objects became invested with exchange rather than use value.[9] Dry-goods merchants exploited the interdependence of cultural forms, especially the legitimate theater as highbrow culture, so that commodities became signifiers of genteel status. Accordingly, middle-class familiarity with theatrical conventions was manipulated in retail literature referring to the stage, store windows decorated as tableaux vivants, plush merchandise dis-played in simulations of living rooms, and elaborate staging of concerts, fashion shows, and pageants. Particularly noteworthy was the attempt to create an atmosphere of cultural refinement. As summed up by Zola's description of the department store as a *cathédrale du commerce moderne*, merchants transferred the experience of spiritual uplift in sentimental culture to consumer goods and the retail environment.[10] A suggestive label, Zola's term also expresses the moral contradictions inherent in modern consumption as experienced by respectable middle-class women.

Edith Wharton's rephrasing of the stricture, "Never buy anything you can do without," to describe shopping as "the voluptuousness of acquiring things one might do without" was a measure of the change in personal identity and ethics required in a consumer culture.[11] Granted, middle-class families had begun to define their status in terms of consumption so that their homes were equipped not only with modern conveniences like electricity, indoor plumbing, and central heating but also with symbols of refinement such as the piano. Signifying the reversal of an earlier movement away from urban congestion and into the confines of the privatized family, the middle-class home now began to resemble the marketplace and vice versa. When John Wanamaker unveiled a second department store in New York in 1907, an exhibit titled "The House Palatial" consisted of a summer garden and twenty-two rooms decorated in the latest styles and with period furniture.[12] Commenting on this erosion of public versus private spheres in *The American Scene* (1907), Henry James observed that the home and the market, both stocked with gleaming consumer goods, looked remarkably alike. A decade earlier, Edith Wharton pointed out the darker side of this analogy in *The Decoration of Homes* (1897) when she asserted that the drawing room, far from being a safe haven, reproduced the clutter, untidiness, and instability of the marketplace.[13]

A sign that consumption as self-gratification represented a moral crisis, retail strategy not only appropriated sentimental uplift but also exploited Orientalist images of exotic lands associated with luxury and sensuality, if not debauchery. During the second half of the nineteenth century, Americans expressed a fascination with travel in their enthusiasm for museum and world's fair exhibits, postal cards, magic lantern slides, stereographs, panoramas and dioramas, Hale's Tours, actuality footage, and so forth. As realist representation of the urban scene demonstrated, touring exotic territory was equivalent to voyeurism rationalized in pedagogical terms. What accounts for this insatiable curiosity about foreign lands and peoples? Why was Orientalism, as Edward W. Said argues, "a Western projection" or a hegemonic discourse that expressed "a systematic accumulation of human beings and territories" in theatrical form?[14] As significant aspects of genteel middle-class culture, the degree of self-control required in the performance of social rituals and the desire to travel to strange, alluring places were surely not unrelated. Orientalism, in other words, was a sign not only of psychic repression but of chronic frustration resulting from the inability to interpret the meaning of coded forms of social intercourse. Wharton, for example, described upper-middle-class life as "a hieroglyphic world where the real thing was never said or done or even thought, but only represented by a set of arbitrary signs."[15] As a result, the mysteriousness of impenetrable social observances was projected onto the enigmatic terrain of the "Other." Wharton's use of the term *hieroglyph* to describe coded rituals in privileged society implies that this psychological projection involved complex visual forms. The pictorial aesthetic of Victorian culture was in effect translated into Orientalist images of exotic and voluptuous civilizations. Vachel Lindsay, not coincidentally, had earlier used the label *hieroglyphic* to describe the explosion of visual imagery in American culture as a whole and in the cinema in particular.[16]

Within exotic shopping emporiums, the installation of hieroglyphic signs required theatrical merchandising displays such as those described by Zola in *Au bonheur des dames*. A site of consumer desire, the department store in the novel was based on the Bon Marché, an edifice with a new wing fittingly located on a street christened Rue Babylone. A carefully staged orchestration of seductive sights greeted crowds of enthralled shoppers:

> [A] sumptuous pasha's tent was furnished with divans and arm-chairs, made with camel sacks, some ornamented with many-colored lozenges, others with primitive roses. Turkey, Arabia, and the Indies were all there. They had emptied the palaces, plundered the mosques and bazaars. A barbarous gold tone prevailed in the weft of the old carpets, the faded tints of which preserved a sombre warmth, as of an extinguished furnace, a beautiful burnt hue suggestive of the old masters. Visions of the East floated beneath the luxury of this barbarous art.[17]

Spectacular displays based on the color, texture, and shape of commodities engulfed sets featuring the domes and minarets of the Middle East. A sheer accumulation of goods labeled "chaotic exotic" by Rosalind H. Williams, such exhibits broke down consumer reserve by appealing to fantasies of a luxurious, sensuous, and effeminate Orient. (The Victorian term for orgasm, it should be noted, was *spending*.) Although Orientalism was "a theatrical stage affixed to Europe" in an appropriation of the Middle East, as Said argues, in fact most of the entire non-Western world was construed as Eastern. The terms *Near, Middle,* and *Far East* implied that cartography was a scientific practice dominated by the vantage point of the West. Contrary to British and French intoxication with the Middle East, Americans became fascinated with Japanese art objects exhibited in world's fairs pavilions. Indeed, Tiffany's capitalized on a passion for Japanese artifacts, such as ceramics, lacquer ware, and bronzes, by importing goods that genteel women purchased to decorate their homes.[18] Understood within this context, DeMille's *The Cheat*, as will be discussed, assumes significant historical dimensions as a drama of gender and race relations in a consumer culture.

As the first important group of shoppers to be seduced by modern consumption, middle-class women, whose families had in the past depended on their economic reserve, now flocked to palatial department stores. Genteel consumers responded to the allure of spectacular displays behind expanses of plate glass, ready-to-wear fashions and home furnishings illuminated by electric lights, staged extravaganzas accompanied by orchestral performance, courteous and attentive service rendered by uniformed staff, and social life conducted in elegant tea rooms and restaurants. As the privatization of women in the domestic sphere had earlier signified the acceleration of industrialism, the erasure of the line between work and leisure in shopping emporiums now represented the rise of consumption. Such a momentous transition to consumer capitalism was not easily accomplished, however. Actors in a powerful drama compared to seduction and rape, women in department stores encountered a site of moral contestation where the "old" middle-class values of self-denial were démodé but not as easily discarded as last year's frocks. Octave Mouret, the entrepreneurial hero of Zola's *Au bonheur des dames*, put the matter succinctly, "the mechanism of modern commerce" depended upon "the exploitation of women."[19]

Although the contest of power ultimately proved unequal, middle-class women engaged dry-goods merchants in the arena of the department store by capitalizing on the slogan, "the customer is always right." Within the opulent environment of emporiums, they demanded courtesies and services lacking in their own homes. Abandoning their scruples, an alarming number of them bought goods their husbands refused to pay for, returned used merchandise, and indulged in theft. As early as 1857, *Harper's Weekly* referred to a "dry-goods epidemic" and "shopping mania . . . as a species of absorbing insanity" to discuss the compulsive and irrational dimension of consumption.[20] Significantly, respectable women arrested for shoplifting were unacknowledged as a sign of the moral contradictions of a consumer culture because the courts dismissed charges against them on the grounds of illness. A disease attributed to female sexuality and emotional instability, kleptomania was the result of medical discourse that provided a rationale for the ethical lapses of genteel women.[21] Albeit gender-biased, this pseudo-scientific dialogue in effect suggested that aberrant shoppers were engaging in a form of commodity fetishism, that is, the transference of desire from human beings to objects. Such conduct was a sign not only of individual pathology but of the increasing abstraction or reification of social relations in consumer capitalism.[22] A drama of frustrated desire involving repressive definitions of gender, class, and ethnicity, consumer behavior became the focus of some of DeMille's most acclaimed films in the 1910s and remained an obsession through the 1920s.

CINDERELLA ON THE LOWER EAST SIDE:
THE GOLDEN CHANCE

Toward the end of 1915, DeMille began to work increasingly with scenarist Jeanie Macpherson on original screenplays, rather than adaptations, and scored impressive hits with both *The Cheat* and *The Golden Chance*. A move that secured his claim to authorship, the decision to collaborate with a scriptwriter rather than to purchase rights to existing works was also cost-effective: Macpherson received $250 for the script of *The Golden Chance,* whereas playwright and novelist Charles Kenyon was paid an advance of $2,000 against 10 percent of the royalties for the adaptation of *Kindling*.[23] As critical acclaim for *The Cheat* and *The Golden Chance* foreshadowed, DeMille's collaboration with Macpherson would be extraordinarily productive during the silent era. The director later summed up their working relationship as follows: "She was not a good writer. She would bring in wonderful ideas but she could not carry a story all the way through in writing. Her name is on many things because she wrote with me. I carried the story and she would bring me many, many ideas."[24]

Due to studio personnel and scheduling problems, DeMille worked simultaneously on *The Cheat* and *The Golden Chance* by filming around the clock in two shifts. Production on *The Golden Chance,* which had commenced on October 26, 1915, was first delayed because of an unsatisfactory script and then halted as a result of difficulties with both the initial director and leading actress. Lasky explained to Goldwyn, "The Goodrich picture . . . has been held up on account of the scenario. . . . Cecil finally gave up trying to put the scenario into shape and he and Jeanie wrote an original which looks very good." As for the leading actress, he remarked, "Cecil claims that Goodrich is often under the influence of liquor and is altogether very stupid." DeMille, who had begun filming *The Cheat* on October 20, decided to assume direction of *The Golden Chance,* as well, to meet a scheduled release date, replaced Edna Goodrich with Cleo Ridgley in the lead, and started shooting the film on November 5. Completed first on November 10, *The Cheat* was released to enthusiastic reviews on December 13. The director continued to work on a tight schedule so that *The Golden Chance,* concluded on November 26, was premiered a mere six weeks after the domestic release of *The Cheat*.[25] Within a relatively short period of time, *The Cheat* was enshrined as part of the canon of silent cinema, especially by enthusiastic critics in war-ravaged Paris. Although overshadowed by the éclat of the earlier feature, *The Golden Chance* also received critical acclaim. Indeed, the two films are comparable in that the moral dilemma represented by women as consumers is displaced onto lower-class and racial components in the body politic. *The Golden Chance* also shows striking parallels with earlier films about tenement life such as *Chimmie Fadden* and *Kindling*. DeMille in fact recycled the set of the Schultzes' apartment in *Kindling* as a slum dwelling in the later release. According to realist conventions exploited in the earlier texts, *The Golden Chance* serves as an exercise in middle-class voyeurism with the heroine in the mediatory role of a tourist. As such, it draws a moral lesson from a conventional juxtaposition of urban rich and poor, whereas *The Cheat* not only focuses on the problematic intersection of race and gender but also prefigures consumption as Jazz Age spectacle.

An updated society drama, *The Golden Chance* introduces the characters during the credits in a succession of medium shots in low-key lighting: Mr. and Mrs. Hillary (Ernest Joy and Edythe Chapman), identified as members of the "Smart Set," are playing chess; Roger Manning (Wallace Reid), shown with his valet, is "A Millionaire" in formal dress and top hat; Jimmy the "Rat" (Raymond Hatton), dangling a cigarette from his lip, is obviously a Bowery bum. Appearing last in the sequence in separate shots are a husband and wife who, in contrast to the first couple, are clearly differentiated with respect to social class and moral standing. Steve Denby (H. B. Carpenter) is introduced in a shot in which a large beer sign dominates a darkened screen until a light gradually reveals him awakening from a drunken stupor. Mary Denby (Cleo Ridgley), identified as "His Wife," appears in a shot that, unlike the rest of the credits, is photographed from a slightly oblique angle to show her leaning out the window of a tenement building to enjoy a ray of sunshine. She waters a scraggly geranium in a pot that shares space on the fire escape with milk bottles and laundry draped over a railing.

An actress who began her career at Universal, Cleo Ridgley typifies the blond, stately, aristocratic woman who starred in director Lois Weber's feature films.[26] Appearing rather incongruous as a slum woman in *The Golden Chance*, she is, according to an insert, a judge's daughter who eloped with a "young city man of questionable reputation." A sentimental heroine in the tradition of country maidens seduced by city slickers, Mary lives to regret her decision. All too predictably, she becomes destitute and faces empty cupboards in a tenement building in a disreputable neighborhood. According to the script, Steve engineers a sex role reversal when he sneers in a dialogue title that was altered in the film, "You needn't think because you're a Van Cortlandt, that you're too good to work!" (The Van Cortlandts were Chimmie Fadden's Fifth Avenue employers in the comedy series.) Steve "indicates angrily—she is to look for a job—and right away—She says nothing, but looks straight in front of her showing the hurt and humiliation of everything he has said. He turns at the door, just as he is about to leave, to ask her emphatically if she understands what he has said about working."[27]

Contrary to the script, Mary herself decides in the film to become a seamstress at the Hillarys' residence, a turn of events similar to the plot of *Kindling*. But, whereas Maggie Schultz expresses outrage at the disparity between rich and poor, Mary is seduced by a sumptuous decor and fashionable gowns and jewelry. Aptly titled the "House of Enchantment," the mansion becomes a site of self-theatricalization and replicates a department store in its enticing display of goods. When she applies for employment,

Mary follows the maid into a living room photographed in an extreme long shot that shows a richly carpeted floor, a writing table next to an elegant floor lamp, a uniformed butler awaiting the instructions of his seated mistress, and a grand staircase with a landing between two flights of stairs.[28] After a brief interview, Mrs. Hillary leads Mary up to the second floor, or the back region of the house, where she will assume her duties as a seamstress. Already enchanted by the decor, the young woman peers curiously about her while ascending the stairs. A tapestry decorates the rear wall of the staircase, and a female statue suggestive of a manikin stands conspicuously in the foreground on the newel post of the bannister at the foot of the landing. The role of the manikin, as Stuart Culver argues, is to mediate between "consumer and commodity by tempting people to confuse themselves with things," surely an example of the reification of human consciousness articulated by Georg Lukács. The plate glass window thus "becomes a stage for the performance of a specific drama of desire."[29] An enactment of just such a drama occurs in *The Golden Chance* as the screen becomes a department store display or a site for the construction of the "new woman."

The transformation of Mary into a showpiece dramatizes a convergence of desire expressed in terms of exchange value in the reification of social relations; that is, human beings are commodified as objects, on the one hand, and objects are invested with human qualities, on the other. Signifying the dominance of the commodity form, the destitute heroine wears fashionable gowns and accessories that represent romance, the millionaire pursues a beautiful woman befitting his status, and the upper-middle-class couple convert social engagements into business deals. Downstairs, in a long shot in front of a large, gilt-framed painting, the Hillarys initiate these transactions by luring Roger Manning to their home with the prospect of meeting "the prettiest girl in the world" as a dinner guest. Paralleling the casting dilemma of the film, in which Cleo Ridgley replaced the female lead, the evening's entertainment requires a substitute for "the prettiest girl," who is indisposed. Upstairs, in the bedroom where she has finished sewing, Mary drapes a beaded gown against her body in a dimly lit shot that enhances her mood of reverie. A cut to the Hillarys, now shown in a closer medium shot, reveals their disappointment about the turn of events. Suddenly, Mrs. Hillary remembers Mary upstairs. Confronted with the proposal that she become a substitute guest as she is leaving the back region, Mary is incredulous and calls attention to her threadbare clothes. As the script indicates, "Mrs. Hillary sees gown, and watching Mary shrewdly holds up the dazzling silk against Mary—indicates how pretty she would look in it, etc. She watches this effect on Mary's face (the lure of things beautiful for a woman) as Mary capitulates."[30] DeMille cuts back and forth between front and back regions of the mansion as a prelude to the evening's entertainment in which all signs of labor will have vanished. A sense of unreality thus pervades performance rituals as the effortlessness of appearances attests to genteel control of the stage, if not the backstage, as a site of social reproduction.

As "The Substitute," Mary is showcased in an impressive entrance in a full-length gown with train, as lateral and frontal shots of her descending the grand staircase are intercut with shots of Roger, including a close-up in profile, mesmerized by her beauty. Upon their introduction, Mary and Roger are immediately linked as a romantic couple in two-shots before, during, and after dinner. DeMille himself sketched camera placements on the script to show the dinner sequence from angles that would emphasize how much the couple are absorbed with each other, as the camera pans left and right to show a guest unable to intrude on their conversation.[31] At the end of the evening's performance, however, Mary confronts her personal dilemma in the back region of the upstairs bedroom. DeMille moves his camera in for a closer medium shot as she removes a borrowed silk slipper and compares it with her worn shoe. As disembodied parts of herself, the footwear symbolizes the role that Mary will enact in the plot, that is, the tenement woman who resumes her former status as a socialite after an unhappy sojourn on the Lower East Side.

The drama of social appearances as an indecipherable hieroglyph continues when Mrs. Hillary hires Mary for a return engagment so that her husband may conclude a business deal with Roger. A revealing shot shows Mr. and Mrs. Hillary playing chess in the foreground and observing the young couple through a draped doorway in the background. DeMille is obviously staging a play-within-a-play in a complicated parlor game that escalates into a moral dilemma when Mary and Roger fall in love. At the end of the evening, Mary looks into the mirror as she is seated before a dresser and gazes at successive reflections of Roger and then her husband, Steve. A woman's personal identity and social status, in sum, is dependent upon the commodities that a man's income secures for her. During the following sequence, which is photographed in extreme low-key lighting and includes striking reverse angle shots in suspenseful moments, Orientalist fantasies about illicit sexuality and luxury abound. Goaded by Jimmy the "Rat," Steve startles Mary in a poorly executed robbery attempt by sneaking into her room in the middle of the night. Fingering her jewels and expensive lingerie with a leer, he asks, "Who's the Guy?" A blackmail scheme that further substantiates the paranoia of the rich regarding the urban masses lures Roger, now informed about Mary's plight, to the Lower East Side, but results in a fatal injury for Steve. When Roger tells Mary in a medium two-shot that her husband is dead, she responds by looking away from him to her left before the final fade-out. With her own demise as a worn-out tenement woman, Mary may now be resurrected as a socialite in a process that rep-

19. As Cinderella in an upper-class drawing room, Cleo Ridgley enchants a millionaire (Wallace Reid) in *The Golden Chance* (1915), an original screenplay by Jeanie Macpherson. *(Photo courtesy George Eastman House)*

20. After playing the role of a socialite at an elegant dinner, Cleo Ridgley sits in front of a dresser and contrasts her worn shoe with a silk slipper. *(Photo courtesy George Eastman House)*

licates fashion cycles. Fashion, according to Walter Benjamin, "is the eternal return of the new."[32]

Critic Peter Milne, who later praised DeMille in *Motion Picture Directing*, noted that the lighting in *The Golden Chance* resulted in "subdued" backgrounds against which "the characters in the foreground stand out in stereoscopic relation." Comparing the film's mise-en-scène to the stereograph, a device that heightened the spectator's sense of voyeurism and illusion of reality, Milne described the director's practice of using black drops to illuminate characters in the foreground.[33] W. Stephen Bush also called attention to "wonderful lighting effects [that] lend an indescribable charm and lustre to numerous scenes in the play. Never before have the lighting effects, i.e. the skillful play with light and shade, been used to such marvelous advantage. The highly critical spectators who saw the first display of the film were betrayed into loud approval by the many and novel effects." Acknowledging that he was at a loss for hyperbole, Bush compared DeMille's mise-en-scène with the paintings of Titian and Tintoretto.[34] Since most of the scenes in *The Golden Chance* take place indoors or at night, a high percentage of the shots were in low-key lighting that enhanced the dreamlike experience of the heroine and, given the Victorian trope of darkness and light, rendered performance rituals morally ambiguous. Further, as critics acknowledged, the lighting casts a luminous glow on sets such as "The House of Enchantment" and "picturesque" slum dwellings as images for middle-class consumption. DeMille's lighting effects, in other words, conveyed moral ambiguity, as opposed to a schematic representation of good and evil, by enhancing desire for commodities that included cinematic images for visual appropriation.

The Golden Chance serves as a primer on the construction of the "new woman" and thus comments on the compromised role of women who are seduced by goods and are themselves commodified in an unending cycle of exchange. According to F. Scott Fitzgerald, the "new woman" in the guise of a flapper was "lovely and expensive and about nineteen."[35] As a consumer, she constituted a threat to male breadwinner status due to an insatiable appetite for material goods. Charles Dana Gibson, whose shirt-waisted Gibson girl was superceded by the flapper, shows such a woman gloating as a man drowns in a *Life* drawing titled "In the Swim Dedicated to Extravagant Women."[36] As historians point out, the word *consumption* originally meant "to destroy, to use up, to waste, to exhaust" and thus signified tuberculosis in the medical lexicon.[37] Despite respectable middle-class status, the "new woman" as consumer was linked to a sinful world of luxury associated with the demimondaine. Although she symbolized modernity with her carefree manner and streamlined dress, the flapper could trace her silent-screen lineage to the vampire who devoured men without conscience to satisfy extravagant whims in films such as *The Vampire* (1913) and *A Fool There Was* (1915).[38]

A discourse on the "new woman," *The Golden Chance* displaces anxiety about female behavior in a consumer culture onto degenerate lower-class males like Steve and Jimmy the "Rat." According to the script, Mary must be shown as a wife "who does not neglect Steve—no matter how bad he is."[39] Steve, however, typifies the irresponsible drunkard censured by temperance crusaders concerned about the welfare of families. Audience reaction to his characterization should be gauged with reference to the fact that by 1911, the Women's Christian Temperance Union had become the largest women's organization in an era characterized by social activism.[40] Steve's decadence not only exculpates Mary for being deceitful but also justifies the existence of social hierarchies. But the heroine is not completely without guilt. A pawn used to attract a millionaire in both the Hillarys' business deals and her husband's blackmail scheme, Mary attempts to retain her integrity but is nevertheless compromised. When Mrs. Hillary offers her a bonus— "You have played your part admirably. Will you accept this as a token of my appreciation?"—she rejects this commodification of a romantic experience. Still, her refusal to accept an additional payment implies that to the extent she was *not* playing the role of a socialite, she was being false to her marriage vows. Despite the scapegoating of drunken, lower-class men, DeMille's resolution of the moral ambiguities of a consumer culture as confronted by women is equivocal. Significantly, the final shot of the film shows Mary looking away from Roger when he tells her that Steve is dead and thus renders the ending inconclusive.

A brief consideration of DeMille's remake of *The Golden Chance*, titled *Forbidden Fruit* (1921), is chronologically out of order in assessing his career but instructive with respect to filming upper-class consumption as spectacle. The Mallory (previously Hillary) mansion now has an arched vestibule with glass doors, gigantic potted plants, and a sunken garden, an elegant space that must be traversed before gaining entry to a high-ceilinged living room that dwarfs its occupants. Mary Maddock (formerly Denby) is still married to a shiftless bum named Steve, but she is no longer the daughter of a judge. Persuading her to play the role of a dinner guest, Mrs. Mallory (Kathlyn Williams) orders her maid to "phone Celeste—tell her to open her shop and send me her best selection of gowns, lingerie, slippers, stockings, gloves, and fans." A parade of uniformed bell boys subsequently arrives with huge packages as Mary (Agnes Ayres) receives the attention of several maids. She is seated at a semicircular dresser in an elegant boudoir with slender columns encircling a bed on a circular carpet. Unrestrained by scruples, the seamstress is delighted by the finery, removes her wedding ring, and admires a large solitaire. She also manages to pass the "ordeal by fork" with minimal assistance and plays the role of a socialite with aplomb. During one sequence, she and Nelson Rogers (formerly Roger) even attend a play-within-a-play titled *Forbidden Fruit*. DeMille interrupts this Cinderella fantasy with an even more sumptuous fairy tale in the form of flashbacks to a magnificent eighteenth-century court that is a feast for the eyes. Indeed, Mary wins forgiveness for her deception by confessing that she could not resist playing Cinderella because she was "unhappy and lonely and heart-hungry," an admission that serves as a pretext for one of the film's glittering flashback sequences. After Steve's death, an epilogue titled "Life's Springtime" provides a resolution when Nelson (Forrest Stanley) arrives with a slipper to claim his Cinderella and kisses her while holding her foot.

What conclusions may be drawn about the nature of a consumer culture from this brief account of the remake in comparison to *The Golden Chance*? First, DeMille escalates the level of conspicuous consumption in *Forbidden Fruit* so that historical flashbacks are required for more ostentatious spectacle than those afforded by contemporary life. Consumption, in other words, represents an endless cycle in which time is but another dimension of waste as history itself becomes commodified. Second, the characters evince little or no compunction about the enjoyment of luxury, although Victorian sentimentalism dictates moralizing attitudes as well as didactic intertitles. Third, Mary Maddock appears to move in the smart set with relative ease, signifying that social mobility is a result of cash rather than cultivation. And last, the commodification of film spectacle, especially in extravagant and outré flashback sequences, leaves very little to the imagination of spectators for whom visual appropriation serves as a substitute for material gratification. DeMille's film language in effect is translated into a readable hieroglyph for a mass audience that is increasingly female and that has limited access to luxury goods as displayed on the screen. Whereas *The Golden Chance* demanded some input from the spectator in response to its moral ambiguity and inconclusive ending, *Forbidden Fruit* simply requires an awestruck audience.

THE "NEW WOMAN" VERSUS
THE NEW IMMIGRANT: *THE CHEAT*

Since the heroine of *The Golden Chance* is familiar to readers of sentimental literature, DeMille's articulation of the moral contradictions of a consumer culture goes further in *The Cheat*, an original screenplay by Hector Turnbull and Jeanie Macpherson.[41] Far more than class distinctions, the significance of racial difference in early-twentieth-century America clarifies the ethical dilemma of remapping gender roles at the site of emporiums laden with Orientalist fantasies. A narrative of an interracial relationship in which a wealthy Japanese merchant (Sessue Hayakawa) brands a socialite (Fannie

21. DeMille used low-key lighting and set design with a Japanese shoji screen to dramatize an interracial relationship in *The Cheat* (1915), acclaimed as one of the great films of silent cinema. *(Photo courtesy George Eastman House)*

Ward) with a hot iron bearing his trademark, *The Cheat* still inspires frisson. Since Japan fought on the side of the Allies during World War I, the villain's ethnic, if not racial, identity was altered in the 1918 reissue that is presently in circulation.[42] An intertitle in the credits preceding a shot of the Japanese actor thus reads, "Haka Arakau, a Burmese Ivory king to whom the Long Island smart-set is paying tribute." DeMille, interestingly, changed the shot of Hayakawa described in the script: "Tori (the Japanese name of the character) is discovered seated near tables, reading magazine or newspaper, and smoking. He is dressed in smart American flannels." According to changes pencilled on the script, the director called instead for a "Scene dyed *Red*—Black Drop—oriental lamp—brazier of coals—Tori takes iron away from object he is branding—turns out light—replaces iron in brazier— his face shown in light from coals—when he puts lid on brazier screen goes black."[43] Tori, costumed in a Japanese robe, is shown in low-key lighting as he inscribes his mark, a shrine gate, on an objet d'art. (Curiously, the Japanese term for a shrine gate is *torii*.) The film thus emphasizes the racial "Otherness" of the Asian merchant, who is both fascinating and repulsive, in the first of several dramatically lit shots that won critical acclaim. Further, this scene, illuminated by the glow of the brazier on the desk and an offscreen light, was to be tinted red (as opposed to amber in the George Eastman House print) to emphasize the character's dangerous sexuality.

Richard Hardy, "a New York Stockbroker" (Jack Dean), is also seated at his desk in the credit sequence, but the shot is tinted blue rather than red or amber. Although the background has been darkened by a black drop, the character, who is feverishly poring over ticker tape and correspondence, is less dramatically lit. The businessman is thus represented as a rather pedestrian and unimaginative character. While the Japanese merchant enjoys wealth and leisure, the American stockbroker has yet to make his mark; he confides to friends who urge him to spend more time away from his desk, "It's for my wife, I'm doing it." An accepted social practice among the elite, the sexual division of labor in a consumer culture dictated that men earn and women spend as a sign of genteel status. Characteristic of middle-class marriage at the turn of the century, as Thorstein Veblen argues, was the role of the woman as a lady of leisure:

> It is by no means an uncommon spectacle to find a man applying himself to work with the utmost assiduity, in order that his wife may . . . render for him that degree of vicarious leisure which the common sense of the time demands. The leisure rendered by the wife . . . invariably occurs disguised under some form of work or household duties or social amenities, which prove . . . to serve little or no ulterior end beyond showing that she does not and need not occupy herself with anything that is gainful.[44]

Such a division of labor, it would appear, was based on traditional gender roles, but the distinction between private and public spheres was collapsing in an era of self-sufficient and energetic "new women." Mrs. Potter Palmer, for example, annexed business circles to Chicago society in fund-raising activities and thereby outmoded the practice of separate spheres for the sexes. Yet heterosexual relations in an elite social setting that contrasted with the sex-segregated world of Victorian culture were not necessarily based on equality.[45] Although DeMille represents Richard Hardy as the victim of his wife's extravagance in *The Cheat,* such a narrative strategy disguises actual control of the purse strings. As Veblen concludes, the wife is "still unmistakably . . . chattel in theory; for the habitual rendering of vicarious leisure and consumption is the abiding mark of the unfree servant."[46]

Significantly, the script of *The Cheat* juxtaposes the figure of the glamorous socialite with her maid in the credits. "Dressed in smart evening gown—Maid fitting the gown to her . . . Edith revolves slowly to get effect as though standing before a mirror. She must be pleased and happy." Although the maid is a minor character likely to be overlooked, her presence in the film is undeniably a reminder of the wife's analogous status. The uniformed servant, in other words, is a stand-in occupying the domestic space appointed for the housewife.[47] As if to underscore this reality, the maid interrupts Edith in the act of taking Red Cross funds to gamble on the stock market in a scene that occurs early in the film. The socialite is seated in front of a dresser, but the mirror shows a reflection of the maid as she brings in folded laundry. DeMille deleted the servant in the credits, however, and introduced Edith in a long shot in which she is seated on an upholstered wicker chair and pets her dog, an animal that Veblen described as a useless and thus ideal token of wealth. So that women in the audience could get a closer look at her feathered headdress and jeweled bodice, Edith stands, advances toward the camera, and greets an unseen guest, a stand-in for the spectator. A bracelet winding up her right arm is molded in the form of a serpent. Although the leisured woman is clearly aligned with the vampire, her fashionable wardrobe and surroundings disguise her actual status both in the home and in a consumer culture.

DeMille's casting of Fannie Ward to play the self-indulgent socialite in *The Cheat* capitalized on the cult of celebrity that was well established in big-time vaudeville, theater, and opera before it was typified by film stars. A stage actress whose career had been interrupted by marriage to a British multimillionaire, described as "actually rolling in gold," Ward personified conspicuous consumption. According to news and magazine articles, "her jewels and gowns created a furor" during the years she graced British society as the mistress of a country house and a London mansion. When she decided to return to the United States in 1907, the actress had in tow "three maids, two automobiles, five dogs, and a wardrobe that, with her jewels, cost a million dollars." Appearing once again on the American stage, Ward dazzled the audience with her elegant attire. "From a purely fashionable standpoint," reported *Theatre*, "the costumes worn by Fannie Ward . . . are both a sensation and an inspiration. They are the last word in modishness. They typify the light hearted woman of fashion with a love for beautiful things and the means to gratify that love." As a film star relocated on the West Coast, Ward acquired a Florentine villa touted as "the most sumptuous photoplayer's domicile in the world." The actress apparently indulged her taste for luxury without experiencing the moral constraints of sentimental culture. Fittingly, she wrote an advice column in which she counseled women, "Express your own personality in every way. And let the world feel you are going to do this because of the individuality of the clothes you wear."[48]

Publicity regarding the details of Ward's elegant attire and villa illustrates the extent to which personal identity and celebrity status were based on commodities acquired in a fashion cycle. That is to say, the Protestant notion of character based on individual ethics and social commitment was being superceded by a modernist concept of personality defined in terms of consumer goods. Such a development further weakened the traditional distinction between home and marketplace, or the Victorian practice of separate spheres for the sexes. Since respectable middle-class women in privatized households did not expect to function outside the domestic sphere, character remained a manly attribute.[49] When personality became a product of consumption, however, women assumed significance in the public sphere but at great cost to themselves. As the embodiment of commodification in theatrical spectacles designed to stimulate acquisitive behavior, they occupied center stage but played a perverse role in the enactment of Orientalist fantasies. According to Williams, the "chaotic exotic" display of department stores was based on sheer accumulation that "becomes awesome in a way that no single item could be." An exotic decor, moreover, is "impervious to objections of bad taste"—taste being an Arnoldian concept with moral as well as aesthetic implications in genteel culture. Such a decor "is not ladylike but highly seductive . . . and exists as an intermediate form of life between art and commerce." Similarly, Said defines Orientalism as "a systematic discipline of accumulation."[50] Williams's distinction between "art and commerce" has limitations in a postmodernist age, but her argument about exotic decor, sensuality, and accumulation is well taken. Zola, for example, compares the orgiastic buying sprees of women on the sales floor with the obsession of an entrepreneur for a virtuous maiden in scenes in *Au bonheur des dames* that exemplify parallel editing. The impassioned relationship between buyers and commodities, in short, is one of temptation, seduction, and finally rape, a drama rendered even more titillating by the taboo of interracial desire in *The Cheat*.

DeMille borrowed an old plot device about gambling used in *Lord Chumley* and in *The Squaw Man* to precipitate the series of events leading to seduction and rape in *The Cheat*.[51] As treasurer of the Red Cross, Edith gambles with funds meant for Belgian refugees, the film's only reference to the events of World War I, so that she may ignore her husband's plea for economies and splurge on fashionable gowns. Symbolically, the Red Cross ball is held at Tori's mansion, described in the script as a "gorgeous combination of modern luxury and oriental beauty." Guests must traverse a Japanese bridge in a richly landscaped garden to leave the mundane world behind and to enjoy the pleasures of an emporium. Although her upper-class home has a living room accented with a dark, velvety portiere, plush upholstered furniture, and a grand piano, Edith is captivated by Tori's mansion, a site replicating exotic displays in department stores. Upon arrival, guests congregate in a large living room decorated with art objects that include a statue of a Buddha in front of a folding screen. Architecturally distinctive, the room is dominated by a magnificent hanging lantern and supported by dark columns with heavy gold ornamentation in Oriental design. Assuming the role of a dry-goods merchant or a museum guide, Tori attempts to seduce Edith with priceless objets d'art during a private tour of the back region or "Shoji Room." According to a report in *Motion Picture News*, this set was filled with "novelties," including a bronze Buddha and "mysterious panels" borrowed from wealthy Japanese in Los Angeles and San Francisco.[52] As detailed in the script:

> This room is the typically Japanese room—In it are Shoji Doors—The Shrine of Buddha—A cabinet where Tori keeps his treasures—A gold screen against which stands silhouetted sharp as an etching, a tall black vase full of cherry blossoms—Near the screen stands the treasure cabinet—and a brazier of coals with small branding iron which has Tori's seal on the end—This brazier has a cover to it—On a table are several artistic curios—Over a seat is thrown a woman's gorgeous kimono—plainly a treasure of great worth—etc.[53]

As Tori opens a sliding door and extends his arms in welcome, Edith enters the room, lit in very low-key lighting, and advances to the foreground where she becomes a showpiece by posing self-consciously like a manikin draped with an exquisite kimono. She refuses, however, to accept the costly garment as a gift in what is obviously a ritual of seduction. As opposed to the ballroom scene tinted in blue, the shots in the Shoji Room are tinted amber to lend the objects a more lustrous glow. Consistent with the architecture of the house which features sliding shoji screens, the couple's movement is lateral as they occupy a series of contiguous but fragmented spaces. As Tori gestures left, they exit the frame and retreat further into the interior of the room. A cut to a medium shot shows them standing before Tori's desk laden with exotic objects. Edith is captivated by the bibelots on display, but when her curiosity about the branding tool elicits an explanation—"That means it belongs to me"—she is palpably uncomfortable and shrinks back. A cut to a longer shot of the same scene effects a change in scale that creates depth as Edith moves to the rear of the room to continue her excursion. A folding screen in the background stands beneath a vase containing a large branch of cherry blossoms whose petals rain down on her.

As if to break the spell of enchantment to anticipate a disastrous turn of events, DeMille suddenly cuts to an extreme long shot of the couple photographed from a slightly oblique high angle that is unsettling. A succession of medium shots are then intercut to show events as they occur in the front region of the ballroom and in the back region of the Shoji Room. Jones, whom Edith has entrusted with the Red Cross funds, is searching for her among the ballroom guests. A cut back to the Shoji Room shows Tori flicking on a light switch to give Edith a better view of the Buddha seated before an incense burner releasing puffs of smoke into the air. Suddenly, Jones intrudes on this backstage tour with devastating news that the charity funds have been lost. Stunned, Edith faints in front of the statue of the Buddha. Switching off a series of lights, Tori renders the interior completely dark as the film is now tinted in blue instead of amber. A cut to a blank screen, the

22. Agreeing to "pay the price" in *The Cheat* (1915), Fannie Ward accepts a ten thousand dollar check from Japanese art collector Sessue Hayakawa to avoid a ruinous disclosure. (*Photo courtesy George Eastman House*)

left half of which is part of the shoji panel, represents an adjacent space outdoors. Gradually, Tori enters the frame as he carries the socialite's body and steals a kiss before she revives. While Edith confides her dilemma to him, suddenly a light in the interior projects the shadows of Richard and Jones, who are conversing inside, against the shoji screen on the left. A reverse angle shot shows the two men on the opposite side of the screen. Richard informs his friend, "I wish I could help you—but I couldn't raise a dollar tonight to save my life." Fearful of disclosure, signified by garish newspaper headlines that appear on the darkened screen to her right, Edith agrees to "pay the price" in exchange for ten thousand dollars. DeMille makes brilliant use of lighting effects, color tinting, set design, and variations in scale and angle of shots to dramatize a ritual of seduction symbolizing the moral contradictions of a consumer culture.

The Shoji Room, at first an exotic spectacle, continues to be the scene of disastrous transactions. As opposed to coded social rituals in genteel drawing rooms, the back region remains a site where financial deals, violent emotions, and sexual desire are undisguised. After learning that her husband's stock investments have yielded a fortune, Edith attempts to renege on her deal by offering Tori a ten thousand dollar check. When he insists, "You cannot buy me off," a violent struggle ensues during which Edith brandishes a samurai sword. Tori brutally seizes her and brands her on the left shoulder with the mark of his possessions. The enraged socialite retaliates by grasping a gun and inflicting a similar wound on her assailant. A startling correspondence between these two antagonists divided by race and gender underscores the film's representation of modern consumption as a form of Orientalism or Western hegemony. Albeit the villain, Tori, like Edith, is a victim whose desire is thwarted by the arousal of desire in others in an unending cycle of exchange. Aside from the symmetry of their wounding each other on the left shoulder, the two characters are shown in matching high angle shots that show the diagonal of their fallen bodies intersecting with the line of the tatami mat. When Richard arrives on the scene moments after Edith's departure, he bursts through the shoji screen with explosive force to find Tori clutching a piece of chiffon torn from a gown. Unquestionably, this violation is a counterpart of the rape that has just occurred and is perpetrated, not coincidentally, against the Japanese merchant by an enraged husband. Attempting to shield his wife from her crime, Richard too engages in duplicity as he assumes blame for the shooting and is imprisoned. When Edith visits him in jail, DeMille projects the shadows of the characters and the vertical bars of the cell onto the rear wall in a succession of riveting shots. As in the scenes in the Shoji Room, the positioning of the figures in terms of light and dark areas of the frame signifies emotional states corresponding to ethical dilemmas. Paralleling this melodrama, it should be noted, were equally histrionic events that blurred the line between reality and representation. Jack Dean and Fannie Ward were married after a lawsuit in which Dean's first wife accused Ward, then a widow, of alienation of affection.

Within the historical context of urban immigration and resurgent nativism in the early twentieth century, what does the dramatic courtroom conclusion of *The Cheat* signify? Specifically, what message is being conveyed in the form of Orientalism as a Western discourse regarding American relations with an emergent Japan? Although Americans responded enthusiastically to Japanese exhibits of precious objets d'art at world's fair pavilions in Philadelphia, New Orleans, Chicago, and Saint Louis, their fascination was a sign of profound ambivalence. As Neil Harris argues, Americans projected their own equivocal response to modernization, industrialism, and immigration onto Japan, a nation whose artwork was still the product of exquisite craftsmanship even as its government began to Westernize.[54] Given anti-Asian sentiment on the West Coast, where the Chinese had long been brutally oppressed, admiration for Japanese artifacts did not translate into a welcome for new immigrants. A negotiated Gentlemen's Agreement with Japan, therefore, restricted further entry of Japanese laborers, and state legislators barred Japanese immigrants from land ownership and citizenship.[55]

The tense courtroom drama that concludes *The Cheat* is highly charged with the politics of nativism and racism characteristic of the era. At the beginning of the proceedings, the camera pans across the jury box to show twelve white men in three-piece suits as representatives of the status quo. As the trial progresses, DeMille uses a number of masked medium close-ups of the principals to reveal their emotional reaction to crucial testimony. During a sensational moment following the announcement of a guilty verdict, Edith proclaims her guilt and disrobes to reveal the scar that vindicates her actions. The sympathetic courtroom crowd, which has become all male in the final shots, erupts in anger and surges forward in a scene recalling a lynch mob. In fact, the script characterizes the situation as a "riot" in which the audience shouts, "Lynch him! Lynch him!" (referring to Tori) and urges men to "right the wrong of the white woman."[56] As noted in *Moving Picture World*, "the wrath of the audience bursts forth with elemental fury and there ensues a scene that for tenseness and excitement has never been matched on stage or screen." Equally impressed, the *New York Dramatic Mirror* described the courtroom scene as "one of the most realistic mob scenes that has ever been produced upon the screen."[57]

Since DeMille himself penciled on the script the clichéd intertitle, "East is East and West is West, and never the twain shall meet," the message of the film about race relations is clear. In sum, *The Cheat* is a statement about the impossibility of assimilating "colored" peoples, no matter how civilized their veneer, and warns against the horrors of miscegenation. When the courtroom crowd attempts to attack Tori, it recalls lynch mobs that murdered blacks with impunity in a segregationist era of Jim Crow laws. Within the context of early-twentieth-century demographics, protest against Asians and African Americans also represented paranoia about the new immigrants from southern and eastern Europe. At the time, Congressman Oscar Underwood called for a literacy test to restrict immigration by claiming that the nation's purity was being threatened by the mixture of Asiatic and African blood coursing in the veins of southern Europeans.[58]

Although nativism and racism are obviously linked in *The Cheat* as a response to the new immigration, the relationship of these political developments to the "new woman" as a consumer is more complex. As homologous threats to the social formation, women and racial groups may be substituted for each other in considerations of the body politic. A lurid aspect of Orientalism as a Western discourse, moreover, is the characterization of the East as effeminate and subject to colonial rape. A sign of their correspondence, Edith and Tori wear similar costumes in the film's early sequences. During an outing, for example, the socialite appears in a striped coat lined with fabric in a bold, checkered pattern, while Tori wears a striped shirt and dons a plaid cap. Yet Edith is rehabilitated as a repentant wife through objectification of her body as a courtroom spectacle, a strategy that reinforces sexual difference to offset the diminution of separate spheres in Victorian culture.[59] Consumer behavior as a sign of modernity, in other words, is recuperated by sentimental values. Such a narrative strategy displaces anxiety about the "new woman," which was considerable, onto the racial "Other." Nevertheless, women's extravagant behavior was stereotyped as childish, if not deceitful. According to the script, when Richard reprimands Edith for a bill totalling $1,450 worth of gowns and negligees, he "indicates some displeasure, but his attitude is that of one talking to a spoiled child—not angry."[60] Yet women's inability to resist merchants and advertisers who lured them to department stores, labeled an "Adamless Eden," surely provoked disquieting thoughts about the nature of female sexuality.[61] Discourse on kleptomania as a function of the womb was, therefore, a symptom of larger concerns regarding the viability of traditional definitions of gender. Attempts to regulate sexual behavior and the body, including the medical categorization of women as kleptomaniacs, were part of tactics to impose order on a pluralistic urban environment. As women's historians demonstrate, such policing attempts intensified during periods of rapid social change and upheaval.[62]

If Edith's questionable behavior is interpreted as a woman's response to her ambiguous role in a consumer culture, what, then, may be said about Tori as a Japanese merchant and art collector? According to Grant McCracken, "the cultural meaning carried by consumer goods is enormously more various and complex than the Veblenian attention to status was capable of recognizing." Commodities do not necessarily constitute the locus of irrational and ungovernable desires, nor are they merely objects acquired during lapses of ethical judgment.[63] Granted, this may be the case today, but a discussion of Progressive Era consumption that does not account for the legacy of sentimentalism and evangelical Protestantism is an exercise in decontextualization. Yet McCracken's observations are useful in decoding the actions of the Japanese merchant as a hieroglyph that requires an investigation of meaning invested in objects. Genteel familiarity with world's fair exhibits as an intertext in middle-class culture accounts for the characterization of Tori as an art dealer. Since his enormous wealth renders consumption meaningless, Tori is no longer a consumer but a collector of rare objets d'art ritualistically branded with the mark of his possession.[64] Although department stores, museums, and world's fairs were interchangeable in terms of architectural design and displays meant to spur consumption, these institutions also served as social agencies with a mission to educate public taste. According to this logic, the Japanese merchant has learned his lesson well and seeks assimilation in American society. For him, Edith is not simply prized as a beautiful woman who represents a tabooed relationship; as the ultimate bibelot, she symbolizes his acceptance as an art collector in an elite society that marks him as alien.[65] Anticipating their rendezvous, Tori is even more sumptuously arrayed than the fashionable socialite. Consequently, when Edith reneges on her bargain, he possesses her by force in accordance with an established ritual signifying ownership. When she later changes her mind and offers herself willingly so that charges against her husband will be dropped, Tori replies impassively, "You cannot cheat me twice." Edith is labeled "The Cheat" because she has denied the Japanese merchant assimilation into privileged white society.

Unquestionably, the enthusiastic reception accorded *The Cheat* was in large measure due to Hayakawa's riveting screen presence. Film critics unanimously singled out his subtle acting style, described as "the repressive, natural kind, devoid of gesticulation and heroics," because it not only contrasted with the melodramatic stage posturing of Fannie Ward and Jack Dean but rendered the villain a complex character. As Hayakawa stated in a fan magazine interview, "If I want to show on the screen that I hate a man, I do not shake my fists at him. I think down in my heart how I hate him and try not to move a muscle of my face. . . . The audience . . . gets the story with finer shades of meaning than words could possibly tell them." The Japanese actor in effect triumphed over the racist characterization of Tori in a script that stereotyped him as bowing with "oriental deference," having "a *slow* Oriental smile" or an "enigmatic smile," registering "sinister satisfaction," and crouching like an animal with "eyes narrowing" and "nostrils breathing hard."[66]

Catapulted into stardom, Hayakawa became one of the most important male stars on Famous Players-Lasky's roster and preceded Rudolph Valentino as an exotic matinee idol for female filmgoers.[67] Predictably, his screen persona remained charged by the fiendish role he played in *The Cheat*, a part that aroused protest in Japan and in Japanese-American communities. Publicity stories emphasized his bellicose nature and gave detailed descriptions of the ritual of hara-kiri. *Photo-Play Journal* informed readers, "You can 'take it from us,' this popular Japanese artist can scrap. His efficiency in the art of belligerency may be due to his fondness for it. In fact, he'd rather fight than eat any day. . . . Sessue is a formidable rival either at boxing or jui-jitsu [*sic*]." *Motion Picture Classic* claimed, "in his customs and manners and conversation he is American to the finger-tips, but one always feels . . . there is the soul of some stern old Samurai."[68] Ultimately, the Japanese were unassimilable, not least because Japan's rise to global power was perceived as a threat to the United States in violation of Orientalism as a hegemonic discourse.[69]

Since canon formation is a political enterprise, an inquiry into reasons for recognition of *The Cheat,* as opposed to other titles in DeMille's filmography, further illuminates the issue of the new immigration in relation to the "new woman." Aesthetic considerations with respect to visual style, such as low-key lighting with dramatic use of shadows or mise-en-scène including a high ratio of medium shots, were obviously significant in the film's reception at a time when the industry sought cultural legitimacy.[70] Critics singled out the film's sensational lighting. According to *Moving Picture World,* "the lighting effects . . . are beyond all praise in their art, their daring and their originality." A reviewer for *Motion Picture News* claimed that "the picture should mark a new era in lighting as applied to screen productions." Sociological issues, however, were hardly negligible in the film's reception and elevation to canon status. The *Photoplay* critic focused on *The Cheat* as "a melodrama . . . full of incisive character touches, racial truths and dazzling contrasts"; he rightly predicted that the story was so novel it would appear before footlights.[71] Charting a reversal of the usual trajectory, *The Cheat* was adapted for the legitimate stage in the United States and as an opera in France (where it was retitled *Forfaiture*). Paramount remade the film twice, and a French filmmaker shot a European version as an homage that also starred Hayakawa.[72] Without minimizing DeMille's superb achievement, the enormous success of *The Cheat* must be understood within the context of an era of rapid urban change that provoked discourse on the "new woman" and the new immigration as ideologically charged subjects.

As a footnote, it should be observed that the acclaim accorded *The Cheat* may well have profited from hindsight. William deMille stated in his account of the early silent film era that *The Cheat* became "the talk of the year." Yet an examination of trade journal literature shows that *Carmen* (1915) received far greater publicity as a result of the screen debut of Metropolitan Opera soprano Geraldine Farrar. Samuel Goldwyn recalled in his autobiography that *The Cheat* catapulted DeMille "to the front" rank of film directors and "was a first real knockout after a number of moderate successes." Again, trade journal literature and DeMille's financial statements indicate otherwise. But *The Cheat* did earn foreign receipts that were considerably higher than those posted for DeMille's earlier features, an indication that overseas reception of the film was quite exceptional. At the time of its release, Jesse L. Lasky did claim that *The Cheat* had "equalled if not surpassed" *Carmen* and rated the film as "the very best photoplay" his company had produced. Indeed, he had written to Goldwyn, "At last we have a picture with a wonderful, absorbing love story, with plenty of drama, and original in theme. Cecil has surpassed all his other efforts as the direction is absolutely perfect." Possibly, William deMille and Goldwyn were influenced in their recollections by French critics like Louis Delluc whose response to *The Cheat* was nothing short of adulation comparable to reception later accorded *Battleship Potemkin* (1925). Astonished by DeMille's brilliant achievement, French intellectuals began to consider film as a serious art form. And as a further sign of bourgeois respectability, *The Cheat* drew crowds for ten months at a theater on the fashionable Boulevard des Italiens.[73]

THE SENTIMENTAL HEROINE VERSUS THE "NEW WOMAN": *THE HEART OF NORA FLYNN*

After filming two more adaptations, *Temptation* (1916) and *The Trail of the Lonesome Pine* (1916), DeMille again collaborated with Hector Turnbull and Jeanie Macpherson on *The Heart of Nora Flynn* (1916). The *New York Times*, interestingly, praised the feature as "an excellent example of the modern photodrama as opposed to the film founded on a story or stage play." DeMille, however, expressed the contradictions involved in the studio's transition from adaptating intertexts in genteel culture to filming original screenplays for a broader audience. Since he was in the habit of personally inspecting exhibition venues, the director called attention to the need to update film titles as marquee attractions. As he wrote to Lasky, "we are inclined to be a little too high-brow. I have noted two pictures . . . playing opposite each other. . . . Going Straight has been jammed all week and A Gutter Magdalene has been starving to death. The Heart of Nora Flynn proved to be an awful lemon as have the titles of many of our recent productions."[74] Whatever the merits of its title, which was indeed sentimental, the film marks a transition in the director's body of work during the Progressive Era. As such, it may be read as a sequel to *The Cheat* in its representation of gender, class, and ethnicity as these intersect in a consumer culture.

The screen in *The Heart of Nora Flynn*, as in *The Cheat*, simulates a display window for the well-to-do whose conspicuous consumption conflicts with personal ethics. During the credits, all the characters, with the exception of playboy Jack Murray (Charles West), are lit against black drops in medium shots as they fantasize about desired objects in a mood of reverie. Mrs. Brantley Stone (Lola May), obviously a lady of leisure, reclines on a chaise longue with a lap dog and takes tea from a silver service. A cut to an extreme close-up shows the details of her lustrous pearls and lace-trimmed negligee as she stares at an image of Jack inside her teacup. By contrast, Brantley Stone, described as "A Man of Means" (Ernest Joy), is introduced in a shot similar to that of Richard Hardy in the credits of *The Cheat*. Seated at his desk, he is busily poring over ticker tape and correspondence, but he smiles when miniature figures of his wife and children appear on his desk. Unfortunately, his happiness evaporates when his wife sends the toddlers away and greets her friend Jack. Appearing next in the credits are the two Stone children, Anne (Peggy George) and Tommy ("Little Billie" Jacobs), seated on a wicker chair and looking at an album. Nolan, a hot-tempered chauffeur (stage and vaudeville actor Elliott Dexter), is working behind the hood of a stately and well-polished limousine. Finally, Marie Doro, a comedienne whose theatrical career was promoted by Charles Frohman, appears in the role of Nora, the "Irish Nurse Maid." Preparing the children's bath, she appears rather wistful. A cut to a medium close-up shows her holding a child's outfit while the superimposed image of the man she hopes to marry, Nolan, appears to her left. (In fact, Doro and Dexter were married for a brief period in real life.) Since the lady of leisure and the Irish maid are the only characters privileged with close-ups, the film announces itself not only as a morality tale about the ethics of the domestic sphere but also as a drama about female desire.

A film that may be construed as *The Cheat* narrated from the viewpoint of the maid standing in for the wife, *The Heart of Nora Flynn* contrasts the self-absorbed "new woman" with the sentimental heroine. At the beginning, Nora instructs Anne, who preys on goldfish, "Have all the fun ye want, darlin' but don't get it by hurtin' someone else"—a lesson the child's self-indulgent mother must learn as well. While Mr. Stone devotes long hours to business deals, Mrs. Stone neglects the children and engages in a dangerous flirtation with Jack. An obliging "man about town" who has just acquired a luxurious, cream-colored roadster, he sends her notes that read, "I've a perfect peach of a new car . . . take a little spin with me. It's the color you like." Unhappily, this situation escalates into a sensational turn of events one evening when Mrs. Stone decides to abandon her husband and children and to abscond with her lover. As in *The Golden Chance* and *The Cheat*, DeMille uses dramatic low-key lighting to construct a tableau that dramatizes the moral dilemma of the characters. Indeed, he specified lighting effects in the script for some of the film's most impressive scenes.[75] A medium long shot of the living room, for example, is lit only by the glow of a table lamp illuminating the lower half of the screen as the couple secretly meet and prepare to depart. A cut to an exterior long shot shows the headlights of Mr. Stone's chauffeured limousine as it speeds toward the house. A cut back to the interior shows the headlights flash through the window and briefly illuminate the surprised guilty couple. Startled, Jack turns off the table lamp to plunge the room into darkness.

Practically exposed with her lover, Mrs. Stone appeals to Nora to hide Jack: "The future of my home—my babies—*everything* is in your hands!" Unfortunately, Jack takes refuge in Nora's room in the back region upstairs while Nolan, infuriated by what he construes as a betrayal, breaks down the door and shoots the scoundrel. As in *The Cheat*, a jealous man spends the night in jail, but the scene is pedestrian compared to the dramatic use of low-key lighting and shadows of despondent figures in the earlier film. DeMille appears in this instance to be quite uninterested in quoting from his own work. Upon his release, Nolan is tailed by reporters who ask, "Did it ever occur to you that your sweetheart has been used as a 'Cat's-paw'?" Despite the chauffeur's entreaties that she reveal the truth to newsmen, Nora appears willing to sacrifice not only her reputation but her employment for the sake of the children. Discharged by an employer who tells his wife, "I won't have *her* kind of woman contaminating you and the children," Nora at first pleads with Mrs. Stone, "You've got to tell Nolan it's you and not me that's bad." Confronted with Mrs. Stone's own desperation at being exposed, however, the maid consoles her in a medium two-shot that conveys an intimacy impossible between two women who are not social equals. A medium shot invites sympathy for Mrs. Stone's dilemma because she is next shown alone in a room with a gilded bird cage. After dismissing the reporters, Nora tells her mistress, "I don't want any thanks, ma'am but you've got to promise not to see him again!" Silently witnessing the pact between the two women, the wounded "man about town" hovers in the extreme lower right hand corner of the frame, a sign of his irrelevance. A cut to the neglected children shows them waiting in the hallway; in the next shot, Mrs. Stone embraces them for the first time in the film.

As for Nora, her real loss is neither her reputation nor her employment, but Tommy. A delightful child, he is inconsolable when she leaves the mansion and he gives her his favorite toy, a wooden duck, as a token of his affection. DeMille orchestrates a heart-wrenching farewell sequence by intercutting medium shots of the sobbing child staring into dappled sunlight, long shots of Nora and Nolan as they walk away from the estate, and a reverse angle shot of Tommy as he lays crumpled on the bench window seat inside his room. The director was so skillful in eliciting performances from child actors that their absence from his later work is regrettable. In the final shot of the film, Nolan comforts an equally desolate Nora by offering her a branch with orange blossoms to signify their future together.

DeMille singles out *The Heart of Nora Flynn* rather than *The Cheat* in his autobiography as a film that "was praised for its lighting effects. 'An automobile charging along a dark street, with only the lights and the reflection of the street lamps on the pavement visible' seems commonplace now," recalls the director, "but it was deemed worthy of special mention in *The Motion Picture News*."[76] A film that relies heavily on intertitles in addition to lighting to convey a moral lesson, *The Heart of Nora Flynn* dramatizes the contradictions of a consumer culture according to a conflicting visual strategy. A scrutiny of the reviews shows that the critics themselves were divided about ambiguities in the film. As the *New York Dramatic Mirror* complained, "one or two of the subtitles could have been greatly improved, as they lent a decidedly false note to an otherwise realistic production." *Variety* described the film as "one of those self-sacrificing yarns, on the 'Peg' lines, in which a little Irish maid . . . saves her mistress from being compromised." The *Motion Picture News* concluded, however, "it is needless to speak of artistry where the DeMilles are concerned. There seems to be a deftness about their touch . . . understood by persons who never even heard the word 'art.' " *Moving Picture World* concurred: "Of the splendid lighting effects, the superb settings and realistic atmosphere it is not necessary to say much on a Lasky production."[77]

Signifying contradictions involved in the redirection of the privatized family outward toward consumption and commercialized leisure, DeMille's discourse on the "new woman" endorsed the values of the "old" as opposed to the "new" middle class. Such ambiguity permeated the film's narrative strategy. As critics observed, the director relied heavily upon the use of intertitles to convey a sentimental message that conflicted with a technically advanced visual style. Although DeMille's mise-en-scène drew upon the legacy of Victorian pictorialism as an intertext, lighting setups not only reinforced moral lessons but also enticed spectators by imparting a luster to expensive commodities like home furnishings and automobiles. The representation of material goods, in other words, was seductive and contradicted didactic intertitles. Silent cinema, like other cultural forms in the genteel tradition, privileged sight as the key to spectacle in an era of increased conspicuous consumption.[78] As symbolized by the self-indulgent "new woman" in *The Cheat* and *The Heart of Nora Flynn*, however, the pleasures of self-gratification were not as yet unambiguously inviting. Guilt was thus displaced, on both a literal and symbolic level, onto the working-class, ethnic, and racial "Other" while the "new woman" was recuperated according to sentimental values.

DeMille later maintained, in his role as a cultural steward, that the cinema promoted understanding across class and ethnic, if not racial, barriers; he asserted: "the screen has made good progress in teaching the lower grades of society that every rich man is not purse-proud and heartless and in disabusing the minds of the upper ten of the belief that every laboring man goes home . . . and beats his wife and children."[79] Yet his Progressive Era films preserved class, ethnic, and racial hierarchies in an articulation of genteel middle-class ideology. To be sure, the traditional line between separate spheres based on gender was also redrawn according to Victorian social practice. As demonstrated by *The Golden Chance, The Cheat,* and *The Heart of Nora Flynn,* however, the "new woman" was constructed as spectacle for display in the front region through spatial exile of the urban "Other" to the back region. Although the Irish, or old, immigrants—unlike the Japanese, or new, immigrants—were assimilable in a future increasingly dominated by popular rather than genteel culture, the director's work attests to fault lines in the body politic during a period of rising nativism and racism. Apart from describing the terrain of the respectable middle-class home as a site of self-theatricalization, the terms *front* and *back region* also serve as a useful metaphor for exploitive class, ethnic, and racial relations in consumer capitalism.

FIVE

The Historical Epic and Progressive Era Civic Pageantry: *Joan the Woman*

A USABLE PAST: CIVIC PAGEANTS AS HISTORICAL REPRESENTATION

DeMille began work on his first historical epic, a production about Joan of Arc starring Geraldine Farrar, before a successful negotiation for the Lasky Company's merger with Famous Players was announced in July 1916. Several weeks prior to shooting, the director was consumed with historical research, scriptwriting problems, casting decisions, costume designs, and construction of elaborate interior and exterior sets.[1] A two-color process, advertised on souvenir programs as the "Wyckoff Process" (also known as the Max Handschiegl process), was developed for use in specific sequences in addition to standard color tinting.[2] For musical accompaniment, DeMille hired David Belasco's composer, William Furst, to write an orchestral score that would be synchronized with various projection speeds.[3] When the director's name was omitted from ads run in *Theatre*, *Vogue*, and *Motion Picture Mail*, Arthur S. Friend, sensitive to the authorship issues involved, mollifed him with an apologetic letter. Friend wrote reassuringly, "We . . . will make the exploitation of your first big picture the most lavish and impressed exploitation ever given to anything offered to the theatres in this country."[4] Accordingly, exhibitors replicated museums in the lobbies of first-run theaters by displaying suits of armor, historical costumes, colorful banners, and murals framed by drapery embroidered with fleur-de-lys.[5] DeMille even furnished his own office in Gothic style and filled it with mementoes from the production. So that he could supervise details of the film's exhibition, the director traveled to New York, where *Joan the Woman* was premiered at the Forty-fourth Street Theatre on Christmas Eve, 1916.

117

23. De Mille and his leading lady, Geraldine Farrar, pose with a statue of Joan of Arc to publicize *Joan the Woman* (1916).

Although widely acclaimed, DeMille's first historical epic, a genre that became his trademark in later decades, did not attract large crowds to the box office. When the filmmaker returned to Los Angeles, Jesse L. Lasky wrote:

> The advertising has been . . . increased until I do not think any production has received quite the newspaper boosting that "Joan" has received. . . . The receipts have been a bit discouraging. . . . It has really puzzled us all—I mean the fact that everyone is talking about the picture and praising it in the highest terms and yet business is nothing like it should be.[6]

Admittedly, the film's length, 10,446 feet—or thirteen reels totalling more than two hours—was excessive; indeed, theater owners complained that they could not schedule the customary two matinees and two evening shows per day. B. Barnett, a states rights exhibitor, wrote to Lasky in May 1917:

> We own the rights for Ohio and Michigan of . . . 'Joan.' We found after having shown same at the principal cities of Ohio, viz, Cincinnati, Cleveland, Toledo, Youngstown, etc., meeting with absolutely no financial success but on the contrary with losses, after having given it the presentation that your organization would have been proud of. . . . I would suggest that this picture be cut down.[7]

A pragmatist, DeMille agreed that states rights buyers be allowed to cut the film to eight reels, a considerable reduction, but he insisted on retaining the prologue and epilogue relating the narrative to trench warfare then occurring in France.[8] Undoubtedly, many exhibitors advertised and retained scenes of historical spectacle, such as the siege of Orléans and the coronation of Charles VII, and cranked up the projection speed for the rest of the film.

Apart from the excessive screening time required by a special feature, the film's title, *Joan the Woman,* proved to be a drawback in exploitation strategies. The director recalled, "Jeanie Macpherson wanted me to use that title and I did. I listened to her arguments and was convinced . . . but it was a mistake, because people did not know that it was Joan of Arc."[9] An auteur whose name became synonymous with historical spectacle, DeMille failed at the box office with his first epic, an effort that did not accrue profit relative to cost nor the amount of time involved in production.[10] The director produced only four features in 1916, compared to thirteen in 1915, because he devoted so much energy to his first costume drama. Scrutinizing the balance sheet, Lasky advised his colleague to "get a subject modern in theme" for his next special.[11] Yet *Joan the Woman* remains an interesting case study because it demonstrates that feature films articulating genteel middle-class ideology had limitations in appealing across class and ethnic barriers. Such was especially the case in marketing constructions of the past as highbrow culture rather than as a legacy transcending cultural diversity. Since history was a lofty and noble subject that represented an ideological consensus among the elite, their conceptualization was not inclusive enough to provide the basis for a broad sense of community. As a matter of fact, working-class unrest and seemingly unassimilable immigrants were threatening social cohesion at a time when there was controversy about military preparedness. On the eve of war the nation was by no means united in its response to German aggression. DeMille's first epic, bracketed by scenes of trench warfare in France, continued the tradition of civic drama that articulated the historical consciousness of the local elite rather than a shared sense of national origins. As such, it was antimodernist both in its vision of an urban society rooted in an idealized past and in its representation of history as an inspirational series of tableaux.[12] Understanding the reasons for the box-office failure of *Joan the Woman* first requires a consideration of civic pageantry as an intertext that defined public history for the genteel classes but excluded the urban "Other."

Linda Nochlin sums up the *Pageant and Masque of St. Louis,* held at the height of the pageantry movement before America entered the war, as "a premonition of Cecil B. DeMille in its ambitious crowd-spectacles—choruses and Pioneers, World Adventurers and 'multitudes of men and women, garbed in the native costumes of all nations,' and reminiscent of Longfellow's Hiawatha in its speech."[13] Although community leaders envisioned pageants as an alternative to the passive consumption of commercialized amusement, historical reenactments undoubtedly influenced filmmakers as intertexts in the production of spectacles. A municipal project sponsored by the cultivated elite, civic drama had histrionic antecedents in upper-middle-class performance rituals that defined the self in relation to others. Amusement that had previously been translated from elegant parlors to ornate theaters now provided the basis for an articulation of history on an immense public stage. As David Glassberg argues, civic pageantry was a continuation, albeit on a monumental scale, of tableaux vivants of historical events reenacted in parlor theatricals and mounted on floats for parades and processions. A movement that attempted to transform recreation into a celebration of local history to instill patriotic, aesthetic, and moral uplift, pageantry was an antimodernist phenomenon in its nostalgic invocation of civic culture as a bulwark against modernization. Although there were some attempts to recognize and include ethnic groups in the festivities, pageants reinforced existing hierarchical relations and projected a conservative view of social change in representations of history as linear progression. A succession of historical episodes as civic drama in effect dramatized the pictorial unfolding of divine revelation as conceptualized by the genteel classes. Despite its conservatism, the pageantry movement was nevertheless related to the New History articulated by Progressive historians, largely sympathetic to urban reform, because both constructions of a usable past emphasized social and economic as well as political issues.[14] Yet a selective and pragmatic approach to history in terms of its present usefulness had implications not only for an agenda of democratic reform but also for the commodification of the past as a form of commercialized amusement. Ultimately, the consumption of spectacle as visual appropriation rather than Progressive historiography, confined within the halls of academe, provided the basis for a shared sense of national identity and historical consciousness advocated by the proponents of civic theater.

Undoubtedly, the most celebrated historical spectacle of the era was the *Pageant and Masque of St. Louis* held in 1914. Written by Thomas Wood Stevens and Percy MacKaye, son of theatrical producer Steele MacKaye and a leading exponent of civic theater, the event was publicized in a manner anticipating DeMille's epics. Roger N. Baldwin of the Civic League of Saint Louis described the enormous setting of the production: "The drama will take place in a great natural amphitheater seating 60,000 persons and 7,500 men, women and children [and a chorus of 750 voices] will take part. The stage, thrown across one of the lagoons left from the World's Fair of 1904, will be the largest ever constructed." (The reproduction of a Mayan temple at center stage prefigures DeMille's even more massive set for an Aztec spectacle titled *The Woman God Forgot* [1917].) Charlotte Rumbold, secretary of the city's Public Recreation Committee, described the production committee as "organized into sub-committees on book, music, cast, costumes, properties, dancing, lighting and wiring, stage management, stage setting, and auditorium." Production expenses for this mammoth reenactment of three centuries of local history exceeded $125,000. Demonstrating an outburst of civic pride, an estimated half-million citizens witnessed four separate marathon performances lasting over five hours. The pageant itself consisted of a series of realistic historical episodes, whereas the masque was an allegory regarding the cosmic significance of the rise and fall of civilizations. Glowing with success, Rumbold characterized the spectacular effort as a "democratization of administration of public recreational facilities." Similarly, Baldwin claimed, "groups of citizens who have never known of one another's existence have been brought together." And yet, unassimilable racial groups such as Native Americans and African Americans, as well as labor unions with suspect ideological beliefs, were not invited to participate. Glassberg concludes that the civic event catapulted Saint Louis into the front ranks of the pageantry movement, but that its "forbidding length and 'highbrow' pretentions did little to endear it among the masses to whom it was directed."[15] A similar conclusion is warranted about the commercial failure of DeMille's first spectacle, *Joan the Woman*.

Although civic theater was sponsored by the genteel classes as a means of articulating a teleological vision of history in relation to a conservative definition of community, the Paterson Strike Pageant of 1913 showed that immigrants and workers could appropriate spectacle for their own ideological purposes. Following the lead of Greenwich Village radicals like John Reed, who had acted in one of Percy MacKaye's productions at Harvard, approximately fifteen hundred Italian, Polish, and Jewish silk workers reenacted scenes from an ongoing, protracted, and bitter strike in Paterson, New Jersey. Robert Edmond Jones, later acclaimed for his set design of Eugene O'Neill plays, staged the pageant in Madison Square Garden, bedecked for the occasion with red banners of the International Workers of the World. John Sloan, who was then a contributor to *The Masses,* painted a two-hundred-foot-wide backdrop representing the silk factory as a grim construction with smokestacks. Dispensing with boundaries signified by the theater curtains of the proscenium stage, the performers emerged from the back region to redefine the public sphere as they sang the *Marseillaise* and the *Internationale* while marching down Fifth Avenue to the Garden. During a reenactment of a May Day parade, they also marched through the audience to eliminate barriers between participants and observers. I.W.W. organizers Bill Haywood and Elizabeth Gurley Flynn delivered stirring speeches as part of a program of five episodes representing the events of the strike. Production costs for this unprecedented spectacle amounted to over $7,000 so that a net gain of only $384 for the strikers' relief fund was reported. Granted, the workers eventually lost their cause, but for a few hours on the night of the pageant, the letters *I.W.W.* flashed in red electric lights to illuminate the public space of the respectable middle class.[16]

After the United States entered the war, the pageantry movement focused on the necessity to create a national allegiance rather than local pride, but motion pictures soon eclipsed such community efforts.[17] Distributed a few months before full-scale mobilization began, DeMille's *Joan the Woman* was prophetic in recasting history in the service of a call to arms. Although the Committee on Public Information established in April 1917 created a mood of intolerance in orchestrating public opinion to support the war, the commercial failure of DeMille's epic demonstrated the need to transcend cultural diversity.[18] By staging magnificent spectacles whose very costliness reinforced a consumer ethos, the prewar pageantry movement unwittingly paved the way for cinematic representations of history with a national appeal. As self-theatricalization in genteel parlors had earlier signified the commodification of social relations, oversized productions of civic drama emphasized the sheer expense of reproducing the historical past. Spectacle based on the consumption of enormous quantities of matériel proved seductive not only to middle-class spectators accustomed to visual appropriation, but, as the Paterson Strike Pageant demonstrated, to the urban "Other" excluded from public history enacted in the public sphere. Pageant leaders, to be sure, shared the goal of Progressive historians to "write the history of the past anew" in order to meet the requirements of succeeding generations, but rewriting history as pictorial dramaturgy also lent itself to the process of reification in a consumer culture.[19] The success of both the pageantry movement and the film industry in inventing a usable past, in other words, meant the commodification of historical images as spectacle. Furthermore, the parallel between monumental reproductions of history—frequently impressive battle scenes—and modern global hostilities underscored the extent to which technological war itself had become a form not only of theater but of obscene consumption involving unprecedented expenditures of men and matériel.

REPRESENTATIONS AND THE BODY POLITIC:
JOAN THE WOMAN

Although social conventions dictated the nature of women's participation as well as their historical representation in community pageants, their presence nonetheless attested to fissures in republican civic culture. An antimodernist response to the dictates of the machine age, pageantry reinforced Victorian sentimental notions of womanhood in an era when the practice of separate spheres was collapsing due to economic and sociocultural changes. According to Glassberg, "the pageant woman symbolizing the community resembled the idealized female image represented in public statues, murals, and posters of the period but was explicitly tied to images of both maternity and maturity."[20] American propaganda efforts on behalf of the war, such as Red Cross advertisements, also emphasized public images of women as inspirational maternal figures. Yet Charles Dana Gibson, head of the Division of Pictorial Publicity for the Committee on Public Information, had invented the Gibson girl, an early, if ambiguous, incarnation of the "new woman." Gibson, however, was hardly sympathetic toward the feminist movement.[21] Contradictions in wartime representations of women are evident in juxtaposing an ad titled "The Greatest Mother in the World," who is cradling an injured soldier, with another ad of a muscular female, clenched fist at her side, declaring "I am Public Opinion." Copywriting on the latter, an advertisement for government bonds, begins with the exclamation, "All men fear me!" A group that worked closely with the Division of Advertising, Gibson's Division thus perpetuated the ambiguous use of female icons as symbolic of motherhood, on the one hand, and as allegorical figures representing tyrannical public opinion or warlike nations, on the other.[22] Such contradictions also inform *Joan the Woman*, an epic that is intertextually related to discourse on civic culture as exemplified both in historical pageants and in wartime propaganda.

Although historical pageantry, like world's fair exhibits, excluded specific racial and working-class components in defining a sense of community, on a symbolic level cultural forms represent marginalized groups including women as homologous entities in the social formation. As discourse on the body politic, therefore, *Joan the Woman* foregrounds the issue of gender with respect to women's emergence in the public sphere and represents the problem of assimilating new immigrants as a threat to the purity of white womanhood. Discontented with the title of the film, which implies romantic melodrama rather than historical epic, DeMille was quite revealing when he recalled, "*Joan the Woman* may have suggested that she was—that they were going to see a story where her chastity was violated or something of that sort."[23] Indeed, a sadistic Catholic prelate, whose characterization raised objections in municipal communities, subjects the Maid of Orléans to sexual threats for persisting in acts of female deviance such as wearing male garments. Such a narrative strategy conflates paranoia regarding women and ethnic minorities in a pluralistic urban culture.

As revealing as DeMille's statement is Macpherson's division of the script into two epochs, the first emphasizing Joan's renunciation of romance, and the second focusing on documented historical events, in order to rationalize the saint's unconventional role. The film thus represents sexual difference not only through a two-part narrative structure but also in terms of two conflicting and intersecting genres. An expressive form associated with the sentimental culture of women, melodrama predominates but remains a problematic mode for realistic reenactments of history. As Christine Gledhill argues, unlike individual actors representing social forces in realist texts, melodramatic figures experience historical events "only as they touch on . . . moral identities and relationships." DeMille's Joan of Arc, for example, achieves military glory, national renown, and spiritual redemption at the cost of romantic fulfillment. Yet rendering the social world in terms of personal dilemmas conflicts with the mode of realism essential to traditional historical film as validated by the critical establishment. According to John L. Fell, "a narrative scheme that plots individual actions so that they relate causally to great, even transcending, events" involves "credibility risks" in "fictional patterns where singular acts have to produce society-restoring consequence. . . . [C]onnections between the two story elements— the macro and micro versions of a writer's cosmos—must be constructed with extreme care."[24] DeMille was able to resolve the narratological problem of civic pageantry as a macrocosm, albeit at the cost of historical veracity, by constructing historicity in uneasy tension with romantic melodrama.

During the Progressive Era, historical pageants constituted a macrocosm because, despite narration, audiences could neither distinguish between foreground and background nor comprehend the symbolic level of events without a program.[25] DeMille, however, bridged the gap between macrocosm and microcosm through the use of cinematic language, especially editing and variations in shot angle and scale due to camera placement. Predictably, a high ratio of medium shots predominated in the sentimental melodrama of "Joan the Woman," whereas extreme long shots and panoramic shots conveyed the masculine epic of Joan of Arc. Furthermore, critics noticed that DeMille employed variations in intertitles to register shifts in mood and genre. Specifically, the director used conventional titles—mostly for dialogue—art titles with drawings to communicate the emotional tone of a sequence, and historical titles that simulated hieroglyphs on stone tablets to convey the historicity of reenacted events. According to *Wid's,* "The titles were very well prepared, there being a number of new ideas incorporated in the decorations. These helped materially in keeping the note of distinction predominantly throughout the film." Similarly, *Moving Picture World* commented, "There are novelties in the titling. Many of the leaders are of raised letters, simulating brass on a dark background. Others are of the atmospheric sort."[26] Additionally, Furst's orchestral score was undoubtedly effective in establishing the proper mood for romantic melodrama as opposed to historical epic. DeMille in fact arranged for the composer to travel to various cities to supervise the film's musical accompaniment.[27] Also noted by critics, the director used his well-known lighting effects with color tinting and a two-color process to foreground specific scenes or sequences. The marketing of special effects in conjunction with woman constructed as spectacle and with historical film requiring advanced technology to achieve realism was hardly coincidental.[28] The Handschiegl two-color process in *Joan the Woman* is especially vivid in the protracted sequence in which the saint is burned to death in the public square. In sum, DeMille employed all the resources at his command as director-general of the Lasky studio to surpass Progressive Era civic pageantry. Yet his first epic failed to attract audiences to the box office, especially in key urban areas, because it appealed to an elitist and orthodox sense of history that excluded the "Other."

DISCOURSE ON FEMININITY: JOAN OF ARC AS A SYMBOL OF GENDER CONFLICT

According to Richard Hofstadter, "American historians in the nineteenth century were in the main a conservative class of men writing for a conservative public." What they wrote "embodied the ideas of the possessing classes about industrial and financial issues, manifested the complacency of white Anglo-Saxon Protestants about social and ethnic issues, and, on constitutional issues, underwrote the requirements of property and of national centralization." Although the professionalization of historiography after 1890 produced a new generation of university-trained historians more sympathetic to social change, the pageantry movement drew on the conservative legacy of the nineteenth century as well as the historicism of the Progressive Era. As custodians of culture, the genteel classes were accustomed to history as orthodoxy based on an ideological consensus, that is, a form of knowledge that inculcated moral and patriotic values in a loyal citizenry.[29] Given the intertext of American historical literature in the early twentieth century, *Joan the Woman* is unmistakably addressed to the educated and privileged middle class. During and after the credits, DeMille precedes the first shot of the film with seven historical intertitles that appear three-dimensional, as if chiseled on stone:

Founded on the Life of Joan of Arc, the Girl Patriot, Who Fought with Men, Was Loved by Men, and Killed by Men—Yet Withal Retained the Heart of a Woman

For seventy years defeat after defeat had followed the French arms, until in the year 1429, France was on the verge of becoming an English province

Charles VII, King of France—deserted by his most powerful nobles—was opposed by his cousin the Duke of Burgundy, whose wealth and soldiers were at England's call

Paris, itself, was in English hands; and Charles, the weakling King, ruled a shabby, debt-ridden little court—unhonored and uncrowned

At this time—when the soul of France was slowly dying—there dwelt in the little village of Domremy, a simple peasant girl, the daughter of Jacques d'Arc

Her name was Joan of Arc, and her life that of the sturdy country maiden as she worked at the hearth or in the pasture

Joan of Arc [a crest appears in upper right hand corner]

DeMille had never before begun a narrative with a succession of intertitles equivalent to voice-over narration in sound films; historical literature that only educated audiences could understand evidently comprised the intertext for such titles. The sentimental tone of the first intertitle which, unlike the rest, is featured in the credits, clearly demarcates the romantic melodrama from the textbook rhetoric of the epic. The mise-en-scène of the first two shots of the film, photographed in low-key lighting, further contrasts the domestic life of the peasant girl confined to the private sphere with the martyrdom of a warrior sacrificed in defense of the public sphere. A telescoping of events for didactic purposes, these two shots juxtapose the beginning and end of the narrative before the plot unfolds. Specifically, Joan is introduced spinning thread in a medium shot which is then contrasted with a full shot of her martyred figure lit by a fleur-de-lys cast against a shadowy wall. As she extends her arms outward and lowers her head, she is obviously the victim of a crucifixion. After a slow fade-out, a historical intertitle informs the audience, "Joan of Arc is not dead. She can never die—and in the war-torn land she loved so well, her spirit fights today." Although there is no mention of either the prologue or epilogue in the script, an art title illustrated with barbed wire links the past with the present, "AN ENGLISH TRENCH SOMEWHERE IN FRANCE."[30]

DeMille constructs his version of a usable past in the prologue by showing a young British officer (Wallace Reid) discovering an ancient sword embedded in the wall of a trench. After volunteering for a suicide mission, the soldier is pensive. An art title with the single word "MEMORY," evoked by the drawing of a British castle on a horizon of fields intersected by a stream, conveys his nostalgia for the bucolic scene that is home. Spending his last moments in a darkened trench lit by a single candle, the soldier is seated on his bunk when a brilliant apparition of Joan of Arc appears to his left. She links the events of the past to the present, as well as melodrama to realistic newsreel footage, by stating rather enigmatically, "The time has come for thee to expiate thy sin against me." Stilted utterances repeated by actors in countless sound epics, it should be noted, underscore the advantage of dialogue titles as archaically inflected speech in silent film; in this instance, the intertitles give further evidence of historical address constructed for a highbrow audience. Plunged "INTO THE PAST," the maid of Domrémy meets Eric Trent, an English nobleman in the service of the Duke of Burgundy during the Hundred Years' War. A French counterpart of the art title, "MEMORY," an extreme long shot shows Joan in a pastoral scene as she tends sheep on a brilliant sunlit day in woods where skyscraping trees form graceful arches. Although they are separated by historical time, nationality, and gender, the British officer and the French peasant girl both have ties to a romanticized vision of a rural landscape. Americans have a quarrel with history, as Hofstadter argues, because they are unable to reconcile a yearning for the agrarian past with modernization as progress. The contradictions of antimodernist civic drama rooted in nostalgia are expressed in *Joan the Woman* in terms of the politics of gender rather than urban class conflict. The peasant maid whose spiritual mission meant a refusal, indeed, a reversal, of traditional gender roles is represented according to a sentimental tradition familiar to genteel audiences. A fan magazine novelization captured Macpherson's concept of the heroine as a woman who foregoes romantic love to become the savior of her country:

> And so she grew to womanhood, with the flame that burned in her heart shining in her wide, grave eyes. . . . And those beautiful, sad-seer eyes of hers glanced once into other eyes, bold and beseeching and loverlike, and the brave heart nearly faltered ere she could look away.
>
> Human love was not for her, nor the touch of her child's groping fingers on her breast, nor the homely, humble joys of home.
>
> "I cannot love you," she told her lover quietly; "I shall not wed any man."[31]

At a time when anxiety regarding the diminution of the Victorian practice of separate spheres for the sexes informed political discourse, *Joan the Woman* exemplified confusion regarding gender roles. For an untutored peasant maid in a remote village, romantic love proves to be as treacherous as court intrigue. DeMille uses Freudian symbolism to show that Joan of Arc assumes the unconventional role of a warrior only because men are cowardly and unprincipled. A timid French deserter named Gaspard (Lawrence Peyton), for example, seeks shelter in Domrémy and flings his sword on the table. Joan carries the weapon out of the room as if she were transfixed by it. When the villagers flee in panic from Burgundian troops led by Eric Trent, DeMille shows the peasant maid in a medium shot as she hands the sword back to Gaspard so that he may "parley" with the invaders. Carrying a child in her arms, she then rushes off to join her family but stops to glance backward; a cut to a point-of-view shot reveals the unmanly Gaspard taking refuge in a barn. A cut back to Joan shows her handing the child to another woman; in the next shot, she occupies the space that Gaspard has abandoned to confront enemy soldiers advancing from the rear. At the head of his troops, Eric Trent, in a reverse high angle shot, first sights Joan with arms outstretched as she entreats him to turn back. Dismounting, he forces her into the barn where Gaspard is hiding. DeMille cuts between interior medium shots of Eric Trent expressing dishonorable intentions and exterior long shots of pillaging soldiers to emphasize sexual assault. Awed by the French maid's fearlessness and spirituality, the invader becomes a gallant courtier but is felled by Gaspard, concealed in the loft, before he can rejoin his men. Joan decides to hide the wounded Englishman to nurse him back to health. Photographed in a slightly high angle medium shot, Joan of Arc and Eric Trent are lit against a darkened loft strewn with straw; while he sleeps in the foreground, she wears his glove and looks inspired. The dim illumination gradually fades except for a spotlight on the face of the saint transported by a vision of her future.

DeMille had no compunction about foregrounding fictional scenes of romantic melodrama seemingly out of place in a historical pageant. As Eric Trent recovers from his wound, for example, he plucks the petals from a daisy and recites, "She loves me. She loves me not." When he later bids Joan farewell, DeMille cuts from a frontal two-shot to an oblique angle to show an apparition of a lighted sword against the Englishman's body. As Eric Trent descends the ladder, the brilliant figure of a courtier representing one of Joan's angels appears to announce, "Prepare thyself, Joan, for thou art to save France." Astounded, the peasant maid drops to her knees as the light from the apparition illuminates the loft. DeMille cuts to a close medium shot of Joan to capture her awed response, but in the next shot her mother emerges from a hut to pluck the feathers from a bird. The director thus juxtaposes domestic scenes with historical tableaux until Joan leaves Domrémy during a nighttime sequence that impressed critics with a two-color process that intensified the orange glow of a candle in a room flooded with ambient moonlight.[32] At the court of Charles VII (Raymond Hatton), where the focus is on historical reenactment rather than romantic melodrama, Joan of Arc inspires French soldiers to follow her into battle. An extreme long shot of the crowded throne room, intercut with English soldiers advancing on Orléans, dramatizes Joan's extraordinary ability as a seer; she announces the siege as superimposed images of the enemy march across the screen. After the call to arms, a historical tableau titled "The Blessing of the Standard" consists of two shots, the second beginning with an iris that opens out to reveal a panorama with clergy in ceremonial robes flanking the screen, Joan holding the consecrated flag in the center, and General La Hire

(Hobart Bosworth) and his troops kneeling in the background. As evidence of research to achieve authenticity in these sequences, the script cites several sources such as *Manners, Customs, and Dress during the Middle Ages,* the *Encyclopedia Britannica,* the *Life of Charles the Bold,* and the *Life of Louis XI.*[33]

After "The Blessing of the Standard," which is constructed in the tradition of historical reenactments in parlor theatricals and civic pageants, DeMille's representation of space becomes more cinematic in the first of his monumental battle scenes, the lifting of the siege of Orléans. Although the director demonstrates finesse in handling extras in the huge crowd scenes that became his trademark, the geography of the conflict is unclear because the French attack an outlying fortress occupied by the English, who are laying siege but have not yet become the conquerors of Orléans.[34] Assisted by a team of ten directors, including his brother William and Oscar Apfel, each in charge of a regiment of one hundred men and armored horses, DeMille produced a spectacle that represented the battle of the sexes as well as the end of a famous siege.[35] Advancing knights carrying banners on horseback and foot soldiers with pikes are photographed in sweeping long shots from frontal, lateral, and reverse angles as they ride over impalements and charge into the English line to engage in hand-to-hand combat. The fighting becomes especially fierce in the moat surrounding the castle as the French, photographed in high angle shots, attempt to scale the wall. After an artillery barrage creates an opening in the stone wall of the fortress, Eric Trent and his men retreat toward the tower as Joan of Arc enters through the breach and is immediately felled by an arrow. About to slay the woman he loves, the Englishman halts with a shock of recognition. DeMille cuts from extreme long shot to medium shot to medium close-up to focus on human feelings in the midst of stirring historical events. When Eric Trent is later brought to Joan as a captive, he surrenders his sword and is obliterated by an iris that focuses on the saint glancing up toward the heavens. According to a historical title, this victory marks the "End of First Epoch." At first-run theaters that projected the entire film, a ten-minute intermission followed.[36]

Although the battle for Orléans is symbolically represented as a sexual assault under the command of a female warrior, especially in scenes in which Joan of Arc storms the castle, the victor herself becomes the prey in "The Second Epoch." Welcomed by the jubilant inhabitants of the city, who had previously been shown close to starvation, Joan leads her troops into the city in one of the few forward tracking shots in the film. She is immediately surrounded by admiring women, one of whom offers her an infant to be embraced. At the very moment of her triumph, however, Joan is reduced to a voyeuristic object as the suspicious eyes of a spy are shown behind the rectangular slot of a door. A reverse shot of the interior reveals the voyeur to be L'Oiseleur (Tully Marshall), a monk in the employ of a British agent

24. Geraldine Farrar as Joan of Arc is surrounded by women, one of whom lifts up her child, after the liberation of Orléans in *Joan the Woman*, DeMille's first historical epic. (*Photo courtesy George Eastman House*)

25. Farrar relinquishes romantic love as represented by Eric Trent (Wallace Reid), a fictional character, in favor of spirituality and martyrdom. (*Photo courtesy George Eastman House*)

named Bishop Cauchon. Following the coronation of Charles VII, another impressive historical tableau, Joan of Arc refuses both filial obligation and romantic love in separate interviews with her uncle and her English prisoner. DeMille ends this sequence with a lyrical set piece in which Eric slowly walks toward the Gothic arches in the rear of the dimly lit cathedral, still strewn with flowers from the coronation. A cut to a reverse shot shows the saint ascending the stairs to the altar where she kneels to dedicate herself to God.

Joan of Arc's demise quickly follows as Eric Trent is enlisted in a plot orchestrated by Bishop Cauchon (Theodore Roberts) and a court advisor nicknamed "The Spider" (George Clary), both agents in the English cause. A forward tracking shot shows the Maid of Orléans, dressed without her usual armor, riding at night with a handful of men to Compiègne. Accompanying her is the superimposed image of the angel of death on horseback. At daybreak she is captured by Eric's men and sexually harassed as a sign of foul play to come. Gaspard, who has become a devoted follower, is stabbed to death as he attempts to defend her honor. Anticipating events with unbecoming glee for a cleric, Bishop Cauchon threatens Joan in a darkened chamber with a boiling cauldron in the foreground. Photographed in extreme low-key lighting, this sequence proves riveting because the Bishop terrifies the saint in the presence of three hooded figures costumed like Ku Klux Klansmen. DeMille thus conflates a Catholic clergyman, symbolizing new immigrants in a Protestant culture, with hooded persecutors in scenes that aroused protest. After she "promises to return to the garb of a woman," Joan is led back to her cell, but the Bishop initiates a scheme to pronounce her "a relapsed heretic" to be burned at the stake. At this point, even L'Oiseleur protests, "Thou art a priest and should seek the salvation of the girl rather than her death!" Cauchon orders a soldier to "place the worst ruffian of thy guard in the cell of Joan the Maid" and, in another highly voyeuristic moment, proceeds to spy on her through a large opening in the floor above the prison chamber. An overhead shot photographed through the aperture shows the brute trying to assault Joan as Eric Trent finally comes to her rescue, but his attempt to save her is foiled.

Condemned to death because she has "resumed the garb of a man," a sure sign of heresy, Joan of Arc spends her final nightmarish hours in a sequence tinted blue and intercut with amber shots of the court of Charles VII in utter debauchery. At dawn, she is carted to the public square where black smoke turns day into night in a stunning two-color process that shows orange flames consuming piles of faggots. Joan triumphantly cries out, "My voices were of God—they have not deceived me!" As clouds of billowing smoke fade out, the epilogue continues the events of the prologue to relate the Hundred Years' War to World War I. The British officer has been fatally wounded during a successful effort to destroy an enemy trench.

As he lays dying in the foreground, a large apparition of Joan, lit against the surrounding darkness of the trenches, appears to dominate the skyline. Aside from linking past and present through the fate of the characters in the romantic melodrama, the prologue and epilogue convey the universal significance of the life of Joan of Arc as an allegory.

CRITICAL DISCOURSES: GENDER AND THE MORAL LESSON OF HISTORY

Although it was unsuccessful at the box office, *Joan the Woman* was one of the most critically acclaimed productions of its time and provoked further discourse on motion pictures as an art form. The film industry and its critics, in other words, were still addressing a genteel audience regarding the cultural legitimacy of cinema. A special production such as *Joan the Woman* thus represented a noteworthy event. According to the *New York Dramatic Mirror,* the film was "perhaps the most dramatic and wholly commendable screen offering of a decade. It is difficult to see how an advance is to be made on this production and it should have the effect of absolutely silencing those critics of the motion picture who affect to regard them as unworthy of serious consideration." *Wid's* agreed that "there is an air of distinction and class about the entire offering which places it in the front rank of big productions, and certainly no one can see this offering without being impressed with the tremendous strides made in the last two or three years by our producers of big films." Peter Milne, critic of *Motion Picture News,* described the film as "a true classic of the screen" that was "so intelligently welded as to give complete satisfaction and to be fully worthy of its classification as a high grade piece of theatrical entertainment at corresponding prices." For filmgoers in Boston, the price of evening tickets ranged from twenty-five cents to one dollar. Sounding a similar note to that in trade journals, the *New York Times* observed "lapses into pure fiction for romantic or melodramatic purposes" but declared "the photodrama takes its place among the half-dozen finest films yet produced."[37] The *New York Evening Sun* trumpeted in a headline that *Joan the Woman* was "One of the Most Artistic and Satisfying Pictures That Ever Has Been Shown." Calling attention to the sheer magnitude of the production, the review linked the film to publicity about historical pageantry as a mode of conspicuous consumption that commodified history:

> It required months of preparation on the part of a score or more assistants to assemble copies of practically everything obtainable in Joan of Arc literature, heraldry and design. Even before the first photographs were made a hundred seamstresses were working daily on the several thousand costumes which were required. . . . It was necessary to provide suits of mail in sufficient number to purchase the entire output of a Pacific coast manufacturer of chain pan and

pot cleaners. Thousands of yards of chain mesh were demanded, and the machinery of the factory worked overtime on the supply. [According to] DeMille, "we had in all some 13,000 separate items of costume, equipage, heraldry, and the like. . . . [W]e built three separate villages, all careful duplicates of the original where the embattlements and the like are accurate to an inch. The interior of the Rheims Cathedral is perfectly executed."[38]

Not surprisingly, DeMille's first historical epic dictated comparisons with those of D. W. Griffith and Thomas H. Ince. Critical discourse on cinema, it should be noted, had advanced by 1917 to the point where film authorship was readily being discussed in reviews of special productions. Although *Moving Picture World* expressed doubts regarding the authenticity of the romantic relationship in *Joan the Woman,* it claimed, "Cecil B. DeMille belongs in the front ranks of the great producers of the day." *Photoplay*'s Julian Johnson compared DeMille's camera work to Michelangelo's use of the chisel in a review that recalled earlier discourse on cinema in relation to traditional art forms. But Johnson also discussed the film in relation to other filmic texts and concluded that *Joan the Woman* had been excelled only by *The Birth of a Nation.* The *New York Review* volunteered in a similar vein, "This production easily ranks with 'Intolerance,' 'Civilization,' and 'A Daughter of the Gods' in size, scope, imagination, drama, photography, and ethical purpose." According to the *Boston Evening Transcript,* DeMille's epic "is not the equal of that unparalleled 'Birth.' Yet it achieves an effect far finer than anything but the Babylonian episodes in 'Intolerance' . . . at what seems . . . a smaller cost of production." *Joan the Woman,* not coincidentally, succeeded *Intolerance* at the Colonial Theatre in Chicago after the Griffith film completed a long engagement. Griffith enjoyed such preeminence in the prewar years of the industry that a congratulatory telegram he sent to Farrar was reproduced in a two-page ad in *Motion Picture News.* The Western Union message read, "I hope you will not consider it a boldness to offer you my most sincere congratulations on this beautiful contribution to our little new and budding art." The director was probably then involved in negotiations to direct films for Artcraft, which Adolph Zukor acquired a few months later to consolidate vertical integration of the industry. DeMille himself acknowledged a communication from Griffith in a letter addressed to Lasky shortly after the film's premiere: "I received a very delightful telegram from Griffith on the subject of 'Joan.' He was most enthusiastic."[39] Despite the fact that it was not a commercial success, *Joan the Woman* consolidated DeMille's status as an author and contributed to the increasing cultural legitimacy of motion pictures.

After winning unanimous acclaim for her debut in *Carmen,* Geraldine Farrar, however, received mixed notices as the star of *Joan the Woman.* Critics who applied standards of realism to historical representation not only fulminated about the fact that she neither looked nor acted like a peasant girl, but disapproved of the romantic melodrama. DeMille in fact suppressed an episode in the script in which Joan's father attempts to marry her to Gaspard, a fiction that would have elicited even more objection.[40] Discourse on historical authenticity signifying a cultural practice that validated realism proved disadvantageous to the actress. Julian Johnson was particularly unkind: "Those who object to Miss Farrar's Joan because she is rising to battle-cruiser weight had best turn to their histories. Joan is described as broad, short, heavy. But Joan had a peasant's face. . . . One of Miss Farrar's eyes reflects Riverside Drive, the other, Fifth Avenue, and her mouth seems to be singing Broadway." George Blaisdell was more insightful when he observed in *Moving Picture World*, "Geraldine Farrar in her interpretation . . . has crossed all the centuries of time, and . . . portrays a woman of regal, dominating presence rather than a simple child of God and of France. . . . We may even feel that had the story adhered to history it would have been of greater strength."[41] As a matter of fact, Farrar projects throughout the film a majestic and commanding dignity befitting a historical tableau or pageant. She easily resembles the sculptured female forms that had been familiar to the public and functioned on an allegorical level in wartime posters. What, then, does the critical response to Farrar as Joan of Arc signify besides a preoccupation with realism as a cultural practice valorized by male critics? A consideration of discourse on gender within a broad social context reveals why the narrative strategy of the film disrupts realist historical representation and privileges sentimental romance.

Aside from introducing a human interest story to the macrocosm of historical pageantry, the romantic melodrama of *Joan the Woman* alleviates spectator anxiety regarding a heroine who achieves sainthood by assuming a masculine role. At a time when controversy regarding the doctrine of separate spheres was being aired in diverse forums, sex-role reversal proved to be a disconcerting issue. Were men indeed being unmanned by the "new woman"? Charles Dana Gibson drew a dinner table scene titled "A Suffragette's Husband" (1911) in which an emasculated male shrinks from the glance of his domineering wife, a weighty figure with a double chin and a stern glance.[42] During the first two decades of the twentieth century, many fashionable women were asserting class and ethnic solidarity against the new immigrants by campaigning for the right to vote and even mounted theatrical spectacles in support of their cause. At the same time, a radical restructuring of female employment or the feminization of clerical work resulted in young middle-class women becoming salaried employees in unprecedented numbers. Furthermore, 40 percent of the college population in 1910 was female. Departing from tradition, a number of college-educated women chose careers and social activism rather than marriage and motherhood. As for married women, they routinely participated in club work and community projects in an era of reform.[43] The multifaceted activities of middle-class women, not to mention their shopping in down-town business districts, had redrawn if not erased the line between public and private spheres.

Anxiety regarding the dynamics of social change as it affected gender roles in middle-class families accounts for critical preoccupation with Joan of Arc as a woman.[44] Critics who responded to sentimental values, inter-estingly, were not concerned about the historical veracity of DeMille's epic. According to the *New York Evening Sun*, "the remarkably well chosen love interest that shows what this woman (who was too great to lose her identity as a woman) was like are touches that have made . . . one of the mightiest pictures of screendom, a close, thrilling personal narrative."[45] The Rever-end Thomas B. Gregory, surely a representative of sentimental culture, argued at length in the *New York American:*

> Perhaps the greatest thing that the picture will accomplish . . . will be the revelation of the greatness of the womanly character when it is really and truly womanly.
>
> We of today are just beginning to see the entrance of woman into the great, wide life of the world from which she has heretofore been debarred; and many are wondering what the result will be. Will woman be able to act her part nobly and well in the great arena toward which she is drifting? And can she go into the battle, into the . . . rough-and-tumble competition and not be ruined? Will she not cease to be woman, becoming . . . God knows what.
>
> The play answers these fears and answers them in a way to encourage us all.
>
> Joan, thrown headlong into the whirl and stress of the world, did not lose her womanliness, her modesty, her beautiful reserve, nor was she in any way corrupted by contact with the world's brutalities and coarseness, its plots and conspiracies.[46]

DeMille solved the narratological problem of civic pageantry as a macro-cosm by casting Joan in sentimental terms as a woman who sacrifices ro-mantic love for a spiritual cause. Although he did not meet expectations for a more realistic historical drama, as some critics complained, his discourse on gender deftly exploited sentimentalism to alleviate anxiety about a sex-role reversal. Yet the director's work remains ambiguous because the male characters in the film are far from admirable, and even despicable. Wallace Reid, who became a dashing matinee idol before succumbing to drug addiction, played a particularly passive, uninspiring, and unheroic role as Eric Trent.

Since critics invested in realism did not perceive Farrar as a symbolic icon and criticized her weight gain, age, and sophistication, the intertextuality of film and publicity material proved to be disadvantageous to the actress. A beautiful and internationally renowned diva with an enthusiastic following, dubbed "Gerryflappers," Farrar led a well-publicized life. She had even been romantically linked with the Hohenzollern crown prince so that she had to deny pro-German sentiment on the eve of war. After she made her Metropolitan Opera debut in *Roméo et Juliette* in 1906, stylish magazines such as *Theatre, Vanity Fair,* and *Harper's Bazaar* featured color photographs of her on the cover and printed articles about her fashionable wardrobe and elegantly furnished home. For example, the caption of a full-page photo in *Theatre* read, "Miss Geraldine Farrar. In A Wonderful Chinchilla and Sable Creation. By Paquin." Farrar had been associated, in other words, with the world of high art, aristocracy, and luxury since her operatic debut at the Berlin Royal Opera in 1901. Furthermore, the soprano was hardly reticent about airing her ambivalent views about marriage. She was widely quoted as having remarked, "I shall never marry, I never intended to marry. . . . I am old fashioned enough to think that a woman should be subordinate to her husband, and I must have my freedom or I can't work." Signifying ambivalence about women's issues, the *Boston Daily Advertiser* ran a headline that labeled Farrar a "Self-Supporting, Independent Working Woman" but attributed to her the following statement: "This feminism, race suicide, etc., what is it but this, that all repressed women are getting discontented and muttering."[47]

Although the validity of these quotations cannot be ascertained, they nevertheless reveal confusion about and hostility toward the "new woman." When Farrar married actor Lou Tellegen in a volte-face, *Photoplay* reported the event as the result of a primordial contest, "Farrar's Real Romance. Cave Man Tellegen's Conquest In A Stone-Age Episode With A Movie Background." "Never did a lovely woman more completely change her mind," began the article, which described Tellegen as "the physical embodiment of the rugged and resourceful man . . . a man's man."[48] Farrar soon regretted her decision even though she did not divorce Tellegen for seven years. In a revealing letter, DeMille wrote to Lasky during the filming of *Joan the Woman:* "Incidentally, a word on Farrar—She seems to have lost a little something of the great spark of genius that animated her last year . . . also, she has gotten pretty plump." Later, he recalled, "I never had any difficulty with Geraldine at all on the pictures that I made with her. Now, on the last one we weren't speaking, but we still didn't have any temperament. We weren't speaking because she married Lou Tellegen. . . . [H]e wanted to direct, so I let him . . . and boy! I put my foot down and said, 'No, he cannot direct any more.' " The director had enjoyed a friendlier relationship with the soprano before her wedding: "the warmth after shooting wasn't there. I didn't go over and hold her hand the way I had before."[49] Despite her marriage, Farrar projected the image of a glamorous and independent diva that, for some critics, interfered with her representation as a spiritual heroine in the sentimental tradition. Yet her engaging persona as a "new woman" resonates in both *Carmen* and *Joan the Woman* as heroines who refuse to submit to traditional prescriptions of womanhood.

Despite evident differences in class, ethnicity, and gender, workers and immigrants represented entities interchangeable with "new" women who were remapping separate spheres as threats to the body politic. Contrary to *The Cheat,* in which racial groups are conflated and scapegoated in Orientalist consumer fantasies, paranoia as a response to social change is displaced in *Joan the Woman* onto the body of the saint burned in the public sphere. Unlike Edith Hardy, the erring socialite whose body is exhibited as a court-room spectacle so that she may be recuperated as a sentimental heroine, Joan of Arc is sacrificed for future redemption. Sadistic Catholic clergy execute her as a deviant woman for assuming masculine prerogatives. Subject to threats of sexual assault and torture, she is finally burned at the stake because church leaders interpret her refusal to confine herself to the domestic sphere as an unnatural ambition to rule. After the liberation of Orléans, for example, L'Oiseleur reproaches her, "Wouldst thou become Queen—that thou lettest the people kneel to thee!" During the trial, the monk testifies that Joan, who wears female apparel for the first time since grasping the sword, is a "weaver of spells" and that "people fall down and worship her." "The Spider" deters Charles VII, a pitiful weakling, from ransoming his military leader because she "would make herself queen and reign in thy stead." A great deal of attention is focused on clothing as a sign of subordinate behavior appropriate for the female gender. Under threat of torture, Joan is forced to sign a statement in which she "promises to return to the garb of a woman."[50] Although the Duke of Burgundy and the English are French foes in the Hundred Years' War—an unhappy alignment given the events of modern trench warfare—a Catholic bishop and hooded inquisitors resembling Klansmen are the ultimate villains.

A sign of the rising tide of nativism in small towns eclipsed by cities in the South, Midwest, and Far West, the Ku Klux Klan reorganized in 1915. Catholics as well as blacks were among its chief targets. DeMille repressed fault lines in the social formation by conflating the Catholic hierarchy with the Klan as conspirators against Victorian womanhood. Although prewar civic pageantry excluded specific racial and working-class groups, movement leaders attempted to project a vision, however antimodernist and nostalgic, of a stable community. Absent in DeMille's spectacle, essentially addressed to the genteel middle class, is not only an articulation of history that transcends cultural differences but a harmonious vision of public life. Catholics, who were themselves divided according to class and ethnicity but faced increasing nativism, censured the film.[51] Anticipating criticism, the Cardinal Film Corporation, formed to produce and distribute *Joan the Woman* during the consolidation of Famous Players-Lasky, printed souvenir programs that

26. As a sadistic bishop, Theodore Roberts threatens Joan of Arc with torture in scenes that aroused Catholic protest and minimized the film's box-office appeal in urban areas. (*Photo courtesy George Eastman House*)

characterized Cauchon as a man who "did not hesitate to misuse the mighty power of the Church to defeat his personal enemies." The program cited the eleventh edition of the Encyclopedia Britannica to describe the ugly fate awaiting the cardinal as his due.[52] Critic Peter Milne referred to the quotation in his review:

> There has been some question raised as to the manner in which those of Catholic faith will accept the character of Pierre Cauchon, the churchman who ultimately causes Joan's downfall. There should be none whatsoever. The Catholic Encyclopedia itself refers to Cauchon as an "unscrupulous and ambitious man" and states in dealing with the various acts of Pope Callixtus III that the sentence passed on Joan . . . was "quashed and the innocence of the Maid of Orleans proclaimed." The Encyclopedia Britannica . . . tells more harshly of Cauchon's fate, in that he was excommunicated posthumously by the Pope, his body exhumed and thrown in the common sewer.[53]

Similarly, another critic commented, "it should be perfectly understandable that this is a representation of an historical character, and not intended as a reflection on any creed or people."[54] The citation of historical data reveals more about the condescension of the privileged classes, however, than it does about Catholic reception of the film. Correspondence involving a Midwest exhibitor, Famous Players-Lasky in New York, and DeMille at his

California studio reveals that the high concentration of Catholics in urban areas meant negative reception of the film. Barnett, the exhibitor, claimed that in the "principal cities of Ohio . . . criticisms expressed in various newspapers was not favorable to the success of the picture, but only on account of the religious atmosphere in the picture. I would suggest that this picture be cut down to at least eight reels, eliminating the religious part in the picture, that is made objectionable to particularly the Catholics." Corresponding with DeMille from the New York office, H. Whitman Bennett suggested some "radical cuts in the latter half of the work" and cited "those episodes and scenes which have caused us so much trouble with the Catholic public." Bennett advocated "entirely eliminating the prison scene and the torture scene, and possibly the earlier part of the burning at the stake" because "we have to face much adverse criticism from unenlightened Catholics."[55] DeMille's confusing reply gives evidence not only of ethnic and religious differences in the country but of his own inability to think in positive terms regarding civic culture:

> It might be better for the States Rights buyer, himself, to make these eliminations as the different parts of the country would probably prefer to see different scenes cut out. That is, in the strong Catholic communities, those scenes relating to the Catholic Church might best be spared; while in the Protestant portions of the country, it might be desirable to retain such scenes.[56]

The director had yet to craft a spectacle that would eclipse cultural diversity in appealing to a shared sense of historical consciousness and national identity.

Although *Joan the Woman* did not appeal to urban working-class and ethnic groups, its enthusiastic reception by educated filmgoers attested to the cultural values of the genteel middle class. A construction of a usable past to educate the public on the eve of war, the film was much admired. The Reverend Thomas B. Gregory noted, "What a mighty aid to the teaching of history the motion picture is destined to be . . . and that, too, through the most royal of all the faculties, that of the sight." Critic Frederick James Smith claimed, "As a work of art this picture should be seen by everyone, but its worth as an instrument of uplift and patriotism is incalculable." A great deal of publicity resulted when Lasky sent the Forty-fourth Street Theatre orchestra to play at a special Washington, D.C., premiere for an audience including Vice-President Thomas R. Marshall, Secretary of State Robert Lansing, the Russian ambassador, and their wives. Ads for the film exploited middle-class belief that public reenactments of history would educate a responsible citizenry. Copy for a two-page ad in *Motion Picture News,* for example, made extravagant claims dwarfing those of pageant officials and anticipated the tone of wartime propaganda: "This picture . . .

may become a great shaping force in this remarkable era. . . . Patriotism and religious fervor . . . will sweep all Europe after the war. . . . the motion picture will outdo the mightiest work ever accomplished by a free press."[57]

DeMille's epic was in fact part of public discourse enlisting support for an embattled France symbolized by Joan of Arc rather than the modernist aesthetic so alienating to Protestant middle-class sensibility. Patriotic appeals associated with the Maid of Orléans were useful in overcoming American prejudice against Parisian avant-garde movements that contravened the sacrosanct notions of genteel culture.[58] An ad, for example, addressed the reader as follows: "Would Joan of Arc Be Burned Today? . . . Is the world freed of the arch-enemies of Truth—Ignorance and Superstition?" Articles even exploited accusations that Farrar was pro-German in sentiment. Attacking persistent rumors, the diva claimed, "I knew when I played Joan of Arc for Mr. DeMille's picture that it would be . . . the greatest of all pro-ally propaganda." Such marketing strategies attest to the commodification of history not only because the past became useful for propagandistic purposes, but, as pageant leaders feared, profitable as commercialized amusement. *Joan the Woman* was exploited, not coincidentally, in a lobbying effort on behalf of Sunday film exhibition in the state of New York. After a special screening for the governor, legislators, staff members, and wives, a straw vote resulted in 425 out of 502 votes in favor of Sunday theater openings. Similarly, Kansas legislators, "many of whom admitted never having seen a motion picture in their lives," adjourned for a special screening of the epic, to which their wives and children were invited, before considering legislation on state film censorship.[59] Publicity about these events in trade journals indicates that although great strides had been made since the advent of feature film, the cultural legitimacy of cinema had yet to be firmly established among the genteel classes in the years before the war.

A spectacle produced after the height of the pageantry movement and before the recruitment of the film industry by the Committee on Public Information (which set up a War Cooperating Committee, including DeMille and Griffith), *Joan the Woman* demonstrated the pitfalls of marketing historical representation.[60] An increasingly pluralistic urban audience, fragmented by class and ethnic differences, was unwilling even under threat of war to accept public history validated by the genteel middle class. Unlike DeMille's earlier features—such as the *Chimmie Fadden* series, *Kindling, The Golden Chance, The Heart of Nora Flynn,* and *The Dream Girl—Joan the Woman* offered neither criticism of the idle rich nor sympathetic figures with whom workers and immigrants could identify. Addressed to educated filmgoers who valued history as a sign of ideological consensus and as a vehicle to Americanize foreigners, the spectacle did not exert broad audience appeal. Lasky discouraged the production of any further epics when he wrote to DeMille, "I had some long conferences with Griffith [who was to direct films for Artcraft] and he frankly admitted that after his experience with 'Intolerance,' . . . the ideal pictures for money making . . . and every other purpose—are subjects of about 6500 feet in length, carefully and elaborately produced."[61] In 1917 DeMille directed two films starring Mary Pickford— *Romance of the Redwoods*, a Western, and *The Little American*, an anti-German propaganda piece—and two films with Geraldine Farrar—*The Woman God Forgot*, an abbreviated epic about the Aztec empire, and *The Devil Stone*, a romantic melodrama with the first of his trademark flashbacks. After *The Whispering Chorus* (1918), an impressive if dated reaffirmation of Victorian sentimentalism, DeMille charted a new course and began to address a national audience in terms of shared consumer values rather than foregrounding intertexts in genteel culture. With the consolidation of his stature as a film author, the director began the "second epoch" of his silent career, an epoch that coincided with the burgeoning of a consumer culture that would bear the inscription of his signature.

SIX

Set and Costume Design as Spectacle in a Consumer Culture: The Early Jazz Age Films

DeMILLE'S "SECOND EPOCH"

In January 1922 Paramount Pictures ran a full-page ad in *Motion Picture News* that displayed a cornucopia titled "Cecil B. DeMille's Horn of Plenty for Exhibitors." Stacks of bundled dollar bills and quantities of loose coins poured from the cone's opening. At the tip of the horn, labeled with the titles of all but two of the director's postwar films, was *Old Wives for New* (1918).[1] Clearly, this first Jazz Age feature marked the beginning of a "second epoch" in the periodization of DeMille's extraordinary film career, an event recognized and even touted by the studio at the time. Apart from the frontier sagas and biblical spectacles of the sound era, the director is mostly remembered today for the stylish sex comedies and melodramas of the late 1910s and early 1920s. Yet he reluctantly changed course, to one that would distinguish his career as a commercial filmmaker, against his own predilections and in response to the repeated urging of his longtime business associate, Jesse L. Lasky.

Although DeMille continued to address the genteel middle-class during the Jazz Age, he also constructed a showcase for ostentatious consumption that appealed to lower-middle-class and working-class female spectators. At the center of his society dramas was the sentimental heroine converted into a sexual playmate, a transformation accomplished by visual strategies emphasizing not only set and costume design but didactic intertitles. The director's mise-en-scène, which had won critical acclaim during the Progressive Era, influenced as well as registered the social change of the postwar decade. As consumption became a pleasurable aspect of modernity, his compositions were less distinguished by dramatic low-key lighting to articulate ethical dilemmas and more renowned for spectacular sets. Scripts give

27. A trade journal advertisement celebrates the lucrative "second epoch" of DeMille's career with the titles of his Jazz Age sex comedies and melodramas.

evidence of these changes. Jeanie Macpherson included details in *Old Wives for New,* for example, of furnishings like an elegant desk in the study of a wealthy businessman, a carved Italian chair in a fashionable boutique, and a festooned canopy in the boudoir of a prostitute.[2] DeMille's Jazz Age texts, in short, represented increasingly ostentatious and even outré levels of consumption both as spectacle for visual appropriation and as a showcase that set fashion trends in apparel and interior decorating.

A barometer of socioeconomic as well as aesthetic changes, DeMille's filmmaking style now exemplified a reversal of the intertextual relationship between cinema and established forms of genteel middle-class culture. During the Progressive Era, the director had legitimated feature film by demonstrating its correspondence to spectacles such as stage melodrama, social photography, world's fair and museum exhibits, and department store displays. As the First World War was drawing to a conclusion, however, he himself became a trendsetter. A sign of rebellion against cluttered Victorian taste, contemporary women's clothing as well as the interior decoration of houses, themselves ascribed with expressive personalities, had been changing even before the war.[3] After the armistice, *Theatre* announced in the flippant tone that characterized discourse on women as consumers:

> Los Angeles now fills the proud position Paris once occupied as the arbiter of fashion. . . .
> More women see deMille's pictures than read fashion magazines. . . . five whole reels just crammed and jammed with beautiful creations. . . .
> And then there are the tips on interior decoration and house-furnishing wherewith the Art Director and his staff . . . adorn each scene. It is within bounds to say that the taste of the masses has been developed more by Cecil B. deMille through the educational influence—
> Good Lord! The beans are spilled. Nobody will read any further than the word "Educational."[4]

Indeed, the consumer revolution of the early twentieth century required massive education to influence and mold public taste, an enterprise undertaken by the advertising industry in its role as a social agency. Significantly, DeMille's early Jazz Age films constituted a useful intertext for middle-class advertisers who, as Roland Marchand argues, considered themselves "apostles of modernity" with a mission to legitimate consumption. The sanctioning of consumer behavior through appeals to Victorian moralism was in fact an essential message in DeMille's pictorial mise-en-scène of the late 1910s and early 1920s. Furthermore, the director's representation of consumer goods such as fashion ensembles and bathroom fixtures, as well as his use of color processes and of Art Deco to signify modernity, were several years ahead of developments in advertising.[5] A discussion of specific texts will clarify the relationship between DeMille's mise-en-scène and magazine ads as etiquette manuals for a consumer culture.

Speaking in patriarchal tones in an autobiography compiled by Donald Hayne and Art Arthur, DeMille is apologetic about relinquishing his ambition to film historical epics in favor of "the art of the theater [which] must be popular." Indeed, he characterizes this transition in his career as an "original sin" and as "a last good-by to integrity and art."[6] Since the director was uncomfortable even in retrospect about momentous changes that enabled him to become an architect of modern consumption, Jesse L. Lasky's influential role as the corporation's vice-president deserves scrutiny. After

the financial disappointment of *Joan the Woman,* Lasky suggested that
DeMille consider "a subject modern in theme" and attached to his correspondence, dated January 1917, a memo from Carl H. Pierce on the subject
of "Costume Stuff." Pierce wrote that "Joan will get over big—a modern
story would have gotten over bigger. . . . What the public demands to-day
is modern stuff with plenty of clothes, rich sets, and action." Two months
later, Lasky recommended that DeMille and Macpherson "write something
typically American . . . that would portray a girl in the sort of role that the
feminists in the country are now interested in . . . the kind of girl that
dominates . . . who jumps in and does a man's work." In August, Lasky urged
DeMille to make an adaptation of David Graham Phillips's novel, *Old Wives
for New* (1908), because it "is full of modern problems and conditions, and
while there are a number of big acting parts, it does not require any one big
star. . . . It would be a wonderful money maker and make a very interesting
picture." As an alternative to Adolph Zukor's costly and escalating contract
negotiations with Mary Pickford, a shrewd businesswoman, Lasky was pro-
posing all-star features that capitalized on the studio's stock company.
Toward the end of the year, he purchased the rights to the Phillips novel
for $6,500, a decision that resulted in further communication with his
director-general on the West Coast: "Personally I would like to see you
become commercial to the extent of agreeing to produce this novel. It will
do twice as much businesss as 'The Woman God Forgot' or 'The Devil Stone'
[two Geraldine Farrar features about the historical past or with a flashback
to a former era] on account of the subject matter and the fame of the novel."
Unrelenting, Lasky wrote a few weeks later: "You should get away from the
spectacle stuff for one or two pictures and try to do modern stories of great
human interest. 'Old Wives for New' is a wonderful title. . . . I strongly
recommend your undertaking to do it."[7]

Accordingly, DeMille began production on the film in March 1918 in
time for a midyear release and set an important trend both in the industry
and in a burgeoning consumer culture. Although Lasky described "an
entire change in the taste of the public" that manifested itself in the
popularity of war pictures as well as "a decided tendency toward lighter
subjects," later that year DeMille made another version of his first film, *The
Squaw Man* (1918). Its title is missing from the cornucopia of riches accruing
from studio productions advertised in *Motion Picture News.* Lasky's reaction
was lukewarm: "I doubt if it will do as much business for the exhibitors as
your other pictures, as the subject seems rather old-fashioned." Still un-
enthusiastic about costume dramas, he encouraged the director to make a
variation of *Old Wives for New* that was titled *Don't Change Your Husband*
(1919). Somewhat defensive, DeMille replied, "The success of 'The Squaw
Man' has convinced me that I can do other revivals of this sort." Most likely,
he was also prodded to direct *Why Change Your Wife?* (1920), the last film in
the trilogy, because Lasky wrote, "It is really better that you produce this

picture than William [credited with the story] on account of your being so strongly identified with 'Don't Change Your Husband.' "[8] DeMille was able to indulge his penchant for historical epics in his trademark flashback sequences, but the vice-president had accurately taken the pulse of postwar filmgoers. Less than five years after the Lasky Company was founded to upgrade cinema for the respectable middle class, Lasky himself was encouraging his director-general to think in terms of production for a broad audience. DeMille thus set an industry trend with the production of *Old Wives for New.* After its success, countless titles hinting at marital problems such as *Rich Men's Wives, Too Much Wife, Trust Your Wife, How to Educate a Wife,* and *His Forgotten Wife* appeared on marquee signs.

THE COMMODIFICATION OF MARRIAGE: *OLD WIVES FOR NEW, DON'T CHANGE YOUR HUSBAND, WHY CHANGE YOUR WIFE?*

Although *Old Wives for New* is an adaptation based on a well-known novel, the credits unequivocally announce that cinema is now on an equal footing with literature. Macpherson is thus acknowledged as the author of the photoplay in the same title that attributes the film to the novelist. DeMille, of course, is credited as the author of the production. (By the time he made *Why Change Your Wife?* the director designed a trademark for his credit, a round medallion with his name etched around the upper half and his profile stamped in the center.) Since Macpherson embroidered the essential plot of *Old Wives for New* in numerous scenarios about the commodification of marriage throughout the silent era, Lasky was astute in recognizing the importance of the novel. Phillips, a best-selling novelist whose stories appeared in widely circulated periodicals like the *Saturday Evening Post,* was ahead of his time in contemplating the impact of modernity upon the upper-middle-class family, specifically, "the bearing of the scientific revolution upon woman and the home."[9] An increasing incompatibility on the part of antagonists Charles and Sophy Murdock, a couple drifting apart in middle age, is shown in the husband's fastidiousness and receptivity to fashion as opposed to the wife's neglect of her appearance and household. Because a woman's home was considered an expression of her personality, Sophy's slovenliness not only affected members of her family, including two grown children, but revealed a serious character flaw. Phillips was sympathetic about her failings, attributed in part to rural family origins, but DeMille proved merciless in deconstructing the sentimental image of the American wife and mother in favor of the "new woman."

Macpherson begins *Old Wives for New* with a symbolic sequence cleverly titled in the script as follows: " 'Life's' Bargain Counter / Across which our destinies are bartered like / so many Sacks of Meal—to 'Fate.' / Some are sold for Dollars / Some for Ambition / Some for Love—but all—are 'Sold.' " As described in the script, "Life," costumed as Harlequin, is "constantly laughing" behind a counter with "tiny figurines of *live* people, grouped in four sections, marked . . . staples, remnants, novelties, and mark-downs. . . . Among these are the main characters of the story. . . . Sophy Murdock—in 'Marked Downs,' Murdock and Juliet in 'Staples'—Berkeley and Jessie in 'Remnants,' Viola in 'Novelties.' " Shopping at the bargain counter, "Fate," costumed as Columbine, purchases some of the figurines and pays "Life" by "lifting a purse full of gold coins" that "shower over the counter."[10] Possibly, this sequence about the commodification and reification of marital relations in a consumer culture was too literal a representation of market-place transactions invading the domestic sphere. Instead, DeMille begins *Old Wives for New* with a didactic intertitle that could be construed as a quote from the novel but was not even a paraphrase and, moreover, could not be attributed to any character in the film:

> It is my belief, Sophy, that we Wives are apt to take our Husbands too much for granted. We've an inclination to settle down to neglectful *dowdiness*—just because we've "landed our Fish!" It is not enough for Wives to be merely virtuous anymore, scorning all frills: We must remember to trim our "Votes for Women" with a little lace and ribbon—if we would keep our Man a "Lover" as well as a "Husband"!

Such was the sermon of the film, a legacy of Victorian pictorialism, ad-dressed to female spectators enjoined to embrace the delights of the con-sumer culture if only to retain their marital status.

After DeMille introduces the main characters in terms of their social status, signified by close-ups of their hands performing various functions, he opens the film with the first of his celebrated bathroom sequences. Although the set design is modest compared to the spacious tiled bathroom with a sunken tub and a shower decorated with a silk curtain in *Male and Female* (1919), the scene was surely impressive for audiences who may have been able to afford an automobile but still lived in homes without bathtubs.[11] DeMille's mise-en-scène includes a tub on the left opposite a door flanked by two wash basins, each with hot and cold water faucets, a mirror, a shelf, and a pair of sconces for illumination; the basin on the left is at a right angle to a stained glass window above a towel bar on the rear wall. Ornate molding decorates the cornice, doorway, window, and mirrors of the room. The flooring consists of alternate black and white tiles in a diamond-shaped pattern. Charles Murdock (Elliott Dexter), dressed in a bathrobe and as-sisted by a valet, opens the window so that a view of the trees contrasts nature with artifice. A fastidious person, he is disgusted to find Sophy's hair clog-ging his basin, not to mention a messy comb and toothbrush that have been carelessly left in his corner of the bathroom. Worse, a close-up from his point of view shows untidy toilet articles strewn haphazardly about his wife's basin and vanity. Sophy (Sylvia Ashton), introduced in the credits as she is eating chocolates and reading the funnies, enters the bathroom in a grumpy mood

28. A flashback in *Old Wives for New* (1918) shows Wanda Hawley as the lovely young woman courted years ago by Elliott Dexter, now a dissatisfied spouse. *(Photo courtesy George Eastman House)*

and slams the window shut. She is wearing a loose bathrobe over her corpulent figure and has carelessly swept her unkempt hair into a knot. Deciding that a bath is not worth the effort, Sophy decides to seek refuge in bed while her family breakfasts downstairs. Murdock seats himself at a table set with silverware and a glass fruit compote but is displeased to find an orange spoon in the wrong place. The maid, who is as slovenly as her mistress, serves overcooked poached eggs with broken yolks. As he rises from the table in disgust, his daughter, who is a more sympathetic character in the novel, murmurs, "I'm sorry dear—if mother would only let *me* run the house!"

Disgruntled, Murdock retreats to his study and stares at a photograph of his wife, shown in an insert, when she was a slender, young woman with masses of blond curls (Wanda Hawley). A dissolve to a picturesque country scene shows how he literally reeled in his bride while she was walking barefoot in the stream—a reference to fishing in the first intertitle of the film. DeMille cleverly juxtaposes past and present tense as Murdock's memory of his lovely young bride is intercut with Sophy, now a middle-aged, obese, and untidy matron, emerging from her room and bursting in on his reverie. Appalled by her aging figure, the offended husband declares, "So-phy—it's a degradation for two people to go on living together who no longer care for each other! I propose that you will take half of all we've got—and that you and I shall release each other." A display of armaments on the panelled wall of the study includes a pistol, a long blade, and a sword. Apparently, the battle of the sexes has commenced. Murdock and his son, Charley, who sides with his mother in the novel's version of the marital breakup, decamp on a hunting expedition. Again, DeMille associates ro-mance with outdoor sportsmanship as the businessman falls in love with Juliet Raeburn (Florence Vidor), the vacationing owner of a fashionable boutique aptly named Dangerfield's.

Sophy is angered to learn that she may indeed have a rival. During a marital argument photographed in low-key lighting, she tears up the pho-tograph of herself as a young bride in a gesture of self-loathing and exclaims, "Have all the fun you want with that younger, fresher woman—But just you remember . . . I'll never divorce you—never!" Who is at fault here? Unlike the unambiguous moral dilemma dramatized by low-key lighting in earlier films such as *The Heart of Nora Flynn,* the scenario of *Old Wives for New* is more complicated. Sophy is self-indulgent, but Murdock, whose relationship with his daughter has incestuous overtones, is in love with a much younger woman. Consequently, low-key lighting becomes a technique increasingly keyed to the emotional mood of a shot rather than the dramatic articulation of moral issues. With respect to the use of genre conventions, however, DeMille is less ambiguous. As in the *Chimmie Fadden* series, he is uninterested in sustaining comedy throughout and resorts to melodrama. Although he employs misogynistic humor to lampoon Sophy, the film takes a melodra-matic turn that equates consumption with sexual lust and sinful behavior as opposed to sentimental romance.

Characteristic of DeMille's visual style in the early Jazz Age comedies and melodramas, set decoration and costumes provide a more reliable sign of personal ethics than dramatic low-key lighting.[12] Several weeks after the hunting trip in *Old Wives for New,* for example, Murdock is shopping with his daughter at Dangerfield's and meets his business partner, Tom Berkeley (Theodore Roberts), who is accompanied by his mistress, Jessie (Julia Faye), and her friend, Viola (Marcia Manon). DeMille's mise-en-scène underscores the interpenetration of home and marketplace or the decline of separate spheres based on gender in that Juliet's boutique resembles a tasteful upper-class residence. A split-level design features a checkerboard, black and white marbled floor, walls framed with moldings and intersected with pilasters and columns, an imposing chandelier, an elegant floor lamp and sconces, dark velvety drapery with tie backs, plush upholstered chairs, and artistic floral arrangements. Yet this well-appointed establishment, as signi-fied by its name, has become the site of questionable transactions in which women's bodies are commodified. Since Juliet retains her scruples and shuns him as a married man, Murdock later joins Berkeley, Jessie, and Viola at a supper club, where a dancer in a harem costume evokes Orientalist fantasies of luxury and sensuality. Unfortunately, Berkeley transfers his attentions to a flirtatious blonde named Bertha (Edna Mae Cooper), and Jessie disrupts their rendezvous to shoot her fickle lover. A sign of lower-class origins as well as loose morals, Bertha's gaudy boudoir, where Berkeley dies, contrasts with Juliet's tasteful boutique. The prostitute has a penchant for garish furniture decorated with gilt rococo curves, ruffled drapery and shiny bedspreads, cheap imitations of art work on wainscoted walls, and kitsch memorabilia.

A complicated scenario, the final events of *Old Wives for New* unravel when Sophy, flattered by Murdock's impecunious secretary, Melville Blagden (Gustav Seyffertitz), decides to undergo a tortuous beauty regimen in order to remarry. A benign representative of a patriarchal order, Blagden regulates female behavior by educating Sophy to redefine herself as a commodity through the consumption of cosmetics, gowns, and accessories. At the film's conclusion, DeMille cuts from Sophy's elegant wedding to Murdock's second marriage in Venice. After having met at an outdoor flower market signifying nature as opposed to artificiality, the businessman and dressmaker have reconciled. Yet the film's affirmation of self-theatricalization and fashion cycles emphasizes the importance of artifice rather than sincerity in sexual and marital relationships. The reification of social relations signified by performance rituals in genteel living rooms, in other words, has now invaded the back regions of respectable households. Far from constituting a safe haven, even the private quarters of well-to-do homes now simulate the marketplace as a site for the commodification of female bodies.

According to a fan magazine article, "So many wives wrote in indignant letters to DeMille about 'Old Wives for New' that C. B. and his clever writer, Jeanie Macpherson, wrote a story from the wives' standpoint." The *Chicago News* described the second film of the trilogy as an attempt "to restore harmony with . . . feminine followers."[13] Although *Don't Change Your Husband* was interpreted as the wife's version of matrimonial strife, in effect the heroine has already been transformed into a "new woman" so that her next lesson is to reduce unreasonable demands on her mate. DeMille begins the film with a humorous intertitle that foregrounds the battle of the sexes to contrast its more intimate scale with the tumult of World War I: "This does not deal with the tread of victorious Armies, nor defeated Huns—but is just a little sidelight on the inner life of Mr. and Mrs. Porter." Leila Porter (Gloria Swanson), an elegant and fastidious woman, finds "several dull gray years of matrimony—getting slightly on her nerves." Oblivious to his wife's discontent, Jim Porter (Elliott Dexter) boasts an expanded waistline, buries

29. Gloria Swanson enjoys an elegant breakfast but finds her second mate as immersed in the news as the first spouse she has just divorced in *Don't Change Your
Husband* (1919). (*Photo courtesy George Eastman House*)

his head behind newspapers, forgets their wedding anniversary, and in-
dulges a taste for green onions.

As in *What's His Name,* the director registers reversals in marital relationships through clever use of mise-en-scène. During a compromising
flirtation with ne'er-do-well Schuyler Van Sutphen (Lew Cody) at a costume
ball, Leila, who appears as Juliet with ropes of pearls in her hair, ascends a
marble staircase with an ornate balustrade on the right side of the screen.
After declaring that she can no longer tolerate her " 'corn beef and cabbage'
existence," Leila descends a marble staircase on the left in the vestibule of
the house she is abandoning. Whereas Jim is seated to her left with his head
buried in the papers after dinner in the opening sequence, in her second
marriage Leila finds Schuyler seated to her right at the breakfast table and
equally immersed in the news. DeMille's mise-en-scène thus dramatizes the
reification of marital relations; that is, marriage partners have in effect
become interchangeable parts attesting to the dominance of exchange value
in commodity production. Yet this transformation, based on the conversion
of the sentimental heroine into the fashionable "new woman," raised
disturbing moral issues. As his version of Freud's enigmatic question, "What
do women want?" the director shows a sphinx and a pyramid in an art title,
"The Eternal Feminine." An equation of mysterious Orientalism with

female self-gratification in a consumer culture, the Egyptian symbols reveal the persistence of the image of the vampire whose extravagance spelled ruin.

Determined to win back his former spouse, Jim shaves off his mustache, adopts an exercise regimen, and acquires a dapper wardrobe. Phillips observes in *Old Wives for New*, ". . . of those external forces that combine to make us what we are, dress is one of the most potent. It determines the character of our associations, determines the influences that shall chiefly surround and press upon us. It is a covering for our ideas no less than for our bodies."[14] Macpherson's blunt rewriting of this quotation in *Don't Change Your Husband* exemplifies the reification of human consciousness in a consumer culture in which human beings are confused with commodities: "Of those external forces which combine to make us what we are, DRESS is the most potent. It covers our *ideas* no less than our bodies—until we finally become the thing we look to be." Social ritual as an indecipherable hieroglyph in genteel living rooms, in other words, has been reduced to a reading of external appearances that reinforces self-commodification. A proliferation of mirror shots in DeMille's Jazz Age films attests to the increasing importance of style over substance.[15] A medium shot shows Jim, for example, standing in front of a mirror while staring at his image in a hand mirror. Although he is a powerful businessman who dominates complex financial negotiations, his pose in this instance resembles that of prostitutes, namely Viola in *Old Wives for New* and Toodles (Julia Faye), Schuyler's mistress in *Don't Change Your Husband*. During the credits of the former film, Viola, a "Painted Lady" with Orientalized features, is seated in front of a dresser and applies rouge as she gazes in the mirror.[16] Similarly, Toodles is presented in the credits as she primps in front of a dresser with a three-way mirror, turns around to face the camera, and kisses an image of herself in a hand mirror. Genteel concern with appearances as a sign of the character and breeding of the "best people" has deteriorated into narcissistic self-absorption. Accordingly, Jim wins back his former wife at the conclusion of *Don't Change Your Husband* by transforming himself into a dapper dinner guest wearing a tuxedo and a fur-collared coat.

Although the scenario of *Don't Change Your Husband* appears to be a variation of *Old Wives for New,* the intensity of moral issues raised by a consumer culture begins to diminish in the midst of pleasurable pursuits. Significantly, the characters in *Old Wives for New* are still troubled by their scruples or exhibit some degree of conscience in their behavior. Juliet, for example, refuses to be involved in a relationship with a man who has deceived her about his marital status. When Sophy wrongly names her as a corespondent in a libelous divorce suit, Murdock goes to extreme lengths to protect her reputation. Even Berkeley, as he lies dying from a gunshot wound in a prostitute's apartment, begs his partner to avoid a scandal that will tarnish his family name. The frivolous characters in *Don't Change Your Husband,* on the contrary, pursue their pleasures without much regard for the consequences of their actions. Leila engages in a flirtation with Schuyler, whom she marries after divorcing Jim, and Schuyler in turn has an affair with Toodles during his marriage to Leila. While the members of the younger set impulsively gratify their whims, their elders, personified by Schuyler's Aunt Huckney (Sylvia Ashton) and an aging bishop (Theodore Roberts), register indignation in point-of-view and reaction shots. DeMille, interestingly, comments on generational differences by representing conscience as the disapproval of middle-aged spectators rather than as an internalized set of behavioral norms. But in *Why Change Your Wife?*, the last film of the trilogy, even the older generation relinquishes adherence to conventional standards of behavior. Aunt Kate (Sylvia Ashton), who is the equivalent of Aunt Huckney in the guise of a chaperon, is no longer alarmed by the flirtatious behavior of young spouses and herself falls prey to the charms of an attentive European violinist.

To dramatize the less inhibited and hedonistic nature of the marital relations in *Don't Change Your Husband,* DeMille conflates exotic visions of distant lands and employs a bizarre mixture of Orientalist motifs in set and costume design. A Middle Eastern backdrop for social entertainment, Leila's living room features ornately carved pilasters, tapestry, carpeting, and a potted palm. An Asian servant in Chinese dress provides drinks in cups carved out of precious jade at an anniversary dinner. Leila, whom Schuyler addresses as "Lovely Chinese Lotus," poses in an off-the-shoulder gown and turban as part of the decor; to complement her ensemble, she carries an enormous fan of peacock feathers. Even more exotic is Schuyler's residence, a mansion that includes a loggia with matching rattan furniture and a study simulating a display window with chinoiserie for the decoration of elegant homes. A scroll hangs on the rear wall, and an Oriental vase stands on the cabinet to its right. A chair in the foreground is upholstered in fabric with a bamboo pattern, and a fringed throw in floral print is artfully tossed over a nearby sofa. On the right side of the floor, partially covered with an Oriental carpet, stands an ornate table with an incense burner. Leila, responding to the pungent aroma filling the air, enters this sybaritic domain at her peril. Delighted by a beaded gown unpacked for a costume party, she drapes the fabric around her body in a pose that recalls Edith's posturing in the Shoji Room of *The Cheat.* The showcasing of women as manikins or commodities serves in both features as a prelude to rituals of seduction. A description of this scene in the script reads even more like the sequence in the earlier film because Schuyler presents Leila with a mandarin coat that has a hypnotic effect: "A change comes over Leila; . . . she seems suddenly to be slipping back into Orientalism; to be taking on a real, subtle, *un-American* personality. She is no longer a laughing Society Woman merely trying on a Chinese Cloak, for fun."[17]

A cultural practice established by halftones, magic lantern slides, panoramas, stereographs, and actuality footage, as well as by department store displays and museum and world's fair exhibits, consumption in the form of visual appropriation was linked to exotic sites. Indeed, picturesque images of the "Other" mediated the disturbing experience of urban pluralism for middle-class consumers who preferred social reality contained within the framework of photographs, plate glass, and theatrical venues. Yet the correspondence of cultural forms in genteel society accounted for the intrusion of the marketplace, simulating an elegant living room, into the back regions of affluent households. Symbolic of the accelerating dissolution of separate spheres based on gender was the fashionable "new woman" who shopped in emporiums laden with enticing Orientalist displays of merchandise. Aestheticized visions of modernity, however, were rooted in a legacy of Victorian pictorialism and thus raised the specter of moral dilemmas. Consumer behavior in effect implied sexual license that was interpreted as un-American, unpatriotic, or uncivilized, even as Americans loosened their purse strings and eased their consciences to buy goods signifying refinement. Preoccupation with bathing rituals and with elegant bathrooms in the latest fashion, as represented in DeMille's celebrated texts, therefore belied anxiety about consumption insofar as it evoked the "Other," including women, as threats to the body politic.[18] Furthermore, commodities that denoted genteel status, like the restraints of sentimental culture against which men rebelled, threatened masculinity. Schuyler in *Don't Change Your Husband,* for example, is a morally bankrupt and effeminate voluptuary because Orientalism remains at the core of his obsession with illicit sexuality and sybaritic luxury. Thus his exclamation about " 'Pleasure'—'Wealth'— and 'Love' " cues the sensational fantasy sequence of the film. A spectacle prefiguring the well-known flashback to a Babylonian court in *Male and Female,* this footage consists of three separate scenes photographed mostly in extreme long shot: Leila seated on a gigantic swing suspended over a swimming pool adorned with masses of flowers and bathing beauties in fishnet stockings; Leila draped in rich fabric and jewels with the well-oiled bodies of black male slaves at her feet in an opulent Oriental court; and Leila clad in flimsy chiffon as she lounges in an Edenic paradise, with Bacchus squeezing grapes into her mouth.

Although DeMille was quite willing to pique the curiosity of prewar audiences, as evidenced in *The Golden Chance* and *The Cheat,* his postwar flashback and fantasy sequences left very little to the imagination. The Jazz Age films, in particular, exemplify Guy Debord's discourse on the "society of the spectacle" as a "*Weltanschauung* which has become actual, materially translated. . . . a world vision which has become objectified." Furthermore, motion picture images as spectacle constituted a form of commodity fetishism, an investment of desire in objects displacing human relations, that represented a confluence of the filmmaker's own fantasies with the burgeoning of consumer capitalism. Granted, the commodification of spectacle was hardly a recent historical phenomenon, but its replication and mass distribution by the cinematic apparatus occurred during a period of accelerated economic development. DeMille's texts thus represented a consumer culture that appealed to the eye, an appeal that had been stimulated for decades by a realist aesthetic enhanced by technological developments such as halftones in periodicals and electric lights in theaters and department stores. Consumption thus became "a hegemonic 'way of seeing,'" as T. J. Jackson Lears and Richard Wightman Fox argue, in that an elite cultural practice eventually dominated the marketing strategies of a nationwide economy.[19] The issue of whether consumer behavior patterns including leisure-time pursuits followed a top-down or bottom-up model is debatable, but the significance of visual appropriation in a postwar decade of increased class and ethnic conflict cannot be underestimated. As the middle class became more immersed in consumption as a way of life, the lower class, especially women, found that the democratization of luxury was accessible for the price of a movie ticket, a price they could still afford at neighborhood venues if not at downtown movie palaces.[20]

A year after the completion of *Don't Change Your Husband,* Lasky prevailed upon DeMille to make *Why Change Your Wife?* Although the director later sought to obtain rights to the film for Macpherson, William deMille received credit for the story and Olga Printzlau and Sada Cowan wrote the scenario.[21] Granted, the film's intertitles are much wittier, but given the similarity of the plot to the previous two films, based on the best-seller by Phillips, Macpherson's influence was probably not inconsiderable. A remodeling of the Victorian sentimental heroine as the centerpiece of a consumer culture, *Why Change Your Wife?* is a variation of *Old Wives for New* and opens with yet another of DeMille's famous bathroom scenes. Robert Gordon (Thomas Meighan) is shaving in front of an oval mirror at right angle to an elegant oval window, decorated with a scalloped and fringed valance, on the rear wall. As his wife Beth (Gloria Swanson) constantly interrupts his toilet, a title informs us "Marriage, like genius, is an infinite capacity for taking pains—" DeMille in fact proved quite daring by showing Robert sitting on the toilet seat twice when Beth demands access to the medicine cabinet behind the mirror and requires help fastening her dress. Unfortunately, Beth's "virtues are her only vices" in a hedonistic era associated with playful flappers, bathtub gin, and raucous jazz. She disapproves of her husband's commodious wine cellar, furnished with leather furniture, a full-size bar, and racks of bottles. When Beth voices concern about postwar issues, such as "the

starving millions in Europe," Robert replies, "Why do you insist that everything I do for *our* happiness robs someone else?" Social problems—not
to mention the primary role of the middle-class family in rearing children—
disappear from DeMille's Jazz Age films as self-gratification displaces noblesse oblige.

Drawing on Orientalist themes about consumption that equate an expensive boutique in the public sphere with the privacy of a woman's boudoir,
DeMille shows Robert visiting a shop, aptly titled Maison Chic, where an Asian
woman in exotic dress greets him at the door. A medium long shot shows
Sally Clark (Bebe Daniels), an attractive model, climbing on top of a dresser
with a three-way mirror to peer out an oval-shaped window, a decorative motif
that links the dressing room of the boutique to the Gordons' bathroom.
DeMille deleted an intertitle in the script that characterizes Sally as a gold
digger "who buys the necessities of her life with her salary and the luxuries
with her alimony" so that she is not entirely unsympathetic but a sexual
playmate in contrast to highbrow Beth. Preparing to model a backless negligee with transparent sleeves and a train trimmed with fur, she removes the
full-length slip beneath the flimsy skirt in a close-up revealing high-buttoned
shoes,[22] places a heart-shaped tattoo on her left shoulder, and daubs perfume
from a bottle labeled in an insert as "Persian Night." Beth, on the contrary,
is outraged that evening when she tries on the negligee and gazes at her image
in the bedroom mirror. Robert insists, "My dearest, since time began dress
has played it's [*sic*] role in love, and woman has worn it to delight her mate."
As in *Don't Change Your Husband,* the seduction of women with expensive
apparel triggers a fantasy or flashback sequence. But DeMille edited out
footage described in the script as follows: "Dissolve to Gloria Swanson as a
wood nymph in cave man days, then an Oriental courtesan . . ." Since a still
photograph of Swanson and Meighan in exotic costumes survives, the director most likely photographed these scenes but deleted them in the final
cut.[23] A marital rupture thus occurs without the disruption of pictorial
moralism instructing women to become commodities, although Beth's indignation is obviously a response to the flashback: "Do you expect me to
share your Oriental ideas? Do you want your *wife* to lure you like a—Oh why
didn't you marry a Turk?" Robert, in a medium shot, smells Sally's perfume
on the sleeve of the negligee and recalls her seductive image, superimposed
on the screen between himself and his incensed wife.

Aside from fashion, an essential aspect of the transformation of the
genteel upper-middle-class woman into a sexual playmate is an appreciation
of popular as opposed to highbrow culture. Anticipating the delivery of the
negligee, Robert decides to play the "Hindustan Fox Trot," a popular
postwar tune with distinct Oriental overtones, but Beth insists, "Try to
cultivate your taste, dear!" and prefers "The Dying Poet." Robert is not only
bored with Beth's dowdy clothes and spectacles, he would also prefer to

attend the follies rather than listen to an adagio performed by Radinoff (Theodore Kosloff), whom he stereotypes as "a wired-haired foreigner." Still dedicated to spiritual uplift, Beth reads books with titles such as *How to Improve Your Mind*. After an inevitable marital rupture occurs, the irate wife removes all traces of her spouse from the living room and tosses in the trash can a copy of *Motion Picture Classic* (an inspired choice for DeMille) and a baseball magazine. She then announces, "I'm going to give my whole life to charity, Aunt Kate. I hate clothes—and men." A satirized version of the genteel woman who believes in social commitment and values highbrow culture, Beth is instantly converted to consumer values during a shopping trip. DeMille cuts between adjacent dressing rooms in a smart boutique to show Beth's angry reaction when she overhears two gossiping women attribute her divorce to her frumpy appearance. Assuming the role of a manikin, she places ornaments in her hair, poses with a feathered fan, and drapes brocade against her body as she gazes at her image in a hand mirror. She then instructs the sales clerk, "I'll take this and six more; and make them sleeveless, backless, transparent, indecent—go the limit!"

Beth's sensational debut as a "new woman" occurs at a fashionable beach resort, where Robert is vacationing with his new wife, Sally. An establishing shot shows musicians playing on a balcony and hotel guests seated at dining tables around a large swimming pool with an island featuring an octagonal fountain. Potted plants and palms, as well as wicker and rattan furniture, convey a tropical atmosphere as the backdrop for romance. An extreme long shot shows Beth standing in an archway that is the entrance to the pool area. She advances to the foreground in a floral-patterned bathing suit and a matching fringed cap, an eye-catching ensemble that attracts instant attention. A long shot next shows Beth conversing with several male admirers, including members of the military in uniform. A cut to a long shot of her seated on the wall of the fountain but hidden under her parasol results in an amusing scene when Robert enters from the right. A close-up of her legs, rendered alluring by stylish high-heeled shoes and an ornate garter wrapped around her left calf, represents his point of view. Unaware that he is admiring his former wife, Robert walks behind her and peers down at her from the left. An angled close-up of her peering up at him through the plastic folds of her parasol results in a shocking yet delightful recognition. When Radinoff, costumed in a leotard with a cape and wearing sandals with straps crisscrossed up to his knees, escorts Beth away, Robert, now thoroughly enticed by his former spouse, angrily slams his cap on the ground.

DeMille orchestrates another divorce and remarriage in a complicated scenario that results in Robert, seriously injured, being nursed in Beth's home while Sally is determined to reclaim her spouse. Due to a head injury, Robert's vision is blurred until Beth's face comes into focus in a close-up, a scene that prefigures the introduction of Christ healing a blind girl in *The*

30. Thomas Meighan is quite disconcerted to discover that his dowdy former wife (Gloria Swanson) has transformed herself into a seductive fashion plate in *Why Change Your Wife?* (1920) *(Photo courtesy George Eastman House)*

King of Kings (1927). An object of struggle between two determined women, Robert lies helpless as they fight over him in a brawl that ends with Sally shattering a mirror and attempting to disfigure Beth. Since she has unmasked herself as being ill-tempered and vindictive, traits previously disguised by self-theatricalization and lavish gowns, Sally concedes defeat and resumes flirting with Radinoff. Beth, in the meanwhile, remarries Robert, wears the negligee she had earlier scorned, and plays the "Hindustan Fox Trot" in the wine cellar. DeMille's patriarchal and didactive voice is heard in the final intertitle: "And now you know what every husband knows: that a man would rather have his wife for his sweetheart than any other woman: but Ladies: if you would be your husband's sweetheart you simply *must* learn to forget that you're his wife." To put it another way, genteel women who exchanged the supportive intimacy of homosocial ties in a sex-segregated Victorian culture to become sexual playmates were still not equal to men, not even in a companionate marriage.[24]

Yet the issue of equality between the sexes was at the heart of the so-called revolution in manners and morals that nevertheless witnessed an increasing commodification of female sexuality. DeMille did hint at the darker aspects of heterosexual relations in a disarmingly blunt intertitle in *Old Wives for New*. After Jessie shoots Berkeley, she confides to Murdock, "I killed him—he was a beast! No man ever knows what another man is with a woman!" Also revealing is a sequence in *Don't Change Your Husband* in which Toodles bursts into the Van Sutphen residence to claim a share of the cash that Jim has paid Schuyler for Leila's solitaire. Giving her husband's mistress half a wad of thick bills, Leila explains, "Don't misunderstand—he *owed* you something—and you are paid! He promised me a few things, too, such as Love and Protection—and he didn't pay! Let's only one of us be cheated!" The use of financial language is extremely apt in a film that dramatizes the increasing commodification and reification of matrimonial life. DeMille, interestingly, cuts from a medium two-shot of Schuyler and Jim looking away from the scrutiny of the camera to a medium long shot of the two accusatory women eyeing the men. For a brief moment, the battle of the sexes takes precedence over class conflict. Although nineteenth-century feminists outraged genteel society by comparing marriage with prostitution in attempts to reform divorce laws, the reification of marital relations based on exchange value, as shown in DeMille's trilogy, implied no less.[25] Furthermore, the displacement of female desire onto fashion and furnishings was yet another expression of commodity fetishism in consumer capitalism. The exploitation of this aspect of the culture of consumption as it related to the composition of the film audience became the focus of Paramount exhibition practices during the 1920s.[26]

DISCOURSE ON THE OLD VERSUS THE NEW MORALITY: THE DEMOGRAPHICS OF FILM AUDIENCES

Significant changes in the demographics of film attendance in the 1920s were related to trends established by the production and exhibition of DeMille's early Jazz Age films. Exhibitors, to be sure, distinguished between middle-class patrons of first-run theaters and working-class and ethnic audiences at neighborhood venues, and between urban centers and small-town or rural areas. During a decade characterized by tumultuous events such as the Red Scare, immigration restriction, prohibition, the Sacco-Vanzetti case, the rise of the Ku Klux Klan, and the Scopes trial, the search for a national market in film distribution and exhibition practices was essential. The exploitation of DeMille's controversial films showed, however, that differences based on class, ethnicity, religion, and geographical region that might segment the audience could be superceded by an appeal to gender. Although the reception of a consumer culture including commercialized amusement was mediated by a variety of subcultures, the director's emphasis on set and costume design appealed overwhelmingly to women. As his brother William noted regarding the democratization of luxury, "Paris fashion shows had been accessible only to the chosen few. C. B. revealed them to the whole country, the costumes his heroines wore being copied by hordes of women and girls throughout the land, especially by those whose contacts with centers of fashion were limited or non-existent." DeMille himself represented this obsession with style in *The Affairs of Anatol* (1921) when a farmer's wife copies a magazine illustration, shown in an insert, to trim an ordinary hat. Since the director became the industry's most important trendsetter in the late 1910s and early 1920s, his emphasis on fashion was surely related to changes in the demographics of the film audience. According to Richard Koszarski, the percentage of men in motion picture audiences began to decline in the 1910s, while the number of women rose from 60 percent in 1920 to 83 percent in 1927.[27]

An analysis of industry discourse shows that exploitation campaigns appealing to women displaced censorship issues in DeMille's texts that might otherwise have segmented the audience. Indeed, the controversy provoked by scenes in *Old Wives for New* was scarcely an issue by the time *Why Change Your Wife?* was exhibited two years later. DeMille later claimed that Zukor, who "spent millions to plaster the country about the purity of Paramount Pictures," released the first film in the trilogy with great reluctance.[28] During the same month that critics were taking note of the director's trendsetting production, Zukor asserted in *Motion Picture News* that "Wholesome dramas, uplifting in character, clean comedies, comedy dramas, and plays dealing with the more cheerful aspects of life will be exclusively chosen for production."[29] *Old Wives for New* had in fact been subject to in-house censorship before its distribution. A few weeks before the film's premiere, Lasky received a detailed memo that proposed a number of cuts in the film. Among the suggestions was deletion of the first intertitle referring to the dowdiness of married women because "it is liable to be misconstrued by the average spectator." Clearly, Famous Players-Lasky was now marketing its product in terms of a broad-based appeal rather than targeting genteel audiences. Also objectionable were close-ups of the wash basins in the bathroom and signs of Murdock's fastidiousness. (These scenes were not cut, however, in the surviving print in the director's nitrate collection bequeathed to George Eastman House.) But the suggestion that DeMille insert an intertitle to indicate that Murdock, contrary to the scenario, did not engage in an affair with Viola was heeded. Further, risqué scenes of Berkeley's rendezvous with Bertha were cut to emphasize Jessie's confrontation with the couple. Perhaps most interesting, given negative Catholic reception of *Joan the Woman*, was deletion of a scene at the film's conclusion in which Jessie seeks refuge in a convent while both Sophy and Murdock remarry. According to the New York office, this scene would be considered "offensive to Catholics, in as much as it implies that a Catholic Institution would receive and protect a murderess."[30]

Critical discourse on *Old Wives for New* and subsequently *Don't Change Your Husband* and *Why Change Your Wife?* did focus on the impact of controversial moral issues on audience reception. A reminder that *Old Wives for New* was condemned by the Pennsylvania State Board because it dealt with the subject of prostitution provides present-day readers with some insight into censorship issues that characterized past cultural formations.[31] Critics disagreed at the time about the extent to which these films violated social conventions, yet their very disagreement reveals a lack of consensus regarding problematic issues such as divorce. R. E. Pritchard, for example, summed up his assessment of *Old Wives for New* in *Motion Picture News:* "There are some risque situations in the story, but these have been handled delicately." Frederick James Smith, however, objected to "scenes of disgusting debauchery" and "immoral episodes" and concluded, "It is extremely difficult to build up a pleasing romance upon a foundation of divorce." Similarly, Edward Weitzel claimed in *Moving Picture World* that "hardly any of the characters command the spectator's respect. Charles Murdock . . . has but little moral stamina, and is surrounded, principally, by well-dressed men and women of no morals at all." Weitzel even suggested censoring objectionable material: "The cabaret scene is too insistent in establishing the moral laxity of its female guests, and other scenes of the same nature would stand cutting." *Variety*'s critic also referred to the possibility of censorship: "There appears to have been some doubt as to the propriety of presenting the picture in total at the Rivoli in New York [a first-run theater]. . . . cutting was no doubt considered." Clearly, the critics recognized that the subject matter of *Old Wives for New* was questionable, if not offensive, but moved their discussion to the high ground of art in order to claim the patronage of the respectable middle class. Pritchard asserted that "it is the kind of picture that will convince those who doubt that the photoplay has reached the artistic plane of the spoken drama." The "Exhibitor to Exhibitor Review Service" in *Motion Picture News* agreed that the "feature will prove objectionable to some of you. Nevertheless, this picture is very artistic."[32]

Don't Change Your Husband elicited another chorus of disagreement among critics in fan magazines and trade journals that is revealing with respect to exhibition practices. Smith stated in *Motion Picture Classic,* "We do not agree with Miss Macpherson's philosophy, but we admire her effort . . . in approaching the realities of things as they are." *Variety* labeled the film "clean and wholesome," but *Motion Picture News* counseled exhibitors, "It suggests the divorce element without your having to go into that, and we wouldn't do so directly, because you are likely to sacrifice some of the intensely human appeal of this picture." As for the fantasy sequence, the journal claimed, "There is a sensuous touch here and there in the scenes that follow. They will offend no one, but they will create a lot of talk for the picture itself." Controversial subjects like prostitution and divorce were evidently difficult for exhibitors to market due to differences in social mores, especially in small towns and rural areas that were increasingly centers of religious fundamentalism. As a matter of fact, the Phillips novel, though published a decade before the film's release, still construes divorce as socially undesirable in contrast to the blasé manner in which DeMille's characters exchange spouses. Apparently, exhibitors engaged in a high wire act by exploiting the sex appeal of a film but taking steps not to offend the sensibility of their patrons. Despite controversy, DeMille's early Jazz Age films played to large and enthusiastic audiences in first-run theaters in major cities. At Grauman's Million Dollar Theatre in downtown Los Angeles, *Don't Change Your Husband* broke all attendance records so that Sid Grauman, departing from established policy, held the picture over for another week. By the time *Why Change Your Wife?* was released in April 1920, Smith gave an indication of the shifting moral standards of the postwar era when he stated, "What a shock Cecil deMille's latest silken orchid drama . . . would have caused but two short years ago." But *Motion Picture News* pointed out that the feature "practically throws that which most people call part of the moral code overboard with its teaching, [and] presents its principal characters as people who have about as much regard for the sanctity of the marriage vow 'as an Arab does for a sun bath.' . . . [F]or an exhibitor with a neighborhood or small town house it may not be an ideal attraction."[33] The trade journal's equation of sexual license with images of Orientalism, however, inadvertently served as part of a parallel discourse comparable to the film as a text on the evils of modernity.

An example of bridging the cultural divide between rural and urban America, the exhibition of *Why Change Your Wife?* was successful in major cities because exploitation avoided mention of divorce and emphasized consumption to appeal to female shoppers. Although these two issues were interrelated, as the film's title implies, exhibitor emphasis on fashion was a clever way to defuse public reaction to controversial moral issues. Sid Grauman, for example, simulated the movie screen by installing oil paintings of captivating stills in downtown Los Angeles shops, surely a reversal of DeMille's construction of the frame as a plate glass window. Such advertising tactics resulted in a special 10:45 P.M. performance that was added to the screening schedule to accommodate overflowing crowds at Grauman's Rialto. Los Angeles was hardly an exception, however. A similar exploitation campaign with window tie-ups in fashionable stores was orchestrated in Memphis with the cooperation of the Chamber of Commerce. A month after the film's release, Paramount ran an ad in *Motion Picture News* that claimed "'Why Change Your Wife?' has broken records in every city in which it has been shown." Constructing an elaborate showcase for the premiere of DeMille's film in New York, Adolph Zukor spent thirty thousand dollars to renovate the Criterion. Indeed, Zukor's strategy of acquiring a financial interest in first-run theatres paid off in terms of the enormous publicity generated for Famous Players-Lasky specials shown at higher admission prices. As *Moving Picture World* remarked about the record-breaking success of *The Affairs of Anatol* in the following year, "a Broadway showing is not always indicative of the attitude of the country, [but] such a run determines a great deal."[34] The exploitation of feature films at movie palaces, especially those appealing to fashion-conscious women, thus influenced nationwide trends in exhibition practices.

Although the industry still relied on small-town exhibitors in the countryside, as well as on neighborhood venues in urban areas, exploitation that stressed window tie-ups in chic department stores and movie ads in magazines like *Saturday Evening Post, Ladies' Home Journal,* and *Colliers* were obviously aimed at respectable middle-class women with disposable incomes. As for working-class and ethnic women, social historians emphasize the importance of filmgoing for a younger generation preoccupied with fashion as a mode of self-representation and assimilation.[35] The film industry's appeal to female spectators was thus a phenomenon that crossed socioeconomic and cultural boundary lines. As early as 1918, *Motion Picture News* suggested that exhibitors display pictures of female stars in elegant costumes to attract women and to persuade their escorts to buy admission tickets. Advertising, moreover, did not cease once members of the audience seated themselves inside the theater and began to enjoy the entertainment. As *Motion Picture News* observed about *Why Change Your Wife?*: DeMille inserted close-ups of commodities including perfume and "a certain talking machine company's records" that functioned as ads in the narrative.[36] Advertisement representing the allure of consumer goods, especially the latest fashion in apparel and home furnishings, was surely related to the demographic fact that throughout the decade the ratio of female to male spectators continued to rise.

In contrast to trade journals counseling exhibitors to downplay controversial issues, fan magazine discourse on DeMille's trilogy, linked by advertising and a reissue of *Old Wives for New,* focused on the relationship between fashion and divorce as a sign of the times.[37] Indeed, the rate of divorce almost doubled during the first two decades of the twentieth century, while expenditures for personal grooming, clothing, furniture, automobiles, and recreation tripled in the second two decades. Divorce was especially common in urban areas in the postwar years when hasty wartime unions were dissolved. Significantly, an increasing number of complaints in divorce suits involved the desire of wives for a more pleasurable life-style and the inability of husbands to provide income for such pursuits. According to the *New York*

Times, "if dissatisfied wives were guided by the argument of 'Don't Change Your Husband,' the divorce courts would be more crowded than they are now." Postwar discourse on divorce as a function of urbanization, secularization of liberal Protestantism, and changing patterns of wage earning and consumption focused on the "new woman."[38] A discourse paralleling DeMille's texts, fan magazines attest that Victorian didacticism was essential to rationalize the transformation of the genteel woman into a sexual playmate. But unlike the scenario of thousands of actual divorce cases, consumption was touted as the solution rather than the cause of marital discord. During the production of *Old Wives for New,* DeMille asserted in a magazine interview that the film provided a "moral lesson to wives." According to the director, "Husbands leave home because their wives are no longer physically attractive. . . . It's simply the most rudimentary example of sex psychology." As for his merciless lampooning of Sophy Murdock as the obese and indolent spouse, he claimed, "It is typically American to . . . idealize the wife, paint her virtues, blacken the man, and think we're standing by the bulwarks of civilization. In reality, we're making men hide their domestic bitterness and seek their comforts . . . secretly."[39]

Upon the release of *Don't Change Your Husband,* DeMille repeated his thoughts in *Motion Picture Magazine* by claiming that "man must have mystery, and, above all, lure, and if his wife doesn't retain it herself, he'll find it elsewhere." Pursuing a similar theme but with an emphasis on Orientalism, *Photoplay* published a short piece about Sessue Hayakawa and his wife, actress Tsuru Aoki, in which "husband-holding" was equated with "pyramid building" and "making Damascus blades" as lost arts! What lessons could be learned from the "wisdom of the Orient"? Captioned photographs showed Aoki waiting on Hayakawa in a solicitous yet refined manner. After the premiere of *Don't Change Your Husband,* Gloria Swanson claimed in *Motion Picture Magazine* that "divorce should be made more easy. . . . Then the wife, knowing she might lose her husband . . . would exert herself to hold him. And . . . the husband would go on paying attention to his wife, bringing her flowers and candy, taking her to theaters." A response to discourse that appeared frivolous but revealed profound changes in matrimonial expectations, *Motion Picture Magazine* published an editorial titled "Cinema Husbands": "Let us have a screenic [*sic*] burial of the movie husband. . . . The average American husband is no fool. The cinema husband is not only a fool but a blind egoist as well."[40]

Perhaps the most revealing fan magazine article that pointed to the contradiction of defining the "new woman" in terms of a Victorian legacy was published after the success of *Why Change Your Wife?* Acclaimed as "the film's greatest authority on matrimonial problems," DeMille claimed in *Photoplay,* "I believe I can do more to prevent divorce, that I am doing more to prevent divorce than any minister or anti-divorce league in the world."

Despite the contemporary and racy tone of his Jazz Age films, the director expressed attitudes about sexual difference and marriage that were Victorian clichés. For example, he asserted, "Sex . . . is a universal problem. It is the one thing one is never free of. If the relations between a man and woman are not right, not harmonious, every other relation of their lives is affected—their home, their children, his business, his usefulness as a citizen." Such distinctions in the use of plural and masculine pronouns implied that separate spheres for the sexes, in a new era of woman's suffrage, was still an ideal arrangement. Furthermore, the filmmaker argued, "Fidelity to the marriage covenant—the most sacred of all obligations— . . . is to be gained only by showing wives how men may be, if not lifted entirely above sex, at least taught to hold it within the bounds of moral law and decency." What exactly were those bounds? DeMille blithely confessed that in eighteen years of marriage, he had never spent a Saturday evening at home, a revelation that attested to the habit of respectable middle-class men visiting brothels.[41] Apparently, a man's sexual nature required a certain amount of discreet tolerance on the part of his wife.

Five months later, DeMille revealed in another piece in *Photoplay,* titled "More About Marriage," that his earlier interview had resulted in an avalanche of mail—presumably from women—surpassing the response to any film he had produced. Fan magazine readers wished to know if Mrs. DeMille, whose photograph was featured in the follow-up article, enjoyed the same privileges on Saturday night that he did. The director asserted, "no matter how willing a man may be to accord his wife complete freedom, men and women are not 'exactly alike'" because "the really good woman . . . is the . . . wise, pure, understanding woman, who . . . tries to kill the beast in man. . . . helping him to overcome the Adam inheritance of lust and dust that eventually lead to ruin." Asserting that a "woman's love that has not much of the maternal is only passion," DeMille appeared to contradict the lesson in his films, dictating that the "new woman" should be a playmate in a companionate marriage.[42]

In sum, the "new woman" who emerged in DeMille's feature films and in fan magazines was, on the one hand, a sexual playmate and herself a commodity and, on the other, a sentimental heroine adhering to an outmoded Victorian legacy. The emphasis on self-theatricalization informing discourse on these contrasting models of femininity ultimately served to validate consumption rather than sexual equality or freedom. A proliferation of discourses on pleasure, as Michel Foucault argues, was linked to a concern "to constitute a sexuality that was economically useful and politically conservative."[43] To put it another way, commodity fetishism, or the displacement of desire onto material goods, proved to be a useful stimulus in the growth of consumer capitalism. Gloria Swanson, an actress who rose to stardom in DeMille's Jazz Age films, thus became an appropriate icon for an era of increased hedonism.[44] She later claimed that "working for Mr. DeMille was like playing house in the world's most expensive department store." A successor to Geraldine Farrar, whose operatic career was associated with highbrow culture, Swanson became Famous Players-Lasky's most important female star and inherited the soprano's leading man, Wallace Reid, in *The Affairs of Anatol*. Aware of the director's crucial role in her career, a relationship parodied in *Sunset Boulevard* (1950), Swanson attracted immediate attention in her first DeMille film, *Don't Change Your Husband*. Lasky rightly predicted that the feature "ought to go a long way towards establishing her as a big possibility." Critic Frederick James Smith echoed Lasky's opinion in his review when he stated, "Gloria Swanson . . . is a distinct discovery." Similarly, *Motion Picture Magazine* labeled her "one of the distinct acquisitions" of the silver screen.[45] Yet fan magazines focused on Swanson's persona as a fashion plate rather than on her stature as an actress. *Motion Picture Classic* labeled her "The Silken Gloria." *Photoplay* described the Oriental look of her exotic hairdos in articles with amusing titles such as "Don't Change Your Coiffure" and "She Changed Her Coiffure." *Variety* kept readers informed about the details of her costume, jewelry, and hairstyle in *Don't Change Your Husband*. And *Motion Picture Magazine* declared, "Gloria believes in the psychology of clothes. Put her in short dresses and bob her hair and she wants to play around like a child. But swathed in an evening gown with her hair high and heavily ornamented—she immediately becomes the society woman. . . . Gloria loves clothes, loves luxuries, *loves fame*."[46] What did Swanson's persona as a glamorous clotheshorse imply with respect to the nature of female self-theatricalization and artifice in a consumer culture? Was preoccupation with the appearance of the "new woman," costumed as man's companion with short skirts and bobbed hair, not a commentary on issues of female sexuality and of equality between the sexes? As feminists advocating dress reform had earlier learned, women's fashions, a sign of sexual difference as well as male prescriptive power, was indeed a barometer of heterosexual relations.[47] DeMille addressed these complex issues in his most exquisite achievement in the postwar decade, *The Affairs of Anatol*.

AMBIVALENCE AS A SIGN OF MODERNITY: *THE AFFAIRS OF ANATOL*

Although Famous Players-Lasky paid Arthur Schnitzler ten thousand dollars for the rights to *Anatol*, a series of seven one-act plays set in fin de siècle Vienna, the credits of the film, represented as the embossed pages of an expensive edition, acknowledge only that the screenplay was "suggested" by the playwright.[48] Jeanie Macpherson receives credit as scenarist but "appreciation of their literary assistance is extended to" Beulah Marie Dix, a writer who was formerly active in the civic pageantry movement, and Elmer Harris. At first, the narrative structure of *The Affairs of Anatol* consisted of discrete episodes titled *Five Kisses,* each written by a different scenarist and starring a separate cast. Lasky was convinced that the film was "typical DeMille material," but he was concerned about the expense of engaging numerous stars and wired the director: "It would of course be absolutely necessary that you get finished script before you start with episode in which you use stars like Hawley, Daniels, Swanson. . . . each episode would probably consume about twelve hundred feet so that you should not require any girl for more than one or two weeks." An elegant spectacle, the film broke box-office records upon its Los Angeles premiere in 1921, but Lasky proved astute in minimizing its cost because the nation's economy was mired in a postwar recession. During production, DeMille relied on Lasky as usual to communicate with Zukor regarding expenses such as the use of the pains-taking Handschiegl color process, and he agreed to retitle the film *The Affairs of Anatol.*[49] Since the director later eliminated one of the five episodes from a production that was becoming too lengthy for the taste of exhibitors, the title change, a result of canvassing theater operators, was fortuitous. According to Lasky, "the picture is too big and important to be called by the . . . trifling title of 'Five Kisses.' The big exhibitors all like the title of 'The Affairs of Anatol' because it is dignified and important and without excep-tion, only the cheap exhibitors of the poorer class voted for 'Five Kisses.' "[50] Apparently, distribution and exhibition practices remained very much in-fluenced by industry perceptions about class and ethnic differences that characterized the film audience.

A sign of the escalating budget of his oversized Jazz Age spectacles, DeMille's production staff began to expand in the postwar period. Aside from hiring additional writers to assist Macpherson with the script of *The Affairs of Anatol,* the director assigned cameraman Karl Struss to work with Alvin Wyckoff, a practice he established on two previous films, *Something to Think About* (1920) and *Forbidden Fruit* (1921). Unquestionably, the most intriguing change in his roster was the departure of Wilfred Buckland, whose decision to form an independent production company as the econ-omy began to decline is puzzling.[51] *Forbidden Fruit,* an extravagant remake of *The Golden Chance,* does not credit an art director even though its gran-diose set decoration prefigures later spectacles. An exquisite work attributed to Parisian designer, Paul Iribe, *The Affairs of Anatol* proved to be a delightful exception in DeMille's pursuit of increasingly outré set and costume design. Whether his decision to engage international talent accounted for Buck-land's departure after a close and lengthy collaboration, dating back to *The Virginian* (1914), is a matter of conjecture.

An artist whose career encompassed the transition from Art Nouveau to Art Deco toward the end of the Belle Epoque, Iribe had designed significant projects for couturiers like Jacques Doucet and Paul Poiret, who set trends by patronizing a streamlined aesthetic. Art Deco did not become common-place until the Parisian Exposition Internationale des Arts Décoratifs et Industriels Modernes (1925), an event that led to an exhibit sponsored by Macy's and the Metropolitan Museum of Art. But emphasis on opulence, symmetry, and functionalism was earlier in evidence on both sides of the Atlantic. Frank Lloyd Wright, for example, popularized a geometric style in the United States that influenced the design of the art titles in *Old Wives for New* in contrast to the more curvilinear Art Nouveau motif employed in *The Cheat*. Although Buckland decorated sets with Art Nouveau furniture, such as Swanson's bed in *Male and Female* and twin beds in *Why Change Your Wife?* he also used a panel of leaded glass in geometric design as the window of the dining room in *Old Wives for New*. Iribe's more streamlined and mini-malist version of a breakfast room in *The Affairs of Anatol* consisted of vertical slats admitting translucent light in the background and a small oval-shaped table with chrome legs. Such designs prompted *Motion Picture News* to observe that the sets in the film were "lavish, sometimes bizarre, and novel."[52] A summation of efforts to render set decoration in terms of aesthetic movements in high art, *The Affairs of Anatol* exhibited an early Art Deco style with antecedents in Art Nouveau to represent ambiguity toward the "new woman" who symbolized modernity.

Since the leading character in the Schnitzler one-act plays is a wealthy aesthete and philanderer who engages in a series of meaningless affairs, the film adaptation, subject to the objections of municipal and state censors, is equivocal. As in DeMille's earlier trilogy about marriage and divorce, cos-tume and set design express the ambiguity of the characters' ethics. Yet *The Affairs of Anatol* unmasks contradictions in the semiotics of performance because appearances that constituted mysterious hieroglyphs in genteel society have deteriorated into signs without a stable set of referents in a consumer culture. Anatol DeWitt Spencer (Wallace Reid), for example, is an urbane and sophisticated young man who resides in an elegant mansion with uniformed servants, but yearns for a rustic setting as a sign of moral certitude. When he goes boating in the countryside, however, his wallet is stolen by a farmer's wife (Agnes Ayres). Furthermore, he becomes involved in several episodes in which he rescues lovely young damsels in distress, a proclivity that he, but not his wife, Vivian (Gloria Swanson), interprets as a sincere act of conscience. Articulating "the decline of the referentials" or the dissolution of a fixed system of referents for verbal and visual signs in everyday language, *The Affairs of Anatol* serves as an intertext for advertisers not only in its set and costume design and use of color, but also in its representation of a moral vacuum resulting from signification that is un-stable if not meaningless.[53]

A dramatization of the new morality of the Jazz Age, *The Affairs of Anatol* renders questionable traditional values based on distinctions between the private and public spheres, not least because its hero is a wealthy and indolent figure. Unlike male leads in previous DeMille texts that show businessmen at their desks, Anatol has only affairs of the heart to preoccupy him. Further, the line between front and back regions of respectable homes has also become indistinguishable so that the marketplace penetrates the most private recesses of the domestic sphere. Anatol, for example, waits impatiently for his young bride, Vivian, to make an appearance so that they may breakfast; instead, he becomes a spectator of her toilet in a series of long and medium long shots that emphasize set decoration in the mise-en-scène. Standing in the high-ceilinged hallway outside Vivian's boudoir, the fidgety husband waits before a sliding door resembling a Japanese fusuma screen with floral decoration. Art Nouveau and Art Deco, it should be noted, were both movements that drew upon Asian artwork converted into Orientalist discourse. When the panel, revealed as a huge mirror in reverse shots, finally slides open, Anatol views the backstage area represented as a spectacle. Vivian rests her foot on a tasseled cushion plumped on an ornate footstool while a French maid gives her a pedicure.[54] She is seated behind a translucent screen with a floral design on a curvilinear edge, a motif echoed by Art Nouveau patterns that decorate the small circular window to the right. A medium long shot shows Anatol, who has entered the room, standing before a luxurious bed at right angle to a modernist design of concentric arches. Assuming a coquettish pose behind the screen, Vivian flirts with her husband in a mirror shot that shows both their reflections in the large semicircular mirror of the dresser in the rear.

When Anatol, Vivian, and their friend, Max (Elliott Dexter), dine at The Green Fan, the decor of the elegant supper club signifies a correspondence between private entertainment and commercialized leisure that represents yet another sign of the collapse of separate spheres. An establishing shot in color shows a limousine driving up to the elegant facade of a pink building topped by two green glass domes with amber light emanating from below and at the entrance. Arranged in the semicircular fan above the entranceway, the name of the supper club appears in bright green letters. A cut to the interior, tinted in amber, shows chorus girls performing on a stage demarcated by four slender pillars topped with fans, an area situated against the backdrop of a gigantic fan displaying a feminine form. The walls of the supper club, obviously a playground for the well-to-do, are decorated with elegant round medallions stamped with fans. A solicitous waiter offers guests a fan-shaped menu that boasts delicacies such as calves' head vinaigrette and cold roast squab. A luxurious Art Deco setting with a semicircular motif, The Green Fan, not coincidentally, replicates the curvilinear screen and mirror

31. Gloria Swanson, as a svelte young bride, begins to quarrel with her wealthy husband (Wallace Reid) at a fashionable Art Deco supper club in *The Affairs of Anatol* (1921). *(Photo courtesy George Eastman House)*

32. An aesthete critical of modernity, Reid attempts to transform a prostitute of lower-class origins (Wanda Hawley) into a "highbrow" who plays the violin. *(Photo courtesy George Eastman House)*

in Vivian's boudoir. As he dines with his wife and friend, Anatol renews his acquaintance with Emilie Dixon (Wanda Hawley), the mistress of an old roué, Gordon Bronson (Theodore Roberts reprising his role in *Old Wives for New*). Since the respectable upper-class home and the elegant supper club are linked rather than contrasted by set decoration, the mise-en-scène renders ambiguous Anatol's project to rescue Emilie from a dissolute life. Indeed, the hero wears on his pinkie finger a snake ring that matches the jewelry adorning the prostitute whom he wishes to save. DeMille does emphasize the socioeconomic, class, and hence moral distinctions between wife and harlot in terms of their costume. Emilie is wearing a shiny evening dress with a full skirt and a lace bodice trimmed with roses, patterned hosiery, and a headband over loose curls. She adorns herself with a diamond necklace and several gold bangles including a bracelet in the form of a snake. Vivian, on the contrary, is well coiffed and projects sleek upper-class elegance as represented later in the decade by Art Deco ads and posters. She is exquisite in a dark, svelte gown with a pearl-trimmed neckline and wears matching jewelry consisting of pearl earrings, necklace, bracelet, and ring.

Attempting to rescue and refashion Emilie as a "highbrow," Anatol installs her in an elegant apartment and pays for her violin lessons. As his price, however, he insists that the former prostitute discard all the expensive jewelry she has accepted from her lover, Bronson. A construction symbolic of modernist aesthetic as well as technological innovation becomes the site of an outmoded but solemn ritual of self-purification. Anticipating the celebration of the Brooklyn Bridge in the 1920s, DeMille shows amber-tinted footage of a frontal shot of the structure at sunrise and then cuts to a medium long shot of Anatol and Emilie stepping out of a limousine in midpassage to gaze at the view.[55] A cut to a panoramic point-of-view shot shows the harbor as the camera pans right to reveal busy tugboats and the breathtaking skyline of the city. Several shots show the two characters on the bridge with crisscrossed steel girders dominating the mise-en-scène. As they stand on the spectacular bridge in sight of the country's greatest metropolis, Anatol instructs Emilie to throw her jewels into the river. Disjunction between symbols of American industrial progress and Victorian morality thus reinforces the film's ambivalent view of modernity.

Anatol's subsequent disillusionment with Emilie, who succumbs to Bronson's gifts and promise of marriage, leads to an interlude that illustrates the recurrent theme of Orientalism in DeMille's texts about consumption. As opposed to the one-act play in which Anatol hypnotizes a lover to inquire about her fidelity, DeMille projects the hero's repressed amoral and sensuous traits onto a Hindu character named Nazzer Singh (Theodore Kosloff).[56] A sensation at one of Vivian's elegant tea parties, held in an immense high-ceilinged living room that accommodates dozens of guests, the turbaned hypnotist performs in a heavily draped area in front of the archway just off the vestibule. Although it is afternoon, the lighting is low-key and the tinting is blue to suggest magical explorations of the unconscious. Anatol is not at all amused, however, when Vivian, shown in close-ups as she falls into a trance, loses her inhibitions and takes off her stockings and shoes to step into an imagined stream of water. Disrupting the act, he orders Vivian restored to her senses and suggests, "Let me take you away from all this rotten, hypocritical crowd! Let's go to some clean sweet place in the Country, where people are honest and decent and find ourselves again!" Since Anatol is being self-righteous while he himself harbors unacknowledged sensual impulses, the low-key lighting conveys an atmospheric mood rather than an unambiguous moral dilemma.

During a quarrel that began while they were enjoying the countryside, Anatol exclaims in a violent outburst in footage now tinted amber, "I give you fair warning . . . I'll go out and find a way to forget!" Upping the ante, Vivian instructs her maid, "My lowest gown—my highest heels, Marie! If there's room for husbands in the Gay White Way—there's room for *wives!*" Anatol amuses himself at "A Certain Roof—where the entertainment provided makes the Feasts of Babylon look like a Cafeteria!" An insert of the program announces "A Tableau Vivant . . . 'The Unattainable' featuring Satan Synne." Against a background of rolling hills and a sharp precipice, a muscular black man in a jewelled costume wields an enormous sword, while, to his left, a woman's prostrate body forms a graceful curve as her long hair and flowing robe spill onto the floor. An intrigued Anatol wanders backstage to meet the star of an Orientalist tableau that inveighs against sins of the flesh by contrasting not only gender but race in a provocative manner. A floral Art Nouveau pattern ornamenting the backstage area, not coincidentally, repeats the decorative motif of Vivian's boudoir. Satan Synne (Bebe Daniels) wears a sensational costume with a long double rope of pearls that is a camp version of the elegant gown Vivian wore to The Green Fan. She mysteriously warns Anatol, in footage now tinted light pink, "the devil's not a man, but a WOMAN!"

DeMille did not require a flashback in *The Affairs of Anatol* because its episodic narrative structure emphasized elements of fantasy that were displacing the realist aesthetic of his prewar films. A fanciful episode toward the end of the film provided an occasion for an extraordinary set piece. Satan's apartment, "The Devil's Cloister," is an Orientalist illustration of high camp in amber-tinted footage. Greeting Anatol at the door is a manacled female slave dressed in a costume appropriated from an Egyptian bas-relief. A mirror shot that repeats an earlier mise-en-scène in Vivian's boudoir shows Anatol as he approaches Satan while she is seated in front of her dresser. A triangular mirror outlined with bat wings is flanked by two lamps in the shape of cobras. Decorating the right side of the vanity is a

33. Julia Faye, costumed like an Egyptian slave to accentuate the Orientalist decor, waits on Bebe Daniels, signifying the decline of referentiality as a prostitute who is in reality a devoted wife. *(Photo courtesy George Eastman House)*

human skull, while on the floor, a large ceramic turtle sits before the chair. Satan is wearing an extravagant headdress and a swirling cape with alternating light and dark stripes bordered with rows of beads. As suggested by shots tinted pink that show Anatol gazing at a reflection of a skeleton in a mirror and then through a transparent curtain of flames at the entrance to the bedroom, the philandering husband is playing with fire. But the line between a respectable upper-class home and an illicit establishment has become indistinguishable, as conveyed by the repetition of set design that links both the backstage area of the cafe and Satan's apartment with Vivian's boudoir. Although Satan's bizarre self-theatricalization emphasizes the reptilian imagery of the Garden of Eden, she ensnares men only to pay for her husband's medical expenses. Disgusted with the truth behind seductive appearances, Anatol exclaims, "If this is what they call the gay life—I'm going back to my wife!" Vivian, however, does not return home until nine in the morning, after spending the evening with Max, and refuses to give an account of her actions. Max does secretly yearn for her, as DeMille earlier conveys in a rare shot-reverse-shot while the couple play chess, but Vivian's outing has been innocent, albeit quite merry. Seizing upon an unexpected visit from Nazzer Singh, Anatol is determined to hypnotize his wife to elicit the truth but decides, when Max intervenes, to trust her after all. Appearances have in fact deceived him throughout the film.

A sequel to DeMille's trilogy about marriage and divorce, *The Affairs of Anatol* represents the collapse of sign systems based on coded distinctions between private and public spheres, and even between front and back regions of respectable homes.[57] As the moral certainties of the Victorian synthesis began to dissolve in an era of increased self-commodification, appearances no longer functioned as a reliable index of character and breeding. Discourse in fan magazines implied that stars like Gloria Swanson assumed new personalities whenever they changed their wardrobes. Given the remapping of spheres based on traditional definitions of gender, at issue was the nature of female sexuality in relation to marriage and the family. As Walter Lippmann argued at the time, birth control and female employment outside the home meant that the sexual experience of women was no longer related to their role as wives and mothers. Further, contraception, which in effect was practiced mostly by educated middle-class women, dictated that sexual intercourse be construed as a pleasurable experience rather than as an obligation for procreative purposes. A companionate marriage was equivalent to childlessness—as DeMille demonstrated in *Don't Change Your Husband* and *Why Change Your Wife?*—and thus required a sexual playmate in view of trends toward a higher marital rate among the younger generation. But a serious ethical dilemma resulted from this transformation of the Victorian woman. As Lippman acknowledged, "The whole revolution in the field of sexual morals turns upon the fact that external control of the chastity of women is becoming impossible."[58] Anxiety about women's extravagant spending on fashionable apparel, represented in DeMille's texts as a prerequisite for the pursuit of pleasure, was more than a concern about household budgets; it also registered suspicion about women's sexual fidelity. When the farmer's wife in *The Affairs of Anatol* uses church funds to indulge her desires, the rage that she inspires in her self-righteous husband, who wields a whip and stomps on her new dress, is telling. A symbol of the consumer culture, the "new woman" raised questions regarding the nature of female sexuality apart from such traditional issues as monogamy and fidelity. As evident in DeMille's representation of upper-class marriage as spectacle that constituted a form of commodity fetishism for female audiences, the consumption of images as well as goods functioned as a substitute for sexual pleasure. Perhaps this was the ultimate irony resulting from the reification of human consciousness and social relations in postwar consumer capitalism. Display windows including the movie screen constituted a "ladies' paradise" or an "Adamless Eden" as the locus of female desire, characterized as infantile and irrational by advertisers and thus subject to manipulation, in a decade touted for a revolution in manners and morals.[59]

ADVERTISING FOR AFFLUENT CONSUMERS: DeMILLE'S TEXTS AS INTERTEXTS

In their study of Middletown, Robert S. Lynd and Helen Merrell Lynd claimed, "It is perhaps impossible to overestimate the role of motion pictures, advertising, and other forms of publicity" in the rising level of expectations sought in living standards.[60] Indeed, film distribution and exhibition practices capitalized on the interrelatedness of these promotional forms to interest female spectators in the latest style in fashion and home furnishings. A closer scrutiny of intertextual issues shows, moreover, that contrary to the prewar years when DeMille sought to legitimate feature films in terms of genteel culture, he himself set trends for advertisers targeting middle- and upper-class readers in the 1920s. The director's visual style, in other words, became associated with escalating levels of conspicuous consumption rather than with technical advances in film as an art form. DeMille remained ambivalent about this transition in his career and objected to ad campaigns that marketed his films as spectacle. Assuming a defensive and contradictory tone, he protested to Lasky in 1922:

> The handling of my pictures, from an advertising standpoint, is not in proper proportion to the importance of the productions nor the amount of money expended thereon. . . . The attitude of the publicity and sales department . . . seems to be that the only thing that there is to talk about in a DeMille picture is the size of the sets and the spectacle generally. . . . I make far more stills than any other company and there is greater attention given to gowns, detail, story and direction than in any pictures made today.[61]

Yet the mise-en-scène of such productions as *Forbidden Fruit* and *The Affairs of Anatol* demonstrates that the director was in effect orchestrating spectacle that displaced the realist aesthetic of his Progressive Era films.

The decline of realist representation in DeMille's Jazz Age films characterized significant trends in the advertising industry as well. An accelerating pace in consumption as well as diminished middle-class sympathy for workers and immigrants were developments related to the waning of realism as a reponse to shocking inequities in urban life. Contrary to the fantasies that pervaded his Jazz Age spectacles, DeMille had earlier stated in a fan magazine that "realism . . . is the most insistent demand of the public."[62] As he had once vitiated realist aesthetic in favor of sentimentalism in films such as the *Chimmie Fadden* series and *Kindling*, DeMille now showcased the life-style of the wealthy. An unusual film like *Saturday Night* (1922) that reiterated prewar discourse regarding class and ethnic divisions, interestingly, upgraded the set decoration of the homes of the poor as well as the rich. Yet the legacy of Victorian genteel culture remained evident in the director's representational strategy throughout the 1920s, albeit pictorialism now served to authenticate the commodified self. DeMille's early Jazz Age films thus provided advertisers with a primer on how to sell consumption as an American way of life. A closer focus on the intertextuality of the director's mise-en-scène and magazine ads first requires a brief overview of the consumer revolution and related developments in the advertising industry.

As Martha L. Olney demonstrates, a consumer durables revolution stimulated by credit financing and massive advertising, which became a fully deductible corporate expense after enactment of a 1917 excess profits tax, occurred during 1922–1929. She argues that a decrease in savings correlated with an increase in expeditures for major durables such as automobiles, household appliances, and radios despite a relative increment in their cost, whereas the purchase of minor durables such as home furnishings, china, artwork, and books declined in the same period. Although Olney does not explore the social significance of this shift in family expenditures, the status symbols of the middle class most likely changed from goods such as furniture and tableware, signifying gentility in social rituals, to an invention that led to a further collapse of separate spheres, the automobile. A big-ticket item, even lower-priced cars like Chevrolets cost 20 percent of a family's annual income and had to be financed on an installment plan. But automobile ownership, as the Lynds point out, was the most important sign of a family's social standing among the younger generation. Within the context of a consumer durables revolution, then, the cultural war of the Jazz Age was a continuation of a basic conflict in values that had been occurring within a broad middle class differentiated between "old" and "new." Since social historians emphasize that working-class and immigrant groups subject to periodic layoffs had neither the disposable income nor the predilection to purchase consumer goods on credit, the democratization of luxury was for them restricted to visual appropriation.[63] By contrast, the respectable middle class not only enjoyed increasingly seductive forms of spectacle, as exemplified by DeMille's feature films, but also had access to levels of consumption that signified a superior social status.

Although filmmakers courted a mass audience in the 1920s, in contrast to advertisers who addressed an upper-middle- and upper-class readership, Famous Players-Lasky developed an exploitation strategy that emphasized premieres at first-run theaters patronized by more affluent filmgoers. Why were DeMille's spectacles major attractions at downtown movie palaces during the Jazz Age? Why, indeed, did the director's mise-en-scène provide a useful intertext for advertisers? As Roland Marchand argues in a study in which he singles out the director, magazine editors and copywriters borrowed from the film industry its image of a public bored with humdrum lives. DeMille articulated a viewpoint regarding the function of spectacle for the lower class that advertisers found relevant in addressing the well-to-do: "Your poor person wants to see wealth, colorful, interesting, exotic—he has an idea of it many times more brightly colored than the reality." An earlier statement reveals that the director also understood the function he performed for audiences as a showman: "The desire [for beauty] is greater than the means of gratification. . . . Give beauty to the world, and you'll be successful."[64] Apart from glamorous representations of upper-class life in widely circulated magazines like *Saturday Evening Post* and *Ladies' Home Journal*, the influence of filmmakers like DeMille on advertising is observable in a number of industry developments during the 1920s.

Particularly significant in the evolution of advertising during the decade was the seductive and streamlined image of the "new woman." As opposed to World War I posters that emphasized maternal and nurturing qualities, the image of a young woman seated before a dresser, a standard shot in *Old Wives for New, Don't Change Your Husband, Why Change Your Wife?, Forbidden Fruit,* and *The Affairs of Anatol,* became formulaic in ads that defined the modern woman. *Ladies' Home Journal*—a Curtis Publishing Company product that pioneered ad stripping in 1896 so that ads were placed in a format with fiction and feature articles—increased its fashion content from 16 percent in 1918–1920 to 30 percent in 1922–1923. A major breakthrough in the use of color in magazine ads for such domestic products as bathroom towels occurred between 1924 and 1928. An emphasis on ensembles in women's apparel and accessories became popular in 1926–1927 and also served as an important theme in home furnishing, especially the decoration of bathrooms as a conspicuous showcase. DeMille's feature films served as significant intertexts for several of these developments. A trendsetter, the director featured elegant table settings, novel bathroom scenes, and ensemble, woven cane bedroom furniture in *Old Wives for New* in 1918. A medium close-up of Swanson sleeping on an embroidered pillowcase trimmed with lace in *Don't Change Your Husband* stressed the importance of fine linens in 1919. For advertisers, the streamlined Art Deco design that DeMille used so inventively with the Handschiegl color process in *The Affairs of Anatol* in 1921 became a signifier of modernity. An increasing use of elements of fantasy in representational strategies was countered, however, by a tradition of realism that was still persuasive in ads as opposed to film spectacle. Without question, the intertextuality of feature film and advertising was most evident in the use of narrative to sell products. Copywriters created social tableaux in the pictorial tradition and employed the conventions of melodrama to dramatize consumer desire for commodities. As *Motion Picture News* observed, DeMille engaged in a reverse practice by inserting product labels in *Why Change Your Wife?*, surely a blatant mode of incorporating advertising in filmic narration. Undoubtedly most important in these narratives was the rationalization of a consumer ethos in terms of the Victorian rhetoric of uplift. Ad men, as Marchand argues, thought of themselves as "apostles of modernity" with a mission to assuage anxiety provoked by modernization and to educate the public, especially women, about the advantages of using products to achieve a distinctive life-style. Ads created by these men were "secular sermons" that bestowed upon goods spiritual qualities transcending the mere satisfaction of material needs. The sacrosanct tone associated with the refinement of highbrow culture, ironically, was transferable to mass cultural forms that stimulated the growth of consumption and commercialized leisure.[65]

A filmmaker who shared the elite socioeconomic background of men in the advertising business, DeMille, too, spoke in terms of a mission that was part of his family's theatrical legacy to use the stage as a pulpit. At the beginning of the 1920s, he articulated a faith in cultural stewardship that belonged to the Progressive Era: "I believe that the people who make up the middle and sometimes the lower elements of human society have a keen grasp on the essentials of drama and life; that their appreciation is worthy of our cultivation." Similarly, he summed up his achievement toward the end of the decade: "I believe I have had an obvious effect upon American life. I have brought a certain sense of beauty and luxury into everyday existence, all jokes about ornate bathrooms and de luxe boudoirs aside."[66] Such sentiment was undoubtedly shared by advertisers who reproduced the director's representational strategy to mediate the experience of modernity for affluent consumers. DeMille himself set an example, as he not only preached uplift through consumption but led a baronial life-style that included a hillside mansion, chauffeured limousine, yacht, and Western style ranch.[67] Yet in response to critics who began to dismiss his productions as ostentatious exercises in set and costume design, he returned to the Bible as an inspiration for *The Ten Commandments* (1923) and articulated a nostalgic vision of America that still resonated in a consumer culture.

SEVEN

DeMille's Exodus from Famous Players-Lasky: *The Ten Commandments* (1923)

ANTIMODERNISM AS HISTORICAL REPRESENTATION:
THE KING JAMES VERSION OF THE BIBLE AS SPECTACLE

When *Motion Picture Classic* published stills from "The Drama of the Decalogue" during the filming of *The Ten Commandments,* it repeated the anecdote that DeMille drew his inspiration for the film from the results of a
Los Angeles Times contest for an original story. An avalanche of mail poured
in from fans eager to see a production with a religious theme. According
to a souvenir program, "The contest revealed . . . that . . . the clean, sober
minds of the vast majority of people are not interested in froth but in the
virile, vital things of life, the epic ideas of all times." Descended from a
distinguished playwright who had written in his diary that he learned Greek
by studying the New Testament, DeMille did not need much prodding to
mount a lavish production about the biblical past.[1] A close analysis of the
acclaimed spectacle shows that it represents not only a summation of the
director's career at Famous Players-Lasky but a preview of his achievement
in the sound era. *The Ten Commandments* thus remains a Janus-faced production that simultaneously looks backward and forward in time. On the
one hand, the biblical epic signifies a return to the antimodernist tradition
of civic pageantry in its representation of a macrocosm and its nostalgia for
the moral certitude and sense of community associated with small-town life.[2]
On the other, the director's technical achievement with respect to use of
color processes, special effects, and colossal set design attests to the reification of religious uplift as spectacle in a modern consumer culture.

A narrative divided into two parts, with separate casts enacting plots in
different historical periods, *The Ten Commandments* appeared innovative but
continued in the tradition of Victorian pictorialism. As industry discourse

179

on the film's production attests, the Biblical Prologue dramatizing the exodus from Egypt attracted considerably more attention than the Modern Story of the Jazz Age. After setting trends in both fashion and filmmaking in the early postwar years, DeMille reverted to a narrative strategy based on intertexts as established forms of middle-class culture. Apart from invoking the tradition of historical pageantry, which reached its apogee in the years immediately before the First World War, he relied upon audience familiarity with the King James Version of the Bible and cited chapter and verse in the art titles. The Biblical Prologue of *The Ten Commandments* thus served as an illustration of the Book of Exodus or the Second Book of Moses in the Old Testament. As such, it appealed to the cultural taste of the genteel classes who were acquainted with the definitive illustrations of the Bible by Gustave Doré, a celebrated artist whose work was published in France in 1865 and subsequently appeared in expensive, gilt-edged editions in Great Britain and the United States. Although this religious iconography was undoubtedly familiar to adherents of liberal Protestantism, which became increasingly secularized in the twentieth century, the rise of fundamentalism meant that the Bible was widely read among the lower-middle and native-born working classes as well.[3] As *Motion Picture News* acknowledged, the casting of the Biblical Prologue required "players of unusual ability as their performance will be carefully watched by millions to whom they are familiar through Biblical reading." The trade journal was obviously not referring to Catholics, who, unlike Protestants, did not emphasize biblical study as a religious practice and, moreover, had adopted the Douay-Rheims translation from St. Jerome's Vulgate as opposed to the King James Version.[4]

Apart from the Bible and Doré's illustrations, DeMille's representation of the exodus has to be considered with reference to yet another intertext, sensational news reports about the discovery of the tomb of King Tutankhamun in November 1922. American newspapers, especially the *Chicago Daily News*, participated in coverage of the excavation that involved the Metropolitan Museum of Art in a significant role. According to Thomas Hoving, the event was "one of the longest-lasting news stories in the history of journalism [and] would continue unabated almost daily and weekly for eight years." A significant component in the construction of an Orientalized Middle East as a site of the mysterious "Other," the discovery of the tomb influenced the exploitation strategy of *The Ten Commandments*. A section in the souvenir program titled "Lost Arts of Egypt," for example, referred to Tutankhamun on the assumption that educated filmgoers were informed about an event touted as "the most sensational in Egyptology."[5] Yet unlike *Joan the Woman*, which offended Catholics and failed to appeal to a broad audience, *The Ten Commandments* drew crowds of moviegoers who were unfamiliar with genteel middle-class culture. The fundamentalist lower-middle and native-born working classes, especially in small towns and rural

34. Gustave Doré's illustrations of the Bible, such as this one of Moses, based on studies of antiquities in the Louvre, provided DeMille with intertexts drawn from highbrow culture.

areas, most likely brought to the filmic text a belief in biblical literalism. As for uneducated spectators, the visual appropriation of unsurpassed spectacle in color was achieved without the mediation of such intertexts as *The Doré Bible* but within the context of both immigrant subcultures and a larger consumer culture. Addressing any possible objections regarding the religious content of the film that might offend a broad moviegoing public, *Variety* assured exhibitors, "It's a great picture for the Jews. It shows the Bible made them the Chosen People, and also (on the statement of a Catholic) it will be as well liked by the Catholics for its Catholicity."[6]

An aspect of consumption anticipated by historical pageants that were ironically organized to offset the lure of commercialized amusement, publicity about the building of Egyptian sets on sand dunes near the coastal city of Guadalupe, California, attests to film production itself as a form of spectacle and commodity fetishism.[7] A report in *Motion Picture News* echoed pre–World War I publicity in print media and newsreels about the expenditure of enormous resources to stage civic pageantry. Exhibitors read about the installation of a twenty-four-square-mile tent city to house 2,500 inhabitants and 3,000 animals, including horses, camels, burros, poultry, and dogs, assembled for scenes of the exodus. A complete utilities system providing water, electricity, and telephones had been built in addition to transportation facilities. Construction of the most impressive structure of the set, a massive entrance to the City of Rameses that measured 750 feet wide and 109 feet high, required 300 tons of plaster, 55,000 board feet of lumber, 25,000 pounds of nails, and 75 miles of cable and wiring. A fact sheet in the souvenir program repeated this preproduction publicity by stressing the extraordinary logistics involved in building the edifice and cited several statistics. After enormous cost overruns that nearly crippled Famous Players-Lasky, DeMille then buried the site in yet another spectacular act of consumption as waste and thereby recycled film history for future archaeological teams that recently excavated the sets.[8] Although not as sensational as the discovery of Tutankhamun's tomb, the excavation of the filmmaker's version of the City of Rameses provided a strange reenactment of the study of antiquities.

Aside from the spectacle created by massive film production that paralleled the representation itself as a commodity form, DeMille's epic evinced other contradictions inherent in antimodernist civic pageantry. Perhaps most obvious was the construction of the Biblical Prologue as a succession of extreme long and long shots with cuts to occasional medium shots of the actors. As such, the epic represented a didactic series of tableaux for the edification of spectators that appeared stylistically regressive rather than producing the "eclipse of distance" characteristic of a more modernist aesthetic.[9] Yet the spectacular use of sets, crowd scenes, special effects, and color that dictated the scale of shots also elicited audience response tinged

35. Charles de Roche as the Pharaoh leaves the City of Rameses, guarded by a massive gate, in the Biblical Prologue of *The Ten Commandments* (1923). *(Photo courtesy George Eastman House)*

with sensation, excitement, and immediacy. For the entrance to the walled City of Rameses, for example, Paul Iribe designed a massive structure that, according to *Motion Picture News,* was the largest set ever constructed for a film. Forming a symmetrical design, the entryway to the city was flanked by a set of two colossal statues seated on a rectangular platform protruding from both the left and right sides of the wall. A set of monumental bas-relief of a horse-drawn chariot on the expanse of wall in turn flanked the twin sculptures of the pharaohs. Approaching this impressive facade was a wide, sweeping avenue lined on both sides with a row of gigantic sphinxes. In the distance, to the left of the massive gate, a pyramid pierced the sky of a limitless, arid landscape. Since DeMille adhered to a tradition of authenticity established by realistic stage melodrama and civic theater, the sets for the interior of the pharaoh's palace represented a curious departure at a time when news accounts stimulated interest in Egyptian artifacts. As opposed to the Doré illustrations based on antiquities in the Louvre, Iribe created a modernist representation with rectilinear Art Deco stairways for the throne room and concentric pointed arches at the base of huge columns in a minimalist design dominated by the towering bust of a pharaoh.

Given that DeMille's representational strategy in the Biblical Prologue appears to regress to an era of antimodernist civic pageantry when audiences viewed spectacle from a distance, what accounts for the chorus of acclaim that greeted the film? A screening of a black and white print is extremely misleading because, as critics stressed, spectators were enthralled by the use of color in scenes of the exodus. Filmgoers who shopped in fashionable department stores had already become accustomed to eye-catching displays of colored lights and merchandise in plate glass windows during the 1910s. DeMille, who clearly influenced advertisers in their use of color after 1924, had previously experimented with color tinting and toning as well as the Handschiegl process with his cameraman, Alvin Wyckoff.[10] Apart from these techniques, the director used a new two-color Technicolor process that had been introduced, not coincidentally, in an Orientalist narrative titled *The Toll of the Sea* (1922) starring Anna May Wong. For reasons that are not entirely clear, DeMille broke with Wyckoff, who had photographed all but the first of his features since the founding of the Lasky Company, and employed a team of five photographers for *The Ten Commandments*. A sixth photographer, Ray Rennahan, was assigned to film scenes in Technicolor, but the director also continued to experiment with the expensive Handschiegl process that involved application of colors like pastel green and platinum yellow with stencilling upon completion of photography.[11] A 1918 report in *Motion Picture News* stressed improvement in this technique so that subtle effects were noticeable in the filmmaker's flashbacks and historical epics starring Geraldine Farrar, notably in *The Woman God Forgot* (1917) and *The Devil Stone* (1917). At the time, DeMille, asserting his role as a cultural custodian, claimed that "color photography . . . can never be used universally in motion pictures, for the eye of the spectator would be put to too great a strain, and the variety of colors would distract . . . from the story values." Five years later, however, *Variety* dismissed the Modern Story of *The Ten Commandments* because it was in "white and black" and remarked, "Were there some manner found to cut back to those enormous scenes in colors . . . it would give the audience another look at what they really want to see in this picture."[12] In sum, the use of color in the Biblical Prologue accounts not only for the technical innovation of *The Ten Commandments* but also explains the high ratio of extreme long shots in the construction of a mise-en-scène that transformed the screen into an artist's canvas.

Although *The Ten Commandments* was one of the first productions to demonstrate innovative two-step Technicolor photography, two versions of the film at George Eastman House, including deteriorating footage of the director's own nitrate print, have color sequences achieved through application of the Handschiegl process. Paolo Cherchi Usai speculates that the director preferred the painstaking stencilling procedure because its effects were more subtle than the less expensive Technicolor used for prints distributed to exhibitors. The transition from standard tinting and/or toning of footage to the Handschiegl process in one of the two prints occurs during scenes of the exodus. An extreme long shot shows Moses (Theodore Roberts) in the middleground as the children of Israel, whose numbers are so vast that they wind across the desert into the horizon, follow him into the unknown. Against the white sand dunes are splashes of color that distinguish items of clothing worn by various followers as they march in exultation. Cuts to several long shots of the crowd show individuals wearing costumes in bright orange and pink. The use of color for this particular sequence in DeMille's nitrate print, however, differs and is more calculated to render dramatic values in chromatic terms. As the Hebrews leave the City of Rameses, for example, a thin vertical strip of blue appears in the center of the screen and increases in width in succeeding shots until it blots out the sepia tint of the footage to convey a sense of liberation.[13] A sequence of masses of people walking into the desert that concludes with a fade-out leaving a blank screen in red, is toned in that color to give a sense of intense heat. DeMille intercuts between blue-tinted shots of Moses, standing with his followers as they complete their passage through the Red Sea, and the pharaoh in hot pursuit in footage toned brown and red so that color values differentiate two opposing armies. Symbolically, the massive stone wall in the background of the art titles disappears upon the liberation of the Hebrews, whereas a bright orange curtain of flames entraps the pharaoh and his chariots. An impressive scene that recalls the burning of the saint in *Joan the Woman,* it represents an effect the director visualized in terms of his first epic when he wrote "like Joan" on the shooting script.[14] Further signifying the clash between two radically different cultures are the elements of fire and water rendered in color and special effects. The pharaoh and his awed charioteer, outlined against an enormous, pastel-colored wall of bluish-tinted green waves, continue their pursuit between parted waters that eventually crash down on the Egyptian host.

As spectacular as the exodus, in essence a magnificent chase sequence, is the intercutting between scenes on the mount in which Moses receives the commandments and scenes in which the children of Israel succumb to bacchanalian revelry and worship a golden calf. DeMille showed his admiration for Doré, whose work remained an inspiration for his mise-en-scène throughout his career, by reproducing the barren, craggy landscape with sheer embankments that dominates so many of the artist's engravings. Again, the director uses color as well as low-key lighting to show Moses, mostly in extreme long shots tinted blue, hammering tablets on the side of a cliff as the words of the commandments appear like thunderbolts against a darkened and windy sky with flashes of lightning toned red. But at the very

36. As the lawgiver Moses, an icon inspired by Doré's illustrations, Theodore Roberts receives the commandments on Mount Sinai while his followers worship a golden calf. *(Photo courtesy George Eastman House)*

moment that Moses receives the law of God to establish a monotheistic patriarchy, his sister Miriam (Estelle Taylor), wearing a jewelled brassiere and serpent bracelets wound around her arms, is burnishing the golden calf in sepia-tinted footage. A symbol of paganism and depraved Orientalism that, it should be noted, is not mentioned in Exodus, she is suddenly afflicted with leprosy and declared unclean.

As allegorical figures symbolizing radically opposed male and female principles, Moses and Miriam are the only characters repeatedly privileged with medium shots that distinguish them as individuals in massive crowd scenes. DeMille did not resolve the narratological problem of historical representation as a macrocosm photographed in extreme long shots until he directed *The King of Kings* (1927). A flashback to the biblical era toward the end of the Modern Story of *The Ten Commandments*, interestingly, minimizes the "eclipse of distance" resulting from a cinematic as opposed to a theatrical articulation of space in terms of shot scale, camera angles, and editing. A recapitulation of the incident in which Christ, standing with his back the camera, heals a woman afflicted with leprosy is photographed not only in extreme long shot but in low-key lighting so that the scene resembles a tableau. Consider this shot in relation to a sequence in *The King of Kings,* photographed four years later and premiered at Grauman's Chinese Theatre, in which Christ (H. B. Carpenter) heals a blind girl. DeMille cuts from an extreme long shot of expectant travelers gathered outside the humble home of the carpenter to a series of medium shots and medium close-ups of the blind girl seeking to be healed. When she finally opens her eyes for the first time, the face of Christ comes into focus in a medium close-up that represents not only her point of view but that of the audience as well. A two-shot then shows the carpenter embracing the young girl in a moment meant to reinforce spectator identification with the Christ figure. By moving his camera in for medium close-ups and close-ups, DeMille humanized biblical characters and thereby bridged the gap between macrocosm and microcosm in historical representations. As in *Joan the Woman,* however, he adopted such a narrative strategy at the expense of historicity because he resorted to dramatizations that either were fictional or could not be authenticated. After this stage in the development of his narration in silent cinema, DeMille incorporated technological advances such as sound and widescreen, but his painterly style, which emphasized frontality or shots mostly perpendicular to the camera and minimal tracking, remained fairly consistent for several decades.[15]

In *The Ten Commandments,* DeMille's failure to resolve filmic narration with respect to the issue of microcosm versus macrocosm is evident in the film's two-part structure. Scenarist Jeanie Macpherson, interestingly, had considered a more episodic narrative in which the commandments would be broken in successive but separate stories until she decided on a Modern Story with a Biblical Prologue. A script that had not bisected historical time may have influenced the director to consider a representational strategy other than one that focused so much attention on the biblical era. Adolph Zukor, who proved himself wrong regarding the box-office appeal of the film, expressed concern about such an approach. Dispatching a telegram to Lasky, who was then on one of his trips to Los Angeles, Zukor noted: "CECIL'S PRODUCTION WILL IN ALL LIKELIHOOD HAVE AN EGYPTIAN AND PALESTINE ATMOSPHERE IT WILL HAVE TO HAVE A TREMENDOUS LOVE INTEREST IN ORDER TO OVERCOME THE HANDICAPS OF ATMOSPHERE I SUGGEST THAT YOU AND CECIL GO OVER THE STORY CAREFULLY." Attempting to reassure Zukor, DeMille, who had previously informed Lasky about his decision to film a two-part feature, wired back, "I can assure you . . . the picture will have those qualities of love, romance and beauty which you so rightly suggest. . . . [I]t will be the biggest picture ever made, not only from the standpoint of spectacle but from the standpoint of humaness [*sic*], dramatic power, and the great good it will do."[16] As critics subsequently noted, however, the spectacle of the "Egyptian and Palestine atmosphere," whose preponderance of extreme long shots did not encourage spectator identification, enraptured the audience while the "love interest" of the Modern Story was eclipsed. In *The King of Kings*, DeMille introduced a "love interest," as he had in *Joan the Woman*, by inventing a fictional relationship between two of its principal characters, Mary Magdalene and Judas.

Despite its being overshadowed by the Biblical Prologue, the Modern Story is thematically related as a narrative about two sons, Dan (Rod La Rocque) and John McTavish (Richard Dix), who respond in opposite ways to the stern upbringing of a fundamentalist mother (Edythe Chapman). The sentimental melodrama begins with a dissolve from an extreme long shot of the children of Israel, terrified by the wrath of God, to a medium shot of the family gathered at a table for a Bible reading. The enormous size of the Bible indicates that it is most likely an illustrated edition, for the mother has been reading Exodus as dramatized in the Biblical Prologue. Dan, an atheist and a dishonest building contractor, eventually violates every one of the commandments to become rich and gratify his whims, including marriage to the woman his brother loves, Mary Leigh (Leatrice Joy), whereas John, a simple carpenter, represents the small-town values that are being eroded in a consumer culture. Although the Modern Story is old-fashioned and clichéd, it is more cinematic than the Biblical Prologue in its use of editing with respect to scale and angle of shots. At least two sequences are particularly striking. In the first, Mary rides an elevator inside the shaft of the construction site of a church to visit John, who is watching her ascend from the top of the scaffolding. Although John's point of view is represented in high angle shots, the audience experiences Mary's ascent in that her point of view is shown not only in repeated low angle shots but in vertical tracking shots of the city's skyline visible through the partially constructed church. As the elevator reaches the top of the scaffolding, the sky comes into full view before Mary alights to greet John. A second sequence focusing on a murder, detailed in the script and quoted by René Clément in *Les Maudits* (1946) and Alfred Hitchcock in *Psycho* (1960), is also striking in its use of low-key lighting, set design, and editing. Dan visits the exotic apartment of his mistress, Sally Lung (Nita Naldi), characterized as a "combination of French perfume and Oriental incense . . . more dangerous than nitroglycerine," to raise funds to stave off a building scandal that has already cost his mother's life.[17] Sally, obviously, is a modern counterpart of Miriam in the Biblical Prologue. After wresting from her a string of pearls that had been an extravagance in better times, Dan is horrified to read a news headline about her escape from a leper colony on Molokai. A long shot in low-key lighting shows Sally, costumed in a sequined gown with kimono-style sleeves and an ornate headdress, gloating as she stands by the draped doorway to the right. Seeking revenge, Dan fires his gun at her. A medium long shot shows the wounded woman react by reaching up to grab the portiere or

37. A male secretary prevents Leatrice Joy from interrupting a rendezvous that her husband is having with his Eurasian mistress in the Modern Story of *The Ten Commandments.* *(Photo courtesy George Eastman House)*

38. As a building contractor who breaks every one of the commandments, Rod La Rocque is about to present Nita Naldi, "a combination of French perfume and Oriental incense," with an expensive string of pearls. *(Photo courtesy George Eastman House)*

drapery. A medium shot and then a close-up show the drapes slowly being torn off the rings to reveal an exotic statue of a Buddha in the background of the adjoining room. Dan has now broken every one of the ten commandments and meets his death in a watery grave—as did the pharaoh's mighty chariot host—in his attempt to escape to Mexico.

The Ten Commandments was premiered in major cities according to the following schedule: Los Angeles on December 4, 1923 (appropriately at Grauman's Egyptian Theatre), New York on December 21, Chicago on February 11, 1924, Philadelphia on February 19, Boston on March 10, and London on March 17.[18] Possibly, the expense of publicity and advertising as well as exploitation at first-run theaters at a time when Famous Players-Lasky was experiencing a financial crisis explains the staggered release dates. Prior to the film's opening in New York, the largest electric sign ever displayed in the city was constructed to show chariots disappear in a chase on the side of the Putnam Building located on Broadway from Forty-third to Forty-fourth Streets. Lasky wrote to DeMille, "We own the Putnam Building and so can devote this space . . . which . . . couldn't be bought for love of money." Audiences, including the notables and celebrities who attended the premiere at the George M. Cohan Theatre, saw gigantic tablets representing the commandments open outward on the stage before the first shot of the credits, showing rays of light emanating from slabs of stone, appeared on the screen. Such a presentation was very costly, as Zukor pointed out to DeMille, and "required an additional outlay of from One Hundred Fifty to Two Hundred Fifty Thousand Dollars."[19] Yet an enormous amount of publicity was necessary not only to stimulate box-office business but to influence critical reception that would affect subsequent runs in major cities.

A clamorous chorus of approval resounded in the New York newspapers following the premiere of *The Ten Commandments*. The *New York Times* asserted, "it is probable [that] no more wonderful spectacle has even been put before the public"; the impressive color sequences were "better and more natural than other such effects we have witnessed on the screen." The Modern Story, however, was dismissed as an "ordinary and certainly uninspiring movie" which, nonetheless, had some "eye-smiting shots." The *New York Morning Telegraph, New York Journal,* and *New York Sun* were not alone in reporting enthusiastic cheers and applause as a sign of audience approval. Critics in trade journals and fan magazines also engaged in hyperbole and repeated superlative assessments of the film. C. S. Sewell summed up in *Moving Picture World,* "This Paramount production easily occupies the position at the top of the ladder of screen achievements," but found that "forceful as is the modern story, it is the biblical section which makes the picture preeminent." Similarly, Adele Whitely Fletcher argued in *Motion Picture Magazine* that the Biblical Prologue, especially the color sequences, represented "one of the most amazing and overpowering sights that we have ever witnessed or ever hope to witness" but had "small praise" for the Modern Story. A number of critics disagreed, however, regarding the merits of the latter. Oscar Cooper claimed in *Motion Picture News* that the prologue "as a spectacle . . . stands alone, because it employs screen artifice as it has never before been employed" but found the Modern Story "powerful, well-knit, and filled with extraordinary acting." Apparently at no loss for words, James R. Quirk proclaimed in *Photoplay* that *The Ten Commandments* was "the best photoplay ever made" and "the greatest theatrical spectacle in history"; indeed, he was even "spellbound" by the Modern Story. Lastly, Julian Johnson, who reviewed films for *Photoplay* before he became head of the Editorial Department of Famous Players-Lasky, wrote to DeMille, "the thing the critics missed . . . is the perfect simplicity of manner in the second part, the life-like details, the startling and realistic dramatic effects."[20]

Critical discourse on *The Ten Commandments,* especially unanimous acclaim for the Biblical Prologue as opposed to mixed reception of the Modern Story, gives evidence of cultural wars signifying ambivalence toward modernity within a broadly construed middle class and native-born working class. In effect, the Biblical Prologue with its intertextual references to historical pageantry, the King James Version of the Bible, Gustave Doré's illustrations, and news stories about Egyptian artifacts constitutes a form of highbrow culture. The Modern Story, however, is not only extremely clichéd in its characterizations but also marred by preachy and risible intertitles. John, for example, warns his wayward brother, "Laugh at the Ten Commandments all you want, Dan—but they pack an awful wallop!" Dan later counters, "I told you I'd break the Ten Commandments and look what I've got for it, SUCCESS! That's all that counts! I'm sorry if your God doesn't like it—but this is *my* party, not His!" As for Mrs. McTavish, who represents fundamentalist adherence to biblical literalism, the *New York Times* commented, "if an old mother reads her Bible it is no reason why a motion picture director should have her carrying around a volume that weighs about a hundredweight." (It was most likely an illustrated edition.) *Variety* simply claimed the Modern Story was "ordinary . . . hoke."[21] But if some critics and cultivated filmgoers found the second part of the film—which comprised roughly two-thirds of an approximate three-hour screening—a disappointment, many in the audience did not.

With the decline of the Red Scare and the passage of an immigration restriction bill that meant the end of most foreign-born peoples in the United States in a generation, cultural fissures within a middle class, broadly defined to include proletarianized white-collar workers, became more visible in the 1920s.[22] Although antimodernist and nativist sentiment prevailed among the elite as well as among the lower-middle and native-born working classes in small towns and rural areas, these groups were nonetheless engaged in a cultural war. Foremost was the challenge posed to an increasingly secularized liberal Protestantism by religious fundamentalism. Whereas the custodians of culture responded to modernity by adopting "a shift from a Protestant to a therapeutic world view" that validated self-realization and thus accommodated the growth of consumer capitalism, segments of the lower-middle and largely nonimmigrant working classes resisted the encroachment of rationalization. American religious movements, as Nathan O. Hatch argues, have traditionally been characterized by a populist impulse that has operated on the periphery of highbrow culture. Forming an alternative subculture, fundamentalists thrived by building their own infrastructure or "extensive network of seminaries, liberal arts colleges, Bible schools, youth organizations, foreign mission boards, publishing houses, conferences, and camps."[23] DeMille's moralizing in the Modern Story, which condemns a consumer culture linked with degenerate Orientalism, undoubtedly appealed to fundamentalists in the country, albeit they, unlike Catholics, did not comprise a sizeable percentage of the urban filmgoing audience. Biblical literalism, in other words, constituted a usable past for social classes that, unlike the cultural elite, were unambiguous regarding the use of popular culture as a representation of their religious views.

Within a decade, DeMille, who began his career as director-general of a production company founded to resituate cinema for a sophisticated clientele, was addressing a mass audience that included fundamentalists as well as urban Catholics. *The Ten Commandments*, with separate narratives set in the biblical past and the present, marks a transitional point in that the director produced highbrow art at the same time that he addressed spectators who would have disapproved of the modernity of his early Jazz Age films. Yet the acclaimed Biblical Prologue, with its references to intertexts in middle-class cultural practice, itself represents a commodity form as spectacle for visual appropriation, however mediated across the divisive lines of gender, class, ethnicity, religion, and geographical region. Particularly noteworthy in this respect is DeMille's popularization of *The Doré Bible,* an expensive and prized edition that appealed to the genteel sensibility. As realist representations based on photographs of Jerusalem and research in the Louvre, Doré's engravings, unlike previous biblical artwork, became well known during the latter part of the nineteenth century. The rich detail of Middle Eastern art surely evoked Orientalist fantasies about traveling to distant exotic places and indulging sensual appetites. Also appealing to the genteel classes who valued performance in parlor games and social entertainment was Doré's sense of theatricality. At the time he was working on the biblical illustrations, the French artist was engaged in staging tableaux vivants for the court of Napoléon III.[24] The most salient characteristics of *The Doré Bible*—realism, Orientalism, and theatricalization—were therefore essential aspects of genteel middle-class culture. To the extent that DeMille popularized Doré's biblical representations, the religious iconography of the elite became dominant but was in turn subject to the homogenizing forces of a consumer culture. In 1945, for example, a two-volume Catholic edition of the Bible, still based on the Latin Vulgate as opposed to the King James Version, was published with Doré's illustrations.[25]

Significantly, the most acclaimed aspect of the Biblical Prologue, DeMille's addition of color to the Doré illustrations, demonstrated the problem of cultural stewardship as practiced by the genteel classes. The use of color in visual media, as Neil Harris argues, became a problematic issue in that it not only signified the refinement and taste of the well-to-do but also constituted a threat to established traditions of iconography. Consequently, the employment of color was desirable only when it did not pander to the vulgar taste of the masses and thereby contravene highbrow culture as spiritual uplift. Such was the case in DeMille's Biblical Prologue. Yet critical discourse on color was only the latest expression of dismay regarding visual representations such as engravings and halftones that were technological advances associated with commercialism. As Harris points out, *Harper's Weekly* complained in a 1911 editorial, "We can scarce get the sense of what we read for the pictures." For decades, the elite classes had been expressing concern that the proliferation of visual media would debase established cultural forms.[26] Since silent cinema, with its narrative and dialogue intertitles, reversed the semiotic ratio or relationship between words and pictures in highbrow publications, as did advertising, it was indeed suspect. *The Ten Commandments* represented a magnificent triumph because DeMille showed that such a reversal could in effect constitute a form of highbrow art with didactic values. But he also demonstrated that culture was a commodity that appealed to a mass audience despite elitist efforts to preserve its sacrosanct status. Although *Motion Picture News* advised exhibitors to emphasize the selling point that the director's film would be "a positive benefit to civilization," eventually the commodification of spectacle would become divorced from the rhetoric of Victorian moralism and confirm the fears of the elite.[27]

Writing an account of the scripting of *The Ten Commandments* for a souvenir program, Macpherson unwittingly reinforced the concern of the genteel classes about the "deverbalization of the forum" that vitiated their concept of culture. She asserted, " 'Seeing is believing' and we believed the spectator would be much more impressed with a story based on the Ten Commandments if he first had seen the history of them . . . during that faraway time of the birth of the Decalogue."[28] The scriptwriter expressed a viewpoint that endorsed the commodification and reification of the biblical past for visual appropriation by film spectators. DeMille's representation of religious experience as spectacle, not coincidentally, provided the advertising industry with intertexts on consumption as a form of self-fulfillment and uplift. When Bruce Barton, son of a clergyman and later a consultant for *The King of Kings,* characterized the function of advertisers in millenarian terms, the translation of religious sentiment into profit was undeniable.[29] Such a development in an industry with a sense of mission to educate the public was not unrelated, however, to the sacralization of culture earlier sought by the elite in order to stave off vulgar materialism and debasement of traditional cultural forms. The rhetoric of spiritual uplift could readily be translated, in other words, not only to products of mass culture but also to advertising strategies that invoked religious doctrine while reifying social relations, surely a sign of a diminished sense of community. A local bank, for example, placed an ad in a souvenir program in which the commandment, "Thou Shalt Not Steal," was quoted to showcase an armored car as a device against those "too weak to resist . . . crime."[30] Appealing to uneasiness about pluralism as well as changing social mores in an industrial environment, the ad attests to lack of social cohesion, a continuing cause for concern among urban reformers. Yet genteel emphasis on spectacle in the form of visual displays and performance as a sign of breeding was not insignificant in setting the stage for alienated human relations in a consumer culture.

To sum up, DeMille's construction of the Biblical Prologue as historical pageantry and the Modern Story as sentimental melodrama was based on an antimodernist aesthetic, but the contradictions within that tradition were manifold. An heir to a theatrical legacy, the director was able to exploit intertextuality in genteel culture because film as spectacle was congruent with existing visual representations such as department store displays, world's fair pavilions, and civic drama, not to mention well-appointed middle-class parlors. "For the sake of appearances," however, was an expression that signified the moral ambiguities involved in simulation or dissimulation as a social and cultural practice. Ultimately, this distinguishing characteristic of genteel middle-class culture became the most essential aspect of what Guy Debord calls "the society of the spectacle." As Debord, following Lukács, points out, "the spectacle is the affirmation of appearance and affirmation of . . . social life as mere appearance." To put it another way, the reality of the social relations of production is obscured or, to be more precise, "mediated by images" and rendered abstract. Accordingly, the representation of reality past and present as consumable images in *The Ten Commandments* testifies to the dominance of spectacle in commodity production. "The real consumer becomes a consumer of illusions."[31] Granted, the antimodernist tradition that DeMille represented was ultimately subverted by its own internal contradictions, but its legacy of spectacle as the ultimate form of commodification still reverberates in today's postmodern culture.

THE COST OF SPECTACLE:
FILM PRODUCTION AS COMMODITY FETISHISM

The Ten Commandments revived DeMille's sagging reputation as a filmmaker at a time when critics were lampooning his society dramas as outré spectacles. Adele Whitely Fletcher observed in *Motion Picture Magazine*, "Just when humorists were finding in the DeMille tales of distorted society life ample material for their somewhat mordant jesting, he comes forth and blazes his name on the roster of the great." Fletcher herself had quoted an amusing line from *Life* when she previously objected to the director's excessive use of flashbacks: "Cecil B. DeMille has sent to India for seven hundred dancing girls, sixty-eight elephants, fourteen Bengal tigers and five maharajahs to be used in the dream episode of his forthcoming production of Sinclair Lewis' novel 'Main Street.' "[32] An analysis of the critical reception of DeMille's texts in another leading fan magazine, *Motion Picture Classic,* is representative of industry discourse and reveals why his reputation, which had consistently been equated with the advance of cinema as an art form, declined in the early 1920s.

In September 1919 Frederick James Smith announced a list of the ten best films of the preceding twelve months in *Motion Picture Classic* and cited four DeMille features: *Don't Change Your Husband, For Better, For Worse, The Squaw Man* (a remake of the famous original), and *We Can't Have Everything.* Smith repeated an earlier assessment in which he claimed, "Just now there's no director as satisfying as . . . DeMille" and praised him for "the most consistent directorial advance." A year later in August 1920, Smith listed DeMille's *Male and Female* and *Why Change Your Wife?* as well as Erich von Stroheim's *Blind Husbands* among the ten best films and noted, "Our biggest disappointment . . . lies in the fact that David Wark Griffith has contributed nothing material to the screen during the [past] twelve months." Perhaps most revealing was his complaint about DeMille: "Lavish and picturesque is his style, but the human note . . . is not there. . . . DeMille is running rife in boudoir negligee. His dramas are as intimate as a department store window." Continuing in the same vein a year later, the critic found "little real warmth and feeling" in *Forbidden Fruit* "because there is little of either in the DeMille method." Harrison Haskins had made a similar observation in *Motion Picture Classic* when he assessed the industry's "big six directors" in 1918: "DeMille falls short in sympathy. . . . He interests, but he doesn't make you *feel.*" When Smith reviewed *Fool's Paradise* in 1922, he described the film as a "mess of piffle" and declared, "Cecil deMille is fast slipping from his luxuriously upholstered seat as one of our foremost directors." After a five-year tenure as *Motion Picture Classic*'s film critic, Smith yielded his byline to Laurence Reid, who promptly dismissed *Adam's Rib* (1923), a society drama featuring a flashback to prehistoric times, as "hokum." Assessing the top directors in 1923, namely, D. W. Griffith, DeMille, Thomas H. Ince, Rex Ingram, Eric von Stroheim, and Ernst Lubitsch, Harry Carr echoed in the fan magazine what had become a refrain in the industry: DeMille has "a silken finish that no other director has ever been able to approach" but his films "always impress you as a story told on a yachting party to well-bred hearers."[33]

A filmmaker whose earlier classics included titles such as *Carmen, Chimmie Fadden Out West, Kindling, The Golden Chance,* and *The Cheat,* that could scarcely be dismissed as set decorations with little human emotion, DeMille had become associated with camp and kitsch productions. Although the early Jazz Age films comprised a novel departure much imitated in the industry, critics responded to the director's continuing orchestration of spectacle with varying degrees of amusement, complaints about commodification, and, ultimately, boredom. An apostle of the consumer culture, like the ad men whose texts he influenced, DeMille gave every indication that he had been thoroughly seduced by film production as a form of commodity fetishism. Although it is impossible to ascertain how the exact figures for the costs and grosses of his features were calculated, the director kept a list, dated April 27, 1928, that gives evidence of the transformation of his filmmaking style in the postwar era. This statistical data is worth considering as an index of change signifying an increased obsession with producing spectacle in an extraordinary film career.

Average cost per feature (excluding *Joan the Woman* as a studio special) during DeMille's tenure as director-general of the Lasky Company remained fairly constant in nominal terms. The total figures are as follows: $15,450.25 in 1913 (for *The Squaw Man*); $17,210.84 in 1914; $16,516.87 in 1915; and $17,760.88 in 1916. Assuming that these sums were not adjusted for inflation and using 1914 as a base year, I conclude that the director's production costs actually declined each year in terms of real dollars. After the merger with Famous Players in 1916, DeMille made two films starring Mary Pickford, whose exorbitant superstar salary inflated budgets so that *Romance of the Redwoods* (1917) and *The Little American* (1917) will not be taken into account here. Starting with the production of *Old Wives for New* in 1918, however, DeMille embarked on a series of all-star features as society dramas that meant relatively low overhead in terms of actors' salaries but escalating expenditures with respect to set and costume design. Average costs per film for each year in the postwar period are as follows: $59,587.36 in 1918; $144,639.88 in 1919; $258,130.04 in 1920; $258,001.05 in 1921; $396,271.89 in 1922; $1,475,836.93 in 1923, the year of *The Ten Commandments;* and $405,516.49 in 1924. Adjusting these figures for inflation and excluding the year 1917 due to Pickford's salary, I conclude DeMille's production budgets increased at an annual rate as follows: 118 percent in 1918 (compared to 1916); 129 percent in 1919; 60 percent in 1920; 58 percent in 1921, a year when a worldwide depression actually meant deflation of the dollar; 55 percent in 1922; and 257 percent in 1923 (for *The Ten Commandments*). Costs for 1924, DeMille's last year with Famous Players-Lasky, were similar to those accrued in 1922.[34]

Although Zukor noted in retrospect that DeMille was an exception to "those who had little respect for the men in the business end of the industry," the director's escalating production budgets caused tension that led to a final rupture. As his filmmaking became increasingly focused on the consumer culture as spectacle, DeMille's correspondence with his longtime colleague, Lasky, became a series of negotiations about budgetary matters. At the end of 1918, the year in which he began to produce society dramas, DeMille wrote to Lasky about a $12,000 cost overrun for *Don't Change Your Husband* and claimed, "The average cost of my pictures to date . . . is $62,243."[35] Less than two years later, in the midst of protracted negotiations for a new five-year contract with the corporation, he wired Lasky:

> I urge the contract provide for an expenditure of not less than one hundred and seventy-five thousand . . . per picture exclusive of weekly advances, the reason . . . being that Male and Female . . . cost one hundred and sixty-thousand . . . and cost of productions has gone up so that I do not want to feel that I must scrimp and pinch . . . and you know my productions are greatly dependent upon their lavish handling.[36]

A shrewd businessman, the director formed Cecil B. DeMille Productions as a partnership in 1920 to negotiate with Famous Players-Lasky for a percentage of net profits realized from the distribution of film rentals worldwide in addition to his usual weekly advances. Such a procedure resulted in considerable friction between the two organizations regarding production costs, accounting methods, audits, and division of profits. DeMille Productions, interestingly, branched out into real estate, securities, and other profitable forms of speculation in addition to filmmaking.[37]

While his attorney, Neil S. McCarthy, dealt with details regarding the relationship between his partnership and the corporation, DeMille continued to press Lasky regarding the budgets of his feature films. Despite a global recession, he wired in May 1921, "the increased magnitude of recent pictures not only of our own but of other companies make it necessary [*sic*] for me to have . . . a minimum of three hundred thousand for each production not including the sixty five hundred dollars weekly" (his advance against a percentage of profits). The Executive and Finance Committee of Famous Players-Lasky countered with a memorandum that limited the director's expenditures to $290,000 including his weekly advances. Due to an economic downturn in the industry and to an anticipated reduction in film rentals, the memo stressed that it would be impossible for a picture to gross $900,000, the minimal amount required to show a profit. A decision to reduce the salaries of studio staff and actors and to cut production costs indicated the gravity of the situation at this time.[38]

A month later, Zukor, noting that DeMille had exceeded his budget for *Fool's Paradise,* stipulated in a modification of the director's contract that the negative cost of his next three productions was to be limited, excluding his weekly advances, to $150,000, $250,000, and $300,000, respectively. DeMille, calling attention to his reputation as "the most consistent money-maker in the business," wired in September, "I cannot and will not make pictures

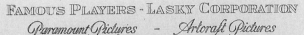

FAMOUS PLAYERS - LASKY CORPORATION

Paramount Pictures - Artcraft Pictures

485 FIFTH AVENUE
NEW YORK CITY

MURRAY HILL 8500
CABLE ADDRESS FAMFILM

OFFICE OF JESSE L. LASKY
VICE PRESIDENT

April 14, 1922.

Mr. Cecil B. DeMille,
Lasky Studio,
1520 Vine Street,
Hollywood, California.

My dear Cecil:-

    As I wired you, I had no difficulty in getting the
Executive Committee to allow you to spend $337,000. for "Manslaughter".
This gave me an opportunity of testing out the feeling here toward
you, and I can assure you again there is nothing in the world for
you to worry about except to make good pictures. Everyone is desir-
ous of giving you a fair deal and that is always the intention, regard-
less of how matters may be reported to you by outsiders or how things
may appear on account of the distance between New York and California.

    I am today instructing Mr. Saunders to send you the gross
returns on the ten pictures you innumerated in your letter of April 6th.
I am also instructing the auditing department, through Mr. Saunders,
to send you the weekly and quarterly reports of bookings, which I understand you are entitled to under paragraph eighth of your contract.

    Regarding myself, I have not been so very happy since my
arrival. You see, you are luckier than I am, old fellow, as you can
always depend on me to go to the front for you, and it is always a
pleasure for me to do it; but I haven't anyone to help me out in my
own problems with the company. You, unfortunately, are at the other
end of the continent and anyway, your position is unique and different.

    The removal of my name from underneath the trademark was
a mistake. I can undoubtedly get it put back if I bring enough pressure
to bear, which I may decide to do. If I brought about such a situation,
you would be left without your name on the trademark and it is that fact
which has kept me from talking to Mr. Zukor, as I feel he will more
readily agree to putting my name back than to putting both of them back
or than to putting your name back.

39. Correspondence from Jesse L. Lasky, vice-president of Famous Players-Lasky and DeMille's colleague for many years. *(Photo courtesy Brigham Young University)*

with a yard stick." Despite Zukor's contractual stipulations, Lasky continued to run interference for the director by securing approval from the Executive Committee for higher production costs even though he had warned him in October, "The company's policy for the next few months will be a most conservative one. There will be no expansion of any kind and . . . investment in theatres, etc. will be gotten rid of, so we can accumulate as much cash as possible." As Lasky confided in a more personal vein in his correspondence the following year, "you are luckier than I am, old fellow, as you can always depend on me to go to the front for you . . . but I haven't anyone to help me out in my problems with the company."[39] In sum, DeMille's determination to acquire a greater percentage of the profits of his features as well as escalating production costs exacerbated his relationship with Zukor and placed Lasky in a precarious position as a middleman. Such a tenuous situation could not withstand the unprecedented cost overruns of *The Ten Commandments.*

When Zukor wired Lasky in April 1923 that he was convinced there should be elements of "love and romance" in *The Ten Commandments,* he also expressed concern that production costs had exceeded $700,000 even before shooting commenced. DeMille volunteered to waive his guarantee to a percentage of the film's profits but not his weekly advances. Zukor remained unimpressed. According to the director's account of events, as expenditures neared $1 million, a bill for $3,000 for the pharaoh's magnificent team of horses sent Elek J. Ludvigh, a corporation attorney, marching into Zukor's office and exclaiming, "You've got a crazy man on that. Look at the cost." Since DeMille served as a board member or an official of several California banks and was acquainted with A. P. Giannini, founder of the financial institution that became the Bank of America, he was able to outflank Zukor and raise $1 million to buy the production outright. A rupture between the two men was momentarily avoided as Zukor backed down, but DeMille's mounting expenditures, which eventually totalled $1.5 million, plunged the corporation into a severe financial crisis. The director agreed in the fall to a retroactive clause in his contract that would reduce the percentage of his profits from five previous productions. Less than two weeks later, Lasky informed DeMille that beginning on October 27, the studio would be closed for a period of ten weeks "on account of the excessive and mounting cost of production and . . . overproduction of pictures throughout the industry." DeMille responded immediately with a memo in which he listed salary reductions and layoffs affecting his staff. The director's decision to retain technicians at half-salary totalling thirty or forty dollars a week, surely a modest sum, and to dismiss clerical workers, seamstresses, and maids who earned even less gives an indication of the magnitude of his expenditures for sets, color processing, and special effects.[40] *Motion Picture News* headlined the story of the layoff of hundreds of Famous Players-Lasky employees not only at the West Coast studio but also in the New York home office, the Long Island studio, and Paramount's exploitation staff in the field. Carl Anderson, president of Anderson Pictures Corporation, astutely summed up the situation in the industry:

> One unit pitted its resources against another, thinking to win favor by the lavishness of their productions. . . . Some producers have been on a wild orgy of spending. . . . There had to come a time when top-heavy production costs would tumble of their own weight. . . . As far back as June, 1921, the . . . Motion

Picture Theatre Owners of America [warned] that production costs were too high.[41]

A short piece about Famous Players-Lasky's denial that DeMille was resigning from his position as director-general of the West Coast studio appeared, interestingly, on the same page.

Although *The Ten Commandments* became a commercial success with gross earnings almost triple its cost, Zukor was determined to curb DeMille's threat to the financial integrity of Famous Players-Lasky when it reopened in January 1924. Since the director's five-year contract was due to expire in 1925, Zukor encouraged him to film his next feature, *The Golden Bed* (1925), at the Long Island studio so that they could both spend time with each other that would be "mutually beneficial and enjoyable." Unfortunately, that studio's facilities proved to be inadequate. As usual, Zukor employed Lasky as a go-between in negotiations and suggested that DeMille accept a lower weekly advance—$3,500 a week as part of negative costs negotiated in advance—and agree to a fifty-fifty division of profits between DeMille Productions and Famous Players-Lasky. Less than two months after this offer was tendered, trade journals simultaneously announced DeMille's departure from Famous Players-Lasky and D. W. Griffith's signing of a long-term contract with the studio in January 1925. After purchasing the Thomas H. Ince Studio in Culver City, DeMille began a new, independent, and short-lived phase in his career as the head of his own production company. But his situation was now comparable to the unenviable fate of Samuel Goldwyn upon the latter's ouster when the Lasky Company merged with Famous Players in 1916. As the director later recalled, "Mr. Goldwyn found himself without any organization at all—flat—nothing. . . . You cannot go out and pick up an organization."[42] DeMille negotiated a contract between his new studio and Producers Distributing Corporation, an organization that almost immediately merged with the Keith-Albee-Orpheum circuit of theaters, but he secured neither the financial backing nor distribution outlets to which he had become accustomed. Furthermore, in a replay of his production of *The Ten Commandments,* he spent two million dollars on *The King of Kings* and precipitated another severe financial crisis that led to his downfall.

Five years after he founded the DeMille Studio, the director abandoned his venture and began a brief tenure at Metro-Goldwyn-Mayer, a corporation that challenged the hegemony of Famous Players-Lasky toward the end of the silent era. Unfortunately, he made three sound films, including two remakes—*Madam Satan* (1930), a society drama featuring the Ballet Méchanique as well as a zeppelin, and a third version of *The Squaw Man* (1931)—that were financial disasters. In 1932 he returned to Famous Players-Lasky, now Paramount Publix Corporation, at a time when both Lasky and Zukor were being outmaneuvered in the latest executive power struggle. Although

DeMille, on the verge of bankruptcy and in the midst of litigation with the Internal Revenue Service, survived to win box-office if not critical acclaim with *The Sign of the Cross* (1932), the decline of his career in the interim underscores the importance of his earlier relationships with Lasky and Zukor. Undeterred in his obsession to mount increasingly lavish spectacles, DeMille had been seduced by film production as a form of commodity fetishism. As such, he represented a nonrational component in the industry in contrast to the sober-minded business sense that Lasky and Zukor brought to film as an entrepreneurial enterprise. DeMille thus contributed to the evolution of filmmaking as commodification in an Orientalist form, that is, the exercise of hypnotic power through the sheer accumulation of objects displayed as spectacle.[43] Indeed, the militaristic connotation of his title as director-general of Famous Players-Lasky signified that the orchestration of stupendous visual display was essentially another aspect of Western imperialism. The filmmaker, not coincidentally, wore jodhpurs and puttees as part of his costume on the set to project an authoritarian image. As opposed to the bureaucratic cost accounting procedures of entrepreneurialism, the Orientalist dimension of filmmaking as an irrational expression of power poses an interesting legacy for the industry today in its phase of multinational corporate competition that transcends geographical boundaries.

DeMILLE'S LEGACY IN A POSTMODERN AGE: *THE TEN COMMANDMENTS* (1956) AS A TELEVISUAL SUPERTEXT

The legacy of DeMille's silent cinema with respect to his productions in the sound era is best characterized as an antimodernist representation of history in the tradition of Progressive Era civic pageantry. Although commodified as spectacle for a mass audience, the director's historical films constituted a usable past by defining progress in Protestant terms and by reinforcing moral and patriotic values in times of crisis. During the economic downturn of the nation's worst depression and the beleaguered years of the Second World War and the Cold War, DeMille revitalized the tradition of Victorian pictorialism by emphasizing the relevance of public history for American citizens. Consequently, his outmoded filmmaking style, which articulated space according to theatrical as opposed to cinematic conventions, proved to be advantageous despite the ridicule it sometimes provoked among critics. DeMille, in other words, minimized the "eclipse of distance" characteristic of a modernist aesthetic and thereby reaffirmed the didactic value of his message. Yet at the same time, he continued to reinforce consumer values by representing history in Orientalist terms as a magnificent spectacle for visual appropriation. Such a representational strategy proved to be especially apt at a time when the United States emerged as a superpower engaged in spread-eagle diplomacy and as a model of consumer capitalism. Consistently exerting an appeal that other filmmakers rarely surpassed, the director established a series of box office records with historical epics about Orientalized empires, such as *The Sign of the Cross* (1932), a bizarre narrative of martyred Christians in ancient Rome; *Cleopatra* (1934), a sumptuous vision of antiquity; and *The Crusades* (1935), a swashbuckler set in an era of Saracen conquest. DeMille also succeeded with Westerns, frontier sagas, and period pieces celebrating American national emergence, like *The Plainsman* (1937), *The Buccaneer* (1938), *Union Pacific* (1939), *North West Mounted Police* (1940), *Reap the Wild Wind* (1942), and *Unconquered* (1947). Fittingly, he culminated his career by returning to small-town American values, as in *The Greatest Show on Earth* (1952), and to the biblical past, as in *Samson and Delilah* (1949) and a remake of *The Ten Commandments* (1956).

A brief consideration of the acclaimed remake, which became one of the industry's three top-grossing films at a time when the studio system was in decline, attests to the relevance of antimodernist historical film for today's postmodern culture.[44] A three-hour, thirty-nine-minute version of the earlier Biblical Prologue photographed in Technicolor and Vista Vision, the epic is the only religious film that is regularly telecast during the Passover and Easter holidays each year. Why is this particular narrative recycled annually as opposed to other historical epics typifying a genre that ironically was exploited to counter television spectatorship in the 1950s and 1960s? What explains the continuing high Nielsen ratings of an antimodernist spectacle that should by all accounts be outmoded on the small screen? First, the film engages in direct address, an oratorical mode congruent with television commercials promoting consumption as personal fulfillment, in order to celebrate American freedom during the Cold War. Unfortunately, DeMille's two-minute stage appearance, initially shown before a foreword and a fade-out to the Paramount logo, is not televised. During this brief prologue, the director inveighs against tyranny and attests to the historical veracity of his work in a theatrical space prefiguring the epic as a tableau. Audiences do listen to DeMille during the course of the film, however, as he narrates the voice-over that describes the founding of a nation based on religious worship and human freedom. Second, despite the visitation of God's wrath upon the children of Israel for worshipping the golden calf and engaging in bacchanalian revelry, the biblical vision of the Promised Land as the land of milk and honey accords with the consumer ethos promoted on television. Picture-postcard shots of Moses (Charlton Heston) seeking refuge under fruit-laden palm trees, moreover, conflate the Promised Land not only with the United States as a "city on a hill," but with southern California as a site of cultural imperialism signified by the studio system. And lastly, as part of a televised "programmed flow" or "supertext" that reedits the epic so that its dramatic tensions are disrupted and resolved by commercials as mininarratives, *The Ten Commandments* is translated into a post-modern electronic form. Constant interruptions of the exodus by ads for food products, beverages, and minivans produce juxtapositions that cele-brate American products, cause unintended hilarity, and alter the meaning of the spectacle.[45] The referent of the film is thus no longer a construction of the past but a commodity.[46] Since the filmmaker broke box office records by commodifying history as spectacle for mass audiences, the disappearance of the historical referent or its displacement by a televised image of a product in a postmodern consumer culture is particularly apt.[47]

A director who was instrumental in legitimating film by establishing the correspondence of cultural forms in the genteel tradition, DeMille did not live to see his most enduring historical epic transformed into a postmodern commodity. Fortuitously, he died in 1959 on the eve of a watershed in American history when a younger generation rebelled against the spread-eagle foreign policy that his frontier sagas and biblical films celebrate in the tradition of civic pageantry. DeMille's sound epics appear dated today because Victorian pictorialism is no longer part of dominant representa-tions, but his legacy survives in the form of television commercials and infomercials as didactic texts and in theme parks with interdependent media reconfiguring or erasing the line between spectacle and spectator.[48] The innovative silent cinema of the 1910s and early 1920s, however, remains the most substantial part of the director's achievement because these texts not only inscribe middle-class cultural practice during a historic moment of transition but also document the evolution of feature film as an art form. As a whole, his work in successive decades continues to be instructive regarding the consumer ethos because it demonstrates that fabricating spectacle became a form of commodity fetishism involving both producer and spectator in a process of reification. Granted, the reception of genteel middle-class culture has been mediated by a variety of working-class and ethnic subcultures, but the increasing dominance of representation in twentieth-century economic, political, and cultural life attests to DeMille's enduring legacy as an architect of modern consumption.

FILMOGRAPHY

THE JESSE L. LASKY FEATURE PLAY COMPANY

The Squaw Man. Scenario and direction by DeMille and Oscar Apfel, based on the play by Edwin Milton Royle. Photographed by Alfred Gandolfi. Starring Dustin Farnum, Winifred Kingston, Red Wing, Monroe Salisbury, Billy Elmer, Joe E. Singleton. Distributed by the Lasky Company. Released on February 13, 1914.

The Call of the North. Scenario by DeMille, based on the play by George Broadhurst and the novel, *The Conjuror's House,* by Stewart Edward White. After his first effort, DeMille hired Alvin Wyckoff as photographer and Wilfred Buckland as art director; both remained his collaborators until the early 1920s. Starring Robert Edeson, Theodore Roberts, Winifred Kingston, Horace B. Carpenter, Florence Dagmar. Distributed by the Lasky Company. Released on August 11, 1914.

The Virginian. Scenario by DeMille, based on the play by Kirk LaShelle and the novel by Owen Wister. Starring Dustin Farnum, Winifred Kingston, J. W. Johnstone, Billy Elmer. Beginning with this release, the Lasky Company distributed its features through Paramount. Released on September 7, 1914.

What's His Name. Scenario by DeMille, based on the novel by George Barr McCutcheon. Starring Max Figman, Lolita Robertson, Fred Montague, Sydney Deane, Cecilia DeMille. Released on October 22, 1914.

The Man from Home. Scenario by DeMille, based on the play by Booth Tarkington and Harry L. Wilson. Starring Charles Richman, Mabel Van Buren, Horace B. Carpenter, Anita King, Fred Montague, Monroe Salisbury, Theodore Roberts. Released on November 9, 1914.

Rose of the Rancho. Scenario by DeMille, based on the play by David Belasco and Richard Walton Tully. Starring Bessie Barriscale, J. W. Johnstone, Dick La Reno, Monroe Salisbury, Jane Darwell. Released on November 30, 1914.

The Girl of the Golden West. Scenario by DeMille, based on the play by David Belasco. Starring Mabel Van Buren, House Peters, Theodore Roberts, Jeanie Macpherson, Anita King. Released on January 4, 1915.

The Warrens of Virginia. Scenario by William deMille, based on his play. Starring Blanche Sweet, House Peters, James Neill, Page Peters, Marjorie Daw. Released on February 15, 1915.

The Unafraid. Scenario by DeMille, based on the novel by Eleanor M. Ingram. Starring House Peters, Rita Jolivet, Page Peters. Released on April 1, 1915.

The Captive. Scenario by DeMille and Jeanie Macpherson. Starring Blanche Sweet, House Peters, Gerald Ward, Page Peters. Released on April 22, 1915.

Wild Goose Chase. Scenario by William deMille, based on his play. Starring Ina Claire, Tom Forman, Helen Marlborough, Raymond Hatton, Florence Smythe, Ernest Joy. Released on May 27, 1915.

Kindling. Scenario by DeMille, based on the play by Charles Kenyon and the novel by Charles Kenyon and Arthur Hornblow. Starring Charlotte Walker, Thomas Meighan, Florence Dagmar, Mrs. Lewis McCord, Raymond Hatton. Released on June 12, 1915.

The Arab. Scenario by DeMille, based on the play by Edgar Selwyn. Starring Edgar Selwyn, Gertrude Robinson, Horace B. Carpenter, Theodore Roberts, Sydney Deane. Released on June 14, 1915.

Chimmie Fadden. Scenario by DeMille, based on the play by Augustus Thomas and the stories by E. W. Townsend. Starring Victor Moore, Camille Astor, Raymond Hatton, Mrs. Lewis McCord, Anita King, Ernest Joy, Tom Forman. Released on June 28, 1915.

Carmen. Scenario by William deMille, based on the story by Prosper Merimée. Starring Geraldine Farrar, Wallace Reid, Pedro de Cordoba, Horace B. Carpenter, Jeanie Macpherson. Released on November 1, 1915.

Chimmie Fadden Out West. Scenario by DeMille and Jeanie Macpherson, based on the stories by E. W. Townsend. Starring Victor Moore, Camille Astor, Ernest Joy, Raymond Hatton, Mrs. Lewis McCord, Florence Dagmar. Released on November 22, 1915.

The Cheat. Scenario by Hector Turnbull and Jeanie Macpherson, based on an original story by Hector Turnbull. Starring Fannie Ward, Sessue Hayakawa, Jack Dean. Released on December 13, 1915.

Temptation. Scenario by DeMille, Jeanie Macpherson, and Hector Turnbull, based on an original story by Turnbull. Starring Geraldine Farrar, Pedro de Cordoba, Theodore Roberts, Elsie Jane Wilson, Raymond Hatton, Sessue Hayakawa. Released on January 2, 1916.

The Golden Chance. Scenario by Jeanie Macpherson. Starring Cleo Ridgley, Wallace Reid, Horace B. Carpenter, Ernest Joy, Edythe Chapman, Raymond Hatton. Released on January 31, 1916.

The Trail of the Lonesome Pine. Scenario by DeMille, based on the play by Eugene Walter and the novel by John Fox, Jr. Starring Thomas Meighan, Charlotte Walker, Theodore Roberts, Earle Foxe. Released on February 14, 1916.

The Heart of Nora Flynn. Scenario by Jeanie Macpherson, based on an original story by Hector Turnbull. Starring Marie Doro, Elliott Dexter, Lola May, Ernest Joy, Charles West, Billy Jacobs. Released on April 24, 1916.

Maria Rosa. Scenario by William deMille, based on the play by Wallace Gilpatrick and Guido Marburg which was based on the play by Angel Guimera. Starring Geraldine Farrar, Wallace Reid, Pedro de Cordoba, Horace B. Carpenter, James Neill. Released on May 8, 1916.

The Dream Girl. Scenario by Jeanie Macpherson. Starring Mae Murray, Earle Foxe, Theodore Roberts, James Neill, Mary Mersch, Charles Welsh. Released on July 17, 1916.

Joan the Woman. Scenario by Jeanie Macpherson. (Production on this epic was begun under Cardinal Film Corporation before Lasky merged with Famous Players.) Starring Geraldine Farrar, Wallace Reid, Raymond Hatton, Hobart Bosworth, Theodore Roberts, Tully Marshall, Charles Clary, Lawrence Peyton. Premiered in New York on December 23, 1916. Released on January 15, 1917.

FAMOUS PLAYERS-LASKY CORPORATION

Romance of the Redwoods. Scenario by DeMille and Jeanie Macpherson. Starring Mary Pickford, Elliott Dexter, Charles Ogle. Released on May 14, 1917.

The Little American. Scenario by Jeanie Macpherson. Starring Mary Pickford, Jack Holt, Raymond Hatton. Released in July 1917.

The Woman God Forgot. Scenario by Jeanie Macpherson. Starring Geraldine Farrar, Wallace Reid, Theodore Kosloff, Hobart Bosworth. Released on November 8, 1917.

The Devil Stone. Scenario by Jeanie Macpherson, based on a story by Beatrice DeMille and Leighton Osmun. Starring Geraldine Farrar, Wallace Reid, Hobart Bosworth, Tully Marshall. Released on December 31, 1917.

The Whispering Chorus. Scenario by Jeanie Macpherson, based on the short story by Perley Poore Sheehan. Starring Kathlyn Williams, Elliott Dexter, Raymond Hatton, Edythe Chapman. Released on March 28, 1918.

Old Wives for New. Scenario by Jeanie Macpherson, based on the novel by David Graham Phillips. Starring Elliott Dexter, Florence Vidor, Theodore Roberts, Julia Faye, Marcia Manon, Gustav von Seyffertitz. Released on May 9, 1918.

We Can't Have Everything. Scenario by William deMille, based on the novel by Rupert Hughes. Starting with this film, Anne Bauchens is credited as the editor of the rest of DeMille's work. Starring Kathlyn Williams, Elliott Dexter, Thurston Hall, Wanda Hawley, Zada l'Etoile. Released on July 15, 1918.

Till I Come Back to You. Scenario by Jeanie Macpherson. Starring Bryant Washburn, Florence Vidor, C. Butler Clonbough, Winter Hall. Released on September 1, 1918.

The Squaw Man. Scenario by Beulah Marie Dix, based on the play by Edwin Milton Royle. Starring Elliott Dexter, Katherine McDonald, Ann Little, Theodore Roberts, Jack Holt, Thurston Hall. Released in December 1918.

Don't Change Your Husband. Scenario by Jeanie Macpherson. Starring Gloria Swanson, Elliott Dexter, Lew Cody, Julia Faye, Sylvia Ashton, Theodore Roberts. Released on January 16, 1919.

For Better, For Worse. Scenario by Jeanie Macpherson, based on William deMille's adaptation of the play by Edgar Selwyn. Starring Gloria Swanson, Elliott Dexter, Tom Forman, Wanda Hawley. Released on April 27, 1919.

Male and Female. Scenario by Jeanie Macpherson, based on the play, *The Admirable Crichton,* by James M. Barrie. Starring Gloria Swanson, Thomas Meighan, Leila Lee, Theodore Roberts, Raymond Hatton. Released on November 16, 1919.

Why Change Your Wife? Scenario by Olga Printzlau and Sada Cowan, based on a story by William deMille. Starring Gloria Swanson, Thomas Meighan, Bebe Daniels, Theodore Kosloff, Sylvia Ashton. Released on May 2, 1920.

Something to Think About. Scenario by Jeanie Macpherson. Photography by Alvin Wyckoff and Karl Struss. Starring Gloria Swanson, Elliott Dexter, Theodore Roberts, Monte Blue. Released on October 3, 1920.

Forbidden Fruit. Scenario by Jeanie Macpherson. Photography by Alvin Wyckoff and Karl Struss. Art direction uncredited. Starring Agnes Ayres, Forrest Stanley, Clarence Burton, Kathlyn Williams, Theodore Roberts, Theodore Kosloff. Released on February 13, 1921.

The Affairs of Anatol. Scenario by Jeanie Macpherson, Beulah Marie Dix, Lorna Moon, and Elmer Harris, based on the series of one-act plays, *Anatol,* by Arthur Schnitzler. Photography by Alvin Wyckoff and Karl Struss. Art direction by Paul Iribe. Starring Gloria Swanson, Wallace Reid, Wanda Hawley, Theodore Roberts, Agnes Ayres, Monte Blue, Bebe Daniels, Theodore Kosloff. Released on September 25, 1921.

Fool's Paradise. Scenario by Beulah Marie Dix and Sada Cowan, based on the story, "The Laurels and the Lady," by Leonard Merrick. Photography by Alvin Wyckoff and Karl Struss. Art direction uncredited. Starring Conrad Nagel, Dorothy Dalton, Mildred Harris, Theodore Kosloff, John Davidson. Released on December 9, 1921.

Saturday Night. Scenario by Jeanie Macpherson. Photography by Karl Struss. Art direction by Paul Iribe. Starring Leatrice Joy, Conrad Nagel, Edith Roberts, Jack Mower. Released on February 5, 1922.

Manslaughter. Scenario by Jeanie Macpherson, based on the novel by Alice Duer Miller. Photography by Alvin Wyckoff. Art direction by Paul Iribe. Starring Leatrice Joy, Thomas Meighan, Lois Wilson. Released on September 25, 1922.

Adam's Rib. Scenario by Jeanie Macpherson. Photography by Alvin Wyckoff. Art direction by Paul Iribe. Starring Anna Q. Nilsson, Morton Sills, Theodore Kosloff, Elliott Dexter, Pauline Garon. Released in March 1923.

The Ten Commandments. Scenario by Jeanie Macpherson. Photography by Bert Glennon, Edward Curtis, J. Peverell Marley, Archibald J. Stout, and J. F. Westerberg. Technicolor photography by Ray Rennahan. Art direction by Paul Iribe. Starring Theodore Roberts, Charles de Roche, Estelle Taylor, Rod La Rocque, Leatrice Joy, Richard Dix, Edythe Chapman. Premiered in Los Angeles on December 4, 1923.

Triumph. Scenario by Jeanie Macpherson, based on the novel by May Edington. Photography by J. Peverell Marley. Art direction uncredited. Starring Leatrice Joy, Rod La Rocque, Victor Varconi, Theodore Kosloff. Released on April 20, 1924.

Feet of Clay. Scenario by Beulah Marie Dix and Bertram Milhauser, based on the novel by Margaretta Tuttle and the play, *Across the Border,* by Dix. Photography by J. Peverell Marley and Archibald J. Stout. Art direction by Paul Iribe. Starring Vera Reynolds, Rod La Rocque, Julia Faye, Richard Cortez, Robert Edeson. Released on September 22, 1924.

The Golden Bed. Scenario by Jeanie Macpherson, based on the novel, *Tomorrow's Bed,* by Wallace Irwin. Photography by J. Peverell Marley. Art direction by Paul Iribe. Starring Lillian Rich, Rod La Rocque, Vera Reynolds, Theodore Kosloff. Released on January 19, 1925.

NOTES

ABBREVIATIONS USED IN NOTES

AMPAS	Margaret Herrick Library, Academy of Motion Picture Arts and Sciences, Los Angeles
DMA, BYU	Cecil B. DeMille Archives, Harold B. Lee Library, Brigham Young University
LMPA	Library and Museum of the Performing Arts, New York Public Library at Lincoln Center
MPC	*Motion Picture Classic*
MPM	*Motion Picture Magazine*
MPN	*Motion Picture News*
MPW	*Moving Picture World*
NYDM	*New York Dramatic Mirror*
RLC	Robinson Locke Collection, Library and Museum of the Performing Arts
USC	Cinema-TV Library, University of Southern California

INTRODUCTION

1. Mrs. H. C. DeMille to C. B. DeMille, 2 December 1914, DMA, BYU.

2. Neil Harris, "Iconography and Intellectual History: The Halftone Effect," in *Cultural Excursions: Marketing Appetites and Cultural Tastes in Modern America* (Chicago: University of Chicago Press, 1990), 304–317. Admittedly, Americanists who ventured into film studies have been criticized by film specialists for faulty readings or lack of readings. See, for example, Jeanne Allen on Lary May in "Palaces of Consumption as Women's Club: En-countering Women's Labor History and Feminist Film

Criticism," *Camera Obscura* 22 (January 1990): 151; or Andy Medhurst on Charles J. Maland in *Screen* 31 (Winter 1990): 458–461.

3. Karen Halttunen, *Confidence Men and Painted Women: A Study of Middle-Class Culture in America, 1830–1870* (New Haven: Yale University Press, 1982).

4. See Edward W. Said, *Orientalism* (New York: Random House, 1978); Michael Rogin, "Making America Home: Racial Masquerade and Ethnic Assimilation in the Transition to Talking Pictures," *Journal of American History* 79 (December 1993): 1050–1077.

5. Georg Lukács, *History and Consciousness: Studies in Marxist Dialectics*, trans. Rodney Livingstone (Cambridge: MIT Press, 1971), 83; Guy Debord, *The Society of the Spectacle* (Detroit: Black & Red, 1977), 36.

6. As this book was going to press, the DeMille Estate and James V. D'Arc secured for the DeMille Archives missing documents, including DeMille's hand-written telegraph messages and copies of letters addressed by DeMille and Jesse L. Lasky to Samuel Goldfish (Goldwyn) in 1914–1915. I am grateful to D'Arc for copies of some correspondence relevant to my study.

7. See my *Cecil B. DeMille: A Guide to References and Resources* (Boston: G. K. Hall, 1985); James V. D'Arc, ed., *The Register of the Cecil B. DeMille Archives* (Provo: Brigham Young University, 1991); *Property from the Estate of Cecil B. DeMille* (New York: Christie's East, 1988).

8. David Bordwell, *Making Meaning: Inference and Rhetoric in the Interpretation of Cinema* (Cambridge: Harvard University Press, 1989), 82, 151–165, passim. For a theoretical reformulation of auteurism, see Tom Gunning, *D. W. Griffith and the Origins of American Narrative Film: The Early Years at Biograph* (Urbana: University of Illinois, 1991), 49–52; Tony Bennett and Janet Woollacott, *Bond and Beyond: The Political Career of a Popular Hero* (New York: Methuen, 1987), 46–47, 65, 233. On the "turn toward textuality" in cultural history, see the introduction in T. J. Jackson Lears and Richard Wightman Fox, *The Power of Culture: Critical Essays in American History* (Chicago: University of Chicago Press, 1993), 1–10. On the ahistorical nature of poststructuralist models in cinema studies, see my "Ethnicity, Class, and Gender in Film: Cecil B. DeMille's *The Cheat*," in Lester D. Friedman, ed., *Unspeakable Images: Ethnicity and the American Cinema* (Urbana: University of Illinois Press, 1991), 112–139.

9. See Jay Leyda and Charles Musser, *Before Hollywood: Turn-of-the-Century Film from American Archives* (New York: American Federation of Arts, 1986). For discussions about DeMille by social and cultural historians, see especially Lary May, *Screening Out the Past: The Birth of Mass Culture and the Motion Picture Industry* (New York: Oxford University Press, 1980), 205–214; Robert Sklar, *Movie-Made America: A Cultural History of American Movies* (New York: Random House, 1975), 91–95. May and Sklar disagree regarding the extent to which DeMille set cultural trends in the postwar period. Although the director's vision was rooted in sentimental culture, as Sklar argues, his films did influence consumer behavior, as May contends. See chapter 1, note 10 in this volume. See also Elizabeth Ewen, *Immigrant Women in the Land of Dollars: Life and Culture on the Lower East Side, 1890–1925* (New York: Monthly Review Press, 1985), 222–223; Kathy Peiss, *Cheap Amusements: Working Women and Leisure in Turn-of-the-Century New York* (Philadelphia: Temple University Press, 1986), 157; Roland Marchand, *Advertising the American Dream: Making Way for Modernity* (Berkeley: University of California Press, 1985), 198; T. J. Jackson Lears, "From

Salvation to Self-Realization: Advertising and the Therapeutic Roots of the Consumer Culture, 1880–1930," in Lears and Richard Wightman Fox, eds., *The Culture of Consumption: Critical Essays in American History, 1880–1980* (New York: Pantheon, 1983), 28.

10. Bennett and Woollacott, *Bond and Beyond*, 44–45, 86, 260–269. The authors differentiate their concept by hyphenating the term *inter-textuality*. On intertextuality, see also John Frow, *Marxism and Literary History* (Oxford: Basil Blackwell, 1986), chap. 6; Janet Staiger, *Interpreting Films: Studies in the Historical Reception of American Cinema* (Princeton: Princeton University Press, 1992), part 1; William Uricchio and Roberta E. Pearson, "'Films of Quality,' 'High Art Films' and 'Films de Luxe': Intertextuality and Reading Positions in the Vitagraph Films," *Journal of Film and Video* 41 (Winter 1989): 15–31; Uricchio and Pearson, *Reframing Culture: The Case of the Vitagraph Films* (forthcoming, Princeton University Press).

11. Henry F. May captures this moment in the title of his work, *The End of American Innocence: A Study of the First Years of Our Own Time 1912–1917* (New York: Alfred A. Knopf, 1959).

12. Dana Polan, "History of the American Cinema," *Film Quarterly* 45 (Spring 1992): 56. For a study that incorporates historical literature on class and gender relations in a reading of silent melodrama rather than subsuming a problematic notion of history in a theoretical construct, see Richard Abel, "Scenes from Domestic Life in Early French Cinema," *Screen* 39 (Summer 1989): 3–28.

CHAPTER ONE: THE LASKY COMPANY AND HIGHBROW CULTURE

1. William deMille to Cecil B. DeMille, 3 September 1913, and William deMille to David Belasco, 25 July 1911, William deMille Papers, New York Public Library, Manuscripts and Archives Division; William deMille, *Hollywood Saga* (New York: E. P. Dutton & Co., 1939), 18. William, unlike Cecil, signed his last name with a lower case d.

2. Adolph Zukor, "Famous Players in Famous Plays," *MPW*, 11 July 1914, 186.

3. See A. Nicholas Vardac, *Stage to Screen: Theatrical Origins of Early Film: David Garrick to D. W. Griffith* (Cambridge: Harvard University Press, 1949; New York: DaCapo, 1987); Rick Altman, "Dickens, Griffith, and Film Theory Today," *South Atlantic Quarterly* 88 (Spring 1988): 321–359. See also Tom Gunning, *D. W. Griffith and the Origins of American Narrative Film* (Urbana: University of Illinois Press, 1991); Gunning, "Weaving a Narrative: Style and Economic Background in Griffith's Biograph Films," *Quarterly Review of Film Studies* 6 (Winter 1981): 11–26. Charles Musser contests Gunning's argument regarding the industry's attempt to woo the middle class in "The Nickelodeon Era Begins: Establishing the Framework for Hollywood's Mode of Representation," *Framework* 22/23 (Autumn 1983): 4–11. See also Musser, *The Emergence of Cinema: The American Screen to 1907* (New York: Charles Scribner's Sons, 1990); Musser with Carol Nelson, *High-Class Moving Pictures: Lyman H. Howe and the Forgotten Era of Traveling Exhibition, 1880–1920* (Princeton: Princeton University Press, 1991). On the class composition of early film audiences, see Janet Staiger, *Interpreting Films: Studies in the Historical Reception of American Cinema* (Princeton: Princeton University Press, 1992), chap. 5; Miriam Hansen, *Babel and*

Babylon: Spectatorship and Silent Cinema (Cambridge: Harvard University Press, 1991);
Judith Mayne, "Immigrants and Spectators," *Wide Angle* 5, no. 2: 32–40; Mayne,
Private Novels, Public Films (Athens: University of Georgia Press, 1988); Charlie Keil,
"Reframing the Italian: Questions of Audience Address in Early Cinema," *Journal
of Film and Video* 42 (Spring 1990): 36–48; William Uricchio and Roberta E. Pearson,
" 'Films of Quality,' 'High Art Films' and 'Films de Luxe': Intertextuality and Read-
ing Positions in the Vitagraph Films," *Journal of Film and Video* 41 (Winter 1989):
15–31; Uricchio and Pearson, *Reframing Culture: The Case of the Vitagraph Quality Films*
(forthcoming, Princeton University Press); Roberta Pearson, "Cultivated Folks and
the Better Classes: Class Conflict and Representation in Early American Film,"
Journal of Popular Film and Television 15 (Fall 1987): 120–128; Douglas Gomery,
"Movie Audiences, Urban Geography, and the History of the American Film," *Velvet
Light Trap* 19 (1982): 23–29; Robert C. Allen, "Motion Picture Exhibition in Man-
hattan, 1906–1912: Beyond the Nickelodeon," *Cinema Journal* 17 (Spring 1979):
2–15; reprinted in John L. Fell, ed., *Film Before Griffith* (Berkeley: University of
California Press, 1983), 144–152; Allen, *Vaudeville and Film 1895–1915: A Study in
Media Interaction* (New York: Arno Press, 1980); Russell Merritt, "Nickelodeon The-
aters 1905–1914: Building an Audience for the Movies," in Tino Balio, ed., *The
American Film Industry* (Madison: University of Wisconsin Press, 1975), 59–82; Garth
S. Jowett, "The First Motion Picture Audiences," in John L. Fell, ed., *Film Before
Griffith*, 196–206; Ben Singer, "The Embourgeoisement Thesis and Silent American
Cinema: Revising the Revisionists" (Paper delivered at Society for Cinema Studies
Conference, New Orleans, 1993).

4. Jesse L. Lasky with Cecil B. DeMille, Agreement, 16 October 1913, DMA, BYU.

5. Lawrence W. Levine, *Highbrow/Lowbrow: The Emergence of Cultural Hierarchy in
America* (Cambridge: Harvard University Press, 1988), 86, 23, 76, parts 1 and 2.
Levine's argument is anticipated by Neil Harris (see note 6 below) and David
Grimsted, *Melodrama Unveiled: American Theater and Culture, 1800–1850* (Chicago:
University of Chicago Press, 1960; Berkeley: University of California Press, 1987, with
an introduction by Levine). See also Paul Dimaggio, "Cultural Entrepreneurship in
Nineteenth-Century Boston: The Creation of an Organizational Base for High
Culture in America," *Media, Culture and Society* 4 (January 1982): 33–50.

6. Neil Harris, "Four Stages of Cultural Growth: The American City," in Arthur
Mann, Neil Harris, and Sam Bass Warner, Jr., *History and Role of the City in American
Life* (Indianapolis: Indiana Historical Society, 1972), 25–49; reprinted in Harris,
Cultural Excursions: Marketing Appetites and Cultural Tastes in Modern America (Chicago:
University of Chicago Press, 1990), 12–28. See also Dale A. Somers, "The Leisure
Revolution: Recreation in the American City, 1820–1920," *Journal of Popular Culture*
5 (Summer 1971): 125–145.

7. Levine, *Highbrow/Lowbrow*, 76, part 3; Daniel Czitrom, *Media and the American
Mind* (Chapel Hill: University of North Carolina Press, 1982), chap. 2; Joan Shelley
Rubin, *The Making of Middlebrow Culture* (Chapel Hill: University of North Carolina
Press, 1992), chap. 1; John S. Gilkeson, Jr., *Middle-Class Providence, 1820–1940*
(Princeton: Princeton University Press, 1986), chap. 6; Levine has been criticized for
not taking into account the pervasive influence of Protestantism on American
culture. See David D. Hall, "A World Turned Upside Down?" *Reviews in American
History*, March 1990, 11–13.

8. Levine, *Highbrow/Lowbrow*, 221–222, part 3; John Higham, *Strangers in the*

Land: Patterns of American Nativism 1860–1925 (1963; reprint, New York: Atheneum, 1981), 113–157. See also Barbara Miller Solomon, *Ancestors and Immigrants: A Changing New England Tradition* (Cambridge: Harvard University Press, 1956; Boston: Northeastern University Press, 1989); David H. Bennett, *The Party of Fear: From Nativist Movements to the New Right in American History* (Chapel Hill: University of North Carolina Press, 1988).

9. See Robert Sklar, *Movie-Made America: A Cultural History of American Movies* (New York: Random House, 1975). Sklar argues that his work is still relevant in "Oh! Althusser!: Historiography and the Rise of Cinema Studies," *Radical History Review* 41 (Spring 1988): 10–35, reprinted in Sklar and Charles Musser, eds., *Resisting Images: Essays on Cinema and History* (Philadelphia: Temple University Press, 1990), 12–35. Donald Crafton and Janet Staiger disagree in a special issue of *Iris*, on early cinema audiences (Summer 1990): 1, 24. See also Lary May, *Screening Out the Past: The Birth of Mass Culture and the Motion Picture Industry* (New York: Oxford University Press, 1980); Garth Jowett, *Film: The Democratic Art* (Boston: Little, Brown, 1976); Roy Rosenzweig, *Eight Hours for What We Will: Workers and Leisure in an Industrial City, 1870–1920* (Cambridge: Cambridge University Press, 1983); Francis G. Couvares, *The Remaking of Pittsburgh* (Albany: State University of New York Press, 1984); Elizabeth Ewen, *Immigrant Women in the Land of Dollars: Life and Culture on the Lower East Side 1890–1925* (New York: Monthly Review Press, 1985); Kathy Peiss, *Cheap Amusements: Working Women and Leisure in Turn-of-the-Century New York* (Philadelphia: Temple University Press, 1986). For an exchange between Sklar and May, see *American Historical Review* 86 (October 1981): 945–946; and 87 (June 1982): 913–915. Among other issues, they disagree about the argument in *Screening Out the Past* that the film industry was the "handmaiden of Progressivism." Rosenzweig and Couvares argue that far from exerting control over mass communications, upper- and middle-class reformers were displaced by the leisure industry. See also Nancy J. Rosenbloom, "Between Reform and Regulation: The Struggle over Film Censorship in Progressive America, 1909–1922," *Film History* 1 (1987): 307–325, and "Progressive Reform, Censorship, and the Motion Picture Industry, 1909–1917," in Ronald Edsforth and Larry Bennett, eds., *Popular Culture and Political Change in Modern America* (Albany: State University of New York Press, 1991), 41–60. On the issue of Progressivism, see Richard L. McCormick's assertion, "we cannot avoid the concept of progressivism—or even a progressive movement—because ... after 1910, the terms were deeply embedded in the language of reformers," in his *Party Period and Public Policy: American Politics from the Age of Jackson to the Progressive Era* (New York: Oxford University Press, 1986), 269. See also Peter G. Filene, "An Obituary for the Progressive Movement," *American Quarterly* 22 (Spring 1970): 20–34; David M. Kennedy, "The Progressive Era," *The Historian* 37 (1975): 453–468; Daniel T. Rogers, "In Search of Progressivism," *Reviews in American History* 10 (December 1982): 113–132. Standard works on the Progressive Era include Richard Hofstadter, *The Age of Reform: From Bryan to F. D. R.* (New York: Alfred A. Knopf, 1955); Robert Wiebe, *The Search for Order 1877–1920* (New York: Hill & Wang, 1967).

10. See Deborah Anne Federhen, Bradley C. Brooks, Lynn A. Brocklebank, Kenneth L. Ames, and E. Richard McKinstry, *Accumulation and Display: Mass Marketing Household Goods in America, 1880–1920* (Wilmington: Union Press, 1986).

11. "Lasky and DeMille Enter Picture Field," *MPN,* 20 December 1913, 15.

12. Interview with Adolph Zukor, 3 April 1957, in Executives, Adolph Zukor

folder, Personal: Autobiography files, DMA, BYU. Because box and folder numbers have been rearranged since I completed most of my research, I have not included that information. See James V. D'Arc, ed., *The Register of the Cecil B. DeMille Archives* (Provo: Brigham Young University, 1991). As for citations of interviews with DeMille, these sessions were tape-recorded for an autobiography that was prepared by Art Arthur and Donald Hayne and that was published posthumously. Unlike the publication, the interviews provide more insight into the director's personality. Unfortunately, the transcripts were cut up and filed according to topics and therefore do not exist in their entirety. See James V. D'Arc, "'So Let It Be Written . . .': The Creation of Cecil B. DeMille's Autobiography," *Literature/Film Quarterly* 14 (1986): 1–9.

13. K. Owen, "The Kick-In Prophets," *Photoplay*, October 1915, in Cecil B. DeMille scrapbook, RLC, LMPA.

14. On auteurism, see John Caughie, ed., *Theories of Authorship* (London: Routledge & Kegan Paul, 1981); David Bordwell, *Making Meaning: Inference and Rhetoric in the Interpretation of Cinema* (Cambridge: Harvard University Press, 1989), 151–165, passim; Roland Barthes, "The Death of an Author," in *Image-Music-Text*, trans. Stephen Heath (New York: Hill & Wang, 1977), 142–148; Michel Foucault, "What Is an Author?" in Donald F. Bouchard, ed., *Language, Counter-Memory, Practice*, trans. Donald F. Bouchard and Sherry Simon (Ithaca: Cornell University Press, 1977), 113–138; Andrew Sarris, *The American Cinema: Directors and Directions, 1929–1968* (New York: E. P. Dutton, 1968). Sarris ranks DeMille as a *metteur en scène*, as do French critics, rather than an auteur. See Jacques Second, "Les Livres," *Positif* 167 (March 1975): 86–87.

15. K. Owen, "Dustin Farnum," *Photoplay*, July 1915, 123; Johnson Briscoe, "Photoplays vs Personality: How the Identity of the Players is Fast Becoming Known," *Photoplay*, March 1914, 39.

16. "Lasky Films Coming Oscar Apfel to Direct Company Leaving for Pacific Coast Soon," *NYDM*, 10 December 1913, 27; "Organize Lasky Forces," *NYDM*, 17 December 1913, 26; Robert Grau, *The Theatre of Science* (New York: Benjamin Blom, 1914), 165–166.

17. David Bordwell, Janet Staiger, and Kristin Thompson differentiate between cross-cutting and parallel editing in *The Classical Hollywood Cinema: Film Style and Mode of Production to 1960* (New York: Columbia University Press, 1985), 48. Eileen Bowser gives a history of editing terms in *The Transformation of Cinema 1907–1915* (New York: Charles Scribner's Sons, 1990), 58–59.

18. "The Squaw Man," *MPW*, 28 February 1914, 1068; "The Squaw Man," *NYDM*, 25 February 1914, 37; Kenneth Macgowan, *Behind the Screen: The History and Techniques of the Motion Picture* (New York: Delacorte Press, 1965), 163. The photo by J. A. Ramsey is reproduced in Paolo Cherchi Usai and Lorenzo Codelli, eds., *The DeMille Legacy* (Pordenone: Edizioni Biblioteca dell'Immagine, 1991), 36–37. According to James V. D'Arc, studio correspondence in the DeMille Archives attests that Apfel was highly valued in 1914 but posed unspecified "problems" in 1915.

19. Interview with DeMille, 25 April 1957, in Biography folder, Personal: Autobiography files, DMA, BYU; Beatrice DeMille, "The DeMille Family in Motion Pictures," *NYDM*, 4 August 1917, 4.

20. *Feet of Clay* folder, Personal: Autobiography files, DMA, BYU.

21. "Getting Belasco Atmosphere," *MPW*, 30 May 1914, 1271. Detailed descrip-

tions of the staging of Belasco plays are in A. Nicholas Vardac, *Stage to Screen;* Lise-Lone Marker, *David Belasco: Naturalism in the American Theatre* (Princeton: Princeton University Press, 1975). Significantly, Belasco does not acknowledge Buckland, who had been his pupil at the Lyceum Theatre School of Acting, later the American Academy of Dramatic Arts, either in his own writing, *The Theatre through Its Stage Door* (New York: Benjamin Blom, 1919), or in William Winter's two-volume biography, *The Life of David Belasco* (1918; reprint, Fairport: Books for Libraries Press, 1970).

22. Script of *The Cheat,* USC; Interview with DeMille, 5 June 1957, in Lighting folder, Personal: Autobiography files, DMA, BYU. See Rudolf Arnheim, *Film as Art* (Berkeley: University of California Press, 1957), 65–73; Peter Baxter, "On the History and Ideology of Film Lighting," *Screen* 16 (Autumn 1975): 96–97; Bordwell, Staiger, and Thompson, *The Classical Hollywood Cinema,* 224–225; Lea Jacobs, "Lasky Lighting," in Cherchi Usai and Codelli, eds., *The DeMille Legacy,* 250–261. For a discussion of color tinting and toning, see Paolo Cherchi Usai, "The Color of Nitrate," *Image* 34 (Spring/Summer 1991): 29–38. Fittingly, when DeMille was made an honorary member of the Society of Motion Picture Art Directors, he claimed that his contribution lay in securing Buckland's talent for film production. (Wilfred Buckland folder, Personal: Autobiography files, DMA, BYU.)

23. DeMille to Lasky, 7 June 1916, in Jesse Lasky 1916 folder; DeMille to Arthur S. Friend, 28 October 1916, in Arthur S. Friend 1916 folder, Lasky Co./Famous Players-Lasky, DMA, BYU.

24. Interview with DeMille, 25 April 1957, in Biography folder, Personal: Autobiography files, DMA, BYU.

25. "Lasky Gets Belasco Plays," *MPW,* 6 June 1914, 1412; "Lasky's First Year," *MPW,* 9 January 1915, 674; Interview with DeMille, 25 April 1957, in Biography folder, Personal: Autobiography files, DMA, BYU.

26. "A New Outlet for Genius," *NYDM,* 17 February 1915, 23; *The Autobiography of Cecil B. DeMille,* ed. Donald Hayne (Englewood Cliffs: Prentice-Hall, 1959), 106.

27. See cover, *MPN,* 20 February 1915; "More Belasco Plays by Lasky," *MPW,* 25 March 1916, 2035; "Close-Ups," *Photoplay,* July 1918, 75.

28. DeMille to Goldfish, 23 July 1914, DMA, BYU (Although Goldfish had not yet changed his name, I refer to him in the text as Goldwyn, as he was known for most of his career.); "Men Who Owe Success to the Movies," *Los Angeles Examiner,* 2 July 1916, in Cecil B. DeMille scrapbook, RLC, LMPA; "Lasky Views the Future," *MPW,* 27 March 1915, 1911.

29. "William C. DeMille with Lasky," *NYDM,* 30 September 1914, 25; William deMille to Anna DeMille, 16 October 1914, William deMille cage file, LMPA.

30. "Lasky Scholarship for College Scenario Course," *MPN,* 6 November 1915, 76; "Lasky Company Offers Scholarship to Columbia Students," *MPW,* 30 October 1915, 765; William deMille to Anna DeMille, 16 October 1914, William deMille cage file, LMPA; Lasky to Goldfish, 11 October 1915, and 2 October 1915, DMA, BYU. Although William deMille wrote satisfactory scripts, apparently he was not an able administrator. Lasky wrote to Goldfish, "We are preparing to let Billy direct . . . and if he doesn't make us a first class picture, we will put him back to writing but not to head the Department." Later, he stated more bluntly, "William was useless as head of the Scenario Department." (Lasky to Goldfish, 11 October 1915, and 25 October 1915, DMA, BYU.)

31. DeMille to Arthur S. Friend, 13 September 1916, in Arthur S. Friend 1916

folder; Lasky to DeMille, 14 September 1916, in Jesse Lasky 1916 folder, Lasky Co./Famous Players-Lasky, DMA, BYU; Julian Johnson wrote in "The Shadow Stage" (*Photoplay*, December 1916, 83), "for months this fine studio . . . has sent out the dullest, most conventional plays." Johnson's observation supports Lasky's contention, "The real reason why Famous Players finally gave in to coming in with us on an even 50-50 basis was because they finally realized that they were in a hole regarding scenarios, stories and productions and could not keep up pace" (Lasky to DeMille, 27 June 1916, in Jesse Lasky 1916 folder, Lasky Co./Famous Players-Lasky, DMA, BYU); Jesse L. Lasky, *I Blow My Own Horn* (London: Victor Gallanez, 1957), 102; DeMille to Goldfish, 17 September 1914, DMA, BYU.

32. "Lasky Makes Radical Move," *NYDM*, 1 July 1916, 46; Lasky to DeMille, 21 July 1916, in Jesse Lasky 1916 folder, Lasky Co./Famous Players-Lasky, DMA, BYU.

33. Lasky to Goldfish, 6 July 1915, DMA, BYU.

34. Program for *Chimmie Fadden*, Strand Theatre, New York, 27 June 1915, *Chimmie Fadden* clipping file, LMPA.

35. R. Grau, "A New Invasion of Filmdom," *Motion Pictures*, September 1915, in Geraldine Farrar scrapbook, RLC, LMPA; Lasky to DeMille, 9 June 1916, in Jesse Lasky 1916 folder, Lasky Co./Famous Players-Lasky, DMA, BYU. As company correspondence shows, Farrar was regarded as a major asset during negotiations for the merger.

36. "Geraldine Farrar for the Screen," *MPW*, 8 May 1915, 879; "Lasky Signs Farrar," *NYDM*, 5 May 1915, 22; Geraldine Farrar, "Why I Went into Motion Pictures," in Geraldine Farrar scrapbook, RLC, LMPA.

37. "Miss Farrar Confers with Belasco," *Musical America*, 14 November 1908, in Geraldine Farrar scrapbook, RLC, LMPA; *Girl of the Golden West* folder, Personal: Autobiography files, DMA, BYU; DeMille claimed that Puccini "borrowed" musical themes in *Butterfly* from William Furst, who was Belasco's composer before he wrote orchestral music for silent film.

38. Irving Kolodin, *The Metropolitan Opera 1883–1966* (New York: Alfred A. Knopf, 1967), 285. Although she expressed doubts about marriage, Farrar married Lou Tellegen in 1916. DeMille gave Tellegen an opportunity to direct that he did not wish to repeat. As a result, Farrar broke with Lasky and signed with Goldwyn (who had formed his own company after Zukor ousted him from Famous Players-Lasky) and subsequently with Pathé; her later films never won the acclaim that she enjoyed in Lasky films. Scripts of Farrar films, DeMille and Goldwyn Collections, USC. See Farrar autobiography, *Such Sweet Compulsion* (New York: Greystone Press, 1938).

39. Although *Carmen* was distributed first, DeMille decided to test Farrar before the camera in *Maria Rosa*, released as her third film; he needn't have worried. Farrar's acting in *Maria Rosa* was impressive, especially in the final sequence when she stabs her husband, who dies while clutching her hair on their wedding day. Julian Johnson wrote in *Photoplay*, July 1916: "Farrar performs such a symphony of glowing love, purple hate, and magnificent murder as our screens have seldom reflected."

40. "New York Papers Praise Carmen," *MPW*, 6 November 1915, 116; "Two Carmens Create Keen Rivalry in Terre Haute," *MPN*, 20 November 1915, 49; "Lasky Co. Expanding," *NYDM*, 30 June 1915, 21; *The Opera Magazine*, October 1915, in Geraldine Farrar scrapbook, RLC, LMPA; *MPN* cover, 9 November 1915.

41. I am describing the George Eastman House nitrate print of *Carmen*, which

is tinted, as was the original, but was reedited as a reissue in 1918. After comparing scripts of *Carmen*, including the original by William deMille and a later version, dated May 18, 1918, with instructions for editing the reissued film, I doubt that the original print exits. Apparently, the extant DeMille silents, preserved in a specially built vault on the director's estate before they were deposited at George Eastman House, are not all original releases. Scripts, Paramount Collection, AMPAS.

42. "Lasky Takes 'Carmen' Fight with Censors to Court," *MPN*, 23 October 1915, 77; "Geraldine Farrar Seen but Not Heard," *New York Times*, 1 November 1915, 11; "Grand Opera's Wildest Sensation since Salome," in Geraldine Farrar scrapbook, RLC, LMPA; Kolodin, *The Metropolitan Opera*, 262; "Hodkinson Ideas Realized in Paramount Films," *MPN*, 27 November 1915, 80; Chicago Strand Theatre Program, *Carmen* clipping file, LMPA. Compared with other Lasky Company pictures distributed by Paramount, ticket prices for *Carmen* were higher.

43. "Geraldine Farrar Scores," *MPN*, 16 October 1915, 43; "Stubbornness of Geraldine," *NYDM*, 1 April 1916, 32; "Miss Farrar as a Movie Carmen," *Hartford Daily*, 4 October 1915, in Geraldine Farrar scrapbook, RLC, LMPA; "Geraldine Farrar's 'Carmen' a Splendid Performance," *NYDM*, 6 November 1915, 28.

44. Kirk Bond, "Eastman House Journal," *Film Culture* 47 (Summer 1969): 45. William deMille was less than charitable when he saw a print of *Carmen* during the sound era: "Looked at with 1935 eyes, our picture was badly photographed, the lighting was childish, the acting was awful, the writing atrocious and—may Allah be merciful—the direction terrible." By the 1930s, however, the DeMille brothers' earlier camaraderie had been superceded by personal, financial, and ideological disagreements. See William deMille, *Hollywood Saga*, 155.

45. Jesse L. Lasky, *I Blow My Own Horn*, 116.

46. "Feature Film," *MPN*, 25 October 1913, 17; Leslie T. Peacocke, "The Practical Side of Scenario Writing," *Photoplay*, May 1914, 132.

47. Jesse L. Lasky, "Accomplishments of the Feature," *MPW*, 11 July 1914, 214. Garth Jowett argues in *Film: The Democratic Art* that "the development of film criticism, and the prominence given to film journalism of all types, was a major factor in the expansion of the industry by attracting a class of patrons curious to see this 'new art' " (98). See also Myron O. Lounsbury, *The Origins of American Film Criticism 1909–1939* (New York: Arno Press, 1973).

48. "The Squaw Man," *MPW*, 28 February 1914, 1068; William A. Johnston, "The Rose of the Rancho," *MPN*, 28 November 1914, 41; "What's His Name," *MPN*, 7 November 1914, 39; "Feature Films of the Week," *NYDM*, 24 February 1915, 29; *MPW*, 1 May 1915, 743; DeMille to Goldfish, 23 July 1914, DMA, BYU.

49. Vachel Lindsay, *The Art of the Moving Picture* (New York: Liveright, 1915). See Nick Browne, "Orientalism as an Ideological Form: American Film Theory in the Silent Period," *Wide Angle* 11 (October 1989): 23–31.

50. W. Stephen Bush, "Kindling," *MPW*, 24 July 1915, 655; "The Golden Chance," *MPW*, 8 January 1916, 255; *New York Dramatic News*, 6 November 1915, in Geraldine Farrar scrapbook, RLC, LMPA; Interview with DeMille, 5 June 1957, in Lighting folder; Interview with DeMille, 3 July 1957, in *The Warrens of Virginia* folder, Personal: Autobiography files, DMA, BYU; Margaret I. MacDonald, "The Director as a Painter and the Players His Colors," *NYDM*, 14 January 1914, 50.

51. Robert M. Crunden, *Ministers of Reform: The Progressives' Achievement in American Civilization, 1889–1920* (New York: Basic Books, 1972), chap. 4; James Lincoln

Collier, *The Rise of Selfishness in America* (New York: Oxford University Press, 1991), chap. 2.

52. *Boston Transcript,* 28 December 1912; William deMille, "Speech before the Drama League at the Plymouth Theater," unidentified clipping; "You Can't Uplift the Drama," *New York Sun,* 28 October 1911, in William deMille scrapbook, RLC, LMPA; "The Heart and Soul of Motion Pictures," *NYDM,* 12 June 1920, in Cecil B. DeMille scrapbook, RLC, LMPA.

53. "Moving Pictures a Social Force," *MPN,* 6 September 1913, 15; MacDonald, "The Director as a Painter and the Players His Colors," 50; "Call of the North," *MPW,* 22 August 1914, 1080; "Close-Ups," *Photoplay,* June 1916, 63–64.

54. "Jesse L. Lasky in Pictures," *MPW,* 3 January 1914, 35; Lasky to Goldfish, 14 January 1915, DMA, BYU; Kenneth Macgowan, *Behind the Screen,* 166; Lasky, *I Blow My Own Horn,* 112. Interestingly, Lasky wrote to Goldwyn, "We have just decided to take Hector Turnbull off all writing entirely as his scenarios are not proving satisfactory, and instead, we are going to have him supply original ideas so that we will have plenty to choose from when we want plays for the other writers to prepare." (Lasky to Goldfish, 19 October 1915, DMA, BYU.)

55. Barbara Beach, "The Literary Dynamo," *MPM,* July 1921: 54–55, 81.

56. William Ressman Andrews, "The Cheat," *MPN,* 25 December 1915, 127; "The Golden Chance," *NYDM,* 29 January 1915, 50; William deMille, *Hollywood Saga,* 139; Samuel Goldwyn, *Behind the Screen* (New York: George H. Doran, 1939), 82; Interview with DeMille, 23 July 1957, in *The Cheat, Chimmie Fadden, Chimmie Fadden Out West* folder, Personal: Autobiography files, DMA, BYU. According to DeMille, "Up to this time, foreign receipts would be $10,000 or $4,000—that sort of thing. . . . *The Cheat* did $41,000 foreign."

57. Cecil B. DeMille with Famous Players-Lasky Corporation, Cecil B. DeMille cage file, LMPA.

58. "The Motion Picture News Hall of Fame," *MPN,* 30 December 1922, 32. Also inducted were Adolph Zukor, Samuel Rothapfel, Mary Pickford, Charles Chaplin, Douglas Fairbanks, George Eastman, Thomas Edison, John D. Williams, Will Hays, and Carl Laemmle.

59. Staiger, *Interpreting Films,* chap. 5, Rosenzweig, *Eight Hours for What We Will,* chap. 8, Ewen, *Immigrant Women in the Land of Dollars,* chap. 12, Peiss, *Cheap Amusements,* chap. 6; Hansen, *Babel and Babylon,* chap. 2, Lizabeth Cohen, *Making a New Deal: Industrial Workers in Chicago, 1919–1939* (Cambridge: Cambridge University Press, 1990), chap. 3; Gunning, *D. W. Griffith and the Origins of American Narrative,* 256–257. On working-class cinema, see Kay Sloan, *The Loud Silents: Origins of the Social Problem Film* (Urbana: University of Illinois Press, 1988); Steven J. Ross, "Struggles for the Screen: Workers, Radicals, and the Political Uses of Film," *American Historical Review* 96 (April 1991): 336–367; Ross, "Cinema and Class Conflict: Labor, Capital, the State and American Silent Film," in Robert Sklar and Charles Musser, eds., *Resisting Images,* 68–107. Ben Singer argues that cinema audiences remained working class during the 1910s in "The Embourgeoisement Thesis and Silent American Cinema: Revising the Revisionists." On modes of production and representation in relation to class, see note 3 above.

60. Douglas Gomery, "The Picture Palace: Economic Sense or Hollywood Nonsense?" *Quarterly Review of Film Studies* 3 (Winter 1978): 24–25. See also Gomery,

Shared Pleasures: A History of Movie Presentation in the United States (Madison: University of Wisconsin Press, 1992), part 1.

61. *Cincinnati Inquirer,* 6 December 1908; *The Bookman,* 1911, in William deMille scrapbook, RLC, LMPA.

62. See Lise-Lone Marker, *David Belasco,* Introduction.

63. *Photoplay,* May 1918, 20–39; November 1914, 55–75; January 1915, 39–56.

64. Charles Musser challenges A. Nicholas Vardac's argument that stage melodrama could easily be adapted without dialogue for the screen in "The Nickelodeon Era Begins," 6.

65. See Rubin, *The Making of Middlebrow Culture*; Janice Radway, "The Scandal of the Middlebrow: The Book-of-the-Month Club, Class Fracture, and Cultural Authority," *South Atlantic Quarterly* 89 (Fall 1990): 703–736. See also Rubin, "Between Culture and Consumption: Mediations of the Middlebrow," in Richard Wightman Fox and T. J. Jackson Lears, eds., *The Power of Culture: Critical Essays in American History* (Chicago: University of Chicago Press, 1993): 163–194. Radway differentiates her study from Rubin's by asserting that middlebrow culture was "a separate aesthetic and ideological production constructed by a particular fraction of the middle class."

66. See Jowett's discussion of the rise of the star system, features, and movie palaces in *Film: The Democratic Art,* chap. 3; Richard deCordova, *Picture Personalities: The Emergence of the Star System in America* (Urbana: University of Illinois Press, 1990).

67. See Rosenzweig, *Eight Hours for What We Will,* chap. 8; Couvares, *The Remaking of Pittsburgh,* chap. 8; Ewen, *Immigrant Women in the Land of Dollars,* chap. 12; Peiss, *Cheap Amusements,* chap. 6; Gilkeson, Jr., *Middle-Class Providence,* chap. 6. See also note 3 above.

68. "William DeMille Talks on the Drama," *MPW,* 9 October 1915, 258; "Close-Ups," *Photoplay,* August 1915, 121.

69. L. C. Moon, "Statistics of the Motion Picture Industry," *MPN,* 16 December 1922, 3024. Exhibition statistics during the period 1916–1922 were considered relatively unchanged.

70. See Richard Koszarski, *An Evening's Entertainment: The Age of the Silent Feature Picture, 1915–1928* (New York: Charles Scribner's Sons, 1990).

CHAPTER TWO: SELF-THEATRICALIZATION

1. Script of *What's His Name,* USC. George Barr McCutcheon, the author of the novel, also wrote the best-seller, *Brewster's Millions,* adapted successfully for the stage, and for film by DeMille and Apfel as the Lasky Company's second release.

2. Daniel Horowitz, *The Morality of Spending: Attitudes toward the Consumer Society in America, 1875–1940* (Baltimore: Johns Hopkins University Press, 1985), 88; these figures are for the year 1912.

3. I refer to private, or domestic, and public spheres as concepts that have informed American women's history. See Linda K. Kerber, "Separate Spheres, Female Worlds, Woman's Place: The Rhetoric of Women's History," *Journal of American History* 75 (June 1988): 9–39. For a reconsideration of Habermas's concept of the public sphere in Enlightenment France with respect to American working-class film attendance, see Miriam Hansen's *Babel and Babylon: Spectatorship in American*

Silent Film (Cambridge: Harvard University Press, 1991). On women's political practice in relation to Habermas's theory, see Mary P. Ryan, "Gender and Public Access: Women's Politics in Nineteenth-Century America," in Craig Calhoun, ed., *Habermas and the Public Sphere* (Cambridge: MIT Press, 1992), 259–288; Ryan, *Women in Public: Between Banners and Ballots, 1825–1880* (Baltimore: Johns Hopkins University Press, 1990).

4. Henry F. May, *The End of American Innocence: A Study of the First Years of Our Time* (New York: Alfred A. Knopf, 1959), 24.

5. On the social history of the middle class, see Mary P. Ryan, *Cradle of the Middle Class: The Family in Oneida County, New York, 1790–1865* (Cambridge: Cambridge University Press, 1981), chaps. 4, 5; Stuart Blumin, *The Emergence of the Middle Class: Social Experience in the American City, 1760–1900* (Cambridge: Cambridge University Press, 1989); Horowitz, *The Morality of Spending*; John S. Gilkeson, Jr., *Middle-Class Providence, 1820–1940* (Princeton: Princeton University Press, 1986); Sam Bass Warner, Jr., *Streetcar Suburbs: The Process of Growth in Boston, 1870–1900*, 2d ed. (Cambridge: Harvard University Press, 1978); Cindy Sondik Aron, *Ladies and Gentlemen of the Civil Service: Middle-Class Workers in Victorian America* (New York: Oxford University Press, 1987); Olivier Zunz, *Making America Corporate, 1870–1920* (Chicago: University of Chicago Press, 1990); Peter Stearns, "The Middle Class: Toward a Precise Definition," *Comparative Studies in Society and History* 21 (July 1979): 392–393; Arno J. Mayer, "The Lower Middle Class as Historical Problem," *Journal of Modern History* 47 (September 1975): 417–418. See also C. Wright Mills, *White Collar: The American Middle Classes* (New York: Oxford University Press, 1956), xvi–xvii; Harry Braverman, *Labor and Monopoly Capital: The Degradation of Work in the Twentieth Century* (New York: Monthly Review Press, 1974), chap. 13.

6. *New York Telegraph* clipping, 10 April 1913, in Cecil B. DeMille scrapbook, RLC, LMPA; Beatrice DeMille, "The DeMille Family in Motion Pictures," *NYDM*, 4 August 1917, 4; Agreement . . . between the John W. Rumsey Co. . . . Cecil B. DeMille and M. Beatrice DeMille, Cecil B. DeMille cage file, LMPA. Beatrice DeMille was Jewish, a lineage her son de-emphasized, but she converted to her husband's Episcopalian faith.

7. Interview with DeMille, 24 September 1957, in Mother folder, Personal: Autobiography files, DMA, BYU.

8. Ryan, *Cradle of the Middle Class*, 51.

9. Ann Douglas, *The Feminization of American Culture* (New York: Alfred A. Knopf, 1977), 1–13; T. J. Jackson Lears, *No Place of Grace: Antimodernism and the Transformation of American Culture 1880–1920* (New York: Pantheon, 1981), chap. 3, part 3; John Higham, "The Reorientation of American Culture in the 1890s," in John Weiss, ed., *The Origins of Modern Consciousness* (Detroit: Wayne State University Press, 1965), 25–48; Ryan, *Cradle of the Middle Class*, chap. 4; Blumin, *The Emergence of the Middle Class*, chap. 5; Richard Sennett, *Families against the City: Middle Class Homes of Industrial Chicago 1872–1880* (Cambridge: Harvard University Press, 1970).

10. See Douglas, *The Feminization of American Culture;* Lears, *No Place of Grace.*

11. See Karen Halttunen, *Confidence Men and Painted Women: A Study of Middle-Class Culture in America, 1830–1870* (New Haven: Yale University Press, 1982); John F. Kasson, *Rudeness and Civility: Manners in Nineteenth-Century Urban America* (New York: Hill & Wang, 1990); Katherine C. Grier, *Culture and Comfort: People, Parlors, and Upholstery, 1850–1930* (Amherst: University of Massachusetts Press, 1988); Kenneth L.

Ames, *Death in the Dining Room and Other Tales of Victorian Culture* (Philadelphia: Temple University Press, 1992); Daniel Horowitz, "Frugality or Comfort: Middle-Class Styles of Life in the Early Twentieth Century," *American Quarterly* 37 (Summer 1985): 240; Horowitz, *The Morality of Spending.* See also Siegfried Giedion, *Mechanization Takes Command* (New York: Oxford University Press, 1948), parts 5, 6.

12. Martha Banta, *Imaging American Women: Idea and Ideals in Cultural History* (New York: Columbia University Press, 1987), chap. 15; David Glassberg, *American Historical Pageantry: The Uses of Tradition in the Early Twentieth Century* (Chapel Hill: University of North Carolina Press, 1990), 33–34; Henry C. DeMille, in Diary folder, Family, DMA, BYU; *The Autobiography of Cecil B. DeMille,* ed. Donald Hayne (Englewood Cliffs: Prentice-Hall, 1959), 24; A. Nicholas Vardac, *Stage to Screen: Theatrical Origins of Early Film: David Garrick to D. W. Griffith* (Cambridge: Harvard University Press, 1949; New York: DaCapo, 1987), 144; Bernard Hewitt, *Theatre U.S.A. 1665 to 1957* (New York: McGraw-Hill, 1959), 253; Oscar G. Brockett and Robert R. Findlay, *Century of Innovation: A History of European and American Theatre and Drama since 1870* (Englewood Cliffs: Prentice-Hall, 1973), 51.

13. Halttunen, *Confidence Men and Painted Women,* chaps. 3–6; Erving Goffman, *The Presentation of Self in Everyday Life* (Garden City: Doubleday & Co., 1959), Conclusion. See also Jean-Christophe Agnew, *Worlds Apart: The Market and the Theater in Anglo-American Thought, 1550–1750* (Cambridge: Cambridge University Press, 1986); Richard Sennett, *The Fall of Public Man: On the Social Psychology of Capitalism* (New York: Alfred A. Knopf, 1977). On character versus personality, see Warren Susman, "'Personality' and the Making of Twentieth-Century Culture," in *Culture as History* (New York: Pantheon, 1984), 271–285. Richard Wightman Fox argues that Susman is too schematic because personality was informed by nineteenth-century concepts of character, in "Character and Personality: The Cult of Liberal Protestantism 1850–1930" (Paper delivered at SUNY Brockport, April, 1988). I focus on character and personality as constituting polarities in order to interpret a specific DeMille text.

14. Gilkeson, Jr., *Middle-Class Providence,* 219–220; Francis G. Couvares, *The Remaking of Pittsburgh: Class and Culture in an Industrializing City, 1877–1919* (Albany: State University of New York Press, 1984), 101.

15. For a discussion of inattention to novels and theatrical work in studies of film adaptations, see Rick Altman, "Dickens, Griffith, and Film Theory Today," *South Atlantic Quarterly* 88 (Spring 1988): 321–359.

16. See Alfred Chandler, *The Visible Hand: The Managerial Revolution in American Business* (Cambridge: Belknap Press, 1977).

17. Brockett and Findlay, *Century of Innovation,* chaps. 1–6.

18. David Grimsted, *Melodrama Unveiled: American Theater and Culture 1800–1850* (Chicago: University of Chicago Press, 1968), 65.

19. Programs for *The Wife* and *Lord Chumley,* in scrapbook, Theater and Business, DMA, BYU.

20. Brockett and Findlay, *Century of Innovation,* 183; Hewitt, *Theatre U.S.A.,* 257.

21. On melodrama as working-class entertainment, see Vardac, *Stage to Screen,* 1–2; Michael Booth, *English Melodrama* (London: Herbert Jenkins, 1965), 13, 52, 187; Peter Brooks, *The Melodramatic Imagination: Balzac, Henry James, Melodrama, and the Mode of Excess* (New Haven: Yale University Press, 1985), xii. On melodrama, see John G. Cawelti, *Adventure, Mystery, and Romance: Formula Stories as Art and Popular*

Culture (Chicago: University of Chicago Press, 1967), 260–295; Griselda Pollock, "Report on the Weekend School in Dossier on Melodrama," *Screen* 18 (Summer 1977): 105–110; Chuck Kleinhans, "Notes on Melodrama and the Family under Capitalism," *Film Reader* 3 (February 1978): 40–47; Martha Vicinus, "'Helpless and Unfriended': Nineteenth-Century Domestic Melodrama," *New Literary History* 13 (Autumn 1981): 127–143; Michael Walker, "Melodrama and the American Cinema," *Movie* 29/30 (Summer 1982): 2–38; Martin Meisel, *Realizations: Narrative, Pictorial, and Theatrical Arts in Nineteenth-Century England* (Princeton: Princeton University Press, 1983); Pam Cook, ed., *The Cinema Book* (New York: Pantheon, 1985), 73–84; Laura Mulvey, "Melodrama In and Out of the Home," in Colin MacCabe, ed., *High Theory/ Low Culture* (New York: St. Martin's Press, 1986), 80–100; Christine Gledhill, ed., *Home Is Where the Heart Is* (London: British Film Institute, 1987), Introduction; Gledhill, "Speculations on the Relationship between Soap Opera and Melodrama," *Quarterly Review of Film and Video* 14 (1992): 103–124; Altman, "Dickens, Griffith, and Film Theory Today," 321–359; Robert Lang, *American Melodrama: Griffith, Vidor, Minnelli* (Princeton: Princeton University Press, 1989); Richard Abel, "Scenes from Domestic Life in Early French Cinema," *Screen* 39 (Summer 1989): 3–28. Film scholars who study melodrama have a tendency to conflate bourgeoisie with middle class and often do not distinguish between the upper and lower middle class.

22. Frank Rahill, *The World of Melodrama* (University Park: Pennsylvania State University Press, 1967), 268.

23. Rahill, *The World of Melodrama,* chap. 28, 261–263; James Smith, *Melodrama* (London: Methuen, 1973), 43.

24. Robert Heilman, *Tragedy and Melodrama* (Seattle: University of Washington Press, 1968), 94–97.

25. Lise Lone-Marker, *David Belasco: Naturalism in the American Theatre* (Princeton: Princeton University Press, 1975), 78–114; Vardac, *Stage to Screen,* 129–135; Brockett and Findlay, *Century of Innovation,* 12.

26. "Review of the Week," *New York Clipper,* 1 September 1888, 393.

27. Henry C. DeMille, *The Wife,* in Robert Hamilton Ball, ed., *The Plays of Henry C. DeMille Written in Collaboration with David Belasco* (Princeton: Princeton University Press, 1940; Bloomington: Indiana University Press, 1965), 117. This collection of plays is volume 17 in the series, *America's Lost Plays,* which also includes William C. deMille's *The Warrens of Virginia.*

28. Nym Crinkle, "The Charity Ball," *Theatre,* November 1889, in scrapbook, Theater and Business, DMA, BYU.

29. Peter Brooks, *The Melodramatic Imagination,* 16, 20.

30. See Halttunen, *Confidence Men and Painted Women;* Kasson, *Rudeness and Civility;* Sennett, *The Fall of Public Man.*

31. "About a Certain School of Plays," *The Illustrated American,* 4 March 1893, Henry C. DeMille clipping file, LMPA.

32. Ibid.

33. Henry C. DeMille, *The Wife,* 59.

34. *New York Sun,* 20 November 1889, in scrapbook, Theater and Business, DMA, BYU.

35. "About a Certain School of Plays," LMPA.

36. *New York Daily Tribune,* 2 November 1887, in scrapbook, Theater and Business, DMA, BYU.

37. *The Spirit of the Times,* 25 August 1888, in scrapbook, Theater and Business, DMA, BYU.

38. *Tid Bits,* 12 November 1887, in scrapbook, Theater and Business, DMA, BYU.

39. Craig Timberlake, *The Bishop of Broadway: The Life and Work of David Belasco* (New York: Library Publishers, 1954), 133.

40. Brockett and Findlay, *Century of Innovation,* 8; Vardac, *Stage to Screen,* xx. On realism represented in a romantic mode, see also Lone-Marker, *David Belasco,* 76, and Michael R. Booth, *Victorian Spectacular Theatre, 1850–1910* (London: Routledge & Kegan Paul, 1981), 74; Gledhill, "Speculations on the Relationship between Soap Opera and Melodrama," 103–109. On realism and representation, see Roland Barthes, "The Reality Effect," in Tzvetan Todorov, ed., *French Literary Theory Today,* trans. R. Carter (Cambridge: Cambridge University Press, 1982), 11–17.

41. *The Spirit of the Times,* 25 August 1888; *The World,* 20 November 1889, in scrapbook, Theater and Business, DMA, BYU.

42. *Graphic,* 25 August 1888, in scrapbook, Theater and Business, DMA, BYU; Brockett and Findlay, *Century of Innovation,* 183; Hewitt, *Theatre U.S.A.,* 261.

43. *New York World,* 24 November 1889, in scrapbook, Theater and Business, DMA, BYU.

44. Jane Tompkins, *Sensational Designs: The Cultural Work of American Fiction, 1790–1860* (New York: Oxford University Press, 1985), 126.

45. *New York Mirror,* 30 November 1889, in scrapbook, Theater and Business, DMA, BYU.

46. *Once a Week,* 17 December 1889, in scrapbook, Theater and Business, DMA, BYU.

47. Minnie Maddern Fiske was courted by Lasky's rival, the Famous Players Company. Unfortunately, DeMille's adaptation is the only silent film extant about the theatrical life that was his family legacy. *Wild Goose Chase,* based on William deMille's play about rebellious young lovers who join a traveling troupe, has not survived.

48. "Max Figman in 'What's His Name,' " *MPW,* 26 September 1914, 1778.

49. Hanford C. Judson, "What's His Name," *MPW,* 7 November 1914, 792.

50. Script of *What's His Name,* USC.

51. Henry Seidel Canby, *The Age of Confidence: Life in the Nineties* (New York: Farrar & Rinehart, 1934), 50; see also Lary May, *Screening Out the Past: The Birth of Mass Culture and the Motion Picture Industry* (New York: Oxford University Press, 1980), 7.

52. Paul Boyer, *Urban Masses and Moral Order in America, 1820–1920* (Cambridge: Harvard University Press, 1978), chap. 13.

53. Ruth Rosen, *The Lost Sisterhood: Prostitution in America, 1900–1918* (Baltimore: Johns Hopkins University Press, 1982), 42.

54. Acting became a more respectable profession for women in the late nineteenth century. See Christopher Kent, "Image and Reality: The Actress and Society," in Martha Vicinus, ed., *A Widening Sphere: Changing Roles of Victorian Women* (Bloomington: Indiana University Press, 1977), 94–116.

55. "Lasky at Los Angeles," *MPW,* 10 July 1915, 239. In 1918, DeMille trained Anne Bauchens to be his editor, and she worked in that capacity until the end of the director's decades-long career.

56. Hanford C. Judson credits Buckland "for having made the scenes" in his review, "What's His Name," in *MPW;* the art director is not credited in the film.

57. Interview with DeMille, 28 June 1957, in *The Squaw Man* folder, Personal: Autobiography files, DMA, BYU.

58. See Rudolf Arnheim, *Film as Art* (Berkeley: University of California Press, 1957), 65–73. Arnheim titles this section "Artistic Uses of Lighting and of the Absence of Color," but Lasky releases were all color tinted. See also Peter Baxter, "On the History and Ideology of Film Lighting," *Screen* 16 (Autumn 1975): 96–98; David Bordwell, Janet Staiger, and Kristin Thompson, *The Classical Hollywood Cinema: Film Style and Mode of Production* (New York: Columbia University Press, 1985), 223–227; Lea Jacobs, "Lasky Lighting," in Paolo Cherchi Usai and Lorenzo Codelli, eds., *The DeMille Legacy* (Pordenone: Edizioni Biblioteca dell'Immagine, 1991), 250–261.

59. Interview with DeMille, 3 July 1957, in *What's His Name* folder, Personal: Autobiography files, DMA, BYU.

60. Script of *What's His Name,* USC.

61. See Ryan, *Cradle of the Middle Class,* chap. 4; Sennett, *Families against the City,* part 3.

62. The Henry C. DeMille School for Girls Founded in 1893, Henry C. DeMille clipping file, LMPA.

63. "What's His Name," *NYDM,* 28 October 1914, 32; untitled *Hartford Current* review, 30 October 1914, *What's His Name* clipping file, LMPA.

64. See Susman, " 'Personality' and the Making of Twentieth-Century Culture."

65. Clyde Griffin, "The Progressive Ethos," in Stanley Coben and Lorman Ratner, eds., *The Development of an American Culture* (Englewood Cliffs: Prentice-Hall, 1970), 129. See Ryan, *Cradle of the Middle Class,* chap. 4; Blumin, *The Emergence of the Middle Class,* chap. 5; Sennett, *Families against the City,* part 3.

66. Horowitz, *The Morality of Spending,* chaps. 5, 6; Blumin, *The Emergence of the Middle Class,* 185–186; Ryan, *Cradle of the Middle Class,* 200–201.

67. Judson, "What's His Name," 792.

CHAPTER THREE: THE LOWER EAST SIDE AS SPECTACLE

1. Money Land and Transportation folder, Family, DMA, BYU.

2. See Albert Habegger, *Gender, Fantasy and Realism in American Literature* (New York: Columbia University Press, 1982), chaps. 7, 11; Alan Trachtenberg, *The Incorporation of America: Culture and Society in the Gilded Age* (New York: Hill & Wang, 1982), chap. 4; Henry F. May, *The End of American Innocence: A Study of the First Years of Our Time 1912–1917* (New York: Alfred A. Knopf, 1959), 48–50.

3. Quoted in Miles Orvell, *The Real Thing: Imitation and Authenticity in American Culture, 1880–1940* (Chapel Hill: University of North Carolina Press, 1989), 106.

4. See Habegger, *Gender, Fantasy and Realism in American Literature,* chap. 11; Jane Tompkins, *Sensational Designs: The Cultural Work of American Fiction, 1790–1860* (New York: Oxford University Press, 1985), chap. 5; Christine Gledhill, "Speculations on the Relationship between Soap Opera and Melodrama," *Quarterly Review of Film and Video* 14 (1992): 107–108; Neil Harris, "Iconography and Intellectual History: The Halftone Effect," in *Cultural Excursions: Marketing Appetites and Cultural Tastes in Modern America* (Chicago: University of Chicago Press, 1990), 304–317.

5. Peter B. Hales, *Silver Cities: The Photography of American Urbanization* (Phila-

delphia: Temple University Press, 1984), chap. 2. See also John F. Kasson, *Rudeness and Civility: Manners in Nineteenth-Century Urban America* (New York: Hill & Wang, 1990), for a discussion of "bird's-eye view" versus "mole's-eye view" (72–80).

6. See Paul Boyer, *Urban Masses and Moral Order in America, 1820–1920* (Cambridge: Harvard University Press, 1978); Warren Susman, "The City in American Culture," in *Culture as History: The Transformation of American Society in the Twentieth Century* (New York: Pantheon, 1984); Trachtenberg, *The Incorporation of America,* chap. 4; William H. Wilson, *The City Beautiful Movement* (Baltimore: Johns Hopkins University Press, 1989).

7. See Wilson, *The City Beautiful Movement,* chap. 3; Trachtenberg, *The Incorporation of America,* chap. 7. According to Trachtenberg, the exhibition excluded African Americans and stereotyped other ethnic groups and women.

8. On fiction, see Eugene Arden, "The Evil City in American Fiction," *New York History* 35 (July 1954): 259–279.

9. Thomas Bender, *Toward an Urban Vision: Ideas and Institutions in Nineteenth Century America* (Baltimore: Johns Hopkins University Press, 1975), 193.

10. George G. Foster, *New York by Gaslight and Other Urban Sketches,* edited and with an introduction by Stuart Blumin (Berkeley: University of California Press, 1990), 93.

11. David Ward, *Poverty, Ethnicity, and the American City, 1840–1925: Changing Conceptions of the Slum and the Ghetto* (Cambridge: Cambridge University Press, 1989), 12.

12. A quote attributed to Gilles Deleuze in Craig Owens, "The Discourse of Others: Feminists and Postmodernism," in Hal Foster, ed., *The Anti-Aesthetic* (Port Townsend: Bay Press, 1983), 80.

13. Quoted in Ward, *Poverty, Ethnicity, and the American City,* 78.

14. See Michel Foucault, *Discipline and Punish,* trans. Alan Sheridan (New York: Pantheon, 1978). See also M. Christine Boyer, *Dreaming the Rational City: The Myth of American City Planning* (Cambridge: MIT Press, 1983).

15. Habegger, *Gender, Fantasy and Realism in American Literature,* preface, chap. 11; Daniel H. Borus, *Writing Realism: Howells, James, and Norris in the Mass Market* (Chapel Hill: University of North Carolina Press, 1989), chap. 5. See also Amy Kaplan, *The Social Construction of American Realism* (Chicago: University of Chicago Press, 1988), Introduction; Trachtenberg, *The Incorporation of America,* chap. 6.

16. May, *The End of American Innocence,* 66.

17. Tompkins, *Sensational Designs,* chap. 5.

18. Orvell, *The Real Thing,* Introduction, part 2; Oscar G. Brockett and Robert R. Findlay, *Century of Innovation: A History of European and American Theatre and Drama Since 1870* (Englewood Cliffs: Prentice-Hall, 1973), 8. Orvell differentiates between the middle-class *culture of imitation* and the *culture of authenticity,* a modernist and intellectual response to the former.

19. Lise-Lone Marker, *David Belasco: Naturalism in the American Theatre* (Princeton: Princeton University Press, 1975), chap. 6.

20. See Kaplan, *The Social Construction of American Realism,* Introduction.

21. Habegger, *Gender, Fantasy and Realism in American Literature,* 11.

22. Apparently, sketches about characters who commented on New York immigrant life were not uncommon. "This was about the same time that 'Bill' Young, prominent magazine authority of the day, discovered 'Chuck' Connors, Mayor of

Chinatown" (unidentified clipping, in Victor Moore scrapbook, RLC, LMPA). See also *New York Times,* 23 June 1895, 27; *New York Times Illustrated Magazine,* 28 November 1879, 13; *New York Times,* 14 June 1902, 405. Townsend also published another series of sketches about urban life, titled *A Daughter of the Tenements* (New York: Lovell, Coryell & Co., 1859). Gunther Barth finds the Chimmie stories valuable precisely because they are based on observation as opposed to invention. See his *City People: The Rise of Modern City Culture in Nineteenth-Century America* (New York: Oxford University Press, 1980), 269. As for the stage play, I have been unable to determine whether the Thomas and Townsend versions were separate works, or if Townsend was involved in writing an adaptation of his stories.

23. Edward B. Watson, *New York Then and Now: 88 Manhattan Sites Photographed in the Past and the Present* (Mineola: Dover Publications, 1976), 16. Although this photo is dated 1893, the play was not, in fact, premiered in New York until 1896.

24. Unidentified clipping, in Victor Moore scrapbook, RLC, LMPA; *The Cheat* folder, Personal, Autobiography files, DMA, BYU. The star of the initial Broadway production in 1896 was Charles H. Hooper.

25. Edward W. Townsend, *Chimmie Fadden, Major Max, and Other Stories* (New York: Lovell, Coryell & Co., 1895), 72, 47–48.

26. Typed script of E. W. Townsend's stage play, in *Chimmie Fadden* folder, Lasky Co./Famous Players-Lasky, DMA, BYU. Although the film script credits the play to Thomas, the film appears to be based on the Townsend play in the DeMille Archives.

27. See Kay Sloan, *The Loud Silents: Origins of the Social Problem Film* (Urbana: University of Illinois Press, 1988).

28. Script of the film *Chimmie Fadden,* USC. Tom Gunning refers to this type of editing as *contrast edit* in *D. W. Griffith and the Origins of American Narrative: The Early Years at Biograph* (Urbana: University of Illinois Press, 1991), 77.

29. Typed script of E. W. Townsend's stage play, in *Chimmie Fadden* folder, Lasky Co./Famous Players-Lasky, DMA, BYU.

30. *"Chimmie Fadden Out West," Variety Film Reviews, 1907–1980* (New York: Garland, 1983), 2 July 1915. See Douglas Gilbert, *American Vaudeville: Its Life and Times* (New York; Dover Publications, 1940); Joe Laurie, Jr., *Vaudeville: From the Honky-tonks to the Palace* (New York: Henry Holt, 1953); Albert F. McLean, Jr., *American Vaudeville as Ritual* (University of Kentucky Press, 1965); Robert W. Snyder, *The Voice of the City: Vaudeville and Popular Culture in New York* (New York: Oxford University Press, 1989).

31. Script of the film, *Chimmie Fadden,* USC.

32. "Garden—Chimmie Fadden," *NYDM,* 18 January 1896, 16.

33. "Chimmie Fadden," *NYDM,* 7 July 1915, 28.

34. W. Stephen Bush, "Chimmie Fadden," *MPW,* 10 July 1915, 322.

35. "More 'Chimmie Fadden' Plays with Moore Coming," *MPN,* 17 July 1915, 190. DeMille constructed his own filmography. Although only two *Chimmie Fadden* films were listed in it, a third title, "The Detective," was produced before the series was cancelled. (Lasky to Goldfish, 29 November 1915, DMA, BYU.)

36. Poster for *Chimmie Fadden Out West, Chimmie Fadden Out West* clipping file, AMPAS.

37. Significantly, Paul West, author of an early adaptation of the Townsend play for the first *Chimmie Fadden* film, was not credited, nor was Jeanie Macpherson, who worked on a number of scenarios for which DeMille alone is credited in bound copies of his scripts. Papers in the DeMille Archives indicate, however, that Macpher-

son, who did receive coauthor credit for *The Captive*, contributed to screenplays for *The Arab, Chimmie Fadden*, and *Kindling*. See Paul West, Script of *Chimmie Fadden, Chimmie Fadden* folder, Lasky Co./Famous Players-Lasky, DMA, BYU; Scripts of DeMille's film, USC. DeMille later attempted to secure Macpherson rights to her stories, including *The Captive, The Golden Chance, Forbidden Fruit, Dream Girl, Romance of the Redwoods, Till I Come Back to You, Little American, The Woman God Forgot, Don't Change Your Husband, Why Change Your Wife? Something to Think About, Saturday Night, Adam's Rib*, and *The Ten Commandments*. (DeMille to Lasky, 12 January 1924, Jesse Lasky 1924 folder, Lasky Co./Famous Players-Lasky, DMA, BYU.)

38. Story treatment of *Chimmie Fadden Out West*, in *Chimmie Fadden Out West* folder, Lasky Co./Famous Players-Lasky, DMA, BYU.

39. "Put Chimmie Fadden into a Movie Play," *New York Times*, 22 November 1915, 12; "Chimmie Fadden Out West," *NYDM*, 4 December 1915, 281.

40. Lasky to Goldfish, 29 November 1915, DMA, BYU. Since the Townsend stories represented "a gold mine for ideas," Lasky was disappointed about having to abandon the series. Yet DeMille's figures show that receipts for *Chimmie Fadden Out West* were comparable to *Chimmie Fadden*, if not to box-office figures for Geraldine Farrar vehicles. See David Pierce, "Success with a Dollar Sign: Cost and Grosses for the Early Films of Cecil B. DeMille," in Paolo Cherchi Usai and Lorenzo Codelli, eds., *The DeMille Legacy* (Pordenone: Edizioni Biblioteca dell'Immagine), 316.

41. See Francis G. Couvares, *The Remaking of Pittsburgh: Class and Culture in an Industrializing City 1877–1919* (Albany: State University of New York Press, 1984); Roy Rosenzweig, *Eight Hours for What We Will: Workers and Leisure in an Industrial City, 1870–1920* (Cambridge: Cambridge University Press, 1983); Lizabeth Cohen, *Making a New Deal: Industrial Workers in Chicago, 1919–1939* (Cambridge: Cambridge University Press, 1990). See also Michael Rogin, "Making America Home: Racial Masquerade and Ethnic Assimilation in the Transition to Talking Pictures," *Journal of American History* 79 (December 1992): 1050–1077.

42. Arthur Hornblow also wrote *A History of the Theatre in America from Its Beginnings to the Present Time*, 2 vols. (New York: J. B. Lippincott, 1919).

43. *Colliers,* 17 February 1912, in Margaret Illington scrapbook, RLC, LMPA.

44. See Barth, *City People*, chap. 3.

45. *Toledo Blade*, 15 July 1911; *New York Telegraph*, 29 January 1912; *Chicago Record Herald*, 13 February 1912; *New York Review*, 9 December 1909; *New York Times*, 10 December 1911; *Green Book*, May 1911, in Margaret Illington scrapbook, RLC, LMPA.

46. See Harris, "Iconography and Intellectual History"; Charles Musser, "Rethinking Cinema's Beginnings: Images, Projection, and Editing" (Paper delivered at George Eastman House, Rochester, September, 1992).

47. John A. Kouwenhoven, *Adventures of America 1857–1900: A Pictorial Record from Harper's Weekly* (New York: Harper & Bros., 1938), 133. See also John Grafton, *New York in the Nineteenth Century: 317 Engravings from Harper's Weekly and Other Contemporary Sources* (Mineola: Dover Publications, 1977); Sally Lorensen Gross, *Toward an Urban View: The Nineteenth-Century American City in Prints* (New Haven: Yale University Press, 1989).

48. Ward, *Poverty, Ethnicity, and the American City*, 17–18.

49. Barbara Novak, *American Painting of the Nineteenth Century: Realism, Idealism, and the American Experience* (New York: Praeger, 1969), 263.

50. William Innes Homer, *Robert Henri and His Circle* (Ithaca: Cornell University Press, 1969), chap. 8; Martin Green, *New York 1913: The Armory Show and the Paterson Strike Pageant* (New York: Macmillan, 1988); James Lincoln Collier, *The Rise of Selfishness in America* (New York: Oxford University Press, 1991), 111–155; Robert M. Crunden, *Ministers of Reform: The Progressives' Achievement in American Civilization 1889–1920* (New York: Basic Books, 1972), 102–115.

51. Alan Trachtenberg, *Reading American Photographs: Images as History: Matthew Brady to Walker Evans* (New York: Hill & Wang, 1989), chap. 4.

52. Collier, *The Rise of Selfishness in America*, 12; Crunden, *Ministers of Reform*, 91.

53. Jacob Riis, *How the Other Half Lives: Studies Among the Tenements of New York* (New York: Charles Scribner's Sons, 1890; Mineola: Dover Publications, 1971). Interestingly, Riis titles one of his chapters "The Street Arab." See also Riis's *The Making of an American* (New York: Macmillan, 1916); Emma Louise Ware, *Jacob Riis: Police Reporter, Reformer, Useful Citizen* (New York: D. Appleton-Century, 1939); James B. Lane, *Jacob Riis and the American City* (Port Washington: Kennikat Press, 1974); Lewis Fried and John Fierst, *Jacob A. Riis: A Reference Guide* (Boston: G. K. Hall, 1977). See also note 59 below.

54. Script of *Kindling*, USC.

55. Kathy Peiss, *Cheap Amusements: Working Women and Leisure in Turn-of-the-Century New York* (Philadelphia: Temple University Press, 1986), 13. See also Elizabeth Ewen, *Immigrant Women in the Land of Dollars: Life and Culture on the Lower East Side, 1890–1925* (New York: Monthly Review Press, 1985).

56. W. Stephen Bush, "Kindling," *MPW*, 24 July 1924, 655.

57. Eileen Bowser, *The Transformation of Cinema 1907–1915* (New York: Charles Scribner's Sons, 1990), 267. According to Bowser, critics saw a relationship between Griffith's lighting effects and the Photo-Secessionists.

58. Carol Schloss, *In Visible Light: Photography and the American Writer 1840–1940* (New York: Oxford University Press, 1987), 107; Trachtenberg, *Reading American Photographs*, chap. 4. On Stieglitz, see Sue Davidson Lowe, *Stieglitz: A Memoir/Biography* (New York: Farrar, Strauss & Giroux, 1983); Waldo Frank et al., eds., *America and Alfred Stieglitz* (New York: The Literary Guild, 1934); Beaumont Newhall, *The History of Photography from 1839 to the Present*, rev. ed. (New York: Museum of Modern Art, 1982).

59. Maren Stange, *Symbols of Ideal Life: Social Documentary Photography in America 1890–1950* (Cambridge: Cambridge University Press, 1989), chap. 1. Stange updated her revisionist interpretation of Riis in "Narrative Strategies in the Documentary Tradition" (Paper delivered at Columbia Film Seminar, New York, February 1992). See also Alexander Alland, Sr., *Jacob A. Riis: Photographer and Citizen* (Millerton: Aperture, 1974); Hales, *Silver Cities*, chap. 4; Ward, *Poverty, Ethnicity, and the American City*, 71–75; Trachtenberg, *The Incorporation of America*, 126–128; Harris, "Iconography and Intellectual History," 314; Kaplan, *The Social Construction of American Realism*, 46.

60. Script of *Kindling*, USC.

61. Grace Kingsley, "Where the Babies Come From," *Photoplay*, December 1915, 80.

62. Ewen, *Immigrant Women in the Land of Dollars*, 136–139.

63. Alland, *Jacob A. Riis*, 28.

64. Ibid., 152–153.

65. *New York American*, 7 December 1911; *Bloomington Telegraph*, 14 February 1912; *Chicago Herald Record*, 13 February 1912; *New York Review*, 9 December 1909; *Vancouver World*, 8 July 1912, in Margaret Illington scrapbook, RLC, LMPA.

66. "Kindling," *MPN*, 24 July 1915, 71; "Reviews of Current Productions," *MPW*, 24 July 1915, 665; *"Kindling," Variety Film Reviews*, 16 July 1915.

67. See Russell Merritt, "Nickelodeon Theaters 1905–1914: Building an Audience for the Movies," in Tino Balio, ed., *The American Film Industry* (Madison: University of Wisconsin Press, 1976), 72; Richard deCordova, *Picture Personalities: The Emergence of the Star System in America* (Urbana: University of Illinois Press, 1990).

68. Charles Kenyon, "Kindling," in Thomas H. Dickinson and Jack R. Crawford, eds., *Contemporary Plays: Sixteen Plays from the Recent Drama of England and America* (Boston: Houghton Mifflin, 1925), 260.

69. Script of *Kindling*, USC.

70. *Boston Transcript*, 16 November 1911, in Margaret Illington scrapbook, RLC, LMPA.

71. Script of *Kindling*, USC.

72. Conversation with James V. D'Arc, November 1993. I am grateful to James Card for a screening of this film.

73. *"Kindling," Variety Film Reviews*, 16 July 1915.

74. Script of *Kindling*, USC.

75. Kevin Brownlow offers a more progressive interpretation of this film in *Behind the Mask of Innocence* (New York: Alfred A. Knopf, 1990), 285–287.

76. Trachtenberg, *The Incorporation of America*, 21–22.

77. Nina Baym, *Woman's Fiction: A Guide to Novels by and about Women in America, 1820–1870* (Ithaca: Cornell University Press, 1978), 45; Susman, "The City in American Culture," 245.

78. See Ruth Perlmutter, "For God, Country, and Whoopee," *Film Comment* 12 (January/February 1976): 24–28.

79. Script of *The Dream Girl*, USC.

80. See Rosenzweig, *Eight Hours for What We Will;* Couvares, *The Remaking of Pittsburgh;* Cohen, *Making a New Deal;* Peiss, *Cheap Amusements;* Ewen, *Immigrant Women in the Land of Dollars.*

CHAPTER FOUR: THE SCREEN AS DISPLAY WINDOW

1. Margaret Gibbons Wilson, *The American Woman in Transition: The Urban Influence, 1870–1929* (Westport: Greenwood Press, 1979), 8. See also James R. McGovern, "The American Woman's Pre-World War I Freedom in Manners and Morals," *Journal of American History* 60 (September 1968): 315–333; Kenneth A. Yellis, "Prosperity's Child: Some Thoughts on the Flapper," *American Quarterly* 21 (March 1969): 44–64; Nancy Woloch, *Women and the American Experience* (New York: Alfred A. Knopf, 1984), chaps. 12, 16; Lois W. Banner, *American Beauty* (New York: Alfred A. Knopf, 1983), chaps. 12, 13; Martha Banta, *Imaging American Women: Idea and Ideals in Cultural History* (New York: Columbia University Press, 1987); Ellen Wiley Todd, *The "New Woman" Revised: Painting and Gender Politics on Fourteenth Street* (Berkeley: University of California Press, 1993), chap. 1; Carroll Smith-Rosenberg, "The New Woman as Androgyne: Social Disorder and Gender Crisis, 1870–1936," in *Disorderly Conduct:*

Visions of Gender in Victorian America (New York: Alfred A. Knopf, 1985), 245–296; Estelle B. Freedman, "The New Woman: Changing Views of Women in the 1920s," *Journal of American History* 56 (September 1974): 372–393. Unlike Todd, Yellis and Banner do not consider the Gibson girl, who was superceded by the flapper, to exemplify an independent "new woman." Smith-Rosenberg, however, focuses not on the flapper but on the androgyne as a "new woman." On silent screen flappers as a *character-type,* a concept used in earlier feminist criticism, see my *Virgins, Vamps, and Flappers: The American Silent Movie Heroine* (Montreal: Eden Press, 1978), chap. 6; Mary P. Ryan, "The Projection of a New Womanhood: The Movie Moderns in the 1920s," in Jean E. Friedman and William G. Shade, *Our American Sisters,* 3d ed. (Lexington: D. C. Heath & Co., 1982), 500–518. According to British usage, the flapper was associated with left-wing politics and disenfranchised working-class women. See Billie Melman, *Women and the Popular Imagination in the Twenties: Flappers and Nymphs* (New York: St. Martin's Press, 1988), chap. 1. On the American flapper as a social activist rather than as a symbol of the sexual revolution, see Stephen H. Norwood, *Labor's Flaming Youth: Telephone Operators and Worker Militancy, 1878–1923* (Urbana: University of Illinois Press, 1990), Introduction. On working-class versions of the "new woman," see Kathy Peiss, *Cheap Amusements: Working Women and Leisure in Turn-of-the-Century New York* (Philadelphia: Temple University Press, 1986), Introduction.

2. Interview with DeMille, 14 May 1957, Biography folder, Personal: Autobiography files, DMA, BYU; "Playwrights All," *Philadelphia Record,* 28 January 1906, in Cecil B. DeMille scrapbook, RLC, LMPA.

3. "Mrs. H. C. DeMille, Champion of the New Dramatist," *NYDM,* 10 July 1912, 12.

4. William Leach, "Transformations in a Culture of Consumptions: Women and Department Stores, 1890–1925," *Journal of American History* 71 (September 1984): 333; John F. Kasson, *Rudeness and Civility: Manners in Nineteenth-Century Life* (New York: Hill & Wang, 1990), 117. See also Leach, *True Love and Perfect Union: The Feminist Reform of Sex and Society* (New York: Basic Books, 1980), chap. 9.

5. Hugh Dalziel Duncan, *Culture and Democracy: The Struggle for Form in Society and Architecture in Chicago and the Middle West during the Life and Times of Louis H. Sullivan* (Totowa: Bedminster Press, 1965), chap. 11; Robert W. Twyman, *History of Marshall Field and Co., 1852–1906* (Philadelphia: University of Pennsylvania Press, 1954), 152–153. On film and consumption, see Charles Eckert, "The Carole Lombard in Macy's Window," *Quarterly Review of Film Studies* 3 (Winter 1978): 1–21; Jeanne Allen, "The Film Viewer as Consumer," *Quarterly Review of Film Studies* 5 (Fall 1980): 481–499; Allen, "Palaces of Consumption as Women's Club: En-countering Women's Labor History and Feminist Film Criticism," *Camera Obscura* 22 (January 1990): 150–158; Mary Ann Doane, *The Desire to Desire: The Woman's Film of the 1940s* (Bloomington: Indiana University Press, 1987), chap. 1; Jane Gaines and Michael Renov, eds., "Female Representation and Consumer Culture," *Quarterly Review of Film and Video* 11 (1989); Anne Friedberg, *Window Shopping: Cinema and the Postmodern* (Berkeley: University of California Press, 1993). Eckert rightly focuses on DeMille in his discussion of Los Angeles as the center of merchandising tie-ups, but the director was publicizing the life-style of the "smart set" well before his postwar cycle of sex comedies and melodramas.

6. Karen Halttunen, *Confidence Men and Painted Women: A Study of Middle-Class Culture in America, 1830–1870* (New Haven: Yale University Press, 1982), 101–105;

Erving Goffman, The Presentation of Self in Everyday Life (Garden City: Anchor, 1959), chap. 3.

7. Georg Lukács, *History and Class Consciousness: Studies in Marxist Dialectics,* trans. Rodney Livingstone (Cambridge: MIT Press, 1971), 91.

8. See Michael B. Miller, *The Bon Marché: Bourgeois Culture and the Department Store, 1869–1920* (Princeton: Princeton University Press, 1981). See also Ralph M. Hower, *History of Macy's of New York 1858–1919: Changes in the Evolution of the Department Store* (Cambridge: Harvard University Press, 1943).

9. Leach, "Transformations in a Culture of Consumption," 326; Rosalind H. Williams, *Dream Worlds: Mass Consumption in Late Nineteenth-Century France* (Berkeley: University of California Press, 1982), 59.

10. Rémy G. Saisselin, *The Bourgeois and the Bibelot* (New Brunswick: Rutgers University Press, 1984), 37–39. See also Susan Porter Benson, *Counter Cultures: Saleswomen, Managers, and Customers in American Department Stores, 1890–1940* (Urbana: University of Illinois Press, 1986), 67; Miller, *The Bon Marché,* 169–173, 186.

11. Quoted in Saisselin, *The Bourgeois and the Bibelot,* 41.

12. Elaine Abelson, *When Ladies Go A-Thieving: Middle-Class Shoplifters in the Victorian Department Store* (New York: Oxford University Press, 1989), 52; Saisselin, *The Bourgeois and the Bibelot,* 47; Neil Harris, "Museums, Merchandising, and Popular Taste: The Struggle for Influence," in *Cultural Excursions: Marketing Appetites and Cultural Tastes in Modern America* (Chicago: University of Chicago Press, 1990), 64–65; Stuart Blumin, *The Emergence of the Middle Class: Social Experience in the American City, 1760–1900* (Cambridge: Cambridge University Press, 1989), 238–240.

13. Jean-Christophe Agnew, "The Consuming Vision of Henry James," in Richard Wightman Fox and T. J. Jackson Lears, eds., *The Culture of Consumption* (New York: Pantheon, 1983), 77; Amy Kaplan, *The Social Construction of American Realism* (Chicago: University of Chicago Press, 1988), 77–78.

14. Edward W. Said, *Orientalism* (New York: Pantheon, 1978), 95, 123; John L. Fell, *Film and the Narrative Tradition* (Norman: University of Oklahoma Press, 1974; Berkeley: University of California Press, 1986), 131–140; Neil Harris, "Pictorial Perils: The Rise of American Illustration," in *Cultural Excursions,* 344; Charles Musser, *The Emergence of Cinema: The American Screen to 1907* (New York: Charles Scribner's Sons, 1990), chap. 1, 429–430. See also Musser with Carol Nelson, *High-Class Moving Pictures: Lyman H. Howe and the Forgotten Era of Traveling Exhibition, 1880–1929* (Princeton: Princeton University Press, 1991).

15. Edith Wharton, *The Age of Innocence* (New York: Charles Scribner's Sons, 1968; New York: D. Appleton & Co., 1920), 45.

16. Vachel Lindsay, *The Art of the Moving Picture* (New York: Macmillan, 1915; New York: Liveright, 1970); Warren Susman, *Culture as History: The Transformation of American Society in the Twentieth Century* (New York: Pantheon, 1973), xxv–xxvi; Miriam Hansen, *Babel and Babylon: Spectatorship in American Silent Film* (Cambridge: Harvard University Press, 1991); Nick Browne, "American Film Theory in the Silent Period: Orientalism as an Ideological Form," *Wide Angle* 11 (October 1989): 23–31.

17. Emile Zola, *The Ladies' Paradise: A Realistic Novel [Au bonheur des dames]* (Berkeley: University of California Press, 1992), 79. For a discussion of the novel, see Rachel Bowlby, *Just Looking: Consumer Culture in Dreiser, Gissing and Zola* (New York: Methuen, 1985), chap. 5.

18. Williams, *Dream Worlds,* 64–78; Said, *Orientalism,* 63; Harris, "Great American Fairs and American Cities: The Role of Chicago's Columbian Exposition," in

Cultural Excursions, 132; Robert W. Rydell, "The Culture of Imperial Abundance: World's Fairs in the Making of American Culture," in Simon J. Bronner, ed., *Consuming Visions: Accumulation and Display of Goods in America, 1880–1929* (New York: W. W. Norton, 1989), 191–216; Zeynep Çelik, *Displaying the Orient: Architecture of Islam at Nineteenth-Century World's Fairs* (Berkeley: University of California Press, 1992), 80–88; Antonia Lant, "The Curse of the Pharaoh, or How Cinema Contracted Egyptomania," *October* 59 (Winter 1992): 86–112; Lant, "Beams from the East: the Orient of Early Cinema" (Paper delivered at Society for Cinema Studies conference, New Orleans, 1993). Lant makes an interesting case for the perception of light as a projection from the East. Yet in sentimental culture, light is symbolically associated with Christian and moral values.

19. Zola, *The Ladies' Paradise,* 47.

20. Quoted in Harris, "The Drama of Consumer Desire," in *Cultural Excursions,* 178.

21. Abelson, *When Ladies Go A-Thieving,* chaps. 6, 7; Miller, *The Bon Marché,* 197–206.

22. On the "hysterization of women" and "psychiatrization of perversions," see Michel Foucault, *The History of Sexuality,* vol. 1, trans. Robert Hurley (New York: Pantheon, 1978), 146–147; see also Louise J. Kaplan, *Female Perversions: The Last Temptations of Emma Bovary* (New York: Doubleday, 1991), chap. 9. On reification, see Lukács, *History and Class Consciousness;* Guy Debord, *Society of the Spectacle* (Detroit: Black & Red, 1977); Martin Jay, *Marxism and Totality: The Adventures of a Concept from Lukács to Habermas* (Berkeley: University of California Press, 1984); Fredric Jameson, "Reification and Utopia in Mass Culture," *Social Text* 1 (1979): 130–148.

23. *Kindling* and *The Golden Chance,* Paramount Collection, AMPAS.

24. Interview with DeMille, 24 September 1957, in *The Girl of the Golden West, The Godless Girl, The Golden Bed, The Golden Chance* folder, Personal: Autobiography files, DMA, BYU. DeMille's claim may not be unfounded as he dispensed with Macpherson during the sound era. But Lasky wrote to Goldwyn, "Cecil actually does little writing himself as Miss Macpherson does all the continuity while Cecil advises and changes the important points or situations in the scenario." (Lasky to Goldfish, 5 October 1915, DMA, BYU.)

25. Scripts of *The Golden Chance* and *The Cheat,* USC; *The Autobiography of Cecil B. DeMille,* ed. Donald Hayne (Englewood Cliffs: Prentice-Hall, 1959), 149–150; Lasky to Goldfish, 25 October 1915 and 4 November 1915, DMA, BYU.

26. *The Golden Chance* folder, Personal: Autobiography files, DMA, BYU.

27. Script of *The Golden Chance,* USC.

28. See Karen Halttunen, "From Parlor to Living Room: Domestic Space, Interior Decoration, and the Culture of Personality," in Bronner, ed., *Consuming Visions,* 158.

29. Stuart Culver, "What Manikins Want: *The Wonderful Wizard of Oz* and *The Art of Decorating Dry Goods Windows,*" *Representations* 21 (Winter 1988): 107–111.

30. Script of *The Golden Chance,* USC.

31. *Ibid.*

32. Quoted in Brook Thomas, "The New Historicism and other Old-Fashioned Topics," in H. Aram Veeser, ed., *The New Historicism* (London: Routledge, 1989), 187.

33. Peter Milne, *Motion Picture Directing* (New York: Falk Publishing Co., 1922), 48; "The Golden Chance," *MPN*, 15 January 1916, 252. See Katherine DiGiulio, "The Representation of Women in 19th and Early 20th Century Narrative Stereographs," *Ideas about Images*, Rochester Film & Photo Consortium Occasional Papers 4 (January 1990): 2–18.

34. W. Stephen Bush, "The Golden Chance," *MPW*, 8 January 1916, 255.

35. Quoted in William Leuchtenberg, *The Perils of Prosperity, 1914–32* (Chicago: University of Chicago Press, 1958), 172.

36. Banta, *Imaging American Women*, 216.

37. Quoted from Raymond Williams in Stuart Ewen and Elizabeth Ewen, *Channels of Desire: Mass Images and the Shaping of American Consciousness* (New York: McGraw-Hill, 1982), 51; Williams, *Dream Worlds*, 6–7.

38. See Saisselin, *The Bourgeois and the Bibelot*, chap. 4. See also Ben Singer, "Female Power in the Serial-Queen Melodrama: The Etiology of an Anomaly," *Camera Obscura* 22 (1990): 90–129.

39. Script of *The Golden Chance*, USC.

40. Woloch, *Women and the American Experience*, 287–293.

41. Turnbull also succeeded Samuel Goldwyn as Jesse L. Lasky's brother-in-law or the husband of Blanche Lasky, who also worked in the scenario department and exercised considerable leverage.

42. A number of Lasky Company features were reissued in 1918. I have not been able to ascertain if this print of *The Cheat* was reedited as was *Carmen*.

43. Script of *The Cheat*, USC.

44. Thorstein Veblen, *The Theory of the Leisure Class* (1899; reprint, New York: Penguin, 1979), 81–82.

45. Duncan, *Culture and Democracy*, chap. 9. See Carroll Smith-Rosenberg, "The Female World of Love and Ritual: Relations between Women in Nineteenth-Century America," *Signs* 1 (1975): 1–29; reprinted in Rosenberg, *Disorderly Conduct*, 53–76.

46. Veblen, *The Theory of the Leisure Class*, 84.

47. See Faye E. Dudden, *Serving Women: Household Service in Nineteenth-Century America* (Middletown: Wesleyan University Press, 1983).

48. "From a London Home of Fashion to the Stage," unidentified clipping, 21 November 1909; *Theatre*, July 1907; *New York Journal*, 3 February 1907; *Theatre*, August 1914; "Fannie Ward's New Home," *Photoplay*, January 1919; Fannie Ward, "The Well-Dressed Girl," *New York Journal*, 2 October 1913, in Fannie Ward scrapbook, RLC, LMPA.

49. Richard Wightman Fox, "Character and Personality in the Protestant Republic 1850–1930" (Paper delivered at SUNY Brockport, April 1988). See also Warren Susman, "Personality and the Making of Twentieth-Century Culture," in *Culture as History*, 271–285.

50. Williams, *Dream Worlds*, 69–71; Said, *Orientalism*, 123.

51. See Robert Hamilton Ball, ed., *The Plays of Henry C. DeMille Written in Collaboration with David Belasco* (Princeton: Princeton University Press, 1940; Bloomington: Indiana University Press, 1965).

52. J. C. Jensen, "In and Out of West Coast Studios," *MPN*, 20 November 1915, 74.

53. Script of *The Cheat*, USC.

54. Harris, "All the World a Melting Pot? Japan at American Fairs, 1876–1904," in *Cultural Excursions,* 29–55. On antimodernist fascination with Japan as "oceanic withdrawal," see T. J. Jackson Lears, *No Place of Grace: Antimodernism and the Transformation of American Culture, 1880–1920* (New York: Pantheon, 1981), chap. 6.

55. In 1907 Theodore Roosevelt negotiated the Gentlemen's Agreement with the Japanese government to specify restriction of the immigration of Japanese laborers. See Yuji Ichioka, *The Issei: The World of the First Generation Japanese-American Immigrants, 1885–1924* (New York: The Free Press, 1988), 71–72, 159–164; Harry L. Kitano, *Japanese American: The Evolution of a Subculture* (Englewood Cliffs: Prentice-Hall, 1969), chap. 2; Roger Daniels, *Concentration Camps USA* (New York: Holt, Rinehart & Winston, 1971), chap. 1. Although Said's concept of Orientalism is an expression of a form of colonialism that Japan escaped (at least until its post-World War II occupation), Japanese immigrants suffered a fate similar to that of the Chinese who preceded them.

56. Script of *The Cheat,* USC.

57. "Two Lasky Features," *MPW,* 25 December 1915, 2384; "Feature Films of the Week," *NYDM,* 25 December 1915, 40.

58. John Higham, *Strangers in the Land: Patterns of American Nativism* (1963; reprint, New York: Atheneum, 1981), 113–157; Higham, *Send These to Me: Immigrants in Urban America,* rev. ed. (Baltimore: Johns Hopkins University Press, 1984), 50–53. See also Barbara Miller Solomon, *Ancestors and Immigrants: A Changing New England Tradition* (Cambridge: Harvard University Press, 1956; Boston: Northeastern University Press, 1989). See also Foucault, *The History of Sexuality,* 147–150. In 1916 a serial titled *The Yellow Menace* was very popular at the box office and novelized for publication in daily installments in newspapers. A Chinese villain named Ali Singh (a name that conflates the Far East with the Middle East), played by a white actor, leads a conspiracy against antialien legislation in episodes with such titles as "The Mutilated Hand" and "The Poisonous Tarantula." See *NYDM,* 12 August 1916, 25. Publicity stories about Margaret Gale, the featured actress, emphasized themes of miscegenation by describing a Chinese prince who courted her while she was filming in Hong Kong. Margaret Gale scrapbook, RLC, LMPA.

59. See Judith Mayne's discussion of *The Cheat* in "The Limits of Spectacle," *Wide Angle* 5 (1983): 6–9, and in *The Woman at the Keyhole: Feminism and Women's Cinema* (Bloomington: Indiana University Press, 1990), 33–36. See also Gina Marchetti, *Romance and the "Yellow Peril": Race, Sex, and Discursive Strategies in Hollywood Fiction* (forthcoming, University of California Press).

60. Script of *The Cheat,* USC.

61. The phrase was attributed to Edward A. Filene. See Benson, *Counter Cultures,* 76.

62. Mary P. Ryan, *Women in Public: Between Banners and Ballots, 1825–1880* (Baltimore: Johns Hopkins University Press, 1990), chap. 2.; Smith-Rosenberg, "The New Woman as Androgyne"; Foucault, *The History of Sexuality,* 145–150; Abelson, *When Ladies Go A-Thieving,* 56; Benson, *Counter Cultures,* chap. 3. On advertisers' increasing appeal to the irrational, see T. J. Jackson Lears, "Some Versions of Fantasy: Toward a Cultural History of American Advertising, 1880–1930," *Prospects* 9 (1984): 349–405.

63. Grant McCracken, *Culture and Consumption: New Approaches to the Symbolic*

Character of Consumer Goods and Activities (Bloomington: Indiana University Press, 1990), 89.

64. On the meaning(lessness) of consumption, see Saisselin, *The Bourgeois and the Bibelot*, chap. 4; McCracken, *Culture and Consumption*, 109–115.

65. On the role of department stores and museums in the process of bibelotization, see Saisselin, *The Bourgeois and the Bibelot*, chap. 4. See also Harris, "Museums, Merchandising and Popular Taste" and "A Historical Perspective on Museum Advocacy," in *Cultural Excursions*, 56–95. On the relationship of museums and department stores today, see Debora Silverman, *Selling Culture: Bloomingdale's Diana Vreeland, and the New Aristocracy of Taste in Reagan's America* (New York: Pantheon, 1986).

66. "Hayakawa Names First Two Productions," unidentified clipping, 6 July 1918, in Sessue Hayakawa scrapbook, RLC, LMPA; Harry Carr Easterfield, "The Japanese Way of Expressing Emotion. As seen through the Oriental eyes of Sessue Haya [*sic*]," *Motion Picture*, April 1918, 34; Script of *The Cheat*, USC.

67. "The Lasky Studio," *NYDM*, 28 October 1916, 35–36; Stephen Gong, "Zen and the Art of Motion Picture Making," Asian-American International Film Festival Program, 1982, 13. On Valentino, see Miriam Hansen, "Pleasure, Ambivalence, Identification: Valentino and Female Spectatorship," *Cinema Journal* 25 (Summer 1986): 6–32; Hansen, *Babel and Babylon*, part 3; Gaylyn Studlar, "Discourses of Gender and Ethnicity: The Construction and De(con)struction of Rudolph Valentino as Other," *Film Criticism* 13 (1989): 18–35.

68. Pearl Gaddio, "A Romance of Nippon Land," *MPC*, December 1916; "Mr. and Mrs. Hayakawa in Their New Shop," *Photoplay*, November 1917; Untitled article, *Photo-Play Journal*, May 1918; Harry C. Carr, "Sessue of the Samurai," *MPC*, January 1919, in Sessue Hayakawa scrapbook, RLC, LMPA. Hayakawa left Famous Players-Lasky in 1918 to organize his own production company, Haworth, but his career declined in the early 1920s. In 1957, he returned to public attention by winning an Academy Award nomination for his role as a Japanese officer in *Bridge on the River Kwai*. Donald Kirihara's study of Hayakawa's American silent film career is forthcoming.

69. A deconstruction of Puccini's *Madama Butterfly* (adapted by the composer from a turn-of-the-century Belasco play in which sets with shoji screens were used), David Henry Hwang's award-winning *M. Butterfly* emphasizes the West's characterization of the East as feminine and rape as a Western ritual. For a discussion of the effeminacy of the Asian hero, see Julia Lesage, "Artful Racism, Artful Rape," *Jump Cut* 26 (1981): 51–55; reprinted in Christine Gledhill, ed., *Home Is Where the Heart Is* (London: British Film Institute, 1987), 235–254.

70. See Barry Salt, *Film Style and Technology: History and Analysis* (London: Starword, 1983), 138, 146, 148. Salt attributes the film's effectiveness to its high ratio of medium shots, though some of the film's most dramatic scenes are in long shot.

71. "Two Lasky Features," *MPW*, 25 December 1915, 2384; "Miss Ward Puts Mirth Aside for Screen Emotion," *MPN*, 25 December 1915, 69; Julian Johnson, "The Shadow Stage," *Photoplay*, March 1916, 102.

72. Paramount remakes increasingly vitiated the issue of miscegenation so that the villain became first an Indian (not Native American) and then a white man. See *The Cheat*, Paramount Collection, AMPAS.

73. William deMille, *Hollywood Saga* (New York: E. P. Dutton & Co., 1939), 139;

Samuel Goldwyn, *Behind the Screen* (New York: George H. Doran, 1939), 82; Interview with DeMille, 23 July 1957, DeMille as starmaker folder, Personal: Autobiography files, DMA, BYU; "Mr. Lasky Says 'The Cheat' Is Greatest Play," *MPW,* 4 December 1915, 1857; Lasky to Goldfish, 29 November 1915, DMA, BYU; Collette, "Cinema: *The Cheat,*" and Louis Delluc, "Beauty in the Cinema," in Richard Abel, ed., *French Film Theory and Criticism: A History/Anthology,* vol. 1 (Princeton: Princeton University Press, 1988), 123–129, 137–139; Delluc, "Les cinéastes: Cecil B. DeMille," *Cinéa,* 21 July 1922, 11; *Homenaje a Cecil B. DeMille,* Filmoteca Nacional de España Para IV Semana Internacional de Cine Religios en Valladolid, April 1959. See also Noel Burch, *Life to Those Shadows,* trans. Ben Brewster (Berkeley: University of California Press, 1990) for detailed technical analyses of the film. Burch, however, repeats Lewis Jacobs's incorrect characterization of the film's didacticism (185). For figures on foreign receipts, see chap. 1, note 56 in this volume. Whether brisk ticket sales in Paris were matched in other European cities is a matter of speculation.

74. *New York Times,* 24 April 1916, *Kindling, Heart of Nora Flynn* folder, Personal: Autobiography files; DeMille to Lasky, 17 June 1916, Jesse Lasky 1916 folder, Lasky Co./Famous Players-Lasky, DMA, BYU.

75. Script of *The Heart of Nora Flynn,* USC.

76. Notes in *Kindling* and *Heart of Nora Flynn* folder, Personal: Autobiography files, DMA, BYU; *The Autobiography of Cecil B. DeMille,* 158.

77. "Feature Film of the Week," *NYDM,* 29 April 1916, 28; *"Heart of Nora Flynn," Variety Film Reviews, 1907–1980* (New York: Garland, 1983), 21 April 1916; "The Heart of Nora Flynn," *MPN,* 6 May 1916, 2721; *MPW,* 6 May 1916, 984.

78. Debord, *Society of the Spectacle,* 18.

79. Edward Weitzel, "Talking It Over with DeMille," *MPW,* 21 December 1918.

CHAPTER FIVE: THE HISTORICAL EPIC

1. DeMille to Lasky, 17 June 1916, Jesse Lasky 1916 folder, Lasky Co./Famous Players-Lasky, DMA, BYU.

2. Memo, 23 February 1956, in David Belasco folder and *Joan the Woman* folder, Personal: Autobiography files, DMA, BYU. DeMille associates the color process in *Joan* with Handschiegl but credits Wilfred Buckland with using Belasco's method of dimming arc lights to produce some of the effects; there is also mention of a lawsuit initiated by Handschiegl.

3. DeMille to Lasky, 21 November 1916, in Jesse Lasky 1916 folder, Lasky Co./Famous Players-Lasky; Interview with DeMille, 12 July 1957, *Joan the Woman* folder, Personal: Autobiography files, DMA, BYU.

4. Telegram, Friend to DeMille, 23 November 1916; Friend to DeMille, 27 November 1916; in Arthur S. Friend 1916 folder, Lasky Co./Famous Players-Lasky, DMA, BYU.

5. "Live Wire Exhibitions," *MPN,* 24 February 1917, 1208; *New York Evening Journal* clipping, in Geraldine Farrar scrapbook, RLC, LMPA.

6. Lasky to DeMille, 6 January 1917, in Jesse Lasky 1917 folder, Lasky Co./Famous Players-Lasky, DMA, BYU.

7. B. Barnett to Lasky, Cardinal Film Corporation, 25 May 1917, in Folder B, Lasky Co./Famous Players-Lasky, DMA, BYU.

8. H. Whitman Bennett to DeMille, 25 May 1917; DeMille to H. Whitman Bennett, 2 June 1917; in Folder B, Lasky Co./Famous Players-Lasky, DMA, BYU.

9. Interview with DeMille, 8 July 1957, in *Joan the Woman* folder, Personal: Autobiography files, DMA, BYU.

10. DeMille kept a list, dated April 27, 1928, of figures identified as cost and gross for each of his films. For *Joan,* the sums are $302,976.26 and $605,731.30, respectively, compared to $23,429.97 and $147,599.81, respectively, for *Carmen,* both specials for which ticket prices were higher than average. A number of questions arise, however, such as whether these figures included reissues and international as well as domestic distribution. Also pertinent to interpreting these figures, which were most likely not adjusted for inflation, is DeMille's lengthy dispute with the Internal Revenue Service. For a reproduction of the chart, see David Pierce, who also raises questions, in "Success with a Dollar Sign: Cost and Grosses for the Early Films of Cecil B. DeMille," in Paolo Cherchi Usai and Lorenzo Codelli, eds., *The DeMille Legacy* (Pordenone: Edizioni Biblioteca dell'Immagine, 1991), 316–317.

11. Lasky to DeMille, 6 January 1917, in Jesse Lasky 1917 folder, Lasky Co./Famous Players-Lasky, DMA, BYU.

12. On antimodernism, see T. J. Jackson Lears, *No Place of Grace: Antimodernism and the Transformation of American Culture 1880–1920* (New York: Pantheon, 1981), xix. Lears points out that his use of the term, *antimodernism,* is equivalent to the way in which literary critics employ *modernism.* Yet some critics use the term, *modernism,* to describe characteristics ascribed to postmodernism. See Marshall Berman, *All That Is Solid Melts Into Air: The Experience of Modernity* (New York: Simon & Schuster, 1982), Introduction. Lears and Berman both stress continuity rather than rupture in defining these terms.

13. Linda Nochlin, "The Paterson Strike Pageant of 1913," *Art in America* 62 (May/June 1974): 68.

14. David Glassberg, "History and the Public: Legacies of the Progressive Era," *Journal of American History* 73 (March 1987): 957–980; Glassberg, *American Historical Pageantry: The Uses of Tradition in the Early Twentieth Century* (Chapel Hill: University of North Carolina Press, 1990); Naima Prevots, *American Pageantry: A Movement for Art and Democracy* (Ann Arbor: UMI Research Press, 1990); Michael Kammen, *Mystic Chords of Memory: The Transformation of Tradition in American Culture* (New York: Alfred A. Knopf, 1991); Paul Boyer, *Urban Masses and Moral Order in America, 1820–1920* (Cambridge: Harvard University Press, 1978), 256–260. Glassberg describes D. W. Griffith's *The Birth of a Nation* in terms of pageantry (155). See also Robert M. Crunden, "Thick Description in the Progressive Era," *Reviews in American History* 19 (1991): 463–467. On Progressive historiography, see Richard Hofstadter, *Progressive Historians: Turner, Beard, Parrington* (New York: Alfred A. Knopf, 1968); John Higham, *History: Professional Scholarship in America* (Englewood Cliffs: Prentice-Hall, 1965), chaps. 2, 3; David Gross, "The 'New History': A Note of Reappraisal," *History and Theory* 13 (1974): 53–58; Peter Novick, *That Noble Dream: The "Objectivity Question" and the American Historical Profession* (Cambridge: Cambridge University Press, 1988), chap. 4; Brook Thomas, "The New Historicism and other Old-Fashioned Topics," in H. Aram Veeser, ed., *The New Historicism* (London: Routledge, 1989), 182–203; Thomas, *The New Historicism and Other Old-Fashioned Topics* (Princeton: Princeton University Press, 1991).

15. Roger N. Baldwin, "The St. Louis Pageant and Masque: Its Civic Meaning,"

The Survey, 11 April 1914, 52; Charlotte Rumbold, "The St. Louis Pageant and Masque," *The Survey,* 4 July 1914, 372, 375; Glassberg, *American Historical Pageantry,* chap. 5, 194.

16. For a description of the pageant, see Nochlin, "The Paterson Strike Pageant of 1913"; Martin Green, *New York 1913: The Armory Show and the Paterson Strike Pageant* (New York: Macmillan, 1988), chap. 7; Anne Huber Tripp, *The I.W.W. and the Paterson Silk Strike* (Urbana: University of Illinois Press, 1987), chap. 6; Steve Golin, *The Fragile Bridge: The Paterson Silk Strike 1913* (Philadelphia: Temple University Press, 1988), chap. 6. Glassberg thinks that Percy MacKaye may have been involved in the preparations of the Paterson pageant (172).

17. Glassberg, *American Historical Pageantry,* chap. 6.

18. See David M. Kennedy, *Over Here: The First World War and American Society* (New York: Oxford University Press, 1980), chap. 1. See also Stephen Vaughn, *Holding Fast the Inner Lines: Democracy, Nationalism, and the Committee on Public Information* (Chapel Hill: University of North Carolina Press, 1980).

19. Quoted from Frederick Jackson Turner, in Novick, *That Noble Dream,* 99.

20. Glassberg, *American Historical Pageantry,* 136–137.

21. Lois W. Banner, *American Beauty* (New York: Alfred A. Knopf, 1983), chap. 8. Banner points out that Gibson's creation was only partially a reform figure.

22. Vaughn, *Holding Fast the Inner Lines,* 149.

23. Interview with DeMille, 8 July 1957, Personal: Autobiography files, DMA, BYU.

24. Christine Gledhill, "Speculations on the Relationship between Soap Opera and Melodrama," *Quarterly Review of Film and Video* 14 (1992): 107–108; John L. Fell, *Film and the Narrative Tradition* (Norman: University of Oklahoma Press, 1974; Berkeley: University of California Press, 1986), 52.

25. Glassberg, *American Historical Pageantry,* 155.

26. *Wid's,* 4 January 1917, 9, *Joan the Woman* clipping file, AMPAS; George Blaisdell, "Joan the Woman," *MPW,* 13 January 1917, 239.

27. DeMille to Lasky, 21 November 1916, in Jesse Lasky 1916 folder, Lasky Co./Famous Players-Lasky, DMA, BYU.

28. Technicolor's two-color process was first used, not coincidentally, in *Toll of the Sea* in 1922, a Madame Butterfly scenario starring Anna May Wong.

29. Hofstadter, *Progressive Historians,* 7, part 1; Novick, *That Noble Dream,* chap. 3.

30. Script of *Joan the Woman,* USC.

31. Dorothy Donnell, "Joan of Arc. A Short Story Written from the DeMille Photo-Spectacle Featuring Geraldine Farrar, Wallace Reid, Hobart Bosworth, and Theodore Roberts," *Motion Picture Story,* December 1916, 102–103.

32. Descriptions of this scene are in reviews of the film. Unfortunately, the George Eastman House print has two-color footage only in the last reel.

33. Script of *Joan the Woman,* USC.

34. Conversation with James Card, October 1992.

35. Interview with DeMille, 3 July 1957, in *Joan the Woman* folder, Personal: Autobiography files, DMA, BYU.

36. Program of *Joan the Woman,* Geraldine Farrar clipping file, LMPA.

37. "'Joan the Woman' a Triumph," *NYDM,* 30 December 1916, 28; *Wid's,* 4 January 1917, 9, *Joan the Woman* clipping file, AMPAS; Peter Milne, "Joan the

Woman," *MPN*, 6 January 1917, 111; "Boston Premier of 'Joan' a Notable Affair," *MPN*, 7 April 1917, 2175; "Spectacular Films for Holiday Week," *New York Times*, 25 December 1916, 24.

38. "One of the Most Artistic and Satisfying Pictures That Ever Has Been Shown," *New York Evening Sun*, undated clipping, in Geraldine Farrar scrapbook, RLC, LMPA. For interpretations of recent historical film, see Vivian Sobchack, "'Surge and Splendor': A Phenomenology of the Hollywood Historical Epic," *Representations* 29 (Winter 1990): 24–49; Janet Staiger, "Securing the Fictional Narrative as a Tale of the Historical Real," *South Atlantic Quarterly* 88 (Spring 1989): 393–413.

39. Blaisdell, "Joan the Woman," 239; Julian Johnson, "The Shadow Stage," *Photoplay*, March 1917, 113; "Production Easily Ranks with the Greatest Known," *New York Review*, undated clipping, in Geraldine Farrar scrapbook, RLC, LMPA; "Mme. Farrar's Joan of Arc in the New Spectacle of the Screen," *Boston Evening Transcript*, 5 February 1917, in *Joan the Woman* folder, Personal: Autobiography files, DMA, BYU; "'Joan' Opens in Chicago on March 28," *NYDM*, 24 March 1917, 29; Ad for *Joan the Woman, MPN*, 3 February 1917, 638–639; "Zukor Absorbs Artcraft," *MPN*, 5 May 1917, 2811; Lasky to DeMille, 10 March 1917; DeMille to Lasky, 25 January 1917; in Jesse Lasky 1917 folder, Lasky Co./Famous Players-Lasky, DMA, BYU.

40. Script of *Joan the Woman*, USC.

41. Johnson, "The Shadow Stage," 115; Blaisdell, "Joan the Woman," 239.

42. Martha Banta, *Imaging American Women* (New York: Columbia University Press, 1987), 139.

43. Ellen Carol DuBois, "Working Women, Class Relations, and Suffrage Militance: Harriot Stanton Blatch and the New York Woman Suffrage Movement, 1894–1909," *Journal of American History* 74 (June 1987): 34–58; William R. Leach, "Transformations in a Culture of Consumption: Women and Department Stores, 1890–1925," *Journal of American History* 71 (September 1984): 338–340; Nancy Woloch, *Women and the American Experience* (New York: Alfred A. Knopf, 1984), chaps. 10, 12; William H. Chafe, *The American Woman: Her Changing Social, Economic, and Political Roles, 1920–1970* (New York: Oxford University Press, 1972), chap. 2.

44. On the reinvention of the saint through the centuries, see Marina Warner, *Joan of Arc: The Image of Female Heroism* (New York: Alfred A. Knopf, 1981).

45. "One of the Most Artistic and Satisfying Pictures That Ever Has Been Shown," *New York Evening Sun*, in Geraldine Farrar scrapbook, RLC, LMPA.

46. Reverend Thomas B. Gregory, *New York American*, undated clipping, in Geraldine Farrar scrapbook, RLC, LMPA.

47. "Our Fashion Department," *Theatre*, December 1910; "'I Shall Stay Single' Says Miss Farrar," *Boston Herald*, undated clipping; *Vogue*, 1 April 1913; *McClures*, December 1913; *Boston Daily Advertiser*, 30 August 1915, in Geraldine Farrar scrapbook, RLC, LMPA.

48. William A. Page, "Farrar's Real Romance," *Photoplay*, April 1916, 28–31.

49. DeMille to Lasky, 12 July 1916, in Jesse Lasky 1916 folder, Lasky Co./Famous Players-Lasky; Interview with DeMille, 24 July 1957, in Directors General folder; Interview with DeMille, 23 July 1957, in *Joan the Woman* folder, Personal: Autobiography files, DMA, BYU.

50. See Warner, *Joan of Arc*, chap. 7.

51. See Jay P. Dolan, *The American Catholic Experience: A History from Colonial Times to the Present* (Garden City: Doubleday, 1985), chap. 5.

52. Program of *Joan the Woman*, Geraldine Farrar clipping file, LMPA.

53. Milne, "Joan the Woman."

54. Unidentified clipping, in Geraldine Farrar scrapbook, RLC, LMPA.

55. B. Barnett to Lasky, Cardinal Film Corporation, 25 May 1917; H. Whitman Bennett to DeMille, 25 May 1917; in Folder B, Lasky Co./Famous Players-Lasky, DMA, BYU.

56. DeMille to H. Whitman Bennett, 2 June 1917, in Folder B, Lasky Co./Famous Players-Lasky, DMA, BYU.

57. Gregory, *New York American*; Frederick James Smith, *New York Evening Mail*, undated clipping, in Geraldine Farrar scrapbook, RLC, LMPA; "Joan at $5 a Seat Has Unusual Premiere at Bradley House in Washington," *NYDM*, 17 February 1917, 30, *Joan the Woman* ad, *MPN*, 20 January 1917, 343.

58. Henry F. May, *The End of American Innocence: A Study of the First Years of Our Own Time, 1912–1917* (New York: Alfred A. Knopf, 1959), 364.

59. Unidentified newspaper ad, in Geraldine Farrar scrapbook, RLC, LMPA; *Joan the Woman* ad, *MPN*, 20 January 1917, 343; " 'I am American First, Last and Always,' She Says," *NYDM*, 24 March 1917, 30; "Officials Praise 'Joan the Woman' at Albany," *NYDM*, 3 February 1917, 40; " 'Joan' Emphasizes Sunday Opening," *MPW*, 10 February 1917, 859; "Kansas Solons Witness 'Joan,' " *NYDM*, 17 February 1917, 23.

60. Vaughn, *Holding Fast the Inner Lines*, 204; see also James R. Mock and Cedric Larson, *Words That Won the War: The Story of the Committee on Public Information, 1917–1919* (Princeton: Princeton University Press, 1939), chap. 6.

61. Lasky to DeMille, 10 March 1917, in Jesse Lasky 1917 folder, Lasky Co./Famous Players-Lasky, DMA, BYU.

CHAPTER SIX: SET AND COSTUME DESIGN AS SPECTACLE

1. Ad in *MPN*, 14 January 1922, 455.

2. Script of *Old Wives for New*, USC.

3. See Karen Halttunen, "From Parlor to Living Room: Domestic Space, Interior Decoration, and the Culture of Personality," in Simon J. Bronner, ed., *Consuming Visions: Accumulation and Display of Goods in America, 1880–1920* (New York: W. W. Norton, 1989), 157–190.

4. *Theatre*, February 1919, in Cecil B. DeMille scrapbook, RLC, LMPA.

5. See Roland Marchand, *Advertising the American Dream: Making Way for Modernity, 1920–1940* (Berkeley: University of California Press, 1985).

6. *The Autobiography of Cecil B. DeMille*, ed. Donald Hayne (Englewood Cliffs: Prentice-Hall, 1959), 212–213. Since DeMille himself did not write his autobiography, I refer to it only when I have corroborating evidence from other sources. Donald Hayne, the only compiler to receive credit, stated in a memo to the director, "The difficulty—or should I say impossibility . . . is in trying to write *autobiographically* about things that I have neither witnessed nor discussed with you in sufficient detail." See James V. D'Arc, " 'So Let It Be Written . . . ': The Creation of Cecil B. DeMille's Autobiography," *Literature/Film Quarterly* 14 (1986): 1–9. William deMille gives his brother more credit than he deserves for starting the cycle of sex comedies and

melodramas in *Hollywood Saga* (New York: E. P. Dutton & Co., 1939), 238–243. DeMille did not list his Jazz Age films, with the exception of *Male and Female* and *Forbidden Fruit,* among his best films. See George C. Pratt, "Forty-Five Years of Picture Making: An Interview with Cecil B. DeMille," *Film History* 3 (1989): 133–145. I am indebted to the late George Pratt for playing the tape recording of this interview for me.

7. Lasky to DeMille, 6 January 1917; Carl H. Pierce to Lasky, memo attached to Lasky's letter; Lasky to DeMille, 5 March 1917; Lasky to DeMille, 10 August 1917; Lasky to DeMille, 27 November 1917; Lasky to DeMille, 27 December 1917; in Jesse Lasky 1917 folder, Lasky Co./Famous Players-Lasky, DMA, BYU.

8. Lasky to DeMille, 26 March 1918; Lasky to DeMille, 6 November 1918; DeMille to Lasky, 23 January 1919; Lasky to DeMille, 23 May 1919; in Jesse Lasky 1918 and 1919 folders, Lasky Co./Famous Players-Lasky, DMA, BYU.

9. David Graham Phillips, *Old Wives for New* (New York: Grosset & Dunlap, 1908), 100.

10. Script of *Old Wives for New,* USC.

11. Robert S. Lynd and Helen Merrell Lynd, *Middletown: A Study in American Culture* (New York: Harcourt, Brace & World, 1929), 256. According to the Lynds, twenty-one out of twenty-six families who owned a car were without bathtubs. See also Siegfried Giedion, *Mechanization Takes Command* (New York: Oxford University Press, 1948), part 7.

12. See Thomas Elsaesser, "Tales of Sound and Fury: Observations on the Family Melodrama," *Monogram* 4 (1972): 2–15; reprinted in Christine Gledhill, ed., *Home Is Where the Heart Is: Studies in Melodrama and the Woman's Film* (London: British Film Institute, 1987), 43–69.

13. Kenneth McGaffey, "The Excellent Elliott," *Motion Picture,* January 1919, 35; W. K. Hollander, untitled article, *Chicago News,* 21 January 1919, in Gloria Swanson scrapbook, RLC, LMPA.

14. Phillips, *Old Wives for New,* 43.

15. See John F. Kasson, *Rudeness and Civility: Manners in Nineteenth-Century America* (New York: Hill & Wang, 1990), 166.

16. On cosmetics, prostitutes, and changing styles, see Kathy Peiss, "Making Faces: The Cosmetics Industry and the Cultural Construction of Gender, 1890–1930," *Genders* 7 (Spring 1990): 143–169.

17. Script of *Don't Change Your Husband,* USC.

18. See Mary Douglas, *Purity and Danger: An Analysis of Concepts of Pollution and Taboo* (New York: Praeger, 1966), chaps. 7–9.

19. Guy Debord, *Society of the Spectacle* (Detroit: Black & Red, 1977), 5; T. J. Jackson Lears and Richard Wightman Fox, *The Culture of Consumption* (New York: Pantheon, 1983), x. On hegemony, see Raymond Williams, "Base and Superstructure in Marxist Cultural Theory," *Problems in Materialism and Culture* (London: Verso, 1980), 31–49; Williams, *Marxism and Literature* (New York: Oxford University Press, 1977), chap. 8.

20. See Roy Rosenzweig, *Eight Hours for What We Will: Workers and Industry in an Industrial City, 1870–1920* (Cambridge: Cambridge University Press, 1983); Francis G. Couvares, *The Remaking of Pittsburgh* (Albany: State University of New York Press, 1984); Elizabeth Ewen, *Immigrant Women in the Land of Dollars: Life and Culture on the Lower East Side, 1890–1925* (New York: Monthly Review Press, 1985); Kathy Peiss,

Cheap Amusements: Working Women and Leisure in Turn-of-the-Century New York (Philadelphia: Temple University Press, 1986); John S. Gilkeson, Jr., *Middle-Class Providence, 1820–1940* (Princeton: Princeton University Press, 1985); Lizabeth Cohen, *Making a New Deal: Industrial Workers in Chicago, 1919–1939* (Cambridge: Cambridge University Press, 1990).

21. DeMille to Lasky, 12 January 1924, in Jesse Lasky 1924 folder, Lasky Co./ Famous Players-Lasky, DMA, BYU.

22. DeMille was allegedly a foot fetishist; his vision of the consumer culture included an extraordinary number of close-ups of women's footwear.

23. *Why Change Your Wife?* script, USC; *Why Change Your Wife?* stills file, AMPAS.

24. Carroll Smith-Rosenberg, "The Female World of Love and Ritual: Relations between Women in Nineteenth-Century America," *Signs* 1 (1975): 1–29; reprinted in Smith-Rosenberg, *Disorderly Conduct: Visions of Gender in Victorian America* (New York: Alfred A. Knopf, 1985), 53–76.

25. On reification, see Georg Lukács, *History and Consciousness: Studies in Marxist Dialectics,* trans. Rodney Livingstone (Cambridge: MIT Press, 1971).

26. For further discussion of these films, see Charles Musser, "DeMille, Divorce, and the Comedy of Remarriage," in Paolo Cherchi Usai and Lorenzo Codelli, eds., *The DeMille Legacy* (Pordenone: Edizioni Biblioteca dell'Immagine, 1991), 262–283; Lary May, *Screening Out the Past: The Birth of Mass Culture and the Motion Picture Industry* (New York: Oxford University Press, 1980), 205–214; Robert Sklar, *Movie-Made America: A Cultural History of American Movies* (New York: Random House, 1975), 91–97. An expanded version of Musser's article will appear as "Divorce, DeMille, and the Comedy of Remarriage," in Henry Jenkins and Kristine Karnick, eds., *Classical Film Comedy: Narrative, Performance, Ideology* (forthcoming, Routledge/AFI). Musser's research has shown that DeMille invented a genre that later became popular not only in film but on stage, further proof of my argument that the director became a trendsetter in the 1920s.

27. William deMille, *Hollywood Saga,* 242; Garth Jowett, *Film: The Democratic Art* (Boston: Little, Brown, 1976), 188; Richard Koszarski, *An Evening's Entertainment: The Age of the Silent Feature Picture 1915–1928* (New York: Charles Scribner's Sons, 1990), 30; Gaylyn Studlar also cites the latter statistic, touted in fan magazines and trade journals, in "The Perils of Pleasure? Fan Magazine Discourse as Women's Commodified Culture in the 1920s," *Wide Angle* 19 (January 1991): 7.

28. *The Autobiography of Cecil B. DeMille,* 214–215; the quote is from a memo by Berenice Mosk, in *Northwest Mounted, Old Wives for New, Plainsman* folder, Personal: Autobiography files, DMA, BYU. DeMille claimed during a court case years later that Lasky attempted to block release of the film and to write it off as a loss. Although Lasky received in-house instructions to cut the film, I doubt he would have prevented the release of a project that was initially his idea and that he persuaded DeMille to undertake. See *United States Circuit Court of Appeals for the North Circuit. Commissioner of Internal Revenues, Petitioner, vs Cecil B. DeMille Productions, Inc., Respondent. Transcript of the Record. In Three Volumes. Upon Petition to Review an Order of the United States Board of Appeals* (San Francisco: Parker Printing Co., 1936), 319–320.

29. Adolph Zukor, "Zukor Outlines Coming Year's Policies," *MPN,* 29 June 1918, 3869.

30. *Old Wives for New,* Paramount Collection, AMPAS. On film censorship, see Francis G. Couvares, "Hollywood, Main Street, and The Church: Trying to Censor

the Movies Before the Production Code," *American Quarterly* 44 (December 1992): 584–616; Couvares, "Contexts and Solidarities: Thinking about Movie Censorship and Reform in the Twentieth Century" (Paper presented at The Movies Begin: History/Film/Culture, Yale University, May 1993).

31. Memo to Al Lichtman, General Manager of Famous Players-Lasky, 28 June 1918, in Jesse Lasky 1918 folder, Lasky Co./Famous Players-Lasky, DMA, BYU.

32. R. E. Pritchard, "Old Wives for New," *MPN*, 8 June 1918, 3453–3454; Frederick James Smith, *MPC*, August 1918, in *Northwest Mounted, Old Wives for New,* and *Plainsman* folder, Personal: Autobiography files, DMA, BYU; Edward Weitzel, "Old Wives for New," *MPW*, 8 June 1918, 1470; *"Old Wives for New," Variety Film Reviews, 1907–1980* (New York: Garland, 1983), 31 May 1918; "Exhibitor to Exhibitor Review Service," *MPN*, 8 June 1918, 3400.

33. Frederick James Smith, "The Celluloid Critic," *MPC*, April 1919, 44; *"Don't Change Your Husband," Variety Film Reviews,* 7 February 1919; "Special Service Section on 'Don't Change Your Husband,'" *MPN*, 1 February 1919, 728; "DeMille's Film Breaks Some Records," *MPN* 9 March 1919, 1353; Frederick James Smith, "The Celluloid Critic," *MPC*, April/May 1920, 50; Ad, *MPN*, 20 March 1920, 2609.

34. "Grauman's Rialto Gets Business by Use of Novelties," *MPN*, 1 May 1920, 3837; "What Brown Did for DeMille's Special," *MPN*, 10 July 1920, 403; Ad, *MPN*, 22 May 1920, 4245; Lasky to DeMille, 19 April 1920, in Jesse Lasky 1920 folder, Lasky Co./Famous Players-Lasky, DMA, BYU; "Famous Players-Lasky Plans Big Campaign," *MPN*, 24 January 1920, 1083; "Getting the Woman Appeal," *MPN*, 7 December 1918, 3358; "The Affairs of Anatol," *MPW*, 24 September 1921, 446. On the cultural wars of the post-World War I decade, see Frederick Lewis Allen, *Only Yesterday* (New York: Harper & Bros., 1931); William E. Leuchtenburg, *The Perils of Prosperity, 1914–32* (Chicago: University of Chicago Press, 1958); Paul A. Carter, *Another Part of the Twenties* (New York: Columbia University Press, 1973); Stanley Coben, *Rebellion against Victorianism: The Impetus for Cultural Change in 1920s America* (New York: Oxford University Press, 1991); Lawrence W. Levine, "Progress and Nostalgia: The Self Image of the Nineteen Twenties," in *The Unpredictable Past: Explorations in American Cultural History* (New York: Oxford University Press, 1993), 189–205. Daniel H. Borus offers a revisionist interpretation in "New Perspectives in the 1920s in the United States" (Paper delivered at SUNY Brockport, April, 1991). On film exhibition during this period, see Koszarski, *An Evening's Entertainment,* chap. 2; Douglas Gomery, *Shared Pleasures: A History of Movie Presentation in the United States* (Madison: University of Wisconsin Press, 1992), chaps. 3–4.

35. See Ewen, *Immigrant Women in the Land of Dollars;* Peiss, *Cheap Amusements.*

36. "Why Change Your Wife?" *MPN*, 8 May 1920, 4062.

37. Famous Players-Lasky ad, *MPN*, 26 June 1920, 4.

38. *Statistical Abstract of the United States* (Washington, DC: Government Printing Office, 1933), 90; Report of the President's Research Committee on Social Trends, *Recent Social Trends in the United States* (New York: McGraw-Hill, 1933), 694; William L. O'Neill, *Divorce in the Progressive Era* (New Haven: Yale University Press, 1967), 20; Elaine Tyler May, *Great Expectations: Marriage and Divorce in Post-Victorian America* (Chicago: University of Chicago Press, 1980), 51, 87; Glenda Riley, *Divorce: An American Tradition* (New York: Oxford University Press, 1991), 133; *"Don't Change Your Husband," New York Times Film Reviews* (New York: Arno Press, 1970), 3 February 1919; Lynd and Lynd, *Middletown,* chap. 10; William H. Chafe, *The American Woman:*

Her Changing Social, Economic, and Political Roles, 1920–1970 (New York: Oxford University Press, 1972), chap. 2.

39. Media Mistley, "Why Husbands Leave Home," *MPC,* July 1918, 54–56.

40. Hazel Simpson Naylor, "Master of Mystery," *MPM,* November 1919, 126; "How to Hold a Husband," *Photoplay,* November 1918, 31; Elizabeth Peltret, "Gloria Swanson Talks on Divorce," *MPM,* December 1919, 74; "Editorial: Cinema Husbands," *MPM,* September 1920, 29.

41. "What Does Marriage Mean As Told by Cecil B. deMille to Adela Rogers St. Johns," *Photoplay,* December 1920, 28–31. DeMille's more well-known liaisons included relationships with Jeanie Macpherson and Julia Faye. The director also owned a ranch in the San Fernando Valley that was called Paradise for reasons other than its idyllic location.

42. Adela Rogers St. Johns, "More about Marriage," *Photoplay* (May 1921): 24–26, 105.

43. Michel Foucault, *The History of Sexuality,* vol. 1, trans. Robert Hurley (New York: Pantheon, 1978), 37.

44. See Richard Dyer, *Stars* (London: British Film Institute, 1979); Richard deCordova, *Picture Personalities: The Emergence of the Star System in America* (Urbana: University of Illinois Press, 1990); Catherine E. Kerr, "Incorporating the Star: The Intersection of Business and Aesthetic Strategies in Early American Film," *Business History Review* 64 (Autumn 1990): 383–410. On female subjectivity as constructed by fan magazine discourse, see Gaylyn Studlar, "The Perils of Pleasure?" 6–32.

45. *Swanson on Swanson: An Autobiography* (New York: Random House, 1980), chaps. 7–8; Lasky to DeMille, 3 January 1919, in Jesse Lasky 1919 folder, Lasky Co./Famous Players-Lasky, DMA, BYU; Smith, "The Celluloid Critic," 44; Hazel Simpson Naylor, "Across the Silversheet," *MPM,* April 1919, 72.

46. Frederick James Smith, "The Silken Gloria," *MPC,* February 1920, 16; Delight Evans, "Don't Change Your Coiffure," *Photoplay,* August 1919, 73; "She Changed Her Coiffure," *Photoplay,* September 1920, 33; untitled article, *Variety,* 7 December 1919, in Gloria Swanson scrapbook, RLC, LMPA; Hazel Naylor Simpson, "Piloting a Dream Craft," *MPM,* April 1921, 87. Although costume design credits for DeMille's films are difficult to ascertain, Alpharelta Hoffman is cited as the designer for *Old Wives for New* in *Northwest Mounted, Old Wives for New,* and *Plainsman* folder, Personal: Autobiography files, DMA, BYU. *MPN* cites Margaretta Hoffman (the first name is an error) as the designer for *Don't Change Your Husband* in "Cecil B. DeMille's New Feature Is Started," 23 November 1918, 3084. Possibly, Mitchell Leisen, who began his career designing costumes for the Babylonian sequence in *Male and Female* and became DeMille's art director later in the 1920s, may also have been involved in costume design. See David Chierichetti, *Hollywood Director: The Career of Mitchell Leisen* (New York: Curtis Books, 1973), 22–28.

47. See Anne Hollander, *Seeing Through Clothes* (New York: Viking Press, 1975). See also Mary Louise Roberts, "Samson and Delilah Revisited: The Politics of Women's Fashion in 1920s France," *American Historical Review* 93 (June 1993): 657–684. French reaction to changes in women's clothing and hairstyles, which were seductively but disturbingly unisexual, was comparable to consternation expressed in American society. Roberts fails to mention that fashion had become an international phenomenon partly as a result of the influence of motion pictures. Paul Iribe, who illustrated Art Deco fashion plates for couturier Paul Poiret, not coincidentally,

became DeMille's art director in the 1920s. See also Paula S. Fass, *The Damned and the Beautiful: American Youth in the 1920s* (New York: Oxford University Press, 1977); Allen, *Only Yesterday*, chap. 5; Leuchtenburg, *The Perils of Prosperity*, chap. 9. See also F. Scott Fitzgerald, "Bernice Bobs Her Hair," in *Flappers and Philosophers* (New York: Charles Scribner's Sons, 1920), 116–140.

48. *The Affairs of Anatol*, Paramount Collection, AMPAS; *Anatol: A Sequence of Dialogues by Arthur Schnitzler; Paraphrased for the English Stage by Granville Barker* (New York: Mitchell Kennerley, 1911).

49. A 16-mm print at UCLA Film and Television Archive preserves the beautiful colors of this process. Unfortunately, the George Eastman House print is in black and white, incomplete, edited out of sequence, and titled in Czech.

50. Telegram, Lasky to DeMille, 9 October 1920; telegram, DeMille to Lasky, 8 January 1921; Lasky to DeMille, 4 October 1921, in Jesse Lasky 1920 and 1921 folders, Lasky Co./Famous Players-Lasky, DMA, BYU; *The Affairs of Anatol*, stills file, AMPAS. On the recession, see Leuchtenburg, *The Perils of Prosperity*, 179; John Izod, *Hollywood and the Box Office, 1895–1986* (New York: Columbia University Press, 1988), 52.

51. *Morning Telegraph*, 12 December 1920, Wilfred Buckland clipping file, AMPAS. The reasons for Buckland's exit during a recession are unclear. In 1946, he shot his mentally ill son and then himself, leaving his modest estate to his landlady and to William deMille.

52. *The Affairs of Anatol*, *MPN*, 27 September 1921, 166. See Victor Arwas, *Art Deco* (New York: Harry N. Abrams, 1980), chap. 1; Richard Guy Wilson, Dianne H. Pilgrim, and Dickran Tashjian, *The Machine Age in America, 1918–1941* (New York: Harry N. Abrams, 1986); Diane Chalmers Johnson, *American Art Nouveau* (New York: Harry N. Abrams, 1979); Bernard Champigneulle, *Art Nouveau*, trans. Benita Eisler (Woodbury: Barron's, 1976); Peter Selz and Mildred Constantine, eds., *Art Nouveau: Art and Design at the Turn of the Century*, rev. ed. (New York: Museum of Modern Art, 1975).

53. Quoted in T. J. Jackson Lears, "From Salvation to Self-Realization: Advertising and the Therapeutic Roots of the Consumer Culture, 1880–1930," in Lears and Fox, eds., *The Culture of Consumption*, 21.

54. As Roland Marchand observes in *Advertising the American Dream*, a French maid was a real sign of conspicuous consumption because domestic servants were overwhemingly ethnic in origin (202).

55. Wilson, Pilgrim, and Tashjian, *The Machine Age in America*, 29. According to the authors, John Marin painted the bridge in the 1910s, and Frank Stella, Walker Evans, and Hart Crane celebrated it in their work in the 1920s.

56. Schnitzler, "A Question of Fate," *Anatol*. A physician as well as a playwright, Schnitzler had published on the subject of hypnotism. See Paul F. Dvorak, ed. and trans., *Illusion and Reality: Plays and Stories of Arthur Schnitzler* (New York: Peter Lang, 1986), xvii.

57. In fact, DeMille discusses this particular film in relation to the trilogy and *Male and Female*. See Pratt, "Forty-Five Years of Picture Making," 139.

58. Walter Lippman, *A Preface to Morals* (New York: Macmillan Co., 1929), chap. 14, 288; Lynd and Lynd, *Middletown*, chap. 10; Fass, *The Damned and the Beautiful*, 69. For studies on sexuality and marriage during this period, see Gilbert Van Tassel Hamilton, *A Research in Marriage* (New York: Albert and Charles Boni, 1929), 80–82, 383; Robert L. Dickinson and Lura Beam, *The Single Woman: A Medical Study in Sex*

Education (New York: Reynal & Hitchcock, 1934), 101, 145; Lewis M. Terman, *Psychological Factors in Marital Happiness* (New York: McGraw-Hill, 1938), 320–321, 367; Katherine B. Davis, *Factors in the Sex Life of Twenty-Two Hundred Women* (New York: McGraw-Hill, 1938), 14, 38–39. On the history of contraception, see Linda Gordon, *Woman's Body, Woman's Right: A Social History of Birth Control in America* (New York: Grossman, 1976). See also John D'Emilio and Estelle B. Freedman, *Intimate Matters: A History of Sexuality in America* (New York: Harper & Row, 1988).

59. Susan Porter Benson, *Counter Cultures: Saleswomen, Managers, and Customers in American Department Stores, 1890–1940* (Urbana: University of Illinois Press, 1988), 76. *The Ladies' Paradise* is the translated title of Zola's novel, *Au bonheur des dames.*

60. Lynd and Lynd, *Middletown*, 82.

61. DeMille to Lasky, 22 September 1922, in Jesse Lasky 1922 folder, Lasky Co./Famous Players-Lasky, DMA, BYU.

62. Unidentified article, *Photoplay*, October 1915, in Cecil B. DeMille scrapbook, RLC, LMPA.

63. Martha L. Olney, *Buy Now, Pay Later: Advertising, Credit, and Consumer Durables in the 1920s* (Chapel Hill: University of North Carolina Press, 1991), chaps. 1–2, 95; Lynd and Lynd, *Middletown*, 137; Borus (Paper delivered at SUNY Brockport); Lizabeth Cohen, *Making a New Deal*, chap. 3; Daniel Horowitz, *The Morality of Spending: Attitudes toward the Consumer Society in America, 1875–1940* (Baltimore: Johns Hopkins University Press, 1985), chap. 7. See also Mary Douglas and Baron Isherwood, *The World of Goods* (New York: Basic Books, 1979); Grant McCracken, *Culture and Consumption: New Approaches to the Symbolic Character of Consumer Goods and Activities* (Bloomington: Indiana University Press, 1990); Jean-Christophe Agnew, "Coming Up for Air: Consumer Culture in Historical Perspective," *Intellectual History Newsletter* 12 (1990): 3–21.

64. Marchand, *Advertising the American Dream*, 198; Barrett C. Kiesling, "The Boy Who Lived in the Haunted House," *MPC*, November 1925, 29; Gladys Hall and Adele Whitely Fletcher, "We Interview Cecil B. DeMille," *MPM*, April 1922, 93.

65. Marchand, *Advertising the American Dream*, chaps. 1–7; Olney, *Buy Now, Pay Later*, 139–152; T. J. Jackson Lears, "Some Versions of Fantasy: Toward a Cultural History of American Advertising, 1880–1930," *Prospects* 9, 384; Christopher P. Wilson, "The Rhetoric of Consumption: Mass-Market Magazines and the Demise of the Gentle Reader, 1880–1920," in Fox and Lears, eds., *The Culture of Consumption*, 39–64; Stuart Ewen, *All Consuming Images: The Politics of Style in Contemporary Culture* (New York: Basic Books, 1988), 47. See also Ewen, *Captains of Consciousness: Advertising and the Social Roots of the Consumer Culture* (New York: McGraw-Hill, 1976); James D. Norris, *Advertising and the Transformation of American Society, 1865–1920* (Westport: Greenwood Press, 1990); Michael Schudson, *Advertising, The Uneasy Persuasion: Its Dubious Impact on American Society* (New York: Basic Books, 1984); Susan Strasser, *Satisfaction Guaranteed: The Making of the American Mass Market* (New York: Pantheon, 1989); Lynne Kirby, "Gender and Advertising in American Silent Film: From Early Cinema to the Crowd," *Discourse* 13 (Spring/Summer 1991): 3–20.

66. Cecil B. DeMille, "The Heart and Soul of Motion Pictures," *NYDM*, 12 June 1920, 194–195; Frederick James Smith, "How Christ Came to Pictures," *Photoplay*, July 1927, 118.

67. DeMille's impressive and costly collection of furnishings and objets d'art was on display before a Christie's auction in New York in 1988. See *Property from the Estate of Cecil B. DeMille* (New York: Christie's East, 1988).

CHAPTER SEVEN: DeMILLE'S EXODUS FROM FAMOUS PLAYERS-LASKY

1. "The Drama of the Decalogue, Pictures from DeMille's The Ten Command-ments," *MPC*, October 1923, 32; *The Autobiography of Cecil B. DeMille,* Donald Hayne, ed. (Englewood Cliffs: Prentice-Hall, 1959), 249; Souvenir program, *The Ten Commandments* clipping file, AMPAS; Henry C. DeMille, in Diary folder, Family, DMA, BYU.

2. See David Glassberg, *American Historical Pageantry: The Uses of Tradition in the Early Twentieth Century* (Chapel Hill: University of North Carolina Press, 1990).

3. On fundamentalism, see Timothy P. Weber, "The Two-Edged Sword: The Fundamentalist Use of the Bible," and Grant Wacker, "The Demise of Biblical Civilization," in Nathan O. Hatch and Mark A. Noll, eds., *The Bible in America: Essays in Cultural History* (New York: Oxford University Press, 1982), 101–138.

4. James Stevens, ed., *A Doré Treasury: A Collection of the Best Engravings of Gustave Doré* (New York: Bounty Books, 1970), viii; *The Doré Bible Illustrations* (New York: Dover Publications, 1974); "Two 'Ten Commandments' Cast," *MPN*, 12 May 1923, 2305. On the Catholic Bible, see Gerald P. Fogarty, S.J., "The Quest for a Catholic Vernacular Bible in America," in Hatch and Noll, eds., *The Bible in America*, 163–180. I wish to thank Bernard Barryte at the Stanford University art museum for discussions regarding Doré's work.

5. Philip Vandenberg, *The Golden Pharaoh* (New York: Macmillan, 1978), 133; Thomas Hoving, *Tutankhamun: The Untold Story* (New York: Simon & Schuster, 1978), 109–110; Souvenir program, *The Ten Commandments* clipping file, AMPAS.

6. *"The Ten Commandments," Variety Film Reviews, 1907–1980* (New York: Garland, 1983), 27 December 1923.

7. For a psychoanalytic account of this phenomenon, see Christian Metz, *The Imaginary Signifier: Psychoanalysis and the Cinema,* trans. Celia Britton (Bloomington: Indiana University Press, 1982).

8. "Paramount Claims Biggest Location Feat," *MPN*, 14 July 1923, 173; Souvenir program, *The Ten Commandments* clipping file, AMPAS. DeMille's sets were excavated in 1983. See Peter L. Brosnan, "Egyptian City Discovered under California Sands," *American West*, September/October 1985, 34–40.

9. See Daniel Bell, *The Cultural Contradictions of Capitalism* (New York: Basic Books, 1976), 99–119.

10. See William Leach, "Strategies of Display and the Production of Desire," in Simon J. Bronner, ed., *Consuming Visions: Accumulation and Display of Goods in America, 1880–1920* (New York: W. W. Norton, 1989), 114–115; Roland Marchand, *Advertising the American Dream: Making Way for Modernity, 1920–1940* (Berkeley: University of California Press, 1985), 120–127.

11. I am indebted to David Parker at the Library of Congress for detailed explanations of these color processes. Although only four photographers are listed

in the film's credits, DeMille names five in his autobiography. The reasons for Wyckoff's departure are puzzling. Years later, he wrote that he "resigned" from DeMille's crew but declined to explain why. (Wyckoff to George Pratt, 10 January 1956.) I am grateful to the late George Pratt for sharing this correspondence with me. Charles Higham claims in his problematic biography, *Cecil B. DeMille* (New York: DaCapo, 1978), that Wyckoff and DeMille differed over the use of lighting and the former's union activities. Given the director's militant and unrelenting opposition to unionism, a rupture over politics is feasible. For more details on production, see Robert S. Birchard, "DeMille and *The Ten Commandments* (1923): A Match Made in Heaven," *American Cinematographer*, September 1992, 77–81; Birchard, "*The Ten Commandments* (1923): DeMille Completes Personal Exodus," *American Cinematographer*, October 1992, 76–80. Unfortunately, Birchard does not cite sources.

12. "DeMille-Wyckoff Add to Color Process," *MPN*, 9 February 1918, 865; "*Ten Commandments,*" *Variety Film Reviews*, 27 December 1923.

13. James Cozart points out in "*The Captive:* Tinting of the Print for Pordenone," a sheet passed out with program materials at Le Giornate del Cinema Muto in Pordenone in 1991, that DeMille experimented with tinting that was not necessarily cued for day-night effect but for emotional tone.

14. Script of *The Ten Commandments,* USC.

15. On earlier representations of Moses, see William Uricchio and Roberta E. Pearson, "'You Can Make *The Life of Moses* Your Life Saver': Vitagraph's Biblical Blockbuster," in Rosalind Cosandey, André Gaudreault, and Tom Gunning, eds., *Une invention du diable? Cinéma des premiers temps et religion* (Sainte-Foy: Les Presses de l'Université Laval, 1991), 197–211.

16. Jeanie Macpherson, "How the Story Was Evolved," Souvenir program, *The Ten Commandments* clipping file, AMPAS; Telegram, Zukor to Lasky, 19 April 1923; Telegram, DeMille to Lasky, 24 February 1923, in Jesse Lasky 1923 folder; Telegram, DeMille to Zukor, 10 May 1924, in 1924 Autobiography, personal correspondence folder, Lasky Co./Famous Players-Lasky, DMA, BYU.

17. Script of *The Ten Commandments,* USC. See also James Card, "The Silent Films of Cecil B. DeMille," in Marshall Deutelbaum, ed., *Image on the Art and Evolution of the Film* (New York: Dover Publications, 1979), 118–119; Card, *Seductive Cinema* (forthcoming, Alfred A. Knopf).

18. Script of *The Ten Commandments,* USC.

19. Lasky to DeMille, 30 August 1923, in Autobiography, Personal correspondence folder; Zukor to DeMille, 14 August 1924, in Jesse Lasky 1924 folder, Lasky Co./Famous Players-Lasky, DMA, BYU; "Premiere of 'Ten Commandments,'" *MPN*, 5 January 1924, 51.

20. "*The Ten Commandments,*" *New York Times Film Reviews* (New York: Arno Press, 1970), 22 December 1923; "What the New York Critics Say," Souvenir program, *The Ten Commandments* clipping file, LMPA; C. S. Sewell, "The Ten Commandments," *MPW*, 5 January 1924, 56; Adele Whitely Fletcher, "Across the Silversheet," *MPM*, March 1924, 51; Oscar Cooper, "The Ten Commandments," *MPN*, 5 January 1924, 74; "The Shadow Stage," *Photoplay*, February 1924, 62; James R. Quirk, "The Ten Commandments," *Photoplay*, February 1924, 42, 128; Johnson to DeMille, 18 January 1924, in Miscellaneous 1924 folder, Lasky Co./Famous Players-Lasky, DMA, BYU.

21. *"The Ten Commandments,"* New York Times Film Reviews, 22 December 1923; *"The Ten Commandments,"* Variety Film Reviews, 27 December 1923.

22. A restrictive quota bill was passed in 1921 and in 1924. See John Higham, *Strangers in the Land: Patterns of American Nativism, 1860–1925* (1963; reprint, New York: Atheneum, 1981), chap. 11. On the proletarianization of white-collar workers, see Harry Braverman, *Labor and Monopoly Capital: The Degradation of Work in the Twentieth Century* (New York: Monthly Review Press, 1974), chap. 13; C. Wright Mills, *White Collar: The American Middle Classes* (New York: Oxford University Press, 1956), 182–188. See also Cindy Sondik Aron, *Ladies and Gentlemen of the Civil Service: Middle-Class Workers in Victorian America* (New York: Oxford University Press, 1987); Olivier Zunz, *Making America Corporate, 1870–1920* (Chicago: University of Chicago Press, 1990). Although there is disagreement as to when the process of proletarianization began, evidence points to the decades after 1880 when there was a dramatic increase in white-collar workers and an increasingly homogeneous work environment.

23. T. J. Jackson Lears, *No Place of Grace: Antimodernism and the Transformation of American Culture, 1880–1920* (New York: Pantheon, 1981), xvii; Nathan O. Hatch, *The Democratization of American Christianity* (New Haven: Yale University Press, 1989), 216, chap. 8.

24. Millicent Rose, Introduction to *The Doré Bible Illustrations*, vii–viii. Rose points out that Cassell, Peter, & Galpin, the firm that owned the rights to *The Doré Bible*, also published a cheaper, illustrated edition with pictures by various artists; it was titled *Cassell's Illustrated Family Bible*.

25. *The Holy Bible* (New York: P. J. Kennedy, 1945). I am indebted to Robert Gilliam for calling my attention to this fact. See my "Antimodernism as Historical Representation in a Consumer Culture: Cecil B. DeMille's *The Ten Commandments*, 1923, 1956, 1993," in Vivian Sobchack, ed., *The Moving Image: Modernism and Historical Representation* (forthcoming, Routledge/AFI), for discussion of a recent advertising campaign that used Doré's illustration of Moses in an ad for kosher chicken. Interestingly, *TV Guide* recently used another Doré illustration of the lawgiver to advertise *Ancient Mysteries;* opposite the page was an ad for a Billy Graham special. See *TV Guide*, September 4–10, 1992, 178–179.

26. Neil Harris, "Color and Media: Some Comparisons and Speculations," and "Iconography and Intellectual History: The Halftone Effect," in *Cultural Excursions: Marketing Appetites and Cultural Tastes in Modern America* (Chicago: University of Chicago Press, 1990), 318–336, 304–317. Harris, who focuses mostly on the sound era in his discussion of film, is incorrect about silents. James Card reminds us that contrary to most prints that survive today, silent film was composed of color-tinted footage, not to be confused with hand coloring. See his *Seductive Cinema*. See also Paolo Cherchi Usai, "The Color of Nitrate," *Image* 34 (Spring/Summer 1991): 29–38. DeMille himself used the terms *dyed* and *toned* rather than *tinted* in interviews tape-recorded for his autobiography. (*Joan the Woman* folder, Personal: Autobiography files, DMA, BYU.)

27. Cooper, "The Ten Commandments," 74.

28. Jeanie Macpherson, "How the Story Was Evolved," Souvenir program, *The Ten Commandments* clipping file, AMPAS. See Lawrence W. Levine, *Highbrow/Lowbrow: The Emergence of Cultural Hierarchy in America* (Cambridge: Harvard University Press, 1988), 47–48.

29. T. J. Jackson Lears, "From Salvation to Self-Realization," in T. J. Jackson Lears and Richard Wightman Fox, eds., *The Culture of Consumption* (New York: Pantheon, 1983), 29–38; Lears, "Some Version of Fantasy: Toward a Cultural History of American Advertising, 1880–1930," *Prospects* 9 (1984): 367.

30. Souvenir program, *The Ten Commandments* clipping file, AMPAS.

31. Guy Debord, *Society of the Spectacle* (Detroit: Black & Red, 1977), 10, 4, 47. See also Georg Lukács, *History and Consciousness: Studies in Marxist Dialectics,* trans. Rodney Livingstone (Cambridge: MIT Press, 1971).

32. Fletcher, "Across the Silversheet," *MPM*, March 1924, 101; Adele Whitely Fletcher, "Across the Silversheet," *MPM*, December 1922, 108.

33. Frederick James Smith, "The Celluloid Critic," *MPC*, April 1919, 44; September 1919, 44–45; "The Screen Year in Review," August 1920, 44; "The Celluloid Critic," April 1921, 80; Harrison Haskins, "The Big Six Directors," September 1918, 16–17; Smith, "The Celluloid Critic," April 1922, 92; Laurence Reid, "The Celluloid Critic," May 1923, 93; Harry Carr, "The Directors Who Bring 'Em In," November 1923, 25.

34. U.S. Department of Commerce, Bureau of the Census, *Historical Studies of the United States: Colonial Times to 1970* (Washington, D.C.: U.S. Government Printing Office, 1975), part 1, 199. I am grateful to Robert J. Smith for assisting me with these calculations. The Lasky Company's first full year of production, 1914, as the base year and the wholesale price index were used to compute inflation. Filming of the studio's first feature, *The Squaw Man,* was begun in December 1913. Figures for cost and grosses in the DeMille Archives are reproduced in David Pierce, "Success with a Dollar Sign: Cost and Grosses for the Early Films of DeMille," in Paolo Cherchi Usai and Lorenzo Codelli, eds., *The DeMille Legacy* (Pordenone: Edizioni Biblioteca dell'Immagine, 1991), 308–317. I have not discussed costs in relation to grosses because the latter figures, as Pierce points out, are more problematic; whether they include foreign as well as domestic rentals, reissues, and so forth cannot be determined. Furthermore, the director had disagreements with Famous Players-Lasky regarding his percentage of profits on films made after 1920 and was involved in litigation with the Internal Revenue Service, two factors that may have influenced his computing of grosses. Zukor's letter to DeMille regarding additional costs for advertising and exploitation leads me to conclude, however, that these expenditures were not part of the production figures. Although it is impossible to determine the shooting ratio of DeMille's films, interestingly, average footage per feature increased with cost in the postwar era. Figures, based on data for all but three features in DeMille's bound shooting scripts, are rather constant before the merger: 4,569 feet in 1914; 4,724 feet in 1915; and 4,822 feet in 1916, excluding *Joan the Woman,* a special that totalled 10,446 feet. Figures averaged for the years following the merger are as follows: 6,221 feet in 1917; 6,184 feet in 1918; 7,661 feet in 1919; 8,377 feet in 1920; 8,722 feet in 1921; 9,374 feet in 1922; 11,756 feet for *The Ten Commandments* in 1923; and 8,833 feet in 1924.

35. Undated memo, in Executives Folder, Personal: Autobiography files; DeMille to Lasky, 27 December 1918, in Jesse Lasky 1918 folder, Lasky Co./Famous Players-Lasky, DMA, BYU.

36. Telegram, DeMille to Lasky, 13 October 1920, in Jesse Lasky 1920 folder, Lasky Co./Famous Players-Lasky, DMA, BYU.

37. *United States Circuit Court of Appeals for the Ninth Circuit. Commissioner of Internal*

Revenue, Petitioner, vs Cecil B. DeMille Productions, Inc., Respondent. Transcript of the Record. In Three Volumes. Upon Petition to Review an Order of the United States Board of Tax Appeals (San Francisco: Parker Printing Co., 1936), 89–96.

38. Telegram, DeMille to Lasky, 13 May 1921; Lasky to DeMille, 21 May 1921; Memorandum of Points Arrived at in Discussion of Cecil B. DeMille's Wire of May 13th in Which He Requested an Increase in His Allowance for DeMille Productions, in Jesse Lasky 1921 folder, Lasky Co./Famous Players-Lasky, DMA, BYU.

39. Zukor to DeMille, 22 June 1921; Telegram, DeMille to Lasky, 22 September 1921; Lasky to DeMille, 4 October 1921; Lasky to DeMille, 14 April 1922; in Jesse Lasky 1921 and 1922 folders, Lasky Co./Famous Players-Lasky, DMA, BYU.

40. Telegram, Zukor to Lasky, 19 April 1923, in Jesse Lasky 1923 folder; Telegram, DeMille to Zukor 10 May 1924, in Autobiography, personal correspondence folder, Lasky Co./Famous Players-Lasky; Undated memo by Berenice Mosk, in Adolph Zukor folder, Personal: Autobiography files; DeMille to S. R. Kent, 12 October 1923, in Miscellaneous 1923 folder; Lasky to DeMille, 25 October 1923; DeMille to Lasky, 25 October 1923, in Autobiography, personal correspondence folder, Lasky Co./Famous Players-Lasky; DMA, BYU.

41. "F.P.-L. Orders Production Shut Down," *MPN*, 10 November 1923, 2225–2226.

42. "Lasky Studio to Reopen Jan. 7; Full Speed Producing Planned," *MPW*, 5 January 1924, 25; Zukor to DeMille, 14 August 1924, in Jesse Lasky 1924 folder; Zukor to Lasky, 2 December 1924, in Autobiography personal correspondence folder, Lasky Co./Famous Players-Lasky, DMA, BYU; "DeMille Leaves Paramount," *MPN* 24 January 1925, 323; *U.S. Circuit Court of Appeals,* 315–316.

43. Edward W. Said, *Orientalism* (New York: Random House, 1978), 123. Perhaps the best filmic text on filmmaking as a form of Orientalism is the documentary about the making of *Apocalypse Now, Hearts of Darkness* (1991), a more revealing film about the Vietnam War than any narrative about the war itself.

44. For a reading of the sound version of the film as a Western, see Marc Vernet, "Wings of the Desert; or, the Invisible Superimpositions," *Velvet Light Trap* 28 (Fall 1991): 65–72. Interestingly, DeMille instructed an orchestra to play "The New World Symphony" as inspirational music while filming the silent version. As is true of several historical epics of the 1950s and 1960s, the remake resonates with Cold War issues. See Michael Wood, *America in the Movies or, "Santa Maria, It Had Slipped My Mind!"* (New York: Basic Books, 1975), chap. 8. DeMille became so ardent in his right-wing political stance that in his recollection of *Why Change Your Wife?* he stated, "The whole theme of all these pictures is the 'happy home—is home life—the home as the central unit of a nation. It's the exact opposite of what communism gives you." (Interview with DeMille, *Why Change Your Wife?* folder, Personal: Autobiography files, DMA, BYU.)

45. On programmed flow, see Raymond Williams, *Television: Technology and Cultural Form* (New York: Schocken, 1975), chap. 4. On the supertext, see Nick Browne, "The Political Economy of the Television (Super) Text," *Quarterly Review of Film Studies* 9 (Summer 1984): 174–183; Sandy Flitterman, "The Real Soap Operas: TV Commercials," in E. Ann Kaplan, *Regarding Television: Critical Approaches—An Anthology* (Frederick: University Publications of America, 1983), 84–96.

46. On the waning of historicity, see Fredric Jameson, "Postmodernism, or the Cultural Logic of Late Capitalism," *New Left Review* 146 (July/August 1984): 58–64;

reprinted as "The Cultural Logic of Late Capitalism," in *Postmodernism, or, The Cultural Logic of Late Capitalism* (Durham: Duke University Press, 1991): 1–54; David Harvey, *The Condition of Postmodernity: An Enquiry into the Origins of Cultural Change* (Oxford: Basil Blackwell, 1989). For a different interpretation of postmodernism and history, see Linda Hutcheon, *A Poetics of Postmodernism: History, Theory, Fiction* (London: Routledge, 1988).

47. For a fuller discussion of the sound remake and its annual telecast, see my "Antimoderism as Historical Representation in a Consumer Culture: Cecil B. DeMille's *The Ten Commandments,* 1923, 1956, 1993." See also Alan Nadel, "God's Law and the Wide Screen: *The Ten Commandments* as Cold War 'Epic,'" *PMLA* 108 (May 1993): 415–430.

48. As demonstrated in *Jurassic Park* and previous hits, Steven Spielberg, along with George Lucas and Francis Ford Coppola, are the most obvious heirs of DeMille's legacy. Significantly, the concept of theme park as urban reality has been realized in Universal City's CityWalk, a totally artificial environment or supermall for yuppie moviegoers that was opened a year after the riot provoked by the Rodney King verdict. See "Will Movie Meccas Do the Right Thing?" *Variety,* 12 July 1993, 1, 69; Peter Bart, "Bite-Sized Reality," *Variety,* 12 July 1993, 3, 5; Hubert Muschamp, "Who Should Define a City?" *New York Times,* 15 August 1993, H32.

INDEX

Designer: U.C. Press Staff
Compositor: Braun-Brumfield, Inc.
Text: 10/12 Baskerville
Display: Baskerville
Printer: Braun-Brumfield, Inc.
Binder: Braun-Brumfield, Inc.